ADDRESSING
MORAL INJURY
in CLINICAL
PRACTICE

ADDRESSING MORAL INJURY *in* CLINICAL PRACTICE

Edited by

JOSEPH M. CURRIER

KENT D. DRESCHER

JASON NIEUWSMA

AMERICAN PSYCHOLOGICAL ASSOCIATION

Published by
American Psychological Association
750 First Street, NE
Washington, DC 20002
https://www.apa.org

Order Department
https://www.apa.org/pubs/books
order@apa.org

In the U.K., Europe, Africa, and the Middle East, copies may be ordered from Eurospan
https://www.eurospanbookstore.com/apa
info@eurospangroup.com

Typeset in Meridien and Ortodoxa by Circle Graphics, Inc., Reisterstown, MD

Printer: Sheridan Books, Chelsea, MI
Cover Designer: Beth Schlenoff Design, Bethesda, MD

Library of Congress Cataloging-in-Publication Data

Names: Currier, Joseph M., editor. | Drescher, Kent D., editor. | Nieuwsma,
   Jason A., editor. | American Psychological Association, issuing body.
Title: Addressing moral injury in clinical practice / edited by Joseph M. Currier,
   Kent D. Drescher, and Jason A. Nieuwsma.
Description: Washington, DC : American Psychological Association, [2021] |
   Includes bibliographical references and index.
Identifiers: LCCN 2020011433 (print) | LCCN 2020011434 (ebook) |
   ISBN 9781433832697 (paperback) | ISBN 9781433833830 (ebook)
Subjects: LCSH: Post-traumatic stress disorder—Treatment. | Psychic
   trauma—Treatment. | Veterans—Mental health.
Classification: LCC RC552.P67 A264 2021 (print) | LCC RC552.P67 (ebook) |
   DDC 616.85/21—dc23
LC record available at https://lccn.loc.gov/2020011433
LC ebook record available at https://lccn.loc.gov/2020011434

https://doi.org/10.1037/0000204-000

Printed in the United States of America

10 9 8 7 6 5 4 3 2 1

With sincere appreciation to the many clinicians, chaplains, colleagues,
and students who have made this book possible and who have molded
our thinking about moral injury, and with a deep awareness of the privilege
it is to learn from and care for morally injured veterans and service members
who allow us to accompany them in their journeys toward healing, belonging,
and meaning in life.

—JOSEPH M. CURRIER, KENT D. DRESCHER, and JASON NIEUWSMA

CONTENTS

CONTRIBUTORS

Stephanie Amaya, MA, Department of Psychology, University of Wyoming, Laramie

Kendal Binion, MS, Department of Psychology, University of Wyoming, Laramie

Abby E. Blankenship, PhD, University of Texas Health Science Center at San Antonio

Michael B. Brennan, PsyD, ABPP, Department of Psychiatry and Behavioral Sciences, Rush University Medical Center, Chicago, IL

Craig J. Bryan, PsyD, ABPP, National Center for Veterans Studies, University of Utah, Salt Lake City

Kristine Burkman, PhD, San Francisco VA Health Care System; UC San Francisco School of Medicine, San Francisco, CA

Mary Butler, PhD, University of Minnesota School of Public Health, Minneapolis

Timothy D. Carroll, MA, Minneapolis VA Health System, Minneapolis, MN

Marilyn A. Cornish, PhD, Special Education, Rehabilitation, and Counseling, Auburn University, Auburn, AL

Joseph M. Currier, PhD, University of South Alabama, Veterans Recovery Resources, Mobile

Kent D. Drescher, PhD, National Center for PTSD (Retired), VA Palo Alto Health Care System, Menlo Park, CA

Afsoon Eftekhari, PhD, National Center for PTSD, Palo Alto VA Health Care System, Menlo Park, CA

Wyatt R. Evans, PhD, VA North Texas Health Care System, Dallas

Jacob K. Farnsworth, PhD, VA Eastern Colorado Health System, Aurora

Matt J. Gray, PhD, Department of Psychology, University of Wyoming, Laramie

Brandon J. Griffin, PhD, Central Arkansas VA Health Care System; University of Arkansas for Medical Sciences, Little Rock

J. Irene Harris, PhD, Edith Nourse Rogers Memorial Veterans Hospital, Bedford, MA; University of Minnesota Medical School, Minneapolis

Kerry Haynes, DMin, BCC, South Texas Veterans Health Care System, San Antonio

Philip Held, PhD, Department of Psychiatry and Behavioral Sciences, Rush University Medical Center, Chicago, IL

Vanessa M. Jacoby, PhD, University of Texas Health Science Center at San Antonio

Kelsey R. Sprang Jones, PsyD, Emory University School of Medicine, Atlanta, GA

Brian J. Klassen, PhD, Department of Psychiatry and Behavioral Sciences, Rush University Medical Center, Chicago, IL

Brett T. Litz, PhD, VA Boston Healthcare System, Boston University School of Medicine, Boston, MA

Shira Maguen, PhD, San Francisco VA Health Care System; UC San Francisco School of Medicine, San Francisco, CA

Keith G. Meador, MD, ThM, MPH, VA Mental Health & Chaplaincy, Vanderbilt University, Nashville, TN

Jason Nieuwsma, PhD, VA Mental Health & Chaplaincy, Duke University School of Medicine, Durham, NC

Natalie Purcell, PhD, MPA, San Francisco VA Health Care System; Department of Social and Behavioral Sciences, University of California, San Francisco, San Francisco, CA

Sheila A. M. Rauch, PhD, Emory University School of Medicine, Atlanta VA Health Care System, Atlanta, GA

David C. Rozek, PhD, UCF RESTORES, University of Central Florida, Orlando

Andrew M. Sherrill, PhD, Emory University School of Medicine, Atlanta, GA

Melissa A. Smigelsky, PhD, VA Mental Health & Chaplaincy, Durham, NC

Erin R. Smith, PhD, VA Ann Arbor Healthcare System; University of Michigan Medical School, Ann Arbor

Timothy J. Usset, MDiv, MPH, Center for Veterans Research and Education, Minneapolis VA Health Care System; University of Minnesota School of Public Health, Minneapolis

Jennifer Schuster Wachen, PhD, National Center for PTSD, VA Boston Healthcare System; Boston University School of Medicine, Boston, MA

Robyn D. Walser, PhD, National Center for PTSD, Menlo Park, CA

Emily Wharton, MS, PGSP-Stanford PsyD Consortium, Palo Alto University, Palo Alto, CA

Everett L. Worthington Jr., PhD, Psychology Department, Virginia Commonwealth University, Richmond

Jennifer H. Wortmann, PhD, VA Mental Health & Chaplaincy, Boston, MA

ADDRESSING
MORAL INJURY
in CLINICAL
PRACTICE

Introduction to Moral Injury

Joseph M. Currier, Kent D. Drescher, and Jason Nieuwsma

Philosophers of science have repeatedly demonstrated that more than one theoretical construction can always be placed upon a given collection of data. History
of science indicates that, particularly in the early developmental stages of a new
paradigm, it is not even very difficult to invent such alternates. . . . So long as the
tools a paradigm supplies continue to prove capable of solving the problem it
defines, science moves fastest and penetrates most deeply through confident
employment of those tools. The reason is clear. As in manufacture so in science—retooling is an extravagance to be reserved for the occasion that demands
it. The significance of crises is the indication they provide that an occasion for
retooling has arrived. (Kuhn, 1964, p. 76)

The post-9/11 era has presented psychologists and other mental health
clinicians with many occasions for retooling paradigms for posttraumatic
stress disorder (PTSD) and other possible trauma-related issues among service
members and veterans (SM/Vs). Recent military conflicts in Iraq and Afghanistan
mark the longest sustained ground combat operations in U.S. history. Due to
an influx of veterans from these campaigns and renewed motivation for
help-seeking among veterans from previous conflicts, PTSD diagnoses in the
Veterans Administration (VA) system roughly doubled within just 5 years after
9/11 (e.g., Rosenheck & Fontana, 2007). As these conflicts persisted, new waves

https://doi.org/10.1037/0000204-001
Addressing Moral Injury in Clinical Practice, J. M. Currier, K. D. Drescher, and
J. Nieuwsma (Editors)

of men and women enlisted to serve their country for varying lengths of time. However, given a record low percentage of U.S. adults (18 years and up) who serve in the military (U.S. Census Bureau, 2014), many veterans have endured exceptionally heavy physical, emotional, and spiritual burdens from their wartime service.

Amid this backdrop, suicide has emerged as a particularly troubling occurrence among SM/Vs. Although a variety of nonmilitary factors may also increase risk of a suicide attempt (Ursano et al., 2017, 2018), SM/Vs have been dying by suicide at roughly twice the rate as nonmilitary persons for over a decade (Kang & Bullman, 2008)—to the point where suicide deaths surpassed combat-related fatalities in active duty personnel in 2012 (Armed Forces Health Surveillance Center, 2014), and roughly 17 to 20 veterans continue to die by suicide each day (U.S. Department of Veterans Affairs, 2018). Importantly, PTSD and other mental health conditions are among many possible chronic risk factors for suicide and other life-threatening health-related conditions (Pompili et al., 2013). However, given that evidence-based practices for PTSD often do not generate the same favorable outcomes in SM/Vs compared with other trauma-exposed groups (Steenkamp & Litz, 2013; Steenkamp et al., 2015), this troubling epidemic has fueled an alarming sense of crisis for many clinicians to retool models and methods of addressing the possible emotional, physical, social, and spiritual burdens of SM/Vs.

Although these statistics for the post-9/11 era are concerning, every sustained period of major ground combat operations in U.S. history has created extraordinary challenges for clinicians or helping professionals tasked with caring for traumatized SM/Vs. Clinical accounts and findings from the Civil War (Pizarro et al., 2006), World War I (Myers, 1915), and World War II (WWII; Archibald & Tuddenham, 1965) highlight the lasting alterations in emotion, cognition, and behavior that may emerge for SM/Vs exposed to the diverse types of traumas that occur in times of war. For example, focusing on the war with the greatest number of casualties of U.S. personnel, a creative archival analysis of the military and medical records of 17,700 Civil War veterans revealed exposure to potential military traumas (e.g., being wounded, percentage of company killed) was associated with worse risk of a range of postwar mental health issues, as well as cardiac and gastrointestinal diseases (Pizarro et al., 2006).

In light of such physical and mental health costs, clinicians caring for SM/Vs from each U.S. military era have attempted to retool paradigms for describing and understanding the trauma-related symptomatology among SM/Vs seeking their care. For instance, the term "soldier's heart" was often used in conjunction with the Civil War, "shell shock" with World War I, and "combat fatigue" or "battle fatigue" with World War II. Building on insights of these prior generations of clinicians and researchers, the term "posttraumatic stress disorder" was not used in mental health professions until the 1970s in response to severe adjustment issues of many Vietnam veterans (Kulka et al., 1990). In turn, although core features of the traumatic stress response in the diagnostic criteria for PTSD have not changed over subsequent decades (reexperiencing, physiologic arousal, behavioral avoidance, and emotional numbing), the specific symptoms and composition of symptom clusters evolved with each iteration of the *Diagnostic and Statistical Manual of Mental Disorders* (*DSM*; Friedman et al., 2011).

The formalization of a PTSD diagnosis after the Vietnam War has fueled innovation in scientific research and clinical practice in many ways. However, when considering the emphasis on moral aspects of military trauma in art and literature dating back to some of human societies' earliest records (Crocq & Crocq, 2000), as well as astute theoretical and clinical observations of traumatologists working with SM/Vs in the pre-PTSD era (e.g., Haley, 1974), an increasing number of voices have questioned why *trauma* has been nearly exclusively defined as a fear-evoking encounter with death or life-limiting injury for oneself and/or others (e.g., Nash, 2019). Although the term "moral injury" is still new in mental health fields, clinicians who cared for prior generations of SM/Vs often discussed the central importance of moral transgressions, betrayal-related events, and the role of ensuing painful moral emotions and cognitions in hindering recovery from posttraumatic issues. For example, after caring for veterans in an outpatient mental health setting in the years after WWII, Futterman and Pumpian-Mindlin (1951) reported the following observation in the *American Journal of Psychiatry*:

> A factor prevalent among our patients was that of guilt around killing, injuring, or striking a defenseless enemy. As long as the killing of enemy soldiers was done during active combat when it was a question of "kill or be killed," there was relatively little guilt. However, if enemy soldiers or noncombatants were shot when they were unarmed, or unprepared for the attack, or while in a seemingly defenseless position, great guilt was engendered. . . . At such times, apparently, the military code and superimposed group conscience, which gave permission to kill or destroy under certain circumstances, was quickly dissipated and replaced by the usual civilian morale and conscience, which places sharp limited on such impulses. Under such circumstances, conflict and guilt were quickly generated, and difficult to master. (pp. 402–403)

In many ways, this account mirrors the observations of clinicians throughout the United States who care for traumatized SM/Vs in this current post-9/11 era. However, like clinicians of earlier military eras retooling their predecessors' models of addressing traumatic stress reactions to be optimally responsive to SM/Vs seeking their help, many clinicians today are struggling to operate neatly within existing paradigms to understand and respond to these types of severe moral challenges in their work.

Specifically, until the recent fifth iteration of the *DSM* (*DSM-5*; American Psychiatric Association, 2013), there was not even a partial acknowledgment of severe moral challenges as a viable precipitating event for enduring traumatic stress reactions. Further, before *DSM-5*, painful moral cognitions and emotions were similarly not reflected in the symptom criteria for PTSD. However, even with the recent restructuring of symptom clusters, addition of new symptoms (e.g., reckless behavior), and the inclusion of Cluster D's negative changes in beliefs and emotions into the diagnostic criteria in a manner that may capture possible outcomes of a moral injury as the construct is loosely defined at this time (e.g., self-condemnation and shame, profound mistrust and anger; Friedman et al., 2011), these issues may only contribute to a PTSD diagnosis if they arise after exposure to an event featuring actual or threatened death, serious injury, or sexual violence. As such, many of the severely morally challenging events for SM/Vs and other trauma-exposed groups (e.g., first responders) that clinicians should anticipate encountering in their therapeutic work currently do not fit neatly into the definition of trauma in *DSM-5*. At present, it is not apparent whether the continuum of morally injurious sequelae cannot be adequately captured by the PTSD diagnostic criteria such that a Kuhnian paradigm shift might be indicated (Litz & Kerig, 2019). Instead, as highlighted in the coming chapters, clinicians are attempting to adapt their models and methods to varying degrees to holistically and effectively heal the possible moral, emotional, social, and spiritual wounds of war.

This book is a testament to the growing number of researchers and clinicians who are studying and developing interventions targeting the prevention and treatment of moral injury. As we discuss later, there are likely more questions than answers about the essential features of moral injury and how to conceptualize, assess for, and treat this underdefined condition in clinical practice. Nonetheless, whether occurring in military service, civilian peacekeeping occupations (e.g., law enforcement), or other situations in which persons witness and/or engage in acts that violate one's basic sense of humanity and morality, unresolved wounds of morally injurious events continue to burden many persons in a manner that might lead to serious health-related consequences and decrements in psychosocial functioning. As such, clinicians working in this current post-9/11 era are seeking to address moral injury now in an efficacious manner based on the emerging clinical research literature. The approaches and interventions in this book were selected largely according to the extent to which they have been deployed and systematically evaluated to date (even if not yet in formal clinical trials), with a recognition that many other psychotherapeutic, sociocultural, and spiritual approaches may also have benefit for persons struggling with moral injury. In so doing, we hope this book will inform and guide mental health clinicians, chaplains, and other helping professionals about relative conceptual issues in moral injury and promising therapeutic approaches to possibly incorporate in their work with morally injured patients who seek their care.

DEFINING MORAL INJURY

In keeping with the varying ways in which military trauma and ensuing traumatic stress reactions have been conceptualized over the centuries, there is presently no unanimous definition of moral injury. Drawing on philosophical and psychological insights from Homer's tragedies (e.g., the story of Achilles in the *Iliad*) to understand the suffering of Vietnam veterans entrusted to his care, Shay (1994) first introduced this concept in the mental health literature following the first Gulf War. However, partly in response to the burgeoning numbers of veterans from recent conflicts in Iraq and Afghanistan seeking treatment for trauma-related issues after 9/11, serious scientific inquiry on moral injury arguably did not begin until the publication of Litz et al.'s (2009) seminal review article. Since then, moral injury has increasingly captured empirical and scholarly attention from psychologists and other mental health professionals, physicians, chaplains, theologians, and philosophers. Although such interdisciplinary appeal offers a unique opportunity for collaboration and innovation, a lack of definitional specificity across fields also creates challenges with reliability and communication. Further, consistent with understanding posttraumatic reactions in general, important distinctions should be made between different aspects of this emerging construct (e.g., exposure, appraisal, outcomes). However, even within a single discipline, such as psychology, clinicians and researchers often do not maintain precision in their terminology. In turn, attempts at both intra- or interprofessional communication between clinicians, researchers, and/or scholars about moral injury can be quite difficult. Therefore, although many of the chapter authors adopt their own terminology and might disagree about the overall process of moral injury development, we now offer preliminary definitions of key terminology that will be used throughout this book.

Potentially Morally Injurious Events

Contrary to the *DSM-5* Criterion A for a PTSD diagnosis, there are no established criteria for the required features of potentially morally injurious events (PMIEs). However, moral injury is thought to emerge after exposure to severely morally troubling events that fit into two general categories on the basis of perceived moral responsibility. First, PMIEs may entail actions or decisions in which SM/Vs somehow transgressed a moral belief or value by what they did or failed to do. Also referred to as *transgressive acts* and *perpetration-based events*, this category was defined by Litz et al. (2009) as "perpetrating, failing to prevent, or bearing witness to acts that threaten to transgress deeply held moral beliefs and expectations" (p. 700). Whether intentionally or not, such events may entail incidents involving mistreatment or harm to civilians (particularly women and children) or inability to prevent death and suffering, as well as killing an enemy combatant or another person. Depending on the context of the situation, SM/Vs might also find themselves in the role of a witness to or victim of others' moral wrongdoing. Shay (1994) captured this second category of PMIEs in a three-part definition: (a) betrayal of "what's right," (b) by someone who holds legitimate authority, (c) in a high-stakes situation. Given the need for interdependency within units and collaboration with indigenous persons in asymmetrical warfare contexts, we suggest Shay's emphasis on leadership malpractice within the military can be expanded to include "betrayal-based events" from other relationships or sources as well (e.g., peers, trusted civilians, authority figures outside the military ranks).

To date, research has revealed three sets of findings for PMIEs with special relevance for clinical practice. First, when accounting for effects of other types of military traumas (e.g., life threat), exposure to PMIEs emerged in many studies as a salient indicator of common mental health conditions in military populations (e.g., PTSD, depression, suicide ideation or attempts; for reviews, see Frankfurt & Frazier, 2016; Griffin et al., 2019; Litz et al., 2009). Second, drawing on qualitative findings from trauma narratives written at the start of evidence-based interventions for PTSD with a therapeutic exposure component, research found self- and other-focused PMIEs were identified as the Criterion A stressors for a substantive subset of military service members seeking care at a large army base (Litz et al., 2018; Stein et al., 2012). Third, beyond the higher conditional risk of mental health conditions in service members with greater exposures to PMIEs, findings from treatment-seeking samples indicated those who identified PMIEs as their most distressing events also reported more complexity in their distress symptom presentations (Litz et al., 2018). In combination with other work (e.g., Bryan et al., 2018; Jordan et al., 2017; Litz et al., 2018; Stein et al., 2012), these findings raise questions about whether PTSD, as traditionally defined and assessed, captures all clinical concerns that may emerge from exposure to PMIEs.

Moral Violation

Notwithstanding the seemingly morally challenging nature of PMIEs, clinicians should refrain from pathologizing the occurrence of such stressors in the dangerous and violent contexts that can characterize military service. Just as longitudinal work suggests the majority of persons who experience events that meet the *DSM-5* Criterion A do not go on to develop chronic PTSD (Galatzer-Levy et al., 2018), SM/Vs who encounter PMIEs may similarly not become morally injured. For example, Jordan et al. (2017) supported a trend toward resilience or recovery with 867 active duty marines from an infantry battalion that engaged in heavy combat operations between 2008 and 2011 in Afghanistan. Specifically, using Nash et al.'s (2013) Moral Injury Event Scale (MIES), they found that only one third of these marines reported exposure to perpetration- and/or betrayal-based PMIEs in the month following their war-zone deployments. Although the MIES may confound exposure and consequences of PMIEs (Frankfurt & Frazier, 2016), it is quite notable that individuals in Jordan et al.'s sample arguably served in the most demanding combat operational roles during one of the most violent and chaotic periods in this lengthy conflict. As such, these findings highlight a need for clinicians to not assume that SM/Vs with even the heaviest levels of combat exposure will inevitably experience their war-zone stressors in terms of a transgressive act or betrayal of trust.

Instead, whether beginning in the immediate aftermath of the event or upon negotiating varying moral conventions and expectations in civilian life, it is assumed that moral injury only develops when an SM/V has appraised the event as somehow being morally wrong or violating deeply held beliefs or values. Further, whether as a perpetrator, witness, or victim, he or she may feel a sense of personal agency about the occurrence of such events or strong desire to see moral violations committed by others punished or rectified. Unlike mental health conditions that are characterized partly by an absence of conscience or concern with living congruently with moral values or beliefs (e.g., psychopathy), the development of moral injury therefore assumes an SM/V possesses an intact moral code or system of personal morality that might be violated. Lancaster and Erbes (2017) supported the importance of moral appraisals in moral injury development. Namely, focusing on 182 war-zone veterans, Lancaster and Erbes found those who evaluated their combat-related actions, comrades' actions, and/or actions of their commanding officers as being morally wrong were more likely to report worse outcomes that align with emerging definitions of moral injury (e.g., PTSD, anger, shame). Importantly, these findings held in the presence of exposure to combat stressors in general, supporting the role of moral violation in the course of moral injury development.

Moral Pain

When considering how moral violation may lead to development of a moral injury, SM/Vs may experience painful moral emotions (e.g., shame, guilt, anger) and cognitions (e.g., moral culpability or responsibility, self- or other-condemnation) in response to PMIEs that cause significant intrapsychic tension and conflict (Farnsworth et al., 2017). Whether this moral pain emerges immediately after the event or later on, Farnsworth et al. (2017) argued that clinicians should at least initially conceptualize these emotional–cognitive reactions as expected, natural, and nonpathological. For instance, as described in Chapter 2, this volume, painful moral cognitions and emotions can be essential for maintaining shared moral beliefs or values that promote and protect the cohesion of human communities. Further, in the aftermath of PMIEs that are viewed as morally wrong, these responses can prompt appraisals and behaviors that facilitate healing and repair ties to one's larger social community (e.g., disclosure of trauma-related difficulties and shared acknowledgment of tragedy). Therefore, moral pain may provide adaptive functions for the larger social group as a whole but sometimes at the expense of an SM/V's relationships and ability to derive a sense of meaning and belonging in culturally sanctioned activities for a time-limited period (e.g., family, work, religion). Put differently, moral pain in itself can represent a healthy response to PMIEs that violate sacred values or beliefs of the SM/V's larger community, while also fueling distressing patterns of thinking and feeling that have to be honored and resolved in a supportive community or social group (Farnsworth et al., 2017).

In these ways, moral pain can be likened to the experience of grief after bereavement. In cases of common or normal grief after the death of an attachment figure, indications of distress (e.g., sadness and crying, cognitive confusion, social withdrawal, reduced productivity) in the initial postloss period can be an unreliable predictor of mental health status and psychosocial functioning in the distant future (Galatzer-Levy et al., 2018). Instead, even with spousal or child bereavement (e.g., Maccallum et al., 2015), longitudinal findings suggest most grievers display a resilient (i.e., little to no distress or impairment after loss) or recovery (i.e., initial increase in distress after loss and return to baseline functioning) trajectory with respect to depression and other bereavement-related conditions (Galatzer-Levy et al., 2018). However, even in the year after a major loss, certain forms or expressions of grief (e.g., intense sorrow and rumination over the loved one's death, persistent and preoccupying longing for deceased) might be indicative of a complicated and prolonged course of suffering that will not resolve without clinical intervention (Prigerson et al., 2009). In such cases, clinicians have to avoid pathologizing anticipated and normal reactions to the loss of a cherished relationship while also deciphering instances when the grieving process has somehow gone awry. Similarly, although moral pain is necessary for a moral injury to develop, not all SM/Vs who experience such cognitions and emotions will need care from mental health professionals and/or possible religious and informal sources in their lives.

Building on these insights, Litz and Kerig (2019) recently offered a useful heuristic model for differentiating between moral stressors of varying levels of magnitude and impact. For example, when considering a constant need for moral judgments and decision making in human societies, certain stressors may represent *moral challenges* but not be viewed as directly relevant to one's life (e.g., lack of responsiveness to children dying by malnutrition in developing world) in a manner that may not cause moral emotions such as anger or disgust. In contrast, Litz and Kerig contended that *moral stressors* (e.g., infidelity or other ways of mistreating a loved one) must precipitate distressing behavioral and psychological consequences that lead to some degree of impairment. For example, someone may ruminate daily or lose sleep over a moral stressor but not be incapacitated or overly define themselves according to the painful experience. In this way, moral stressors likely occur less frequently than moral challenges and have a greater probability of moral pain and possible dysfunction in life roles and relationships. However, according to Litz and Kerig, moral stressors should not be equated with PMIEs in that they are less likely to entail salient threats to personal integrity or loss of life in a manner that might lead to severely painful moral thoughts or emotions that could constitute injurious and scarring experiences in themselves.

Moral Injury

Unfortunately, whether due to the severity of PMIEs, lack of psychosocial resources, or other factors (e.g., premilitary trauma exposure, personality, moral development), many SM/Vs do not negotiate moral pain in a manner that supports meaning making and social connectedness. In such cases, SM/Vs may display a trajectory of chronic emotional, social, and spiritual suffering characterized by severe impairments in psychosocial functioning and a range of potentially self-destructive behaviors (e.g., self-handicapping, social isolation, substance abuse, suicide attempt). Building on Shay's (1994) insights about moral injury being a character wound from a betrayal-related event, Litz et al. (2009) provided this working definition of moral injury:

> disruption in an individual's confidence and expectations about one's own or others' motivation to behave in a just and ethical manner . . . brought about by perpetrating, failing to prevent, bearing witness to, or learning about acts that transgress deeply held moral beliefs and expectations. (p. 700)

Further, Litz et al. suggested aspects of the PTSD symptom criteria would characterize the long-term impact of morally injurious events (i.e., intrusive reexperiencing of event, behavioral avoidance of painful thoughts or emotions and triggering contexts, and emotional numbing), as well as self-harm or self-handicapping (e.g., poor self-care, substance abuse, lack of social or professional advancement) behaviors and enduring changes in identity. More recently, Farnsworth et al. (2017) defined moral injury as the "expanded and additional psychological, social, and spiritual suffering stemming from costly dysfunctional and or unworkable attempts to manage, control, or cope with the experience of moral pain" (p. 392).

At present, there is a lack of consensus about the specific symptoms or outcomes that may signify this state of being morally injured. However, to distinguish between perpetration- and betrayal-based outcomes, Griffin et al. (2019) highlighted possible continua of moral injury according to the extent to which SM/Vs appraise themselves as (a) committing moral violations and (b) being the victim of another person's transgressive behavior. Further, drawing on an anonymous survey and in-depth interviews with subject experts, Currier et al. (2018) found agreement that self-directed forms of moral injury appear to be characterized by feelings of pervasive shame and guilt; beliefs and attitudes about being unlovable, unforgivable, and incapable of moral decision making; and self-handicapping behaviors. In contrast, in cases of betrayal or witnessing others' acts of moral wrongdoing for which they do not feel personally responsible, subject experts agreed that betrayal-based or other-directed outcomes of a moral injury might include feelings of anger and moral disgust, beliefs and attitudes related to mistrust of others, and revenge fantasies about the responsible person(s). Others have also posited that moral injury typically includes PTSD symptoms (e.g., Litz et al., 2009). However, as highlighted in the upcoming chapters, subject experts disagree as to whether the PTSD diagnostic framework should be retooled to account for distress symptoms associated with a possible moral injury.

PLAN FOR THE BOOK

With these definitions and concepts in mind, this book is intended to support clinicians who are seeking to serve as instruments of healing and change with morally injured SM/Vs and other patients. The editors of this book are clinical psychologists with varying professional backgrounds in clinical practice and research with SM/Vs and civilian traumas. Following his internship and fellow-ship at a large VA medical center when the initial waves of Iraq and Afghanistan veterans were first enrolling in VA health care, Joseph M. Currier has contin-ued serving these men and women in an academic career at a research uni-versity and partnerships with community-based organizations. Also someone who trained at a VA medical center, Jason Nieuwsma has served SM/Vs via training and education, research, and administration with VA's Mental Health and Chaplaincy program office for the past decade. Now (partly) retired, Kent D. Drescher has devoted the past quarter-century to caring for veterans in numerous ways, both within a major VA medical center and a community-based program. In many cases, we serve as lead authors on chapters that are within our areas of professional expertise. However, in most cases, we invited lead-ing mental health experts from VA medical centers, academic medical centers, universities, and community-based organizations to author chapters in their relative areas of expertise with respect to theory and practice for moral injury. In so doing, we proudly assembled a set of authors who are on the frontlines of caring for morally injured SM/Vs and advancing scientific understandings of this construct in the process. Although these subject experts also have backgrounds in clinical or counseling psychology, this book was intended for clinicians from all mental health disciplines, chaplains, and other helping pro-fessionals who are seeking direction in promoting recovery from moral injury in their work with military-connected populations and possible other trauma-exposed groups.

Notwithstanding a shared commitment to science–practice integration with respect to moral injury, you will see a diversity of views and opinions about whether mental health fields are in a state of crisis that may lead to a possible paradigm shift with respect to moral injury. For example, in some cases, authors conceptualize moral injury as a traumatic theme or aspect of PTSD, whereas others assume the conditions are interrelated but separate. You will also find the authors using different language at points about varying components of the moral injury construct (e.g., moral injury outcomes vs. moral injury–based distress). In many ways, this diversity of viewpoints highlights the absence of a paradigmatic framework and comprehensive model for moral injury that may guide clinical practice and research in the decades to come. Looking ahead, it is likely that many of the chapter authors will support this scientific work of discovery and operationalization. However, in the absence of a con-sensus definition at this time, we ensured synchrony across the authors on these basic components of the moral injury construct when inviting them to contribute to this book:

- Military service can entail morally troubling situations that violate SM/Vs' deeply held moral values and beliefs, whether through perpetrating, witness-ing, or being victimized via such events.

- These perceived moral violations elicit strong moral emotions and cognitions directed toward self or others. When a moral injury occurs, these thoughts and emotions may endure and motivate unhelpful or dysfunctional behaviors that impact social or relational, psychological, and spiritual well-being. In many cases, mental health diagnoses such as PTSD and major depressive disorder can co-occur and be interrelated.

- In cases when a moral injury develops, SM/Vs have appraised the morally injurious event(s) as being morally wrong and often feel a sense of personal agency related to the occurrence of the event(s) or have a strong desire to see those violations committed by others punished or rectified.

Beyond these points of agreement, authors nonetheless make different assumptions and statements about moral injury. In an era of polarization of thought leaders with divergent ideas (Lukianoff & Haidt, 2018), we hope this book will promote the necessary respect and dialogue among clinicians and researchers for advancing evidence-based practices for moral injury that may truly support SM/Vs and other trauma-exposed groups in the years to come.

In designing the table of contents and recruiting the chapter authors, this book was not intended to privilege any particular theoretical orientation or conceptual framework. Rather, whether in a controlled outcome study or another type of intervention trial, we opted to prioritize treatment models in which proponents had taken steps to clearly describe and formalize their therapeutic procedures (e.g., manualization), evaluate outcomes with potentially morally injured patients in some manner, and disseminate their research findings to the public. With this said, few of the treatments in this book would likely satisfy established standards for determining best practices in mental health care (e.g., one or more well-designed randomized clinical trials). Further, this commitment to science–practice integration led to an overrepresentation of approaches that are based on cognitive behavior therapy (CBT) models. In keeping with an unfortunate trend in psychotherapy research for proponents of non-CBT approaches to less frequently operationalize, describe, and evaluate their methods, a similar pattern appears to be emerging in the clinical research literature on moral injury—likely for similar reasons (e.g., epistemological differences, lack of funding or other resources). However, beyond a strong reliance on focal components of empirically supported treatments for PTSD (e.g., imaginal exposure, revising unhelpful cognitions), many of the CBT-based treatments in this book also incorporate approaches from alternate theoretical models that have not been emphasized as often in the clinical research literature (e.g., experiential strategies in emotion-focused therapy; Greenberg, 2015).

For readers who are not trained in CBT or align with other theoretical orientations, many of the treatments in this book are rooted in well-established understandings of trauma, stress, and psychopathology. Specifically, many of the authors believe that, unless definitive evidence indicates that existing scientifically supported approaches and models for PTSD do not work for moral injury, we should rely on them whenever possible. For example, multiple chapters rely on seminal ideas by Beck (1983), Foa and Kozak (1986), Lazarus and Folkman (1984), and other historically prominent figures about stress-related responses and the interplay between cognition, emotion, and behavioral attempts at coping with traumatic events.

Recently, when considering the application of Lazarus and Folkman's ideas to moral injury, in particular, Nash (2019) raised concerns about using a stress-appraisal-coping framework to explain why some individuals disconnect from others and experience decrements in psychosocial functioning after a morally injurious event. Specifically, if clinicians assume the choice of coping strategies is fully under an individual's control, Nash cautioned that overreliance on the idea of maladaptive coping with these traumas threatens to stigmatize moral injury when it occurs and reduce the likelihood of help seeking and engagement in the types of treatments in this book. Nash raised concerns that CBT-minded researchers and clinicians, in particular, should consider in their work. However, many of this book's contributors likely vary in their alignment with a stress-appraisal-coping framework, and we, the editors, attempted to include a diversity of theoretical models without evaluating them per se. Further, even in chapters with a broad grounding in CBT, authors often suggest alternate frameworks for conceptualizing moral injury or highlight that painful trauma-related cognitions about morally injurious events may not always be inaccurate or distorted in nature.

Although chapter authors represent many of the best clinical minds and hearts for addressing moral injury, we must also offer a final disclaimer that many of the pressing questions facing clinicians will not be resolved in this book: What is moral injury? What is not moral injury? What are the necessary and sufficient features of moral injury? How can these features differentiate nonclinical manifestations of moral reactions to transgressive acts and/or betrayals? What are unique nonoverlapping features of moral injury relative to PTSD and other common mental health conditions in SM/Vs (e.g., depressive and anxiety disorders), if any? What are the unique collateral consequences of moral injury compared with these existing mental health conditions? Should moral injury symptoms or outcomes be characterized as manifestations of an underlying disease or medical syndrome or in a less traditional framework in mental health disciplines today? When should military leaders and peers, family members and nonmilitary friends, and/or clinicians be concerned that an SM/V, employee, or loved one needs help to prevent chronic or disabling problems from arising from a PMIE? What threshold should be crossed for clinicians to target moral injury, and how can they evaluate the success of their helping efforts? In this process, how can clinicians be certain they are not pathologizing moral pain when treating moral injury in their work? More broadly, what does moral injury say about society and the justness of wars in general? To what extent are leaders and members of society complicit in morally questionable acts of their fellow citizens?

In the absence of scientifically based answers to satisfy these foundational questions, this book will not provide a definitive compendium of best practice guidelines for caring for morally injured persons. Instead, we compiled convergent and divergent views of addressing moral injury from leading experts who are advancing theoretical models and suggestions for clinical practices at this early stage of intervention development and dissemination. In so doing, this book will hopefully aid clinicians by summarizing the major scholarly and empirical contributions in this increasingly variegated area and structuring the conversation about how to care for morally injured SM/Vs and possible civilian groups in the coming decades. Looking ahead, addressing these larger aims will also ideally enhance the efficacy of clinicians who are looking for practical guidance now about how to conceptualize moral injury and apply therapeutic strategies that afford the greatest probability of supporting men and women who are seeking their help. Rather than simply restating findings that have been adequately summarized in other scholarly sources (e.g., Frankfurt & Frazier, 2016; Griffin et al., 2019; Litz et al., 2009), we encouraged the authors to assume a more practically oriented approach in organizing their chapters and to utilize material from their clinical cases to illustrate conceptual points and potential therapeutic strategies that others may also apply.

This book is organized to flow from more conceptual concerns related to treating moral injury to specific intervention models that have been subject to some scientific inquiry to date. Accordingly, Chapters 1 and 2 describe prominent possible conceptual frameworks for understanding moral injury that could inform the clinician's process of selecting and delivering treatment methods (CBT, social functionalism). Next, this book addresses religious and spiritual (Chapter 3) and forgiveness (Chapter 4) issues in moral injury followed by a possible framework for case conceptualization with value for clinicians working from different theoretical models (Chapter 5) and discussion of unavoidable issues facing clinicians who desire to care for morally injured persons (e.g., cultivating a therapeutic alliance, managing vicarious trauma; Chapter 6). In turn, the "meat" of this book entails discussions of emerging evidence-based interventions for treating moral injury, five of which are based in a CBT framework (Chapters 7–11) and two spiritually integrated approaches with potential benefit for SM/Vs with certain cultural values and beliefs (Chapters 12 and 13). Last, we attempt to synthesize the authors' insights and offer ideas for advancing scientific and clinical work in the concluding chapter (Chapter 14). By the end of this book, clinicians will not become experts in treating moral injury. However, we are all learning together, and we hope that all of us may grow more equipped to facilitate recovery from moral injury and identify promising clinical models for which additional education and training might be pursued in the future.

REFERENCES

American Psychiatric Association. (2013). *Diagnostic and statistical manual of mental disorders* (5th ed.). https://doi.org/10.1176/appi.books.9780890425596

Archibald, H. C., & Tuddenham, R. D. (1965). Persistent stress reaction after combat: A 20-year follow-up. *Archives of General Psychiatry, 12*(5), 475–481. https://doi.org/10.1001/archpsyc.1965.01720350043006

Armed Forces Health Surveillance Center. (2014). Surveillance snapshot: Manner and cause of death, active component, U.S. Armed Forces, 1998–2013. *Medical Surveillance Monthly Report, 21*(10), 21.

Beck, A. T. (1983). *Theory and treatment of depression: Towards a dynamic interactionism model.* Leuven University Press.

Bryan, C. J., Bryan, A. O., Roberge, E., Leifker, F. R., & Rozek, D. C. (2018). Moral injury, posttraumatic stress disorder, and suicidal behavior among National Guard personnel. *Psychological Trauma: Theory, Research, Practice, and Policy, 10*(1), 36–45. https://doi.org/10.1037/tra0000290

Crocq, M. A., & Crocq, L. (2000). From shell shock and war neurosis to posttraumatic stress disorder: A history of psychotraumatology. *Dialogues in Clinical Neuroscience, 2*(1), 47–55.

Currier, J. M., Farnsworth, J. K., Drescher, K. D., McDermott, R. C., Sims, B. M., & Albright, D. L. (2018). Development and evaluation of the Expressions of Moral Injury Scale–Military Version. *Clinical Psychology & Psychotherapy, 25*(3), 474–488.

Farnsworth, J. K., Drescher, K. D., Evans, W., & Walser, R. D. (2017). A functional approach to understanding and treating military-related moral injury. *Journal of Contextual Behavioral Science, 6*(4), 391–397. https://doi.org/10.1016/j.jcbs.2017.07.003

Foa, E. B., & Kozak, M. J. (1986). Emotional processing of fear: Exposure to corrective information. *Psychological Bulletin, 99*(1), 20–35. https://doi.org/10.1037/0033-2909.99.1.20

Frankfurt, S., & Frazier, P. (2016). A review of research on moral injury in combat veterans. *Military Psychology, 28*(5), 318–330. https://doi.org/10.1037/mil0000132

Friedman, M. J., Resick, P. A., Bryant, R. A., & Brewin, C. R. (2011). Considering PTSD for *DSM-5. Depression and Anxiety, 28*(9), 750–769. https://doi.org/10.1002/da.20767

Futterman, S., & Pumpian-Mindlin, E. (1951). Traumatic war neuroses five years later. *The American Journal of Psychiatry, 108*(6), 401–408. https://doi.org/10.1176/ajp.108.6.401

Galatzer-Levy, I. R., Huang, S. H., & Bonanno, G. A. (2018). Trajectories of resilience and dysfunction following potential trauma: A review and statistical evaluation. *Clinical Psychology Review, 63*, 41–55. https://doi.org/10.1016/j.cpr.2018.05.008

Greenberg, L. S. (2015). *Emotion-focused therapy: Coaching clients to work through their feelings.* American Psychological Association. https://doi.org/10.1037/14692-000

Griffin, B. J., Purcell, N., Burkman, K., Litz, B. T., Bryan, C. J., Schmitz, M., Villierme, C., Walsh, J., & Maguen, S. (2019). Moral injury: An integrative review. *Journal of Traumatic Stress, 32*(3), 350–362. https://doi.org/10.1002/jts.22362

Haley, S. A. (1974). When the patient reports atrocities: Specific treatment considerations of the Vietnam veteran. *Archives of General Psychiatry, 30*(2), 191–196. https://doi.org/10.1001/archpsyc.1974.01760080051008

Jordan, A. H., Eisen, E., Bolton, E., Nash, W. P., & Litz, B. T. (2017). Distinguishing war-related PTSD resulting from perpetration- and betrayal-based morally injurious events. *Psychological Trauma: Theory, Research, Practice, and Policy, 9*(6), 627–634. https://doi.org/10.1037/tra0000249

Kang, H. K., & Bullman, T. A. (2008). Risk of suicide among US veterans after returning from the Iraq or Afghanistan war zones. *JAMA, 300*(6), 652–653. https://doi.org/10.1001/jama.300.6.652

Kuhn, T. S. (1964). *The structure of scientific revolutions.* University of Chicago Press.

Kulka, R. A., Schlenger, W. E., Fairbank, J. A., Hough, R. L., Jordan, B. K., & Marmar, C. R. (1990). *Trauma and the Vietnam War generation: Report of findings from the National Vietnam Veterans Readjustment Study.* Brunner/Mazel.

Lancaster, S. L., & Erbes, C. R. (2017). Importance of moral appraisals in military veterans. *Traumatology, 23*(4), 317–322. https://doi.org/10.1037/trm0000123

Lazarus, R. S., & Folkman, S. (1984). *Stress, appraisal, and coping.* Springer.

Litz, B. T., Contractor, A. A., Rhodes, C., Dondanville, K. A., Jordan, A. H., Resick, P. A., Foa, E. B., Young-McCaughan, S., Mintz, J., Yarvis, J. S., & Peterson, A. L. (2018). Distinct trauma types in military service members seeking treatment for posttraumatic stress disorder. *Journal of Traumatic Stress, 31*(2), 286–295. https://doi.org/10.1002/jts.22276

Litz, B. T., & Kerig, P. K. (2019). Introduction to the Special Issue on Moral Injury: Conceptual challenges, methodological issues, and clinical applications. *Journal of Traumatic Stress, 32*(3), 341–349. https://doi.org/10.1002/jts.22405

Litz, B. T., Stein, N., Delaney, E., Lebowitz, L., Nash, W. P., Silva, C., & Maguen, S. (2009). Moral injury and moral repair in war veterans: A preliminary model and intervention strategy. *Clinical Psychology Review, 29*(8), 695–706. https://doi.org/10.1016/j.cpr.2009.07.003

Lukianoff, G., & Haidt, J. (2018). *Coddling of the American mind: How good intentions and bad ideas are setting up a generation for failure.* Penguin Press.

Maccallum, F., Galatzer-Levy, I. R., & Bonanno, G. A. (2015). Trajectories of depression following spousal and child bereavement: A comparison of the heterogeneity in outcomes. *Journal of Psychiatric Research, 69,* 72–79. https://doi.org/10.1016/j.jpsychires.2015.07.017

Myers, C. S. (1915). A contribution to the study of shell shock. *The Lancet, 185*(4772), 316–320. https://doi.org/10.1016/S0140-6736(00)52916-X

Nash, W. P. (2019). Commentary on the Special Issue of Moral Injury: Unpacking two models for understanding moral injury. *Journal of Traumatic Stress, 32*(3), 465–470. https://doi.org/10.1002/jts.22409

Nash, W. P., Marino Carper, T. L., Mills, M. A., Au, T., Goldsmith, A., & Litz, B. T. (2013). Psychometric evaluation of the Moral Injury Events Scale. *Military Medicine, 178*(6), 646–652. https://doi.org/10.7205/MILMED-D-13-00017

Pizarro, J., Silver, R. C., & Prause, J. (2006). Physical and mental health costs of traumatic war experiences among Civil War veterans. *Archives of General Psychiatry, 63*(2), 193–200. https://doi.org/10.1001/archpsyc.63.2.193

Pompili, M., Sher, L., Serafini, G., Forte, A., Innamorati, M., Dominici, G., Lester, D., Amore, M., & Girardi, P. (2013). Posttraumatic stress disorder and suicide risk among veterans: A literature review. *Journal of Nervous and Mental Disease, 201*(9), 802–812. https://doi.org/10.1097/NMD.0b013e3182a21458

Prigerson, H. G., Horowitz, M. J., Jacobs, S. C., Parkes, C. M., Aslan, M., Goodkin, K., Raphael, B., Marwit, S. J., Wortman, C., Neimeyer, R. A., Bonanno, G. A., Block, S. D., Kissane, D., Boelen, P., Maercker, A., Litz, B. T., Johnson, J. G., First, M. B., & Maciejewski, P. K. (2009). Prolonged grief disorder: Psychometric validation of criteria proposed for *DSM–V* and ICD-11. *PLOS Medicine, 6*(8), Article e1000121. https://doi.org/10.1371/journal.pmed.1000121

Rosenheck, R. A., & Fontana, A. F. (2007). Recent trends in VA treatment of posttraumatic stress disorder and other mental disorders. *Health Affairs, 26*(6), 1720–1727. https://doi.org/10.1377/hlthaff.26.6.1720

Shay, J. (1994). *Achilles in Vietnam: Combat trauma and the undoing of character.* Atheneum.

Steenkamp, M. M., & Litz, B. T. (2013). Psychotherapy for military-related posttraumatic stress disorder: Review of the evidence. *Clinical Psychology Review, 33*(1), 45–53. https://doi.org/10.1016/j.cpr.2012.10.002

Steenkamp, M. M., Litz, B. T., Hoge, C. W., & Marmar, C. R. (2015). Psychotherapy for military-related PTSD: A review of randomized clinical trials. *JAMA, 314*(5), 489–500. https://doi.org/10.1001/jama.2015.8370

Stein, N. R., Mills, M. A., Arditte, K., Mendoza, C., Borah, A. M., Resick, P. A., & Litz, B. T. (2012). A scheme for categorizing traumatic military events. *Behavior Modification, 36*(6), 787–807. https://doi.org/10.1177/0145445512446945

Ursano, R. J., Kessler, R. C., Naifeh, J. A., Herberman Mash, H., Fullerton, C. S., Bliese, P. D., Zaslavsky, A. M., Ng, T. H. H., Aliaga, P. A., Wynn, G. H., Dinh, H. M., McCarroll, J. E., Sampson, N. A., Kao, T.-C., Schoenbaum, M., Heeringa, S. G., & Stein, M. B.

(2017). Risk of suicide attempt among soldiers in army units with a history of suicide attempts. *JAMA Psychiatry*, *74*(9), 924–931. https://doi.org/10.1001/jamapsychiatry.2017.1925

Ursano, R. J., Kessler, R. C., Naifeh, J. A., Herberman Mash, H. B., Nock, M. K., Aliaga, P. A., Fullerton, C. S., Wynn, G. H., Ng, T. H. H., Dinh, H. M., Sampson, N. A., Kao, T. C., Heeringa, S. G., & Stein, M. B. (2018). Risk factors associated with attempted suicide among US Army soldiers without a history of mental health diagnosis. *JAMA Psychiatry*, *75*(10), 1022–1032. https://doi.org/10.1001/jamapsychiatry.2018.2069

U.S. Census Bureau. (2014). *Introduction to veteran statistics from the U.S. Census Bureau.* https://www.census.gov/content/dam/Census/library/working-papers/2014/demo/2014_Holder-vets.pdf

U.S. Department of Veterans Affairs. (2018). *VA national suicide data report 2005–2016.* Office of Mental Health and Suicide Prevention.

1

A Cognitive Behavioral Model of Moral Injury

David C. Rozek and Craig J. Bryan

Every day we make decisions that are guided by our moral rules of living. As we grow, learn, and experience different life events, our moral lens develops and becomes more nuanced. These views of the world impact and are influenced by our interactions with others. When a traumatic event happens, shifts in beliefs can occur. At times, the traumatic event can go against one's morals, creating a moral injury. As noted in the editors' Introduction and throughout this book, there are several definitions of moral injury that include experiences in which an individual perpetuates, fails to prevent, is witness to, or learns about situations that transgress moral beliefs (Drescher et al., 2011; Litz et al., 2009). In addition, moral injury can occur from a perceived betrayal of justice, especially from an authority figure or someone held in high esteem (Garran, 2009; Shay, 1994; see also the Introduction and Chapter 2, this volume). Understanding how to conceptualize moral injury from a cognitive and behavioral orientation can help improve trauma-focused treatments and treatment planning for individual patients.

Conceptualization of moral injury requires an understanding of the differences and overlap of posttraumatic stress disorder (PTSD) and moral injury (see Chapter 5, this volume). Although there is a significant overlap in symptoms (e.g., anger, depression, substance use, sleep disturbance), moral injury has its own clinical presentation (for a full review, see Griffin et al., 2019). For example, focusing on a sample of National Guard members, moral injury has been shown to be uniquely characterized by guilt, shame, anger, anhedonia,

https://doi.org/10.1037/0000204-002
Addressing Moral Injury in Clinical Practice, J. M. Currier, K. D. Drescher, and J. Nieuwsma (Editors)

and social alienation, whereas PTSD was uniquely characterized by startle reflex response, memory loss, self-reported flashbacks, and sleep disturbances (Bryan et al., 2018). It is important to note that there currently is not a separate diagnosis of moral injury in the *Diagnostic and Statistical Manual of Mental Disorders* (5th ed.; *DSM-5*; American Psychiatric Association, 2013), and some have argued against its inclusion as a diagnosis (e.g., Farnsworth et al., 2017). Often, individuals experiencing symptoms of moral injury are diagnosed with PTSD. However, these differences should be considered in the treatment plan and conceptualization of patients when treating an individual who was exposed to a potentially morally injurious event (PMIE).

COGNITIVE BEHAVIORAL THEORY: UNDERSTANDING MODES

Cognitive behavior therapy (CBT) originated from Beck's (1967, 1983) diathesis–stress model of depression. Diathesis–stress models rely on the interaction of two concepts, diatheses and stressors, to explain the development of disorders (Monroe & Simons, 1991). In its simplest form, CBT considers how life events—specifically, perceived stressors—interact with vulnerabilities to explain the development of symptoms. This emphasis on the interaction between diathesis and stress helps explain the fact that neither everyone who carries a vulnerability, nor everyone who experiences aversive life circumstances, develops psychopathology. Different combinations of stressors and predispositions are theorized to result in psychopathology based on the diagnosis.

In refining the cognitive model, often described as a *mode theory*, Beck and Haigh (2014) provided a more nuanced framework for understanding the processes of psychopathology. Mode theory provides a structural model designed to help organize and conceptualize risk and protective factors that exist for moral injury (Beck & Haigh, 2014; see Figure 1.1). According to mode theory, each individual has certain predispositions or vulnerabilities based on static risk factors, usually couched in demographic and historical variables. In the presence of an activating event, the mode can be "turned on" and manifests as a network web of symptoms and patterns across cognitive, emotional, behavioral, and physical domains. An individual's mode may present differently following activating events (e.g., a more stressful event may lead to a more severe acute mode). Mode theory has been applied to a variety of mental health issues (e.g., depressive mode, anxious mode, suicidal mode), and the generic components of mode theory are described in more detail next. Gathering information related to predispositions, activating events, and acute modes is helpful in conceptualizing a patient's case and to guiding treatment interventions and decision making.

Predispositions

Predispositions, or baseline risk factors, are stable facets that are typically historical in nature. For example, gender, age, race, genetics, abuse history, previous

FIGURE 1.1. Generic Moral Injury Mode

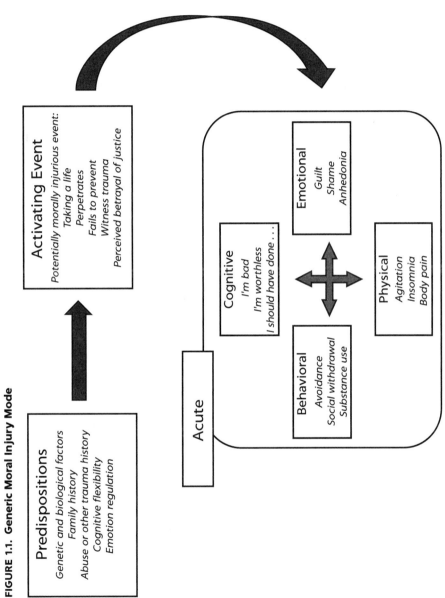

psychiatric illness, and personality traits can increase the probability of a particular psychological mode (e.g., a depressive mode, an anxious mode, or a moral injury mode). Understanding predispositional protective factors such as social support is also important because this can be a risk or protective factor. Moreover, baseline cognitive flexibility and emotion regulation can play a pivotal role in the development of psychopathology symptoms and maladaptive behavior (e.g., Bryan & Rozek, 2018; Joseph, Moring, & Bira, 2015). *Cognitive flexibility*, or the ability to switch between tasks, manage problems, and see alternative solutions, can be a protective factor—or the alternative, cognitive inflexibility (i.e., rigid thinking), can be a risk factor. Without being able to adapt and change their way of thinking, when a traumatic event that goes against their thoughts and/or morals occurs, individuals will not be able to accept such events and the thoughts stemming from them. In many ways, this can keep people "stuck" as they try to figure out how the trauma could have happened to them (e.g., Resick et al., 2017). Baseline *emotion regulation*, or the ability to manage and respond to emotions, can be both a protective and risk factor as well. If an individual is unable to manage emotions in an effective way before a traumatic event, it is unlikely that the trauma will help the level of emotion regulation. Therefore, difficulties in regulating emotions may confer risk to individuals who are exposed to a traumatic event and are more likely to develop symptoms.

Activating Event

According to mode theory, predispositional risk factors lead to the activation of the acute mode if activated by a stressor or contextual stimulus. Activating events can include environmental stressors (e.g., relationship problems, work stress), internal experiences such as physical sensations (e.g., pain), cognitive or psychological experiences (e.g., intrusive memories), and emotional stress (e.g., negative emotions). It is more likely that the stressor will become an activating event if it matches one of the predispositional risk factors. For some individuals, it may take a combination of stressors to trigger an activating event. Although controlling stressors in life is not often possible, it is important for clinicians to understand what potential stressors could occur that might lead to the activation of the acute mode.

Acute Mode

In the presence of an activating event, the acute mode can be activated and manifests as an interconnected web of symptoms and behavioral patterns (see Figure 1.1). This activated mode is often the clinical presentation of the patient to the clinician, especially when symptoms are at their peak level of intensity or severity. The acute factors can be organized into cognitive, behavioral, emotional, and physiological domains that are interactive and, under typical conditions, seek to maintain homeostatic balance. When change in one domain occurs, the other domains also experience change, but in a manner that facilitates a return to homeostasis for the entire system. For example, increased negative emotion might lead to the activation of cognitive reappraisal and behavioral coping strategies that serve to counterbalance and reduce the negative emotions, consistent with a negative feedback loop. This negative feedback loop facilitates recovery following a stressful or traumatic event, including PMIEs.

When the mode is activated, it is reinforced and becomes sensitized to future activation. The increased likelihood of future reactivation of the same mode has been supported in several forms of psychopathology (Beck & Haigh, 2014). Because the various domains (i.e., cognitive, emotional, behavioral, physical) are interactive, under these conditions, activation of one domain can lead to activation of the other domains, leading to a positive rather than a negative feedback loop. This creates a "downward spiral" effect that can lead to increased symptoms and create negative habits for an individual. In this way, repeated exposure to PMIEs (and other stressors and/or traumas) increases the likelihood of manifesting chronic and persistent symptoms of moral injury. Interventions should target one or more domains of the mode to undo these effects, which can lead to a positive cascading effect wherein the whole system loses intensity, and the individual can return to baseline.

Overall, the mode theory provides a simple yet practical theory-based model to conceptualize patients who might be struggling with a moral injury. It provides structure and discerns different categories of risk factors and symptoms (i.e., cognitive, behavioral, emotional, physical) that can be targeted in treatment. Many cognitive- and behavioral-based treatments use mode theory to guide clinicians on their decisions and to provide structure to patients.

MORAL INJURY MODE

Although mode theory has been applied to many forms of psychopathology, there has not been a focus on moral injury. Research has focused on characterizing different aspects of moral injury; however, it has not yet been put into a simple conceptual model that can easily inform clinical practice. Because many clinicians and patients find that using a simple model to organize clinical information can help the progression of treatment (Rudd et al., 2009), articulating the moral injury mode can serve as a way to do so. The moral injury mode follows the description of mode theory, and case examples of taking patient information and organizing it into the moral injury mode are described later. The moral injury mode provides a cognitive behavioral framework for describing the clinical presentation of moral injury and for guiding treatment planning. Although research aimed at better understanding moral injury continues to progress (Griffin et al., 2019), the current data offer some insight that can provide an initial conceptualization of moral injury.

Predispositional risk factors for moral injury likely include demographic risk factors, such as being a member of the military or a first responder, two occupations that put individuals at higher risk of encountering PMIEs. Although these groups are not the only individuals who experience moral injury, they are at higher risk of experiencing PMIEs, given the nature of their occupation. Additional predispositional risk factors include deficits in emotion regulation and cognitive flexibility, both of which lend vulnerability to developing and experiencing symptoms of psychopathology, including moral injury. For example, individuals who are rigid in their thinking and then experience a situation that is out of their control and violates their moral precepts are more likely to develop the symptoms of moral injury because their rigid thinking works against them when trying to process the trauma. Although these risk factors do not necessitate the onset of moral injury, they do provide increased risk and may increase the likelihood of activating the acute moral injury mode during a stressor.

The activating event for the moral injury mode is a PMIE. As highlighted in the Introduction, common examples of these events include injuring or killing a person, exposure to the aftermath of a violent situation, and betrayal (Griffin et al., 2019; Litz et al., 2009). This initial PMIE activates the acute moral injury mode and will directly challenge many of the morally related schemas and core beliefs developed through childhood and early adulthood. Additional activating events may include stressors and situations that somehow remind the individual of the PMIE. For example, if the PMIE was taking the life of a child in combat, seeing children could subsequently activate or intensify the acute moral injury mode. Although stressors and activating events cannot be avoided, understanding the additional "triggers" after the moral injury occurs can help a clinician plan potential behavioral and cognitive interventions during treatment.

This exposure to a PMIE can activate the acute mode, and once this mode is activated, it becomes easily reactivated. The acute moral injury mode comprises cognitive, emotional, behavioral, and physical domains that mutually interact, as illustrated in Figure 1.1. Although each individual will have variation, there are common overlapping features in each domain. Within the cognitive domain, acute factors for moral injury include automatic thoughts, underlying assumptions, and core beliefs that occur in response to a stressful situation, especially those that remind the individual of the morally injurious event. Common cognitions include thoughts related to "I'm a bad person," "I should not have done that," and "People will be disgusted by me if they know what I've done." Individuals might have core beliefs related to guilt and shame, such as "I'm a bad person/a monster" and "I should have done more to stop/end/prevent it." The strong emotional domain may include feelings of guilt and shame as hallmark symptoms. Moreover, grief, along with other emotional responses such as anger, anxiety, and depression, may be present as well. Within the behavioral domain, the acute moral injury mode often includes social alienation and isolation, avoidance, and substance use. For the physical domain, the moral injury mode may include insomnia and nightmares, as well as somatic experiences, including muscle tension, body aches, and pain.

The moral injury mode is slightly different from other psychopathology modes. The activating event for the moral injury mode is a PMIE. When people are exposed to such an event, their moral injury mode may be activated depending on the intensity and content of the traumatic event, as well as their predisposition. Once activated, the moral injury mode is often reactivated or intensified by other common life stressors. Because of this, a clinician should be acutely aware of and ask about PMIEs. If the original trauma and mode are classified as another form of psychopathology, the clinician might not target the correct domains and mechanisms during treatment. Ultimately, both cognitive and behavioral interventions can be used to help individuals with moral injury understand their mode and learn coping strategies and interventions that target one or more domains to help "deactivate" the mode.

TREATMENT IMPLICATIONS

The goal of the moral injury mode as a conceptualization model is to provide clinicians with a tool to help conceptualize and ultimately choose interventions that match. Each domain (i.e., cognitive, emotional, behavioral, physical) of the moral injury mode provides a point of intervention that several cognitive- and behavioral-based interventions target. Although each individual with moral injury will have differences in their moral injury mode, there will be similarities and commonalities in the mechanisms maintaining the symptoms.

Using the moral injury mode as a clinician is helpful to structure case conceptualization. The mode allows for the four domains—cognitive, emotional, behavioral, and physical—to be discrete categories. This is important because the clinician will want to understand how different domains interact with each other, and appreciating how the domains are separate but interact can inform treatment. For example, it might be that one particular thought (e.g., "I'm a monster") is the hallmark indicator of the downward spiral. From that, guilt and shame levels increase, which leads individuals to isolate themselves from family and friends. The isolation then reinforces strong negative emotions, setting off additional negative thoughts. Learning and exploring the timeline of how the domains interact can provide useful information on how to intervene.

As the clinician gains more insight into and data about the individual's moral injury mode, choosing treatment interventions that match the presentation will likely increase the effectiveness of treatment. If a patient presents with strong cognitive distortions and insight combined with a lack of physical symptoms (e.g., tension), using cognitive interventions to target the distorted thinking is likely more useful than teaching relaxation techniques. Similarly, if avoidance of family is causing guilt and shame to increase, the clinician may choose behavioral activation and exposure techniques to help reduce the maladaptive behaviors. Although the moral injury mode provides the structure and organization, there is not necessarily only one "correct" intervention choice. In fact, that is why the moral injury mode can be essential in treatment.

Once a clinician teaches an intervention skill, the moral injury mode can be updated to understand the impact of the intervention. This provides the clinician with feedback from the patient on how the treatment is working.

The moral injury mode is useful for clinicians to organize their conceptualization, and it can also be used as a framework for patients. Clinicians can provide the structure of the moral injury mode to the patient, and then each intervention and skill the clinician teaches to the patient can be framed within the moral injury mode. This allows the patient to understand better why the clinician is teaching them a specific skill. For example, if a clinician teaches a relaxation technique such as mindfulness or breathing exercises, the clinician can explain how these interventions are directly targeting the physical symptoms being experienced. Patients who clearly understand this rationale are more likely to use these skills and understand how their treatment is being personalized and targeted to their acute moral injury mode.

Using the moral injury mode in cognitive- and behavioral-based interventions is useful in targeting the underlying mechanisms of moral injury, as well as personalizing the treatment. Cognitive and behavioral therapy has become a family of therapies (e.g., CBT, cognitive therapy, exposure-based interventions, behavioral activation, dialectical behavior therapy). Even when focused on one disorder—for example, PTSD—manuals vary on what techniques are used and in what order. Two common treatments for PTSD are cognitive processing therapy (CPT; Resick et al., 2017) and prolonged exposure (PE; Foa et al., 2007). Both CPT and PE belong in the family of CBT, and both are effective in reducing PTSD symptoms; however, they focus on different aspects of PTSD. CPT targets cognitions and teaches an individual how to reappraise in a more realistic and balanced manner (see Chapter 8, this volume). Alternatively, PE focuses on behaviors by using exposure-driven techniques (e.g., in vivo, imaginal) to create habituation to the traumatic event (see Chapter 7).

As highlighted in Chapter 5, research has shown that PTSD and moral injury are related but distinct constructs (Bryan et al., 2018; Griffin et al., 2019). Because of this, some have proposed that existing evidence-based treatments for PTSD may not be effective in treating moral injury (e.g., Litz et al., 2016). However, as discussed in many chapters in this book, others have suggested that common evidence-based treatments for PTSD (i.e., CPT and PE) can be effective in treating moral injury if the conceptualization of moral injury is integrated into the underlying theory of the intervention (Held et al., 2018).

Using the moral injury mode to enhance treatment is essential for these treatments to reduce the individual's symptoms. For example, in PE or other exposure-based interventions, targeting the morally injurious event can reduce guilt and shame by integrating more contextual information, which may shift the individual's understanding of the event. Pairing this with in vivo work that targets behaviors that are debilitating (e.g., social isolation) addresses both cognitive and behavioral domains of the moral injury mode. Similarly, in CPT, targeting the core beliefs and cognitions stemming from the morally injurious event that drive guilt and shame should be the focus of treatment (cognitive domain). Using cognitive restructuring and reappraisal interventions on these specific cognitions can help reduce symptoms. Through Socratic questioning and other cognitive restructuring techniques, the clinician and patient can work to accurately and realistically evaluate the morally injurious situation. Ultimately, CPT does not necessarily make the person believe what happened was "good" or "right" but instead provides context for the situation, challenges the negative and unrealistic cognitions, and allows the individual to experience the natural emotions that should come and go from the situation that occurred. Both PE and CPT for moral injury are discussed in depth in other chapters in the book.

Using evidence-based treatments that are effective for symptoms of moral injury can be helpful. It is important for clinicians to use the moral injury mode to conceptualize the individual's case and target interventions on what matters in keeping the acute mode active to maximize the effectiveness of treatment. Using this information provides both the clinician and patient with information on how the treatment is working and what to target in therapy.

CASE CONCEPTUALIZATION CLINICAL EXAMPLES

The following case examples illustrate how the cognitive behavioral model, or moral injury mode, can be used to conceptualize a patient. This conceptualization can be used to guide treatment decisions for cognitive and behavioral interventions such as CPT and/or PE. Case conceptualization is constantly updated with new information that a clinician obtains throughout treatment. At times, certain behaviors and/or cognitions will be the focus of treatment, and once they are managed, treatment will shift to a new target.

The Case of Jackson

Jackson is a 44-year-old South Asian American man who previously served in the United States Army from 2004 to 2013. He is a father of two children and was deployed to Iraq three times as part of the infantry. He received a General Discharge Under Honorable Conditions. Before coming into therapy, Jackson had "hit rock-bottom" and felt distant and cut off from his wife and children. On engaging in therapy, Jackson told his clinician, "I'm a monster," and had strong feelings of guilt and shame. He noted that these feelings started after his last deployment in Iraq. Jackson talked about his childhood as positive, and he had a supportive family. He noted having a history of depression that often manifested as low self-esteem and confidence (e.g., "I'm not good enough"), although he felt able to manage it. His family and friends noticed a difference in his mood and behavior following his last deployment.

Jackson's primary concern and symptoms revolved around feeling cut-off and distant from people, including his family and friends. He often avoided participating in activities that involved his children, which caused his wife to become angry with him. When pushed to do activities with his family, Jackson became angry and overwhelmed. He reported being sad and anxious most of the time nearly every day. Jackson drank alcohol to help him "feel less" when he was stressed and to reduce the tenseness that seemed constant. He continued to work and had transitioned into a telework job so he did not have to interact directly with other people. Jackson had stopped engaging with his friends because he was worried they would see him have an "episode" of high emotions and then ask more about his past. Jackson had difficulty sleeping at night and could rarely get to sleep or stay asleep for more than a couple of hours at a time. He denied nightmares but noticed racing thoughts and images that continuously ran through his mind at night. Jackson was worried that although he was "keeping it together," he could not continue for much longer.

Moral Injury Trauma Description

After meeting his clinician for an intake and an additional session, Jackson disclosed multiple traumatic events related to his deployments. As an infantry soldier, he was exposed to several combat situations, including being shot at, his convoy being ambushed, and carrying wounded and dead soldiers back to safety. Although many of these situations had impacted his way of thinking, Jackson reported that one event was the most troubling to him. Jackson recounted a particular event when he had entered into a combat zone outside the wire. As his convoy was moving, a group of children was in the street playing. This made him nervous because part of his job was to ensure the safety of his convoy, including eliminating any potential threats. Instead of moving out of the street when his convoy rolled in, the children started running at the vehicles. Jackson's initial reaction was to raise his gun, and he reported feeling horrified that he would even think of raising his gun toward a child. When he thought about lowering his weapon, his commanding officer told him and others to fire on the children. Jackson recalled pulling the trigger, and as he shot at the children, an improvised explosive device exploded that was attached to one of the children. Talking about this with Jackson activated intense emotions, especially anger directed toward himself. He kept repeating, "I'm a monster," "I should not have shot at them," and "People would be disgusted if they knew what I did over there."

Case Conceptualization

The traumatic event Jackson described met Criterion A of the *DSM-5* diagnosis for PTSD. It also was an example of a morally injurious event. Taking the lives of children was against Jackson's moral code, and he felt at fault for the deaths of the children. This activating event triggered the onset of his acute moral injury mode.

When looking at Jackson's presentation and history, several predispositions were seen. First, Jackson was a member of the army and deployed to a combat zone and thus was at higher risk of experiencing a PMIE. He reported a history of depression and exposure to other traumas that happened while deployed. Although these may or may not be important in his current presentation, they were a significant piece of historical information. His previous depressive episodes may present differently than his current symptoms, and his negative core beliefs related to his self-esteem may be reinforced by his traumatic event. Jackson also disclosed some protective factors such as supportive parents and family and a positive childhood history.

Jackson's acute moral injury mode was activated, and he reported symptoms in each domain. In the cognitive domain, he alluded to having a core belief of "I'm bad" because he reported several thoughts on that theme (e.g., "I'm a monster"). These were directly linked to his emotional domain, where he felt intense levels of guilt and shame, as well as depression and anxiety. In his behavior domain, Jackson avoided situations that would remind him of the trauma and that could potentially reveal his emotions to others. Jackson's avoidance of his children was also important because it impacted the family dynamic and his relationships with people he considered important in his life. He also was using alcohol to manage his emotions and thoughts, which could lead to more negative outcomes. Physically, Jackson mentioned sleep disturbance and insomnia-related symptoms, as well as feeling on edge and tense. These symptoms had negatively impacted his occupational and social functioning.

The Case of Dana

Dana was a 28-year-old Latina woman who worked as an emergency medical technician (EMT) in rural Iowa. She lived with her biological parents and was a caretaker for her mother, who had advanced-stage pancreatic cancer. Her four siblings and their children all lived within a few miles of each other, and Dana and her family members were well known and active in their community. Dana presented for therapy because she was having anger outbursts after an incident at work that she was refusing to discuss with her family. The only information Dana provided her family was that they would hate her if they knew what she had done. Dana stopped caring for her mom, which led to fights within her family. She stopped attending community activities and slowly started isolating herself from her friends and family. Dana's family had previously suggested therapy to her because Dana had been on many scenes of gruesome accidents, and they were concerned about how this could impact her mental health. They also had noticed that during her time as an EMT, she had become more rigid in her way of thinking, as well as displaying increased anger. After the latest work incident, Dana's family noticed even more behavioral changes with her lack of desire to be active with her family or community.

Dana's primary concern and symptoms revolved around her anger, guilt, shame, and wanting to be left alone. She reported feeling "weak and fragile" and that she "shouldn't be trusted ever again." She was aware of her behavior change in avoiding and isolating herself from her family and explained the rationale for this as "It will only help them if I stay away." Dana was also concerned with intrusive thoughts related to her work and recent traumatic experiences. She also noted having vivid nightmares and that she would often try not to sleep to avoid the dreams. She had recently been put on administrative leave due to several instances when she fought with a coworker on the scene of accidents. Dana had active thoughts about killing herself because she believed she was "useless and a burden to others." She denied any previous attempts or a specific plan or intent and said these thoughts started after a recent event at work.

Moral Injury Trauma Description

Dana did not want to share what had happened at work and expressed that she could never be forgiven for what she had done. After building a strong therapeutic relationship, Dana was willing to talk more about her trauma from her EMT job. She reported that she was responding to a call of a car accident in which two cars had hit head-on and there were reported injuries. Each car was filled with a family, including children. Dana had no other information other than that several EMT crews had been dispatched, although she was the closest by far. Arriving first on the scene, she saw one of the two cars had rolled and was upside-down. She began to assess the injuries of each of the people and realized that there were only two serious injuries. The first was a child who was in critical condition, and the second was the child's mom, who was also in critical condition. Dana assessed that the mother had a better chance of survival, and because the other EMTs were 20 minutes out, Dana had to then choose who to provide medical care to—the mother or the child. She followed protocol, which was to provide care to the individual with a better chance of survival based on her assessment. Dana knew that if she did this and provided care to the mother who had a better chance of survival, this choice would likely mean the child would die. Dana told the mother that her child was going to be okay to keep the mother calm. As she expected, when the other ambulance arrived on the scene, the child had passed away. Dana remembered the mother telling her to provide aid to the child rather than herself. She recalled having thoughts about how unfair the world was and how she should not have to make this decision. Dana also felt ashamed that she could not have saved both and continuously questioned her decision on that scene, as well as every decision she made at work after that.

Case Conceptualization

Dana's morally injurious event put her in a situation in which she felt that she had to decide who lived and died. Although she did not know whether she could have saved the child's life, she questioned her judgment and had lost trust in herself. This was the event that activated and reinforced the moral injury mode for her. Her symptoms also overlapped with PTSD, and the traumatic event met Criterion A of the *DSM-5* diagnosis for PTSD.

There were several predispositional factors from Dana's case. She was a first responder with a job that entailed being called to traumatic events. In her line of work, she often had to make medical decisions that impacted the lives of others and had to do so under pressure. At times, she had to decide who to provide medical care to, even though her goal was to save every life. Through this work, she had been exposed to several traumatic events, which possibly made her more vulnerable to developing symptoms of psychopathology. She had other life stressors, including familial health issues, and she was also a caregiver herself. Dana's family had noticed some mental health concerns, which could be a risk factor. She had several protective factors, including strong family and community support and a healthy childhood based on her reported closeness with her family.

Dana's acute moral injury mode was activated by her trauma related to choosing which patient to provide care for and lying to the mother of the child. In the cognitive domain, Dana reported thoughts such as "I'm worthless," "No one should trust me," "I'm weak," and even other thoughts related to suicide. In her emotional domain, she felt strong levels of guilt, shame, and anger at herself and others. Behaviorally, Dana had socially withdrawn from her previously active lifestyle. She had confrontations at work and with her family. Her stark change in behavior related to her family (e.g., caregiving to her mother) signified a change in her behavior. In her physical domain, Dana had insomnia-related symptoms such as difficulty falling asleep, nightmares, and difficulty returning to sleep. Overall, Dana's life view had negatively changed following her traumatic event in a manner that hindered her psychosocial functioning.

CONCLUSION

In the cases of both Jackson and Dana, the active moral injury mode provided multiple options for intervention. The cognitive domain could be targeted with interventions that focus on identifying how thoughts and emotions are related, followed by skill building in learning to restructure the negatively biased thoughts. By changing the thoughts, the emotions would also be expected to change in valence and/or intensity (see Chapter 8). The clinician and patient may choose to focus on behavioral-based approaches such as imaginal and in vivo exposure related to the trauma (see Chapter 7). This directly targets avoidance, commonly seen in moral injury and PTSD, and reduces the negative emotional response when put into situations that remind the individual of the trauma. In the physical domain, skills such as relaxation, mindfulness, and breathing techniques may improve physiological symptoms that interfere with the patient being able to focus on cognitive and behavioral interventions. Each of these interventions directly targets one domain of the moral injury mode and reduces the intensity of the whole system. An individual may benefit from a combination of all of these interventions, and the clinician should track how the moral injury mode responds during treatment.

Overall, moral injury has its own clinical presentation and is individually different for each patient. Understanding and organizing these symptoms in the moral injury mode can provide a foundation for a clinician to determine the best course of treatment. Even in established evidenced-based treatments (e.g., CPT, PE), it is important to conceptualize the patient to target and focus interventions on factors that contribute to the moral injury mode.

REFERENCES

American Psychiatric Association. (2013). *Diagnostic and statistical manual of mental disorders* (5th ed.). https://doi.org/10.1176/appi.books.9780890425596

Beck, A. T. (1967). *Depression: Clinical, experimental, and theoretical aspects.* University of Pennsylvania Press.

Beck, A. T. (1983). *Theory and treatment of depression: Towards a dynamic interactionism model.* Leuven University Press.

Beck, A. T., & Haigh, E. A. (2014). Advances in cognitive theory and therapy: The generic cognitive model. *Annual Review of Clinical Psychology, 10,* 1–24. https://doi.org/10.1146/annurev-clinpsy-032813-153734

Bryan, C. J., Bryan, A. O., Roberge, E., Leifker, F. R., & Rozek, D. C. (2018). Moral injury, posttraumatic stress disorder, and suicidal behavior among National Guard personnel. *Psychological Trauma: Theory, Research, Practice, and Policy, 10*(1), 36–45. https://doi.org/10.1037/tra0000290

Bryan, C. J., & Rozek, D. C. (2018). Suicide prevention in the military: A mechanistic perspective. *Current Opinion in Psychology, 22,* 27–32. https://doi.org/10.1016/j.copsyc.2017.07.022

Drescher, K. D., Foy, D. W., Kelly, C., Leshner, A., Schutz, K., & Litz, B. (2011). An exploration of the viability and usefulness of the construct of moral injury in war Veterans. *Traumatology, 17*(1), 8–13. https://doi.org/10.1177/1534765610395615

Farnsworth, J. K., Drescher, K. D., Evans, W., & Walser, R. D. (2017). A functional approach to understanding and treating military-related moral injury. *Journal of Contextual Behavioral Science, 6*(4), 391–397. https://doi.org/10.1016/j.jcbs.2017.07.003

Foa, E. B., Hembree, E. A., & Rothbaum, B. O. (2007). *Prolonged exposure therapy for PTSD: Emotional processing of traumatic experiences, therapist guide.* Oxford University Press. https://doi.org/10.1093/med:psych/9780195308501.001.0001

Garran, A. M. (2009). Commentary on the reaction panel in response to the keynote lecture presented by Dr. Jonathan Shay titled the trials of homecoming: Odysseus returns from Iraq/Afghanistan. *Smith College Studies in Social Work, 79*(3–4), 310–313. https://doi.org/10.1080/00377310903130340

Griffin, B. J., Purcell, N., Burkman, K., Litz, B. T., Bryan, C. J., Schmitz, M., Villierme, C., Walsh, J., & Maguen, S. (2019). Moral injury: An integrative review. *Journal of Traumatic Stress, 32*(3), 350–362. https://doi.org/10.1002/jts.22362

Held, P., Klassen, B. J., Brennan, M. B., & Zalta, A. K. (2018). Using prolonged exposure and cognitive processing therapy to treat veterans with moral injury-based PTSD: Two case examples. *Cognitive and behavioral practice, 25*(3), 377–390. https://doi.org/10.1016/j.cbpra.2017.09.003

Joseph, J. S., Moring, J. C., & Bira, L. M. (2015). Cognitive flexibility as a key factor in the conceptualization and treatment of PTSD. *Current Psychiatry Reviews, 11*(3), 180–192. https://doi.org/10.2174/1573400511666150629104921

Litz, B. T., Lebowitz, L., Gray, M. J., & Nash, W. P. (2016). *Adaptive disclosure: A new treatment for military trauma, loss, and moral injury.* Guilford Press.

Litz, B. T., Stein, N., Delaney, E., Lebowitz, L., Nash, W. P., Silva, C., & Maguen, S. (2009). Moral injury and moral repair in war veterans: A preliminary model and intervention strategy. *Clinical Psychology Review, 29*(8), 695–706. https://doi.org/10.1016/j.cpr.2009.07.003

Monroe, S. M., & Simons, A. D. (1991). Diathesis–stress theories in the context of life stress research: Implications for the depressive disorders. *Psychological Bulletin, 110*(3), 406–425. https://doi.org/10.1037/0033-2909.110.3.406

Resick, P. A., Monson, C. M., & Chard, K. M. (2017). *Cognitive processing therapy for PTSD: A comprehensive manual.* Guilford Press.

Rudd, M. D., Joiner, T. E., Jr., Trotter, D., Williams, B., & Cordero, L. (2009). The psychosocial treatment of suicidal behavior: A critique of what we know (and don't know). In P. M. Kleespies (Ed.), *Behavioral emergencies: An evidence-based resource for evaluating and managing risk of suicide, violence, and victimization* (pp. 339–350). American Psychological Association. https://doi.org/10.1037/11865-015

Shay, J. (1994). *Achilles in Vietnam: Combat trauma and the undoing of character.* Scribner.

2

A Social–Functional Perspective on Morality and Moral Injury

Kent D. Drescher and Jacob K. Farnsworth

With the recent emergence of the construct of moral injury, a primary source of dialogue has been how moral injury fits within diagnostic frameworks and how to address it clinically. Perhaps even more important are models for understanding the mechanisms that determine the onset and impact of moral injury in specific cases. To set the stage for this discussion, we share a composite story of moral injury, with key elements derived from multiple clients.

> Adam is a 28-year-old White marine veteran who was deployed twice to Afghanistan and often worked on forward operating bases. A major element of his battalion's mission was "winning the hearts and minds" of the local population. This involved building relationships with Afghani security officers and local leaders to help discourage alliances with insurgents. Early in his second deployment, Adam learned that some Afghani officers were bringing young boys onto the base and sexually assaulting them in the barracks. One day, Adam noticed a 9-year-old boy with bloodstains on his cotton pants, crying as he left the base. Enraged, Adam talked to his gunnery sergeant about the abuse. The gunnery sergeant ordered Adam not to intervene or confront the Afghanis perpetrating the abuse, saying, "Look, we need these guys on our side. We're not here to change their culture." For the rest of the deployment, Adam tried to avoid the barracks used by the Afghani men but continued to see this child around the forward operating base.
>
> Following his military discharge, Adam began noticing intense feelings of protectiveness when he was around children. He began carrying a concealed pistol to help him feel safe, and he has pulled his weapon several times on parents who

https://doi.org/10.1037/0000204-003
Addressing Moral Injury in Clinical Practice, J. M. Currier, K. D. Drescher, and J. Nieuwsma (Editors)

he felt were being overly harsh with their children in public. Adam frequently has intrusive memories of the boy with bloodstained pants and deeply regrets not intervening. He told his therapist that previous therapists encouraged him to remember the potential consequences had he disobeyed his gunny's orders, but this has not seemed to change how he thinks or feels.

Perhaps the question most pertinent to this chapter is how to understand the elements of Adam's experience that are evoking enduring suffering and problematic behaviors. What theoretical models might provide a useful framework for understanding the mechanisms that determine the onset and impact of such moral injuries in the lives of military personnel and their loved ones? In a number of ways, the field of clinical psychology can be viewed as unprepared to address such moral questions effectively. In our experience gleaned from conversations with colleagues and trainees, few received explicit, focused instruction in moral psychology or guidance as to how to incorporate a client's moral principles and address moral conflicts in the context of therapy. The most consistent element of psychology training in morality seems to be found in the ethical principles that insist clinicians respect client diversity. In practice, this includes taking care to avoid imposing clinician values and moral beliefs on the client during the therapeutic process. An unintended consequence of this emphasis may be that some clinicians are wary of exploring issues of values and moral beliefs with clients and may omit these issues from assessment and treatment plans. Perhaps as a corollary to these emphases, psychology as a field has moved away from moral models of mental health (e.g., addiction) in favor of a medical model that deemphasizes concepts such as character and virtue in definitions of wellness (Martin, 2006).

Although acceptance of the medical model and increased attention to ethical guidelines has benefited clients, it has also left providers without a well-elaborated set of tools for conceptualizing and intervening with morally complex issues in the therapeutic environment. For example, in cases like Adam's, providers and clients may both be left unsatisfied with therapeutic approaches that focus primarily on challenging distorted or exaggerated cognitions because this type of moral distress appears rooted in dilemmas that pit an array of personal, social, and military values against one another (Farnsworth, 2019). Another challenge for the field is that clinical practice has historically focused on the needs, distress, and internal functioning of the individual, whereas, as is reviewed next, morality can be seen as being intrinsically social and relational. Moral dilemmas and violations inherently reflect how one individual's actions impact others and vice versa. Because of these historical realities, individually focused assessment and case conceptualization may tend to limit awareness of client moral relational issues when they occur. Because of these limitations, clinical training programs, theoretical orientations, and even evidence-based intervention protocols may fail to provide adequate frameworks for clinicians to understand and intervene effectively regarding moral issues.

Understanding the psychological phenomenon of moral injury requires that scientists and clinicians first understand morality, including the contexts in which it operates and the social functions it serves. The purpose of this chapter is to describe social functionalism, one evolution-based framework for understanding human morality, and its utility for conceptualizing the construct of moral injury. Evolution-based theories of morality, rather than describing the normative content of morality, focus instead on understanding how morality has functioned across time to ensure not just the survival but the flourishing of the human species. In this vein, a social–functionalist definition of morality has been put forward by Jonathan Haidt: "Moral systems are interlocking sets of values, practices, institutions, and evolved psychological mechanisms that work together to suppress or regulate selfishness and make social life possible" (Haidt, 2008, p. 70). In this definition, the moral emotions and cognitions that are among those "evolved psychological mechanisms" that play a key role in human morality are a subset of the larger array of human emotions and cognitions. As we discuss in the following sections, social functionalism can serve as a primary model for examining cognitions and emotions that may emerge in moral injury.

SOCIAL FUNCTIONS OF EMOTION

Social–functionalist accounts of emotion make several assumptions (Keltner et al., 2006). First, they assume that human beings are social creatures who evolved to engage in survival challenges together. They also assume that emotions and associated evaluative cognitions are a primary means of coordinating social relations in the service of meeting these survival challenges. Finally, they assume that emotions are dynamic and continuously mediate an individual's moment-to-moment relationship with his or her ever-changing social environment (Keltner & Haidt, 1999). From a social–functionalist perspective, the overarching function of emotion is, as Haidt (2008) stated, "to make social life possible" (p. 70). A social–functional approach to morality as a whole, and military-related moral injury in particular, thus accounts for these evolved functions of emotions in the regulation of collaborative human behavior in social contexts, such as war-zone deployments. Next, we discuss the evolved functions of morality for communal living before turning to the specific instance of military trauma.

   Social–functional accounts of emotion suggest that distinct emotions evolved to help manage three main challenges and opportunities (Goetz & Keltner, 2007). The first is actual physical survival. Emotions such as fear and anger helped to avoid and/or survive encounters with predators, whereas disgust helped avoid encounters with contamination that might lead to disease. The second challenge has to do with enhancing reproductive opportunities and protecting offspring until they can fend for themselves. Emotions such as love, sympathy, and compassion have evolved for this purpose. Finally, given the highly social nature of human beings, emotions have evolved to help navigate the various threats and opportunities of living together in social groups. For example, when maintaining cooperative alliances that were essential for individual survival, guilt may have evolved as a mechanism for identifying violations of reciprocity and motivating behavior designed to repair trust. Moreover, emotions assist in maintaining group organization and helping group members know their place within the social hierarchy. Emotions such as embarrassment and shame serve an appeasement function that indicates awareness of lower hierarchical status, whereas pride acknowledges increased social status. Thus, social functionalism argues that specific emotions evolved to help humans solve both individual problems as well as those generated by communal living. As a result, there can be an array of social functions for distinct emotions depending on the level at which interactions are examined. Next, we review these functions, starting at the individual level and then progressing through dyadic, group, and finally, cultural–social contexts.

When viewed at the level of the individual, emotions have two main functions (Levenson, 1994). The first is an alerting function. The awareness of physiological sensations associated with emotion focuses an individual's attention on situations or opportunities in the social environment that might benefit from or even necessitate behavioral actions. The second function provided by some emotions is the rapid physical preparation for context-appropriate actions. For example, the emotional experience of anger moves blood away from the body's core and into the extremities (i.e., hands, arms). In the case of anger, this is thought to be preparatory for fighting and survival (Keltner & Haidt, 1999). Evolution has hardwired this physical preparation to make it rapidly available at points when survival threat is imminent, and it would be expected that active combat situations would also trigger these emotional responses.

Beyond matters of individual survival, there are different social functions for emotion when considered from the relational perspective of two people. At this level, emotions aid in communication with and understanding others. The automatic outward expression of emotion via facial expression (Matsumoto et al., 2008), bodily posture, movement, and gesture (Dael et al., 2012), as well as through auditory cues (e.g., nonlanguage sounds and speech prosody; Bachorowski & Owren, 2008), provides crucial information about an individual's emotions and intentions. In addition, nonverbal emotional expression often automatically elicits emotions (both complementary and reciprocal) in other people nearby. For example, anger displays in one person elicit fear responses in others. The elicited emotions also serve to motivate appropriate behavioral responses in those same individuals. Finally, emotional expression by one person functions to either incentivize or discourage social behavior on the part of other individuals (Keltner & Haidt, 1999). Given that military operations are largely conducted by small teams of service members working close to one another, such interpersonal functions of emotion are likely to be highly salient.

At the level of large groups, emotions have several important evolved functions. Overall, emotions help varying collections of individuals who share goals and identities meet objectives. Some theorists have suggested that emotional experience enhances cooperation by helping identify group members and defining group boundaries (Keltner & Haidt, 1999). Collective emotional experience (e.g., political rallies, communal religious worship, military basic training) may give individuals a sense of shared identity, whereas group emotions directed outward toward individuals outside the group may reinforce a sense of "otherness" toward them (e.g., indigenous populations in foreign war zones). Accordingly, although shared positive moral experiences may reinforce group identity, emotions directed outward are often negative other-directed moral emotions.

Variations in emotional experience by group members may also help define individual roles and status within a hierarchy. Members with high status (e.g., commissioned and noncommissioned officers) will experience emotions such as elevation or pride, whereas others experience emotions consistent with submission or lower status (e.g., sense of deference and awe one might feel at meeting an honored world leader). Animal research has suggested that emotional experience may help negotiate specific challenges that arise within groups. For example, emotions of affiliation may arise at times before the distribution of valuable resources (e.g., two marines sharing their last meal ration). Such emotions solidify social bonds at times when a group may be especially vulnerable to threats or conflicts, either internally or externally (Keltner & Haidt, 1999).

The social functions of emotion can also be examined from the level of culture. This level of analysis differs from the prior level of the group by looking at how emotion is shaped over time by historical factors and how emotional experience and expression are embedded within, impact, and perpetuate cultural institutions and their symbols (D'Andrade, 1984). Emotion has an important role in mechanisms through which individuals adopt cultural identities. Specific cultural beliefs about what are appropriate versus deviant emotions appear to motivate culturally desirable behavior. For instance, embarrassment motivates conformity to social roles deemed "proper" within the culture (e.g., real men do not cry in public). In contrast, disgust motivates the exclusion of those who violate important cultural values (e.g., ostracizing service members who shirk their responsibilities to the unit). Cultural expectations about emotional experience and expression strengthen and perpetuate cultural traditions, power structures, and hierarchies, while sometimes ostracizing and viewing groups with different practices as "other," resulting in conflict and even war (Keltner & Haidt, 1999).

SOCIAL FUNCTIONS OF MORAL EMOTIONS

Having reviewed the general functions of emotions for individual and group survival, we now turn our attention to specific classes of moral emotion. To clarify at the outset: Moral emotions can be considered a subset of the larger array of human emotional experience. Like other emotions, moral emotions are experienced and coordinated in a context of social connectedness (Rimé, 2009). Research generally categorizes emotional states as negative or positive on the basis of eliciters, action tendencies, modes of expression, and characteristic nervous system response. Though not exclusively, negative emotions are often elicited in the presence of perceived threat and may activate the sympathetic nervous system (i.e., fight–flight) in preparation for action. Negative emotion is also thought to function protectively by shrinking the array of thought–action choices to maximize the likelihood of escaping or neutralizing the threat. Physical expression (e.g., facial, posture) of negative emotion nonverbally alerts others to the threat, which elicits corresponding or reciprocal emotions within group members, motivating their actions as well. In contrast, positive emotions are less likely to emerge under conditions of threat or danger, tend to engage the parasympathetic nervous system (e.g., relaxation response), and function to "undo" the physiological activation produced in the experience of negative emotion. Positive emotions are theorized to broaden the array of thought–action choices, maximize awareness of situational opportunities, and build lasting resources at all levels of social functioning (Fredrickson, 2001).

In general, moral emotions can be characterized along this same negative–positive dimension. However, moral emotions are distinguishable from non-moral emotions on the basis of their overarching social function related to the preservation of group and dyadic relations (Haidt, 2003). Thus, although fear, sadness, and pleasure may occur in moral contexts, social–functional accounts do not consider them moral emotions per se because they are more directly tied to individual rather than group survival. In contrast, as is elaborated later, moral emotions directly help individuals navigate a complex, dynamic web of varying social relationships by helping group members discourage selfishness, encourage prosocial behaviors, and maintain social connections to enhance the likelihood of group survival.

Self-Conscious Moral Emotions

A primary function of moral emotions is helping individuals navigate complex and dynamic social relationships by helping them prevent or recover from the disdain and hostility of other members of the social group (Haidt, 2003). The emotions of guilt and shame notify individuals of infractions of social and moral norms and function to motivate behaviors likely to reduce conflict and restore group homeostasis. These behaviors include acts of reparation, seeking forgiveness, and submission, as well as withdrawal and social isolation. Because a perceived violation of individual and community moral standards lies at the core of current conceptualizations of moral injury (Drescher et al., 2011; Litz et al., 2009), these emotions are thought to be a frequent consequence of exposure to morally injurious events. To the degree these emotions endure and the individual's attempts to manage them are ineffective, they may lead to individual dysphoria, social alienation, and relational dysfunction, along with an increased likelihood of mental health disorders.

Guilt

The moral emotion of *guilt* involves a negative evaluation of a specific action and is associated with distress, regret, and remorse over the perceived infraction

(Tangney et al., 2007). Guilt is elicited by perceived moral violations of social relations that threaten one's relationship with the harmed individual or group (Clark & Mills, 1979; Fiske, 1991). Guilt motivates prosocial behavior, such as accepting responsibility and initiating restorative actions in response to the violation (Tangney et al., 2007), and is not generally linked with psychological disturbance. In contrast to research in civilian populations, research on combat-related guilt has shown that it is associated with reduced psychological functioning and serves as a risk factor for posttraumatic stress disorder (PTSD) and other disorders (Henning & Frueh, 1997). Furthermore, research has identified associations between combat-related guilt and negative psychological outcomes following potentially morally injurious events (e.g., killing, atrocities; Bryan et al., 2013; Maguen et al., 2012). These discrepancies between guilt in nonmilitary samples and guilt related to combat suggest that different moral emotions might have been assessed in these studies. Most veteran studies have not measured and differentiated between guilt over specific transgressions and the more generalized emotion of shame. This raises the possibility that findings on combat-related guilt might be confounded by unmeasured shame. Future research should include measures of guilt (defined more narrowly in the moral emotions literature) and the more psychologically damaging emotion of shame.

Shame
Although guilt and shame are often used interchangeably and viewed as synonyms, shame can be differentiated from guilt. Research in civilian populations suggests that *shame* involves a broad negative evaluation of the self that is accompanied by feelings of worthlessness and fear of exposure. Whereas guilt focuses outwardly on specific transgressions, shame focuses inwardly on the self (Tangney et al., 2007). Whereas guilt tends to motivate behaviors aimed at restoring a relationship, shame tends to motivate behaviors of hiding and withdrawal. Guilt has been found to increase empathy for others, whereas shame functions to reduce empathy for others because of its preoccupation with self-discomfort (Joireman, 2004). In civilian samples, shame has been associated with anger, aggression, and substance abuse (Tangney & Dearing, 2002), whereas guilt tends not to be related to these behaviors (Tangney et al., 1996).

Research on shame within military populations is sparse and just emerging. Bryan and colleagues (Bryan, Morrow, et al., 2013; Bryan, Ray-Sannerud, et al., 2013, 2018) have undertaken a series of studies with military veterans on the role of moral emotions in suicidality, PTSD, and moral injury. One study (Bryan, Ray-Sannerud, et al., 2013) found that both guilt and shame were associated with worse suicidal ideation, with guilt having the strongest association even after accounting for the effects of PTSD and depression symptoms. Another study indicated that shame interacted with the association between hopelessness and suicidal ideation and that another moral emotion, pride, buffered this relationship. This finding suggests the potential benefit of positive moral emotions (Bryan, Ray-Sannerud, et al., 2013). A third study found that moral injury was distinguishable from PTSD and that moral emotions such as guilt, shame, and anger were most associated with moral injury, as was social alienation (Bryan et al., 2018). Similarly, Jordan and colleagues (2017) found that shame and guilt marginally mediated the relationship between perpetration-based morally injurious events (MIEs) and PTSD, whereas anger mediated the relation between betrayal-based MIEs and PTSD. All these findings are consistent with evolved moral emotions serving situation-specific social functions, which also may increase the risk of psychological conditions reflective of moral injury, such as PTSD.

Other-Condemning Moral Emotions

In contrast to self-conscious moral emotions, Haidt (2003) also identified a subset of emotions that occur in response to another person's violations of moral values and expectations. This group of emotions includes anger, contempt, and disgust, which function to discourage selfish conduct or actions by others that might threaten the cohesiveness of the social group (Hutcherson & Gross, 2011).

Anger

Evidence indicates that *anger* is elicited by the perceived intentional violation of one's personal freedoms (Rozin et al., 1999; Russell & Giner-Sorolla, 2011). It is characterized by an aggressive approach toward others to discourage or end acts that are perceived as immediate threats to the self or one's goals (Hutcherson & Gross, 2011). Anger is known to be highly prevalent among military service members returning from war. Reports suggest that up to half of all returning service members experience problems with anger (Taft et al., 2012). Longitudinal evidence from combat-deployed military personnel showed that anger increased significantly from pre- to postdeployment, suggesting the importance of stressful war-zone experiences in rates of postdeployment anger (Koffel et al., 2012). Similarly, a qualitative study of military personnel returning from Iraq or Afghanistan noted MIEs (e.g., violation of conscience, betrayal of trust) as one of three common precipitants of anger (Worthen & Ahern, 2014)

Disgust

Evidence increasingly suggests that moral *disgust* is an elaboration of the body's physical reaction to objects perceived as disease threats (e.g., rotten food; Chapman & Anderson, 2013). Bodily disgust is typically associated with feelings of revulsion, and its core action tendency is the expulsion of the toxic substance. Moral disgust is likewise elicited by people or actions that are perceived to desecrate something deemed sacred (e.g., political or religious symbols) or contaminate one's sense of moral purity, and has been positively associated with more severe moral judgments (Haidt et al., 1997). Research has found moral disgust reactions to be highly resistant to change (Hutcherson & Gross, 2011).

Contempt

Contempt is arguably the least understood of the other-condemning moral emotions. Some researchers have suggested that contempt is associated with appraisals of another person's incompetence. Relying on incompetent assistance during a crisis could place one at increased risk. Contempt may function to diminish interaction with individuals that cannot be trusted to contribute helpfully to the survival of the social group (Hutcherson & Gross, 2011).

Rozin et al. (1999) argued that these three other-condemning moral emotions function to distinguish behaviors that violate three particular moral ethics. From this perspective, humans experience contempt at violations of the community (disrespect of hierarchy and social responsibilities), anger is elicited by violations of autonomy (disregard of personal rights and freedoms), and disgust is elicited by violations of sanctity (disrespecting something deemed sacred or causing degradation to self or community; Rozin et al., 1999).

Positive Moral Emotions

Positive moral emotions serve similar functions as painful moral emotions for providing information, evoking emotional responses in others, and incentivizing others' behavior. Interpersonally, positive emotions perform at least three social functions. First, they help shape social interactions by providing information to others, evoking positive emotional responses in others, and incentivizing others' behavior. Visible displays of emotion convey information about the sender's current emotion, intended behavior, and perceptions about the relationship with the target. They also provide information about the environment beyond the relationship that allows group members to coordinate actions that enhance opportunities. Displays of emotions elicit both reciprocal and matching emotions from others in the social community. For example, expressions of distress elicit compassion from observers (Goetz et al., 2010). *Empathy*, which can be defined as experiencing the emotion of another, may contribute to moral functioning and helping behaviors (Singer & Lamm, 2009). Finally, displays of positive emotion can incentivize prosocial behavior by others (Keltner & Kring, 1998). For example, parental displays of positive emotion can act as rewards for children that reinforce positive behavior. Similarly, infants smile when parents engage in behavior that aids in achieving the child's goal. Laughter among adults appears to reward many forms of desirable social behavior among interacting groups.

Although negative moral emotions play a predominant role in conceptualizing moral injury, social–functionalist models of morality have important implications for understanding the role of positive moral emotions as mechanisms of moral healing. Litz et al. (2009) defined recovery from moral injury as "successful integration of the moral violation into an intact, although more flexible, functional belief system" (p. 701). As noted earlier, many positive emotions function to "undo" activated sympathetic nervous system arousal systems by engaging a parasympathetic relaxation response. Interpersonally, Fredrickson's (2001) broaden and build theory predicts that positive emotions broaden awareness of social opportunities and motivate actions that may facilitate social connection and strengthen social relationships. The positive moral emotions of compassion, gratitude, awe or elevation, and pride each carry potential benefits that may address some of the pain and social alienation seen in moral injury.

Compassion

Gilbert (2014) defined *compassion* as "a sensitivity to suffering in self and others, with a commitment to try to alleviate and prevent it" (p. 19). It appears compassion originates within the attachment system, where it is evolutionarily adaptive in facilitating altruism toward one's closest social relations. Although people can and do feel compassion for strangers, it is most easily and frequently felt for those in close proximity or social connection. After being elicited by suffering, compassion directs attention to the needs of those who are weak and motivates beneficial actions toward others, even behaviors costly to the self (Oveis et al., 2010). Research has suggested that compassion increases the perceived similarity between self and others and awareness related to providing care to others (Oveis et al., 2010).

Gratitude

Gratitude has been defined as an emotion composed of two elements: (a) awareness that one has experienced a positive outcome that (b) came from an external source (Emmons & McCullough, 2003). The practice of intentional gratitude has been a part of religious and spiritual traditions for thousands of years. McCullough and colleagues (2001) hypothesized that gratitude is a moral emotion with three primary functions. First, gratitude functions as a moral barometer that provides information about particular changes in one's social relationships. It brings awareness of positive benefit from another person that strengthens the relationship. Moreover, gratitude motivates the recipient to behave more benevolently in the future. Third, gratitude expression functions as a reinforcer of moral behavior for others. Appreciative acknowledgment encourages others to continue behaving benevolently. Armenta and colleagues (2017) suggested that gratitude functions as a motivator of self-improvement and positive changes within the social group. They noted that increases in social connectedness, emotional experiences of elevation and humility, and awareness of one's lower social status function as mechanisms for self-improvement behaviors. One indicator of gratitude's potential benefit for moral injury is that intentional gratitude has been put forward as a therapeutic intervention (Emmons & Stern, 2013).

Awe and Elevation

Elevation and awe have been described as "self-transcendent" moral emotions in that they broaden an individual's awareness of the social and physical world around them. *Elevation* is described as a feeling of warmth elicited in response to witnessing human goodness. It motivates one toward better living and pro-social actions (Keltner & Haidt, 2003). On a larger scale than elevation, the emotion of *awe* has been characterized as having two elements: vastness and accommodation. *Vastness* refers to that which is much larger than or beyond the experience and frame of reference of the self. Vastness can relate to physical size but also social size, such as being in the presence of great authority, fame, or prestige. In cognitive psychology, *accommodation* refers to changes in mental structures that cannot assimilate some new experience. In the context of awe, the experience of vastness forces an inability to make sense of the experience requiring a restructuring of one's understanding. Experiences of awe can be disorienting or even frightening because they are associated with feelings of smallness, confusion, and powerlessness. Transformative moral experiences of awe are exemplified in religious texts, such as Moses in the presence of the burning bush. Keltner and Haidt (2003) suggested that awe can be elicited by social (e.g., encounter with fame), physical (e.g., spectacular landscape), and incongruent cognitive experiences (e.g., seeing an object levitate). Though research on the emotions of awe and elevation is limited, it has been suggested that awe can powerfully motivate prosocial behavior and increase social connection, which may be reparative for moral injury (McGuire et al., 2019).

Pride

Social hierarchies are universally part of human experience. Young children seem to be aware of and function within social hierarchies that provide practical solutions to resource allocation and work sharing within communities. Self-conscious emotions help individuals to track appraisals of their social rank. As mentioned previously, embarrassment and shame signal submissiveness and awareness of diminishing of social rank. In contrast, *pride* signals gains in status in relation to others. Pride is elicited by favorable comparisons of the self to valued standards and the behavior of others (Oveis et al., 2010). Pride has been defined as an emotion "generated by appraisals that one is responsible for a socially valued outcome or for being a socially valued person" (Mascolo & Fischer, 1995, p. 66). Like the distinction made in shame and guilt between one's self versus one's behavior, many researchers distinguish between two types of pride. One type is viewed as pride in behavioral accomplishment where an individual experiences positive feelings as a result of virtuous actions. The second type of pride, sometimes called *hubris*, elicits an elevated view of the self (Tangney et al., 2007).

SOCIAL-INTUITIONAL ACCOUNTS OF MORALITY

Moral foundations theory (MFT; Graham et al., 2013) attempts to integrate findings of evolution, anthropology, and modern neuroscience fields into a testable theory of human morality. MFT postulates that biologically based intuitive reactions dominated by moral emotion are foundational for human morality and address particular evolutionary challenges that humans faced. Learning and reasoning are thought to play a secondary role that directs intuitions toward particular social norms and cultural expectations. MFT posits the existence of moral intuitions that are innate, rapid, emotion-based responses designed to alert individuals to moral violations related to specific evolution-based human challenges. Initial evidence of the biological basis of intuitional morality has emerged from studies of moral reactions in preverbal infants (Van de Vondervoort & Hamlin, 2016).

Proponents of MFT postulate the existence of at least five moral "foundations" (i.e., virtue or violation pairs) that each correspond to an adaptive challenge faced by early humans. These foundations are as follows: (a) caring versus harm toward innocents—the need to protect and care for young, vulnerable, or injured members of the community; (b) reciprocity versus cheating—which allows the community to experience benefits through cooperation and mutual reciprocity and addresses the problem of "free riders"; (c) group loyalty versus betrayal—which protects the group from internal threats that could fracture the group; (d) authority versus subversion—which maintains a functional community and a beneficial leadership hierarchy where roles and responsibilities at all levels are clear; and (e) purity versus degradation—evolutionarily the disgust mechanism that prevented disease outbreaks that was seemingly modified to prevent desecration of important shared values and ideals. Given the importance of these five domains to human survival, this theory proposes that evolution incorporates them universally and innately in human beings during development.

Each of these five moral foundations can be identified as being salient for military-related trauma. For example, in the context of war, individuals experiencing imminent life threat must make rapid life-changing decisions that may result in death or serious injury. Moral conflicts in which every situational option may result in moral harm are common during war-zone service, leaving service members with painful questioning of their combat-related decisions and actions. In the instance of Adam, violations of several moral intuitions are present. The sexual abuse of children likely violated both the harm and the purity and sanctity intuitions. Adam likely experienced disgust and anger directed toward the perpetrators, as well as guilt at his inaction. Moreover, the gunnery sergeant's response to Adam's inquiry about punishing the perpetrators may be perceived as a betrayal of the moral foundation of authority because leadership abdicated their responsibilities to those under their stewardship and control. Thus, moral intuitions are relevant to understanding mechanisms by which morally disruptive military situations might result in moral injury.

A social–functional model of morality, as emphasized in MFT, makes potentially important contributions to understanding the etiology and mechanisms through which moral injury develops. For example, the social nature of human morality means that an individual's morality is not a unified singular experience across either time or relationship. Rather, the tangled web of overlapping and intersecting roles, relationships, and identities that individuals have within multiple groups creates a high degree of complexity in moral decision making. For example, during the same period, a deployed service member can be in a distressed long-distance marital relationship, develop intensely close friendships with fellow unit members, create a relationship of trust with a local civilian translator, seek counsel from a chaplain as part of a religious community, and begin to feel parental-like caring for a young local child who keeps approaching the unit to sell DVDs. Each of those relationships potentially carries distinct moral obligations. In some instances, a moral obligation within one relationship might create stress or even violate a moral responsibility for other relationships, thereby generating a host of moral conflicts due to intersecting or even conflicting moral obligations.

Particularly for military personnel, primary moral communities can shift over time in the course of training, deployment cycles, and military-to-civilian transition. When an individual enters the military and undergoes basic training, that experience intentionally strips away their civilian identity and creates a new social identity complete with moral values and beliefs. Basic training is stressful by design, removing important aspects of one's past life, including hairstyle, clothing, contact with family and friends, and personal belongings. An entirely new set of rules is enforced for getting up, going to bed, grooming, and caring for belongings, as well as personal space, eating, movement, communicating, and physical activity. A new set of moral values is taught and enforced (e.g., U.S. Marine Corps' core values of "honor, courage, and commitment"). All of this occurs in a high-stress, physically exhausting environment wherein even small protocol violations are punished harshly, sometimes not just a single individual but the entire unit for the actions of that individual. Training focuses on building tight unit cohesion wherein individuals see unit members as essential for their own survival and begin the process of moral disengagement from previously held moral values, particularly toward those deemed to be "enemies." In this way, recruits are incorporated into their new military community.

On deployment and entry into a war-zone environment, the tight-knit bonds created during training create small moral communities with clear boundaries for group membership that may begin differentiating moral responsibilities toward those within the unit, as opposed to those outside. Missions undertaken during deployment result in direct and indirect exposure to enemy combatants and civilian noncombatants and may result in the experience of MIEs, which then generate powerful moral emotions and judgments that may reshape a service member's moral attitudes and identities. This process may proceed across a series of months or even years and extend across multiple deployments. Few service members escape unscathed from combat service, and most people are changed by it in some manner.

Eventually, a third transition occurs, beginning when service members leave their units, are discharged from military service, and return home to civilian family and friends. Though there may have been extended periods with family between deployments, for many service members, discharge marks a permanent separation from their military community. However, although entry into the military was associated with an intense and deliberate formation of new moral identities and communities for an extended period, no such formal transition exists for those leaving the military. Instead, at discharge, service members generally receive lecture-based briefings, a warning of possible challenges related to civilian reintegration, and the offer of assistance with potential self-identify problems. Though well-meaning, for many service members, these procedures represent an abrupt expulsion compared with the months-long, intensive socialization process reflected in their entry into the military.

This rapid transition is therefore experienced by many service members as that of being jettisoned out of one moral world and into another while being expected to proceed as though nothing has changed. Unfortunately, because most civilians have no concept of military culture or values, service members might feel easily misunderstood or conflicted about the clash between civilian and military moral norms. What's more, these conflicting worldviews may lead many service members to experience moral dissonance, as they compare their civilian identities and moral norms with the norms and behaviors that accompanied their military experiences. Without the support of other veterans or professionals, many service members find it difficult to reconcile the past and present in a way that allows them to reintegrate into the moral community of their family and friends.

IMPLICATIONS OF SOCIAL FUNCTIONALISM FOR UNDERSTANDING MORAL INJURY

From a clinical perspective, awareness of the social–functional model offers a number of important implications for psychotherapy. First, this model of morality can help clinicians develop more awareness of client moral challenges and, when appropriate, affirm the role that morality plays in the client's social and personal flourishing. Second, an awareness of the functional role of morality can help broaden clinician perspectives and expand awareness of the potentially adaptive role that painful moral emotions can play in alerting clients to the impact of events and behavior of self and others. This may temper the tendency of those in helping professions to routinely pathologize distressing emotional experiences. Third, awareness of the social functions of morality may also help increase clinician comfort with moral pluralism as an aspect of human diversity to be engaged with competently. Fourth, to the degree that morality overlaps with religious and spiritual traditions, clinicians working with moral injury may have to reinforce their competencies in working with this aspect of diversity (see Chapter 3).

The social nature of morality also raises important critiques for how mental health providers conceptualize treatment more broadly. A social–functional perspective suggests that evolution ensures the survival of species as opposed to individual survival, resulting in a perspective that acknowledges both the advantages, as well as the occasional disadvantages, of social connection. The social–functional perspective also notes the role that moral emotions play in helping individuals negotiate their varying roles across multiple communities and helping the community to maintain a homeostasis that benefits the group. Inherent in that understanding is the fact that moral emotions can so severely impact the flourishing of an individual that they withdraw from or are excluded from their communities, thereby resulting in distress, loss of potential resources, and failure to thrive. Such a model may help provide balance for clinicians in moving away from strictly intrapersonal therapeutic approaches toward those that will more actively address clients' social relationships and their embeddedness in larger communities.

The social–functional model of morality also has implications for moral injury research. Awareness of this model may spur the use and development of clinical measures of social alienation, as well as the connection between moral identities, values, and measures of well-being and psychological flourishing. Moreover, the use of measures developed for examination of moral foundations could examine how the prioritization of those moral intuitions shift for military personnel over the course of enlistment, careers, and post-military as they reengage with their family and former social communities. Studies using military samples may explore how these variables interact with group cohesion, particularly during and after war-zone deployments.

CONCLUSION

Although the preceding discussion focused on military and veteran populations, social models of morality also have implications for the field of mental health in general. Developing assessments of moral emotions and judgments that do not assume psychopathology or treat these experiences simply as symptoms are important steps toward recognizing their evolutionary value. Such assessments would enable the development of clinical interventions that facilitate client prosocial behavior, social engagement, and flourishing as opposed to a narrower focus on symptom reduction. In parallel to this client focus, research examining clinician attitudes toward morality and their level of comfort in addressing moral issues therapeutically would similarly be beneficial for the field of mental health. Finally, increased research attention to the impact of selfless (prosocial) versus selfish behaviors on individuals, relationships, and community life stands to benefit both clients, providers, and society at large.

REFERENCES

Armenta, C. N., Fritz, M. M., & Lyubomirsky, S. (2017). Functions of positive emotions: Gratitude as a motivator of self-improvement and positive change. *Emotion Review, 9*(3), 183–190. https://doi.org/10.1177/1754073916669596

Bachorowski, J., & Owren, M. K. (2008). Vocal expressions of emotion. In M. Lewis, J. M. Haviland-Jones, & L. F. Barrett (Eds.), *Handbook of emotions* (3rd ed., pp. 196–210). Guilford Press.

Bryan, C. J., Bryan, A. O., Roberge, E., Leifker, F. R., & Rozek, D. C. (2018). Moral injury, posttraumatic stress disorder, and suicidal behavior among National Guard personnel. *Psychological Trauma: Theory, Research, Practice, and Policy, 10*(1), 36–45. https://doi.org/10.1037/tra0000290

Bryan, C. J., Morrow, C. E., Etienne, N., & Ray-Sannerud, B. (2013). Guilt, shame, and suicidal ideation in a military outpatient clinical sample. *Depression and Anxiety, 30*(1), 55–60. https://doi.org/10.1002/da.22002

Bryan, C. J., Ray-Sannerud, B., Morrow, C. E., & Etienne, N. (2013). Shame, pride, and suicidal ideation in a military clinical sample. *Journal of Affective Disorders, 147*(1–3), 212–216. https://doi.org/10.1016/j.jad.2012.11.006

Chapman, H. A., & Anderson, A. K. (2013). Things rank and gross in nature: A review and synthesis of moral disgust. *Psychological Bulletin, 139*(2), 300–327. https://doi.org/10.1037/a0030964

Clark, M. S., & Mills, J. (1979). Interpersonal attraction in exchange and communal relationships. *Journal of Personality and Social Psychology, 37*(1), 12–24. https://doi.org/10.1037/0022-3514.37.1.12

Dael, N., Mortillaro, M., & Scherer, K. R. (2012). Emotion expression in body action and posture. *Emotion, 12*(5), 1085–1101. https://doi.org/10.1037/a0025737

D'Andrade, R. G. (1984). Cultural meaning systems. In R. A. Shweder & R. A. LeVine (Eds.), *Culture theory* (pp. 88–119). Cambridge University Press.

Drescher, K. D., Foy, D. W., Kelly, C., Leshner, A., Shutz, K., & Litz, B. T. (2011). An exploration of the viability and usefulness of the construct of moral injury in war veterans. *Traumatology, 17*(1), 8–13. https://doi.org/10.1177/1534765610395615

Emmons, R. A., & McCullough, M. E. (2003). Counting blessings versus burdens: An experimental investigation of gratitude and subjective well-being in daily life. *Journal of Personality and Social Psychology, 84*(2), 377–389. https://doi.org/10.1037/0022-3514.84.2.377

Emmons, R. A., & Stern, R. (2013). Gratitude as a psychotherapeutic intervention. *Journal of Clinical Psychology, 69*(8), 846–855. https://doi.org/10.1002/jclp.22020

Farnsworth, J. K. (2019). Is and ought: Descriptive and prescriptive cognitions in military-related moral injury. *Journal of Traumatic Stress, 32*(3), 373–381. https://doi.org/10.1002/jts.22356

Fiske, A. P. (1991). *Structures of social life*. Free Press.

Fredrickson, B. L. (2001). The role of positive emotions in positive psychology. The broaden-and-build theory of positive emotions. *American Psychologist, 56*(3), 218–226. https://doi.org/10.1037/0003-066X.56.3.218

Gilbert, P. (2014). The origins and nature of compassion focused therapy. *The British Journal of Clinical Psychology, 53*(1), 6–41.

Goetz, J. L., & Keltner, D. (2007). Shifting meanings of self-conscious emotions across cultures: A social-functional approach. In J. Tracy, R. Robins, & J. P. Tangney (Eds.), *The self-conscious emotions: Theory and research* (pp. 153–173). Guilford Press.

Goetz, J. L., Keltner, D., & Simon-Thomas, E. (2010). Compassion: An evolutionary analysis and empirical review. *Psychological Bulletin, 136*(3), 351–374. https://doi.org/10.1037/a0018807

Graham, J., Haidt, J., Koleva, S., Motyl, M., Iyer, R., Wojcik, S. P., & Ditto, P. H. (2013). Moral foundations theory: The pragmatic validity of moral pluralism. *Advances in Experimental Social Psychology, 47*, 55–130. https://doi.org/10.1016/B978-0-12-407236-7.00002-4

Haidt, J. (2003). The moral emotions. In R. J. Davidson, K. R. Scherer, & H. H. Goldsmith (Eds.), *Handbook of affective sciences* (pp. 852–870). Oxford University Press.

Haidt, J. (2008). Morality. *Perspectives on Psychological Science, 3*(1), 65–72. https://doi.org/10.1111/j.1745-6916.2008.00063.x

Haidt, J., Rozin, P., McCauley, C., & Imada, S. (1997). Body, psyche, and culture: The relationship between disgust and morality. *Psychology and Developing Societies, 9*(1), 107–131. https://doi.org/10.1177/097133369700900105

Henning, K. R., & Frueh, B. C. (1997). Combat guilt and its relationship to PTSD symptoms. *Journal of Clinical Psychology, 53*(8), 801–808. https://doi.org/10.1002/(SICI)1097-4679(199712)53:8%3C801::AID-JCLP3%3E3.0.CO;2-I

Hutcherson, C. A., & Gross, J. J. (2011). The moral emotions: A social–functionalist account of anger, disgust, and contempt. *Journal of Personality and Social Psychology, 100*(4), 719–737. https://doi.org/10.1037/a0022408

Joireman, J. (2004). Empathy and the self-absorption paradox II: Self-rumination and self-reflection as mediators between shame, guilt, and empathy. *Self and Identity, 3*(3), 225–238. https://doi.org/10.1080/13576500444000038

Jordan, A. H., Eisen, E., Bolton, E., Nash, W. P., & Litz, B. T. (2017). Distinguishing war-related PTSD resulting from perpetration- and betrayal-based morally injurious events. *Psychological Trauma: Theory, Research, Practice, and Policy, 9*(6), 627–634. https://doi.org/10.1037/tra0000249

Keltner, D., & Haidt, J. (1999). Social functions of emotions at four levels of analysis. *Cognition and Emotion, 13*(5), 505–521. https://doi.org/10.1080/026999399379168

Keltner, D., & Haidt, J. (2003). Approaching awe, a moral, spiritual, and aesthetic emotion. *Cognition and Emotion, 17*(2), 297–314. https://doi.org/10.1080/02699930302297

Keltner, D., Haidt, J., & Shiota, M. N. (2006). Social functionalism and the evolution of emotions. In M. Schaller, J. Simpson, & D. Kenrick (Eds.), *Evolution and social psychology* (pp. 115–142). Psychosocial Press.

Keltner, D., & Kring, A. M. (1998). Emotion, social function, and psychopathology. *Review of General Psychology, 2*(3), 320–342. https://doi.org/10.1037/1089-2680.2.3.320

Koffel, E., Polusny, M. A., Arbisi, P. A., & Erbes, C. R. (2012). A preliminary investigation of the new and revised symptoms of posttraumatic stress disorder in *DSM-5*. *Depression and Anxiety, 29*, 731–738. https://doi.org/10.1002/da.21965

Levenson, R. W. (1994). Human emotion: A functional view. In P. Ekman & R. J. Davidson (Eds.), *The nature of emotion: Fundamental questions* (pp. 123–126). Oxford University Press.

Litz, B. T., Stein, N., Delaney, E., Lebowitz, L., Nash, W. P., Silva, C., & Maguen, S. (2009). Moral injury and moral repair in war veterans: A preliminary model and intervention strategy. *Clinical Psychology Review, 29*, 695–706. https://doi.org/10.1016/j.cpr.2009.07.003

Maguen, S., Metzler, T. J., Bosch, J., Marmar, C. R., Knight, S. J., & Neylan, T. C. (2012). Killing in combat may be independently associated with suicidal ideation. *Depression and Anxiety, 29*(11), 918–923. https://doi.org/10.1002/da.21954

Martin, M. W. (2006). *From morality to mental health: Virtue and vice in a therapeutic culture.* Oxford University Press. https://doi.org/10.1093/0195304713.001.0001

Mascolo, M. F., & Fischer, K. W. (1995). Developmental transformations in appraisals for pride, shame, and guilt. In J. P. Tangney & K. W. Fischer (Eds.), *Self-conscious emotions: The psychology of shame, guilt, embarrassment, and pride* (pp. 64–113). Guilford Press.

Matsumoto, D., Keltner, D., Shiota, M. N., O'Sullivan, M., & Frank, M. (2008). Facial expressions of emotion. In M. Lewis, J. M. Haviland-Jones, & L. F. Barrett (Eds.), *Handbook of emotions* (3rd ed., pp. 211–234). Guilford Press.

McCullough, M. E., Kilpatrick, S. D., Emmons, R. A., & Larson, D. B. (2001). Is gratitude a moral affect? *Psychological Bulletin, 127*(2), 249–266. https://doi.org/10.1037/0033-2909.127.2.249

McGuire, A. P., Nosen, E., & Lyons, J. A. (2019). Benefits of moral elevation in veterans with PTSD and moral injury: A proposed theoretical framework and pilot study. *Military Behavioral Health, 7*(3), 315–326. https://doi.org/10.1080/21635781.2018.1540316

Oveis, C., Horberg, E. J., & Keltner, D. (2010). Compassion, pride, and social intuitions of self-other similarity. *Journal of Personality and Social Psychology, 98*(4), 618–630. https://doi.org/10.1037/a0017628

Rimé, B. (2009). Emotion elicits the social sharing of emotion: Theory and empirical review. *Emotion Review, 1*(1), 60–85. https://doi.org/10.1177/1754073908097189

Rozin, P., Lowery, L., Imada, S., & Haidt, J. (1999). The CAD triad hypothesis: A mapping between three moral emotions (contempt, anger, disgust) and three moral codes (community, autonomy, divinity). *Journal of Personality and Social Psychology, 76*(4), 574–586. https://doi.org/10.1037/0022-3514.76.4.574

Russell, P. S., & Giner-Sorolla, R. (2011). Moral anger, but not moral disgust, responds to intentionality. *Emotion, 11*(2), 233–240. https://doi.org/10.1037/a0022598

Singer, T., & Lamm, C. (2009). The social neuroscience of empathy. *Annals of the New York Academy of Sciences, 1156*(1), 81–96. https://doi.org/10.1111/j.1749-6632.2009.04418.x

Taft, C. T., Creech, S. K., & Kachadourian, L. (2012). Assessment and treatment of posttraumatic anger and aggression: A review. *Journal of Rehabilitation Research and Development, 49*(5), 777–788. https://doi.org/10.1682/JRRD.2011.09.0156

Tangney, J. P., & Dearing, R. L. (2002). *Shame and guilt.* Guilford Press.

Tangney, J. P., Miller, R. S., Flicker, L., & Barlow, D. H. (1996). Are shame, guilt, and embarrassment distinct emotions? *Journal of Personality and Social Psychology, 70*(6), 1256–1269. https://doi.org/10.1037/0022-3514.70.6.1256

Tangney, J. P., Stuewig, J., & Mashek, D. J. (2007). Moral emotions and moral behavior. *Annual Review of Psychology, 58*(1), 345–372. https://doi.org/10.1146/annurev.psych.56.091103.070145

Van de Vondervoort, J. W., & Hamlin, J. K. (2016). Evidence for intuitive morality: Preverbal infants make sociomoral evaluations. *Child Development Perspectives, 10*(3), 143–148. https://doi.org/10.1111/cdep.12175

Worthen, M., & Ahern, J. (2014). The causes, course, and consequences of anger problems in veterans returning to civilian life. *Journal of Loss and Trauma, 19*(4), 355–363. https://doi.org/10.1080/15325024.2013.788945

3

Religious and Spiritual Issues in Moral Injury

Joseph M. Currier, Timothy D. Carroll, and Jennifer H. Wortmann

Morally injurious events and other types of traumas may affect military service members and veterans (SM/Vs) not only physically, psychologically, and socially but also spiritually. Celtic theologians long ago coined the term *thin places* to capture situations or experiences in life in which a perceived boundary between temporal and eternal worlds becomes diffuse. In many ways, definitions of moral injury similarly point to a *thin construct*—not due to a lack of substance or utility, but because moral injury may compel biomedically oriented clinicians to consider the variegated role of religious faith and/or spirituality (R/S) in SM/Vs' suffering and healing. A growing number of studies reveal diverse ways in which R/S can influence rates and severity of commonly diagnosed mental health conditions in SM/Vs (e.g., posttraumatic stress disorder [PTSD], major depressive disorder; Koenig et al., 2017; Smith-MacDonald et al., 2017). In addition, emerging models of moral injury suggest R/S concerns represent an essential feature of the clinical picture for many SM/Vs (e.g., Litz et al., 2009). However, because of limited opportunities for graduate school education and clinical training in R/S (Shafranske & Cummings, 2013; Vieten et al., 2013), psychologists and other clinicians are often unprepared to conceptualize this cultural domain in their work with SM/Vs.

This lack of knowledge about the potential interplay between R/S and moral injury is problematic in light of a sizeable subset of SM/Vs for whom R/S shaped identity, relationships, and lifestyle decision making. Recent findings from a nationally representative sample of 3,151 veterans from multiple

https://doi.org/10.1037/0000204-004
Addressing Moral Injury in Clinical Practice, J. M. Currier, K. D. Drescher, and J. Nieuwsma (Editors)

service eras indicated nearly half were religiously affiliated and/or engaged in spiritual activities and/or practices (e.g., prayer, service attendance) on a weekly or more frequent basis (Sharma et al., 2017). Focusing on smaller samples from the southern United States, other work similarly found high rates of affiliation with organized religious groups (60%–80%), weekly service attendance (40%–50%), engagement in prayer or other practices (50%), moderate to greater importance of R/S in life (70%–90%), and belief in the existence of God or higher power (60%–70%; Currier, Pearce, et al., 2018; McLaughlin et al., 2010). Importantly, although conventionally religious ties are higher in the U.S. South, these findings mirror patterns of R/S in nationally representative samples of the general population as a whole (Ellison & McFarland, 2013; Pew Research Center, 2014). Moreover, in keeping with an increasing subset of the U.S. population who self-identify as "spiritual but not religious," the Military Leadership Diversity Commission (MLDC; 2010) reported greater diversity in beliefs and behaviors (e.g., no conventionally religious ties) in younger persons who enlisted after 9/11.

Whether working with morally injured SM/Vs or other military-connected groups, these findings affirm the need for mental health professionals to understand patients' R/S backgrounds in the service of providing culturally competent assessment and psychotherapy or counseling (American Psychological Association [APA], 2007; Vieten et al., 2013). As such, the goals of this chapter are to enhance clinicians' (a) conceptual knowledge about possible R/S issues in moral injury and (b) ability to negotiate clinical and ethical concerns that could emerge from pursuing culturally competent care with respect to R/S. Throughout the chapter, we draw on material from a recent case in which Timothy D. Carroll served as the therapist and Joseph M. Currier as the supervisor.

CASE EXAMPLE

Matthew was a 34-year-old White man who self-referred for therapy at a community-based clinic due to a range of psychological, relational, and spiritual issues in the year following his separation from the U.S. Army. The older of two brothers, he was largely raised on military installations around the world because his father was a career soldier. Matthew's nuclear family consisted of his wife and two children (ages 6 years and 2 years). On entering treatment, he described familial and relational difficulties (e.g., anger outbursts, avoidance of emotional intimacy with wife and children) that had resulted in a period of separation. Matthew's family dynamics were further complicated by his youngest child's ongoing struggle with a chronic and life-threatening medical condition involving frequent surgeries and hospitalizations, which also depleted his resources. However, beginning with a strong commitment to Protestant Christianity in his family of origin, his faith system continued to serve as a source of identity, strength, and hope in his life, and he expressed a preference for Timothy Carroll to address spiritual concerns in his treatment. Specifically, he participated in a men's fellowship group each week, attended worship services, and volunteered in several capacities at a large Baptist church. In addition, he prayed and read and studied the Bible and other spiritually oriented texts on a near-daily basis.

Matthew served for nearly a decade as a medic with a special forces unit that completed numerous combat operations in support of recent campaigns in Iraq and Afghanistan. He was medically discharged due to serious physical and psychological injuries (i.e., mild traumatic brain injury, disfigurement) several months before seeking care. At the time, Matthew was also given a medical directive to remain nonambulatory after a sixth reconstructive knee surgery. Restricted from any physical activity with few meaningful engagements, Matthew began to experience serious trauma-related symptomatology that well exceeded the clinical thresholds on the PTSD Checklist for *DSM-5* (total score = 59; Wortmann et al., 2016), Patient Health Questionnaire (total score = 14; Kroenke et al., 2001), and Generalized Anxiety Disorder-7 scale (total score = 16; Spitzer et al., 2006). Although he reported exposure to many life-threatening events for himself and others, Matthew was primarily troubled by potentially morally injurious events (PMIEs) that were impairing functioning in familial, social, and vocational domains. In particular, he carried deep regret for his inability to revive 20 of the U.S. soldiers who died under his care in combat. Further, Matthew discussed carrying "demons" related to thousands of patrols and other highly dangerous operations that resulted in the deaths of more combatants and noncombatants than he could remember.

Among the PMIEs he encountered during his war-zone deployments, Matthew's most distressing event entailed taking the life of a child who was running munitions to embedded combatants in a firefight. Ultimately, he reported struggles reconciling his wartime behavior (e.g., killing other parents' children) with his present life roles (e.g., parenting his children). In turn, Matthew endorsed having frequent nightmares and other reexperiencing symptoms related to this event, avoiding both internal and external reminders of his morally injurious events, being on edge and irritable, and having dysphoric beliefs, cognitions, and emotions (e.g., self-condemnation and shame, sense of being unforgivable or unworthy of love or care from others). Also, Matthew was no longer finding pleasure in things he once enjoyed and was experiencing sleep deficits, a sense of letting loved ones down, and concentration difficulties. He further reported that his suffering was a deserved punishment for his "sins." Thus, he internalized his wartime actions as being representative of the core features of his personhood, which disrupted a formerly secure relationship with God. Specifically, he considered himself to have become too wretched to warrant grace from God. To this end, he stated, "I don't deserve to be forgiven for annihilating families." From a diagnostic standpoint, Matthew met the criteria for PTSD with secondary depressive symptomatology at the time of seeking treatment.

CONCEPTUALIZING RELIGION AND SPIRITUALITY

The U.S. R/S landscape has shifted in numerous ways over the past half-century in ways that may create challenges for clinicians working with morally injured SM/Vs such as Matthew. Because of powerful sociocultural forces (e.g., individualism, consumerism, immigration) and highly visible instances of misconduct and betrayal on the part of religious leaders, U.S. society as a whole has grown skeptical about organized religions (Ellison & McFarland, 2013). Despite decreases in conventionally religious ties, personalized expressions of religiousness, pluralism in religious practices and beliefs, and syncretism or amalgamation of practices and beliefs from historically distinct traditions have nonetheless increased. In turn, unlike cultural shifts in other Western industrialized nations, R/S continues to shape the fabric of relationships and identity for most Americans (Pew Research Center, 2014). However, unlike in eras before the Vietnam War, these constructs have grown differentiated and are often pitted against each other. For example, whereas religion traditionally denoted a "broad-band construct" comprising both individual (e.g., meaning in life, attachment to God or divine) and institutional (e.g., doctrines, rituals) elements, it has increasingly come to be viewed as a more "narrow-band construct," exclusively capturing external, extrinsic features (Hill et al., 2000; Zinnbauer et al., 1999). In contrast, spirituality has emerged as a favored term for internal, intrinsic features and loftier experiences of transcendence, peace, and purpose that are more often valued in the United States.

In this present-day context, there is an overwhelming number of definitions of R/S, many of which could present barriers for addressing moral injury in a culturally competent manner. Research has suggested that R/S carries differing meanings and connotations for many SM/Vs (Oman, 2013). For instance, early work by Zinnbauer et al. (1997) found that the constructs yielded divergent patterns of correlations with psychological factors. That is, whereas highly religious persons reported authoritarianism, orthodoxy, and church attendance at higher levels, spirituality ratings were more positively linked with mysticism and personal beliefs and practices. However, other findings revealed that most persons who self-identified as being religious also labeled themselves as spiritual, and conceptions of transcendent realities overlapped across their descriptions of R/S (Zinnbauer et al., 1997). From a clinical standpoint, these findings highlight that SM/Vs could label themselves as religious and/or spiritual for many idiosyncratic reasons. As such, clinicians should adopt each patient's preferred language in matters of R/S and seek to understand specific beliefs, values, and practices that lead them to apply these labels at different points in life (if at all). In Matthew's case, he viewed himself as a religious and spiritual person due to the importance he placed on both communal rituals (i.e., communion, church attendance) and symbolic professions of faith (i.e., baptism, evangelism), as well as internally focused practices such as belief in a loving and forgiving God, prayer, and regular Bible reading.

Pargament (2007, 2013) offered an integrative framework for clinicians to resolve this tension between flexibility in honoring patients' diverse views of R/S along with a need for consistency in conceptualizing the constructs. According to Pargament, spirituality is best defined as a search for the sacred that may assume an array of forms and pathways. "Search," the first component in this definition, implies spirituality does not refer to static beliefs, values, or behaviors. Instead, this construct can be conceptualized as a journey in which people are highly motivated to discover something of sacred value in life, conserve or hold onto a sense of sacredness, and transform understandings of the sacred amid life's inevitable transitions, losses, and stressors. Hence, the "sacred" not only encapsulates concepts of God or the divine but also extends to other objects, goals, and relationships that assume a spiritual character or transcendent qualities in some manner. Clinically speaking, an SM/V's views of sacredness, therefore, represent socially influenced perceptions of ultimate truth, transcendent reality, and/or divine being or object (Hill et al., 2000). Hence, the sacred cannot simply be equated with something an SM/V deems as important in life; this term should be reserved for objects, goals, or relationships that assume transcendent qualities in some manner. For example, although Matthew's postmilitary pursuit of becoming a physician was highly important, he viewed his role as a father as a sacred gift from God that transcended these career goals.

Rather than creating a false dichotomy or polarizing R/S, Pargament (2007, 2013) also principally conceptualized religion in terms of searching for sacredness in life. However, in this integrative framework, religion uniquely captures instances in which a patient's spiritual journey occurs within the context of institutions and traditions that have been established over human history to guide and facilitate connection with culturally determined sacred objects, goals, and relationships (i.e., facilitate spirituality). Whether physical, psychological, social, or spiritual, religion can be directed to the attainment of a seemingly limitless collection of valued objects, goals, and relationships that might be imbued with significance in a given institution, tradition, and/or culture. Moreover, beyond shaping adherents' understandings of the sacred, religions offer pathways to reach these destinations that may assume ultimate value (e.g., prayer, moral teachings). In keeping with the multiplicity in spirituality, clinicians should conceptualize religion across multiple dimensions (e.g., emotions, cognition, behavior), cultural and social levels (e.g., national, ethnic, familial), and valences (e.g., adaptive, maladaptive) that could affect an SM/V's discovery of, connection with, and transformation of the sacred. When considering the role of religion in coping with emotionally painful issues, Pargament et al. (2013) stated,

> It is important to consider not only *how much* religion is involved in coping, but also *how* religion is involved in coping; specifically, the *who* (e.g., clergy, congregation members, God), the *what* (e.g., prayer, Bible reading, ritual), the *when* (e.g., acute stressors, chronic stressors), the *where* (e.g., congregation, privately), and the *why* (e.g., to find meaning, to gain control) of coping. (pp. 562–563)

Pargament's (2007, 2013) conceptions raise several implications for conceptualizing spiritual and religious issues in moral injury. For example, SM/Vs will more likely invest in pursuits that hold ultimate value, attempt to protect such dimensions of their lives when threatened, and derive greater satisfaction from pursuing objects, goals, and relationships that have somehow been imbued with spiritual meaning. However, when confronted with morally injurious events, SM/Vs could experience more severe health-related consequences when sacred aspects of life are perceived as lost or desecrated in some manner (Pargament et al., 2005). In such cases, these events might be equated with more than traditional biomedical outcomes related to emotional distress or behavioral dysfunction; moral injury might represent a violation of an SM/V's sacred core or spiritual center. In turn, chronic issues with moral injury may strain motivation to (re)discover sacredness in life, precipitate a painful sense of disconnection with the sacred, and/or lead to struggles with R/S that create barriers to healing and recovery. In Matthew's case, taking the life of a child in combat disrupted his sacred relationships with his children. Indeed, this act represented a violation of both a perceived holy mandate from his faith tradition against killing (i.e., "Thou shalt not kill") and a personal and culturally situated desire to protect vulnerable children like his son from any harm. In turn, Matthew questioned how he could restore a connection with his children as an earthly father after acting in ways that desecrated God's law and created disconnection in his relationship with God as an eternal father.

RELIGION, SPIRITUALITY, AND MORALITY

R/S and morality are often closely intertwined for persons in the United States (Graham & Haidt, 2010; McKay & Whitehouse, 2015). As Matthew's case illustrates, moral beliefs can be based on a sacred text and/or central authority that explicates expected and proscribed patterns of thinking, feeling, and/or behaving. Although religious traditions rely on varying authority structures and modes of interpretation, many hold a set of writings as a source of revelation for how people should live and relate with themselves, God or the divine, and others—both in and outside of their social group. Even in nonreligious traditions with less developed moral codes (e.g., secular humanism), SM/Vs' beliefs might be shaped by written materials, podcasts, blogs, or other sources that apply a spiritual worldview to life's challenges. In so doing, religious traditions and secular philosophical approaches to morality may vary in the extent of their canon of written moral codes and the amount of latitude adherents are afforded to interpret such writings versus deferring to their local, regional, or global authorities (Wortmann et al., 2017). However, SM/Vs might lack awareness of R/S features of their implicit belief systems or not have reflected on where, how, and from whom they learned a moral code. In such cases, SM/Vs who do not view themselves as R/S could rely on R/S traditions to form moral judgments about their military experiences. Clinicians should eschew assumptions and ask open questions to help SM/Vs articulate their implicit beliefs and their origins.

Clinicians should also appreciate the distinction between objective and subjective forms of guilt in working with SM/Vs who perpetrated morally injurious events. In many cases, SM/Vs may view themselves as being objectively guilty for violating a moral or ethical code, possibly outlined in a sacred text, and also feel subjectively distressed by the infraction. Because Matthew interpreted the Old Testament (Exodus, Deuteronomy) to prohibit killing a child, he perceived himself as objectively guilty at the time of treatment. Further, whereas other SM/Vs may not feel subjectively guilty for a moral infraction against a spiritual authority, Matthew felt a debilitating sense of shame about his actions in combat. However, possibly due to a lack of commitment to and knowledge about their faith tradition, SM/Vs might also hold destructive views that are not supported by religious authorities or orthodox teachings. In such cases, they could wrongly deem themselves as objectively guilty or internalize an undue degree of remorse. In addition, other SM/Vs may not view themselves as objectively guilty and nonetheless feel morally distressed or corrupted. It is not within the clinician's role to determine whether an SM/V is objectively guilty from a theological or philosophical standpoint; rather, clergy, chaplains, or other spiritual professionals might be needed when the accuracy of an SM/V's understanding of their tradition's moral code is somehow problematic (see Chapter 13, this volume). Importantly, in the same way that R/S can shape SM/Vs' moral codes, R/S traditions have doctrines, procedures, and rituals for resolving objective and subjective guilt (e.g., confession, repentance; for a fuller discussion, see Wortmann et al., 2017).

Beyond cases when SM/Vs feel responsible for perpetrating violence or not limiting others' actions, moral injury may also occur when SM/Vs are victimized or witness others' acts of moral wrongdoing. In such cases, SM/Vs may experience feelings of profound anger, resentment, and moral disgust toward the responsible persons that impair their health and well-being (see Chapter 4). Clinicians should recognize that R/S traditions often view forgiveness as a moral imperative and offer resources for forgiving the offenders (e.g., scriptural examples and teachings about forgiveness, community support). When considering certain behaviors that may follow from anger and betrayal (e.g., revenge seeking), R/S traditions rarely sanction proportionate violence or retaliation. However, Wortmann et al. (2017) suggested R/S SM/Vs may view anger with greater suspicion than guilt and shame. In turn, clinicians may encounter difficulties in encouraging expression and processing of anger with SM/Vs who view their R/S traditions as prohibiting such a response. Particularly in cases of victimization or a serious betrayal of trust, a moral obligation to forgive or ambivalence about feeling angry may hinder an SM/V's recovery. In such cases, clinicians might need training in forgiveness and to team with a spiritual professional who is clinically and theologically trained (see Chapter 13).

SPIRITUAL RESOURCES AND STRUGGLES

Research has established behavioral, social, and psychological dimensions of R/S that may prevent mental health conditions in SM/Vs (e.g., PTSD) and/or serve as sources of strength when such issues emerge (Smith-MacDonald et al., 2017). For example, SM/Vs can incorporate private practices (e.g., prayer, meditation) for transcending distress and experiencing positive emotions (e.g., peace, joy). In addition, most approaches to R/S proscribe unhealthy behaviors many SM/Vs implement to avoid painful thoughts and emotions and restore a sense of equilibrium (e.g., substance misuse). In fact, without overlooking a possible spiritual nature of human beings, many religious traditions have opposed dualistic views that downgrade the sacredness of the physical body (e.g., Christianity's refutation of Gnosticism). In keeping with the role of R/S in shaping moral beliefs (Wortmann et al., 2017), SM/Vs might imbue healthy lifestyle practices with spiritual meaning (e.g., daily exercise). However, morally injured SM/Vs could struggle to live congruently with spiritually motivated standards of moral behavior. In fact, from a psychospiritual developmental perspective, Harris et al. (2015) suggest religious and/or spiritual SM/Vs in early adulthood often function with concrete expectations about "right" versus "wrong" behavior and may lack adequate knowledge about their faith tradition or philosophical system to resolve moral violations in adaptive ways. In turn, like Matthew's moral struggles, SM/Vs may disengage from behaviors that once supported their health and well-being.

From a social standpoint, faith communities can promote strong relationships with people from diverse backgrounds who share similar understandings of the divine or sacred. Regardless of whether such groups are affiliated with a religious tradition, social bonds are usually governed by a leadership hierarchy of some sort, revered texts and doctrines, rituals and practices—any of which can be imbued with spiritual meanings that also mirror aspects of military culture. Further, given the collectivistic nature of many religions, commitment to fellow adherents can also serve as an ultimate value. In turn, SM/Vs may receive and offer help with practical needs, as well as accountability for pursuing a shared mission or journey together (e.g., knowing God, enjoying nature, raising children, fighting poverty or injustice). Consistent with the sense of belonging and purpose SM/Vs can experience from serving shoulder-to-shoulder with their comrades or battle buddies, faith communities also provide opportunities for sacred relationships. However, in cases of moral injury, SM/Vs might experience conflicts with fellow adherents or mistrust for authority figures or tradition as a whole. In other cases, whether as witness or perpetrator, SM/Vs could believe their morally injurious events will contaminate understandings of God or the sacred in their social groups. In turn, SM/Vs might withdraw from previously meaningful connections out of a perceived sense of loyalty to preserve the cohesion of the faith community and success of its transcendent mission.

Beyond these horizontal bonds with other people, R/S might also affect a vertical connection with God or a higher power that similarly serves as a source of strength and struggle. In fact, despite decreasing ties to organized religions, nearly 90% of the U.S. population reports an abiding belief in God (Pew Research Center, 2014). Moreover, possibly due to the cultural impact of Judeo-Christian traditions, most theistically minded persons in the United States believe God is a person with whom they might have a relationship. Consistent with relational dynamics with other attachment figures, theistic believers like Matthew may develop complex views about God's attributes and experience times of both emotional closeness and distance or tension. In any of these situations, cultivating a close connection with God can represent a ultimate value that defines SM/Vs' spiritual meaning systems and search for significance in life. However, in cases of moral injury, SM/Vs may feel angry, abandoned, and/or disqualified from pursuing a loving bond with God. In turn, questioning God's character and/or capability of ordering the universe may worsen their distress and undermine beliefs, practices, and relationships that once emerged from this specific understanding and/or means of connecting with the sacred. On this point, latent profile results from two samples of war-zone veterans supported the importance of divine struggles in the context of moral injury (Currier et al., 2019). Of the forms of struggle described by Exline et al. (2014), emotional tension with God or divine emerged as the most striking feature of profiles of morally injured veterans who were also seriously struggling with R/S at the time.

In psychological or cognitive terms, R/S can also offer a robust interpretive framework for making meaning of morally injurious events in emotionally and intellectually satisfying ways (Park et al., 2016). For example, although individual communities differ in acknowledgment and adequacy of teachings on darker themes of human existence, most religions offer explanations for trauma that may promote a sense of coherence, identity, and control in periods of suffering (i.e., theodicies). Hence, in the aftermath of severe violations of moral beliefs, SM/Vs might be primed to humbly accept their finitude as imperfect persons, seek forgiveness and growth, and experience God's solidarity with them and/or compassionate presence in their suffering. In turn, such transcendent modes of appraisal could alleviate guilt feelings and limit the counterfactual reasoning and other types of rumination that interfere with recovery. However, because of the nature and magnitude of traumas, lack of faith maturity or psychosocial resources, and/or numerous other factors, SM/Vs may struggle to maintain a stable or satisfying faith system that can support a sense of ultimate meaning posttrauma. When SM/Vs cannot find understanding, Park et al.'s (2016) reciprocal meaning making model asserts they may encounter additional losses of close relationships, practices, and other psychospiritual resources that once guided and motivated their spiritual journeys. Notably, when considering ways that SM/Vs may struggle with their faith, a growing research base identified issues with ultimate meaning as a powerful indicator of suicide risk, PTSD, and other mental health conditions in this population (e.g., Currier, McDermott, et al., 2018).

Addressing spiritual resources and struggles was a crucial part of Matthew's treatment. For example, Matthew experienced intimacy and social bonds in his men's fellowship group. This milieu provided opportunities for broader and deeper connections with civilians (other than his therapist and immediate family). Coupled with his involvement in this "church family," these settings allowed him to experience acceptance from others and build a sense of competence in his ability to function as a respected member of his community. Further, serving in practical roles such as church security allowed Matthew to use his professional training to support the community. He also leaned on scriptural readings to draw hope for his future (i.e., the prospect of forgiveness and redemption for sin) and work through problems in his marriage in a healthy manner. Although Matthew derived meaning and security from cultivating a close connection with Jesus Christ, he also felt abandoned, distant, and periodically angry in this relationship. At the start of treatment, he doubted whether divine forgiveness might apply to him, and he struggled to release the shame, guilt, and self-condemning cognitions from his moral struggles. Unable to experience grace for himself, Matthew's self-image was defiled and, by extension, picturing himself as a valued child of God was almost unthinkable. This spiritual disconnect was compounded by a growing sense of emotional disengagement from his family that left him in a state of severe isolation.

ETHICAL CONCERNS

A thorough discussion of ethical concerns in addressing R/S with morally injured SM/Vs is beyond the scope of this chapter. However, before offering suggestions for assessment, several aspirational values and practical issues should be mentioned. First, whether from a multicultural view honoring the role of R/S in shaping identity or a more pragmatic one based on amassing evidence for many ways in which R/S can affect recovery, clinicians are ethically responsible for addressing this domain. At a minimum, clinicians have to offer a spiritually supportive atmosphere, gauge the role of R/S in SM/Vs' daily lives, and conceptualize the impacts of R/S resources and struggles on the presenting problem (APA, 2007; Vieten et al., 2013). Particularly in cases of spiritual struggles, clinicians may not be equipped to target beliefs, practices, and relationships that might hinder recovery. In such cases, clinicians should refer and collaborate with chaplains, clergy, or other pastoral professionals (see Chapter 13). Nonetheless, even when clinicians are equipped to offer spiritually integrated care, SM/Vs must possess an understanding of the rationale, timeline, and possible consequences for incorporating R/S before any such interventions are implemented (i.e., informed consent). In turn, whether R/S serves as a source of strength and/or struggle, clinicians have to respect SM/Vs' autonomy in establishing treatment tasks and goals that possibly negate R/S. In these cases, clinicians could agree not to assume a spiritually integrated approach while expressing concern about possible avoidance-based coping and/or requesting permission to revisit the topic at a later point in treatment (see Chapter 12 for an example).

From an ethical standpoint, clinicians should also recognize a negative bias against R/S that may emerge from philosophical assumptions related to the primary biopsychosocial model in mental health professions. Beginning with a push in the Enlightenment to distance scientific endeavors from religion, naturalism dictates clinicians contextualize all aspects of professional expertise in terms of processes, relationships, and events that can somehow be observed in the natural world. Hence, despite empirical advancements in the applied psychology of R/S, even religiously oriented clinicians might be reluctant to reconcile biomedical appraisals of moral injury with sacred beliefs and values of SM/Vs who seek their care. In extreme cases, clinicians might be prejudiced against metaphysical views that seem "unscientific" and cannot be easily assimilated into a naturalistic paradigm. However, given the force of multiculturalism, clinicians likely more often attempt to avoid bias through pursuing a posture of acceptance and neutrality about R/S. Although done with good intentions, a stance of respectful neutrality might threaten to marginalize metaphysical views that usually shape R/S in one way or another (e.g., theism; Slife, Starks, & Primosch, 2014). Specifically, because prejudices against nonnaturalistic paradigms about health and illness have become so institutionalized, this strategy could inadvertently increase the risk of discriminating against some SM/Vs via neglecting the most sacred beliefs, practices, and relationships in their experiences of moral injury.

Although value conflicts might emerge in any clinical endeavor, these philosophical issues might be particularly relevant for moral injury. From a strict naturalistic paradigm, treatment goals are to alleviate suffering and enhance health according to established syndromes or conditions based on observable emotions, thoughts, behaviors, and/or physiologic data. In this role, ethically minded clinicians might, therefore, feel limited to conceptualizing moral injury apart from philosophic or theological notions about determinants of morality (e.g., What is the purpose of human existence? What is a good life?). Kinghorn (2012) captured this predicament:

> [Traditional psychological models of moral injury] do not wish to deny the sociocultural frameworks that give rise to guilt and shame in particular soldiers, but their disciplinary context does not allow them to speak about these phenomena in anything other than psychological and cognitive terms . . . they cannot engage in *thick* [emphasis added] descriptions about the appropriate ends of human life. . . . They also cannot name any deeper reality that moral assumptions and the rules that engender them might reflect. Moral suffering must therefore be considered formally as a psychological phenomenon only. (pp. 66–67)

From a thin view of morality, R/S only represents a crucial domain to the extent it supports clinicians in alleviating SM/Vs' moral suffering and improving their functioning. However, most persons do not simply choose R/S beliefs, practices, or relationships as tools to reach pragmatic ends in life. Instead, Kinghorn urged clinicians to approach R/S as a "meaning-defining context in its own right" (p. 67) that may lead to painful thoughts and emotions that seemingly conflict with assumptions about mental health in a naturalistic paradigm. For example, although most religions emphasize doctrines and teachings that are not comforting on the surface (e.g., human sin, divine judgment), they also offer means of repentance, forgiveness, and reconciliation after even the most extreme forms of moral wrongdoing or transgressive acts (Wortmann et al., 2017).

Culturally speaking, a lack of formal training opportunities throughout clinicians' professional journeys likely serves as a perpetuating factor for instrumentalizing R/S. Research has suggested that psychologists, in particular, embrace religious forms of spirituality at far lower rates than SM/Vs who might seek their care (Shafranske & Cummings, 2013). Beyond the professionally sanctioned paradigm of naturalism, lack of personal experiences with R/S could further lead clinicians to overlook or avoid beliefs, practices, and relationships SM/Vs deem as sacred. However, just as exposure to trauma does not afford professional skills to treat PTSD, having a strong commitment or background in a faith tradition does not ensure competence in addressing R/S with SM/Vs who share this cultural identification. In fact, given the individualized and idiosyncratic nature of R/S in the United States (Ellison & McFarland, 2013), perceived synchrony might lead clinicians to underestimate discordant beliefs in such cases. Although shared beliefs or values can ease rapport building in some cases, cultural differences in this domain may actually aid clinicians in managing their biases via careful assessment of R/S in SM/Vs' lives. Ethically speaking, like negotiating other areas of cultural diversity (e.g., military culture) and gaining expertise in an evidence-based assessment or intervention, clinicians should engage in activities that promote the acquisition of knowledge and skills for working with SM/Vs from diverse R/S backgrounds (Vieten et al., 2013).

Integrity issues represent a final ethical concern in addressing R/S resources and struggles with SM/Vs. Particularly when clinicians develop competence in this area, they could be in danger of blurring boundaries in their professional role and/or functioning outside their scope of practice as a mental health expert. For example, when treating a religious SM/V who possibly shares the same faith identification, an otherwise competent clinician could function more as a clergy person or theological expert than relying on emerging evidence-based interventions for moral injury. In such cases, clinicians should avoid confusing dual role relationships with SM/Vs that detract from the efficacy of the treatment. In Matthew's case, as an example, a highly memorable moment occurred at midtreatment when he was baptized in a small gathering at his Evangelical Christian church. Although Matthew ascribed responsibility to God for his spiritual transformation, he viewed the therapeutic work with Timothy Carroll as one of the vehicles for this healing. As a sign of his appreciation, he invited Mr. Carroll to attend the intimate baptism ceremony with church leaders, family, and close friends. After many supervisory conversations and consultation with a trusted colleague, we determined Mr. Carroll's presence held too much risk of interfering with Matthew's further engagement in exposure-based interventions and strategies for self-compassion. However, in light of his physical absence and the need to maintain authenticity with his own sacred beliefs and values, Mr. Carroll provided the following letter for Matthew:

> I am humbled to have been included in this sacred work of yours—this journey toward knowing grace and the healing power of forgiveness. You and your family have made many sacrifices over these years. You have known the pain of loss, death and heartache with a depth that only a warrior can. But you have taught me that, for you, death will not have the final say. Yes, your victory is in the renewal of spirit. Although freely given, it has come at a cost. For this renewal is not a death of the shadows you have known, but hopefully a movement into a new relationship to suffering and honoring of the profound wisdom those stories might hold for all of us. Your countless acts of courage are inspiring and life-giving. It is my hope that you will now take on the role of life-receiver as you seek to embrace renewal in your life. I celebrate with you and your family today.

ASSESSMENT SUGGESTIONS

The proper attitudes, knowledge, and skills to assess SM/Vs' R/S backgrounds are crucial components of culturally competent mental health care (APA, 2007; Vieten et al., 2013). To this point, we have provided an overview of the potential role of R/S in moral injury. In so doing, we described both substantial elements (e.g., beliefs, practices), as well as processes (e.g., weakening of faith, spiritual struggle), related to R/S that could help or hinder recovery. With this conceptual background in mind, the goal of this section is to offer practical guidance for conducting an initial assessment of SM/Vs' R/S backgrounds that can inform case formulation and treatment planning (for a more comprehensive approach to spiritual assessment, see Pargament, 2007). Whether as a source of strength or struggle, R/S represents only one aspect of SM/Vs' lives that might demand clinical attention. Clinicians will ideally assess this cultural domain in the context of an interview that covers other sources of identity, morality, and purpose in life. Drawing on Pargament's (2007) work, clinicians might incorporate the following five sets of questions to develop an initial picture of the substance of SM/Vs' faith background and identity:

1. Do you see yourself as a religious and/or spiritual person? If so, in what ways? Do you prefer the terms "religious" or "spiritual" when referring to yourself at this point in your life? Was there a point in time when you preferred another term for yourself?

2. Are you affiliated with a religious or spiritual denomination or community? If so, which one? Has your connection with religious or spiritual groups changed since serving in the military? If so, in what ways?

3. Has your problem(s) affected you religiously or spiritually? If so, in what ways? Reflecting back on your life, has your faith or spirituality grown stronger or weaker since serving in the military? If so, in what ways?

4. Has your religious faith or spirituality been involved in the ways you have coped with your problem(s)? If so, in what ways? Are you currently drawing strength from your faith or spirituality? If so, in what ways?

5. Whether as a source of strength or struggle, how important is it to include your religious faith or spirituality in your care? Do I have permission to inquire about religious or spiritual concerns in your life if I believe they might support or hinder your recovery from the problem(s) that led you to seek my help?

The first two sets of questions clarify whether SM/Vs view their lives through an R/S lens as well as their preferred language for this cultural domain. In cases when SM/Vs view themselves as an R/S person, Question 1 might illumine specific beliefs, relationships, and practices that hold sacred or transcendent value. In such cases, R/S may shape their thoughts, emotions, actions, decisions, relationships, and coping strategies in numerous ways. For example, Matthew identified himself as both spiritual and religious. However, further exploration at intake revealed he delineated the two domains and struggled to experience spiritual aspects of faith. For example, although he drew strength from religious activities, including church attendance and Bible readings, he felt a void of spiritual meaning in his life (e.g., little sense of connection with God and his children). Given rates of religious involvement in SM/Vs (Currier, Pearce, et al., 2018; McLaughlin et al., 2010; Sharma et al., 2017), Question 2 then assesses whether their search for the sacred is rooted in a particular religious tradition. When compared with older military eras, post-9/11 SM/Vs more often pursue spirituality apart from organized religion (Ellison & McFarland, 2013; MLDC, 2010; Pew Research Center, 2014). However, beyond understanding SM/Vs' current ties to such a tradition or community, clinicians should also inquire whether they disaffiliated or disengaged from any formal religious groups and the reasons for such changes (Currier et al., 2019). That is, regardless of whether a morally injured SM/V has accepted or rejected a given religion, his or her identity could still be influenced by the beliefs, values, and teachings of the tradition.

When R/S has shaped an SM/V's identity, relationships, or lifestyle decision making, the next two sets of questions assess the salience of R/S to both the presenting problem and solution to the issues that prompted him or her to seek treatment. Question 3 seeks to elucidate whether the SM/V conceptualizes moral injury or other mental health concerns from a distinctly R/S perspective. For example, when reflecting on their suffering, SM/Vs might view moral injury in terms of a loss of faith, violation of a sacred core or spiritual center (e.g., closeness with God or higher power), and other forms of spiritual struggles discussed earlier. When moral injury has affected an SM/V spiritually, clinicians may inquire whether he or she experienced any changes in this cultural domain that go beyond any ties with conventionally religious groups. However, because those who struggle spiritually typically draw on R/S in healthy ways, responses to Question 4 indicate whether R/S serves as a source of strength and resource in the recovery process. For instance, although Matthew's Christian faith provided social connections, ritualistic predictability, and guidance for moral behavior in the military-to-civilian transition, it also fueled his painful moral emotions and cognitions regarding his capacity for violence as a warrior and emotional distance from God. Given the role of faith in shaping identity, Timothy Carroll had to affirm these strengths while also allowing Matthew to work through faith-related concerns in treatment.

Beyond assessing the substance of an SM/Vs' faith system, Pargament (2007) asserted that clinicians should also seek to understand their location in the process of searching for the sacred. As Matthew's case exemplifies, SM/Vs may have cultivated a stable and existentially satisfying faith system that long served as a source of coherence, identity, and predictability. Although moral injury may cause impairment in psychosocial functioning, these persons may assimilate their morally injurious experiences into their faith system in a manner that does not threaten their sacred core (Park et al., 2016). However, as highlighted in Matthew's difficulties in receiving divine forgiveness, SM/Vs could also seek treatment in a state of spiritual distress in which they are struggling to conserve or transform their understanding and/or ways of connecting with the sacred. Possibly due to avoidance-based coping, SM/Vs might have grown disengaged from seeking transcendence and significance in religious or non-religious contexts. In such cases, responses to Questions 2 and 3 may reflect disaffiliation with a formal religious tradition and/or weakening of beliefs, relationships, and/or practices that were once associated with spiritual meaning. Last, whether at the start or further along in treatment, SM/Vs may also reengage in the process of redefining their sacred core or rediscovering sources of transcendence or significance. Whatever the status of an SM/V's search for the sacred, clinicians should assess any marked changes in his or her spiritual journey with respect to moral injury.

Importantly, SM/Vs will not discuss sacred matters with clinicians who do not embody the necessary attitudes and respectful posture toward R/S (Pargament, 2007; Vieten et al., 2013). Just as clinicians may stifle an SM/V's emotional processing with their own fear in revisiting the trauma narrative, a dry or mechanical approach to assessing R/S concerns will also not suffice in promoting disclosure. That is, in light of a historical bias against R/S in mental health professions, SM/Vs may worry that clinicians will view their faith negatively. Particularly in instances of spiritual struggle, R/S could be a deeply personal area that SM/Vs will only share if the clinician can cultivate a trusting bond with them. Further, even SM/Vs who place ultimate value on R/S might struggle to clearly articulate their R/S experiences in a clinical interview. However, just because they appear uncomfortable or cannot find words to describe the possible hows, whats, whens, and/or whys of their faith system, it does not mean R/S is unimportant. In reflecting on his theistic faith, Blaise Pascal (1966) stated, "The heart has its reasons, which reason does not know. We feel it in a thousand things. . . . This, then, is faith: God is felt by the heart, not by the reason" (p. 154). When considering the possible role of R/S in treating moral injury, clinicians must gain the capacity to both value and affirm the "heart" of an SM/V's faith system, even if such sacred matters are mysterious, not articulated clearly, or do not make sense from a scientific or naturalistic view.

With this said, recent findings call for a patient-centered approach in addressing R/S concerns in psychotherapy or counseling. Drawing on two community samples with diversity in their R/S backgrounds, Currier, Pearce, et al. (2018) found SM/Vs generally viewed incorporation of R/S as "somewhat" important in their care. When compared with more explicit approaches to addressing R/S (e.g., using R/S language or concepts, reading or reciting religious scriptures, conducting a meditation exercise with R/S images and concepts), SM/Vs preferred open-ended or exploratory strategies (e.g., assessing R/S beliefs and values, exploring R/S history and any changes in beliefs and values, affirming R/S as source of strength, exploring relationship with God or higher power). When focusing on the roughly one quarter of both groups who reported clinical levels of PTSD and/or depressive symptomatology, other results suggested members of ethnic minority groups and/or those who were highly religious, had a strong belief in God, and were struggling with R/S more often preferred a spiritually integrated approach. However, even when considering the highly R/S SM/Vs in the study, Currier, Pearce, et al. (2018) also found that many of them preferred a more traditional psychological approach that did not include R/S integration. As such, Question 5 will aid clinicians in not precipitously steering treatment according to their assumptions in a manner that neglects SM/Vs' actual preferences and perceived needs in their care.

CONCLUSION

In conclusion, clinicians working with morally injured SM/Vs should assume a patient-centered approach in which they are not ignorant of R/S concerns but also do not assume this cultural domain should be targeted in every case. In this chapter, we provided an overview of the complex role of R/S in SM/Vs' lives; varied ways in which R/S beliefs, relationships, and practices could affect recovery from moral injury; ethical issues with addressing R/S in mental health care; and suggestions for assessing this cultural domain. In so doing, we drew on therapeutic work with Matthew in which spiritual concerns were a crucial aspect of his recovery. In total, he participated in 12 individual therapy sessions over a 4-month period, two of which included his wife. These sessions entailed a reliance on imaginal and in vivo exposure interventions and emotion-focused imaginal dialogues with his youngest child and the wife of a fallen comrade. Although clinicians should avoid simplistic notions that all morally injured SM/Vs will struggle with and/or draw strength from R/S, culturally competent care for moral injury necessitates a conceptual understanding of this domain, as well as the necessary attitudes and skills to assess R/S, address spiritual concerns in treatment, and/or collaborate with chaplains, clergy, or other pastoral professionals as needed.

REFERENCES

American Psychological Association. (2007). *Resolution on religious, religion-based and/or religion-derived prejudice.* https://www.apa.org/about/policy/religious-discrimination.pdf

Currier, J. M., Foster, J. D., & Isaak, S. L. (2019). Moral injury and spiritual struggles in military veterans: A latent profile analysis. *Journal of Traumatic Stress, 32*(3), 393–404. https://doi.org/10.1002/jts.22378

Currier, J. M., McDermott, R. C., McCormick, W. H., Churchwell, M. C., & Milkeris, L. (2018). Exploring cross-lagged associations between spiritual struggles and risk for suicidal behavior in a community sample of military veterans. *Journal of Affective Disorders, 230*, 93–100. https://doi.org/10.1016/j.jad.2018.01.009

Currier, J. M., Pearce, M., Carroll, T. D., & Koenig, H. G. (2018). Military veterans' preferences for incorporating spirituality in psychotherapy or counseling. *Professional Psychology, Research and Practice, 49*(1), 39–47. https://doi.org/10.1037/pro0000178

Ellison, C. G., & McFarland, M. J. (2013). The social context of religion and spirituality in the United States. In K. I. Pargament (Ed.), *APA handbook of psychology, religion, and spirituality: Vol. 1. Context, theory, and research* (pp. 21–50). American Psychological Association. https://doi.org/10.1037/14045-002

Exline, J. J., Pargament, K. I., Grubbs, J. B., & Yali, A. M. (2014). The Religious and Spiritual Struggles Scale: Development and initial validation. *Psychology of Religion and Spirituality, 6*(3), 208–222. https://doi.org/10.1037/a0036465

Graham, J., & Haidt, J. (2010). Beyond beliefs: Religions bind individuals into moral communities. *Personality and Social Psychology Review, 14*(1), 140–150. https://doi.org/10.1177/1088868309353415

Harris, J. I., Park, C. L., Currier, J. M., Usset, T. J., & Voecks, C. D. (2015). Moral injury and psycho-spiritual development: Considering the developmental context. *Spirituality in Clinical Practice, 2*(4), 256–266. https://doi.org/10.1037/scp0000045

Hill, P. C., Pargament, K. I., Wood, R. W., McCullough, M. E., Swyers, J. P., Larson, D. B., & Zinnbauer, B. J. (2000). Conceptualizing religion and spirituality: Points of commonality, points of departure. *Journal for the Theory of Social Behaviour, 30*(1), 51–77. https://doi.org/10.1111/1468-5914.00119

Kinghorn, W. (2012). Combat trauma and moral fragmentation: A theological account of moral injury. *Journal of the Society of Christian Ethics, 32*(2), 57–74. https://doi.org/10.1353/sce.2012.0041

Koenig, H. G., Boucher, N. A., Oliver, J. P., Youssef, N., Mooney, S. R., Currier, J. M., & Pearce, M. (2017). Rationale for spiritually-oriented cognitive processing therapy in active duty military and veterans with posttraumatic stress disorder. *Journal of Nervous & Mental Disease, 205*(2), 147–153. https://doi.org/10.1097/NMD.0000000000000554

Kroenke, K., Spitzer, R. L., & Williams, J. B. W. (2001). The PHQ-9: Validity of a brief depression severity measure. *Journal of General Internal Medicine, 16*(9), 606–613.

Litz, B. T., Stein, N., Delaney, E., Lebowitz, L., Nash, W. P., Silva, C., & Maguen, S. (2009). Moral injury and moral repair in war veterans: A preliminary model and intervention strategy. *Clinical Psychology Review, 29*(8), 695–706. https://doi.org/10.1016/j.cpr.2009.07.003

McKay, R., & Whitehouse, H. (2015). Religion and morality. *Psychological Bulletin, 141*(2), 447–473. https://doi.org/10.1037/a0038455

McLaughlin, S. S., McLaughlin, A. D., & Van Slyke, J. A. (2010). Faith and religious beliefs in an outpatient military population. *Southern Medical Journal, 103*(6), 527–531. https://doi.org/10.1097/SMJ.0b013e3181de0304

Military Leadership Diversity Commission. (2010). *Religious diversity in the U.S. Military* (Issue Paper No. 22). https://www.hsdl.org/?view&did=716143

Oman, D. (2013). Defining religion and spirituality. In R. F. Paloutzian & C. L. Park (Eds.), *Handbook of the psychology of religion and spirituality* (pp. 23–47). Guilford Press.

Pargament, K. I. (2007). *Spiritually integrated psychotherapy: Understanding and addressing the sacred.* Guilford Press.

Pargament, K. I. (2013). Searching for the sacred: Toward a nonreductionistic theory of spirituality. In K. I. Pargament (Ed.), *APA handbook of psychology, religion, and spirituality: Vol. 1. Context, theory, and research* (pp. 257–273). American Psychological Association. https://doi.org/10.1037/14045-014

Pargament, K. I., Falb, M. D., Ano, G. G., & Wachholtz, A. B. (2013). The religious dimension of coping: Advances in theory, research, and practice. In R. F. Paloutzian & C. L. Park (Eds.), *Handbook of the psychology of religion and spirituality* (pp. 560–579). Guilford Press.

Pargament, K. I., Magyar, G. M., Benore, E., & Mahoney, A. (2005). Sacrilege: A study of sacred loss and desecration and their implications for health and well-being in a community sample. *Journal for the Scientific Study of Religion, 44*(1), 59–78. https://doi.org/10.1111/j.1468-5906.2005.00265.x

Park, C. L., Currier, J. M., Harris, J. I., & Slattery, J. (2016). *Trauma, meaning, and spirituality: Translating research into clinical practice.* American Psychological Association. https://doi.org/10.1037/15961-000

Pascal, B. (1966). *Pensees.* Penguin.

Pew Research Center. (2014). *Religious Landscape Study.* https://www.pewforum.org/religious-landscape-study/

Shafranske, E. P., & Cummings, J. P. (2013). Religious and spiritual beliefs, affiliations, and practices of psychologists. In K. I. Pargament, A. Mahoney, & E. Shafranske (Eds.), *APA handbook of psychology, religion, and spirituality* (Vol. II, pp. 23–41). American Psychological Association. https://doi.org/10.1037/14046-002

Sharma, V., Marin, D. B., Koenig, H. K., Feder, A., Iacoviello, B. M., Southwick, S. M., & Pietrzak, R. H. (2017). Religion, spirituality, and mental health of U.S. military veterans: Results from the National Health and Resilience in Veterans Study. *Journal of Affective Disorders, 217*, 197–204. https://doi.org/10.1016/j.jad.2017.03.071

Slife, B. D., Starks, S., & Primosch, M. (2014). Questioning the presumption of naturalism in the social sciences: A case study. *Pastoral Psychology, 63*, 339–353. https://doi.org/10.1007/s11089-013-0534-8

Smith-MacDonald, L., Norris, J. M., Raffin-Bouchal, S., & Sinclair, S. (2017). Spirituality and mental well-being in combat veterans: A systematic review. *Military Medicine, 182*(11–12), e1920–e1940. https://doi.org/10.7205/MILMED-D-17-00099

Spitzer, R. L., Kroenke, K., Williams, J. B. W., & Löwe, B. (2006). A brief measure for assessing generalized anxiety disorder: The GAD-7. *Archives of Internal Medicine 166*(10), 1092–1097.

Vieten, C., Scammell, S., Pilato, R., Ammondson, I., Pargament, K. I., & Lukoff, D. (2013). Spiritual and religious competencies for psychologists. *Psychology of Religion and Spirituality, 5*(3), 129–144. https://doi.org/10.1037/a0032699

Wortmann, J. H., Eisen, E., Hundert, C., Jordan, A. H., Smith, M. W., Nash, W. P., & Litz, B. T. (2017). Spiritual features of war-related moral injury: A primer for clinicians. *Spirituality in Clinical Practice, 4*(4), 249–261. https://doi.org/10.1037/scp0000140

Wortmann, J. H., Jordan, A. H., Weathers, F. W., Resick, P. A., Dondanville, K. A., Hall-Clark, B., Foa, E. B., Young-McCaughan, S., Yarvis, J. S., Hembree, E. A., Mintz, J., Peterson, A. L., & Litz, B. T. (2016). Psychometric analysis of the PTSD Checklist-5 (PCL-5) among treatment-seeking military service members. *Psychological Assessment, 28*(11), 1392–1403.

Zinnbauer, B. J., Pargament, K. I., Cole, B., Rye, M. S., Butter, E. M., Belavich, T. G., Hipp, K. M., Scott, A. B., & Kadar, J. L. (1997). Religion and spirituality: Unfuzzying the fuzzy. *Journal for the Scientific Study of Religion, 36*(4), 549–564. https://doi.org/10.2307/1387689

Zinnbauer, B. J., Pargament, K. I., & Scott, A. B. (1999). The emerging meanings of religiousness and spirituality: Problems and prospects. *Journal of Personality, 67*(6), 889–919. https://doi.org/10.1111/1467-6494.00077

4

Forgiveness as a Mechanism of Repair Following Military-Related Moral Injury

Brandon J. Griffin, Marilyn A. Cornish, Shira Maguen, and Everett L. Worthington Jr.

The literatures on moral injury and forgiveness have developed largely independent of each other despite repeated acknowledgment that forgiveness (or its absence) likely plays a role in the onset and maintenance of the problematic outcomes that characterize moral injury. We extend prior theory (Litz et al., 2009; Shay, 2014) by proposing in this chapter an adapted stress-and-coping model that (a) recognizes acts or events for which individuals hold themselves or others morally responsible as potential stressors, (b) identifies moral pain as dysphoric cognitions and emotions that result from appraisal of an act or event as a moral transgression (Farnsworth et al., 2017), (c) hypothesizes that stress-related problems may occur if intense or persistent moral pain results from transgressions that are perceived to be more severe or not amenable to repair, and (d) conceptualizes forgiveness as a method of coping with moral pain intended to facilitate moral repair. Whether it is directed toward oneself or others, we argue that forgiveness is adaptive insofar as it facilitates accurate appraisal of responsibility for perceived transgressions coupled with the release of transgression-related psychological and emotional distress.

https://doi.org/10.1037/0000204-005
Addressing Moral Injury in Clinical Practice, J. M. Currier, K. D. Drescher, and J. Nieuwsma (Editors)
In the public domain.

WHAT IS MORAL INJURY?

Despite the growing interest in moral injury, neither a consensus definition of morally injurious outcomes nor a compilation of potentially morally injurious events has yet to emerge in the literature. Litz and colleagues (2009) theorized that moral injury might stem from "perpetrating, failing to prevent, bearing witness to, or learning about acts that transgress deeply held moral beliefs and expectations" (p. 697). Shay (2014), however, maintained that moral injury could result from a betrayal of justice by a person of authority or by oneself in a situation with important consequences. These conceptualizations cover a variety of phenomenologically distinct but not mutually exclusive types of exposure that could include being a perpetrator, victim, or witness of an immoral act. Similarly, subjective reports from military personnel suggest that immoral acts for which individuals hold themselves or others responsible, which in the military setting can include using disproportionate violence against enemy combatants, causing harm to civilians or civilian life, failing to prevent harm to others, or being betrayed by trusted individuals or institutions, are potential sources of psychological and functional problems (Schorr et al., 2018). Efforts to identify problematic outcomes that result from being personally responsible for an immoral act versus witnessing others' immoral acts versus being the victim of others' immoral acts are ongoing and complicated by high rates of exposure to multiple morally injurious and traumatic events among military personnel.

Yet the consensus is that moral injuries characterized by an array of psychological and behavioral, social, religious and spiritual, and physiological problems are a possible consequence of exposure to potentially morally injurious events, just as posttraumatic stress disorder (PTSD) is a possible consequence of exposure to potentially life-threatening events (Galatzer-Levy et al., 2018; Griffin et al., 2019). But not every exposure to an immoral act results in a moral injury. Whether exposure to a potentially morally injurious event results in a moral injury may depend on how moral distress is experienced. Farnsworth and colleagues (2017) suggested that moral pain—in other words, the "experience of dysphoric moral emotions and cognitions" (p. 392)—might naturally occur in response to immoral acts and motivate reparative responses (e.g., apology); thus, moral pain can be indicative of an intact moral conscience. Yet, reparative efforts may be obstructed, for instance, if parties involved in a transgression are deceased, out of reach, or not in a close and continued relationship. In situations like these, when consequences of a perceived transgression are high and repair seems unlikely, intense and persistent moral pain can contribute to an array of problems.

BRIDGING THE MORAL INJURY AND FORGIVENESS LITERATURES

The dearth of studies that examine moral injury and forgiveness may be due, in part, to the lack of an orienting model designed to integrate these complex bodies of research. For this reason, as is depicted in Figure 4.1, we propose an

FIGURE 4.1. Adapted Stress-and-Coping Model of Moral Injury and Forgiveness

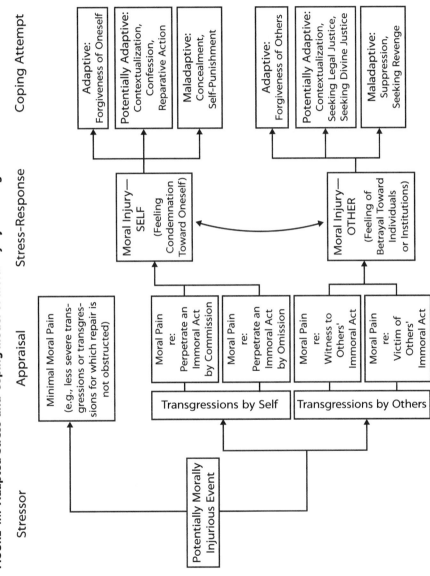

adapted stress-and-coping model of moral injury and forgiveness. For a review of other conceptualizations of forgiveness within a stress-and-coping framework, see Strelan (2019).

According to Lazarus and Folkman (1984), who first proposed the stress-and-coping model, individuals encounter stressors or potentially distressing stimuli. When a person encounters a stressor, he or she appraises the severity of the stressor (primary appraisal), as well as resources that are available to manage the stressor (secondary appraisal). Next, stressors that are appraised as sufficiently threatening and not able to be resolved by available resources elicit a stress response. The stress response motivates the individual to implement some coping attempt to restore equilibrium. Finally, Lazarus and Folkman's model is recursive, such that coping attempts feedback to influence appraisals of the stressor and the stress response. To the extent that attempts to cope do not restore homeostasis, the person will likely experience stress-related threats to health and well-being. We elaborate on how this process might unfold in the context of moral injury and forgiveness.

Stressor

First, a potentially morally injurious event might function as a stressor. Military personnel may encounter ethically ambiguous and challenging events in the course of their service. Although there is currently no objective standard with respect to what events are potentially morally injurious, Frankfurt and Frazier (2016) suggested that immoral acts violate one's personal beliefs about what is acceptable conduct—that is, one's beliefs about right and wrong. Individuals might hold themselves personally responsible for actions that violated a formal moral code (e.g., commission of a war-zone atrocity), but violation of an objective ethical standard is not required. For instance, a service member might have performed their duty with excellence but still believe that they transgressed some expectation of morally good conduct (e.g., maintaining a security perimeter at the site of a terrorist attack as ordered while being unable to provide life-saving support to injured civilians). Or they may blame themselves for a perceived failure to act (e.g., not preventing a fellow service member from sustaining a serious injury). Military personnel may also witness (e.g., observe others use excessive violence during an interrogation) or be the victim of (e.g., experience harassment or assault by one's fellow service members) immoral acts for which others are responsible. In sum, the extant literature on moral injury suggests that exposure to an immoral act as a perpetrator, witness, or victim could be considered a potential stressor.

Appraisal

Next, individuals appraise the severity of the immoral act, considering factors such as personal agency (e.g., whether the act or event was intended or unanticipated, whether there was limited time or information to make a decision in the presence of emotional duress) and amount of harm or suffering that resulted from the event. Importantly, decisions may be appraised as morally right by one ethic (e.g., rules of engagement) but wrong by another ethic (e.g., civilian law, religious or spiritual code). Active military personnel may find it difficult to selectively deactivate civilian ethics in favor of military ethics during combat, and veterans may form ex post facto moral judgments of their military actions relative to civilian ethics when they separate from military service and return to civilian life (Harris et al., 2015).

The appraisal process may also include the formation of secondary appraisals about the likelihood that the immoral act is amenable to repair. For instance, a service member might consider whether it is possible to offer or receive an apology or restitution. In many cases of military-related moral injury, individuals perceive amends making to be impossible. A service member or veteran who feels personally responsible for an immoral act may be unable to contact those who were harmed by a perceived transgression if the victim is geographically isolated or deceased. Also, victims of offense may be out of touch with their transgressors if they are no longer attached to their operational units, or they choose to remain out of contact with past wrongdoers to maintain personal safety. Overall, immoral acts that individuals appraise as more severe and not amenable to repair may contribute to intense and persistent moral pain.

Stress Response

In the third step, intense and/or persistent moral pain is theorized to contribute to a stress response characterized by an array of psychological conflicts, emotional dysregulation, and functional problems. One's commitment to his or her core moral beliefs and values when juxtaposed with a perceived violation or immoral act may become a source of rational and appropriate dissonance (Gray et al., 2017). In fact, preliminary evidence can be adduced to highlight how the stress response associated with moral injury might differ from a stress response associated with other trauma types. Litz and colleagues (2018) interviewed treatment-seeking military service members ($N = 999$) to solicit a description of the deployment-related event(s) they described as the military-related event that currently caused them the most distress. Independent evaluators coded each event description into at least one of six categories: life threat self, life threat–others, aftermath of violence, traumatic loss, moral injury–self, and moral injury–others. Distress reported by veterans who had violated their values (moral injury–self; 7% of the sample) differed from distress reported by those whose personal safety was threatened (life threat–self; 42% of the sample). Those with perpetration-based concerns (i.e., moral injury–self) reported greater hindsight bias and responsibility ($d = 1.06$), reexperiencing of symptoms ($d = 1.19$), perceived wrongdoing ($d = 0.94$), negative cognitions directed at oneself ($d = 0.32$), self-blame ($d = 0.58$), and posttraumatic sadness ($d = 0.49$) compared with those whose safety was threatened (i.e., life threat–self). In addition, when compared with those exposed to events that may have resulted in their own serious injury or death (i.e., life threat–self), those who witnessed or were the victim of others' wrongful actions (i.e., moral injury–others; 18%) reported greater peri- ($d = 0.36$) and posttraumatic ($d = 0.33$) betrayal and humiliation (see also Ramage et al., 2016). The stress response may contribute to a variety of other deficits as well, such as relationships at home or work characterized by interpersonal conflict or isolation, and some individuals may experience existential issues, such as feeling abandoned by God, questioning the purpose of their life, and a foreclosing on their future.

Coping Attempts

Fourth, individuals are motivated to implement coping attempts intended to reestablish equilibrium by relieving the stress response. Attempts to cope may be maladaptive, potentially adaptive, or adaptive. Examples of maladaptive coping attempts could include efforts to conceal or avoid discussion of one's regretted actions or inactions or attempts to suppress thoughts and feelings about others' betrayals; these avoidance strategies are maladaptive in that they prevent resolution of moral pain. Others may try to affirm their values by punishing the perceived wrongdoer, whether by denigrating themselves (if they are personally responsible for an immoral act) or seeking revenge against another person or institution (if others are responsible for an immoral act). These attempts are maladaptive in that they elicit a persistent emotional burden of condemnation toward oneself or others.

Other coping attempts may have mixed success. Contextualization of one's or others' actions—for example, acknowledging that the chaos of combat can impede sound moral judgment—may help to reduce feelings of shame, guilt, anger, or fear connected to a transgressive event. However, such attempts at contextualization may not necessarily address or may even diminish the importance of one's core moral beliefs and values. Other coping methods might address the moral pain more directly. Those who construe their actions as evidence of a personal failure might hope to alleviate moral pain by doing enough good in the world to "balance the scales," and those who were victimized by others may wait for legal or divine justice to rectify the harm they experienced. These attempts may be effective if they alleviate moral pain. In many cases, however, the void may seem impossible to fill, formal channels of justice may not be available, or there may be lingering demoralization despite efforts to atone.

Thus, we face the question at the crux of moral repair: How might a person who was exposed to a gross violation of their moral beliefs and values cope in a way that reduces the burden of moral pain without minimizing their commitment to their core beliefs and values? Although other coping attempts could be effective, forgiveness is an important mechanism of moral repair because forgiveness facilitates meaningful interpretation of moral pain rooted in perceived violation of a moral standard and promotes alleviation of transgression-related psychological and emotional burdens (and potentially social or religious or spiritual problems).

CLINICAL APPLICATION OF FORGIVENESS FOR MORAL INJURY

Researchers have acknowledged the importance of forgiveness in the assessment and treatment of moral injury (e.g., C. J. Bryan et al., 2016; Litz et al., 2009; Maguen et al., 2017; Wortmann et al., 2017). A select few empirical studies have also provided evidence that the clinical application of forgiveness for moral injury is a productive area of inquiry. For instance, in a clustering analysis that examined symptom profiles among treatment-seeking veterans, difficulty forgiving oneself, others, and situations, along with trauma-related guilt and PTSD symptom burden, were associated with exposure to potentially morally injurious events (Smigelsky et al., 2019). In addition, Witvliet et al. (2004) found that difficulties forgiving oneself and others were moderately positively associated with PTSD and depression severity in a sample of veterans seeking psychological services ($N = 213$).

Preliminary evidence also shows that forgiveness as a method to cope with a perceived transgression may promote meaning making, which is an important facet of recovery from trauma-related conditions such as PTSD and moral injury. In a sample of German soldiers ($N = 1,097$), 13% of participants reported a need to forgive others, and another 13% reported a need to be forgiven themselves (Bussing et al., 2018). Associations between the need to clarify unresolved aspects of life with desires to forgive and be forgiven were mediated by soldiers' beliefs that they needed to talk about their worries and concerns. In addition to granting and receiving forgiveness, self-forgiveness may buffer some of the most disastrous outcomes associated with moral injury. A. O. Bryan et al. (2015) found that American military personnel and veterans ($N = 474$) who were more forgiving of themselves were less likely to attempt suicide. We expand on this promising but preliminary set of studies, with a specific focus on the dimensions of forgiveness that involve forgiving oneself and forgiving others. There may be other dimensions of forgiveness, such as seeking and receiving divine forgiveness, that are relevant to moral injury but have less often been the focus of scientific investigation.

Self-Forgiveness

For those who report holding themselves personally responsible for an immoral act, there has been an explosion of interest in self-forgiveness (for reviews, see Woodyatt et al., 2017). Historically, some scholars expressed the concern that self-forgiveness may function as a moral disengagement strategy by which wrongdoers could minimize the consequences of their harmful actions; however, more recent investigations indicate that self-forgiveness may be an essential process in healthy psychological development (Woodyatt & Wenzel, 2014; cf. Vitz & Meade, 2011). Much of this debate regarding the moral appropriateness of self-forgiveness has ensued due to a lack of conceptual precision in scholars' definitions of self-forgiveness (e.g., is self-forgiveness just letting oneself off of the proverbial hook, or does it require acceptance of responsibility for the consequences of one's actions?). For this reason, Webb et al. (2017) conducted a comprehensive review of articles on self-forgiveness ($N = 177$), 85 (48.02%) of which offered a unique definition of the construct. Conceptual components were distilled to produce a single definition:

> Self-forgiveness occurs over time and is a deliberate, volitional process initiated in response to one's own negative feelings in the context of a personally acknowledged self-instigated wrong, that results in ready accountability for said wrong and a fundamental, constructive shift in one's relationship to, reconciliation with, and acceptance of the self through human connectedness and commitment to change. (p. 221)

Like Webb and colleagues' emphases on accepting responsibility for an immoral act and accepting oneself as flawed but capable of growth, Griffin et al. (2018) described two processes that are essential to self-forgiveness: (a) reorientation toward positive values and (b) restoration of personal esteem. In the absence of either of these, what occurs is not self-forgiveness. To accept responsibility and seek to atone for a perceived transgression by denigrating oneself is self-punishment, and to maintain a positive sense of self-esteem by deflecting responsibility for one's actions is self-exoneration. Thus, for a service member or veteran to practice self-forgiveness, they must seek to accept responsibility and commit to change but also replace self-condemning emotions with self-affirming emotions.

Griffin et al. (2016) theorized that self-forgiveness may provide a framework by which to satisfy fundamental needs for belonging and esteem that moral pain often obstructs. First, the social reconnection hypothesis suggests that reorientation toward positive values, particularly by accepting personal responsibility, seeking to make amends, and committing to change, may reduce perceived or actual rejection by others for violated values imbued with social significance (e.g., if the value a veteran believes he violated was internalized from close others, such as family of origin, romantic partners, or religious or spiritual organizations). Second, the personal restoration hypothesis suggests that the process of enhancing esteem, especially replacing self-condemning emotions with self-affirming emotions, may increase psychological well-being and decrease stress-related issues. Empirical evidence has supported these hypotheses. For instance, in their meta-analytic review of 65 independent samples ($N = 17{,}939$), Davis et al. (2015) found that self-forgiveness was associated with greater psychological well-being ($r = .45$) and life satisfaction and meaning ($r = .43$) lower anger ($r = -.41$), guilt ($r = -.50$), and shame ($r = -.60$) and greater perceived social support ($r = .43$) and feeling forgiven by others ($r = .41$).

Several interventions designed to promote self-forgiveness have been developed (for a review, see Cornish et al., 2019). We focus on Cornish and Wade's (2015a) model that clinicians may use to guide individual therapy patients through a four-component process designed to promote self-forgiveness. The first step, *responsibility*, aims to set the occasion for forgiveness by inviting participants to accept responsibility for a specific perceived offense without blaming themselves for things beyond their control. The second step, *remorse*, focuses on facilitating meaningful interpretation of offense-related negative emotions (e.g., guilt and shame). Shame responses directed at nonmodifiable aspects of the self might be targeted for reduction in this step. Negative emotion directed at one's behavior (i.e., guilt) may be directed toward enhancing motivation for amends making and removal of barriers to reparation. The third step, *restoration*, is an action-oriented step in which individuals seek to make amends for the consequences of their perceived transgression and to reconnect to the values they identified as having violated. The fourth step, *renewal*, invites the patient to appreciate his or her intrinsic worth as a person and ability to grow by learning from past mistakes.

In a preliminary randomized trial, community-dwelling adults ($N = 26$) were randomly assigned to participate in an immediate or delayed treatment option using the aforementioned treatment model manualized for administration across eight 50-minute individual psychotherapy sessions using an emotion-focused therapy framework. Improvements over the course of treatment in self-condemnation, self-forgiveness, psychological distress, and self-compassion were observed relative to the wait-list control, with moderate to large effect sizes (Cornish & Wade, 2015b). Although Cornish and Wade (2015a) suggested that military veterans with combat-related regrets may be good candidates for the self-forgiveness model, their intervention trial (Cornish & Wade, 2015b) did not include any veterans in the sample.

As discussed in Chapter 11, impact of killing (IOK) is a treatment model that explicitly incorporates self-forgiveness in the treatment of military-related moral injury (Maguen et al., 2017). Multiple sessions focus on self-forgiveness, which is conceptualized as a key ingredient in healing from moral injury due to killing in war. Therapeutic work is dedicated to understating an individual's framework for self-forgiveness, exploring myths and barriers to self-forgiveness, and participating in exercises aimed at fostering self-forgiveness (e.g., writing letters to the deceased or a younger version of oneself), with a subsequent focus on making amends and maintaining gains. Veterans participating in qualitative interviews after IOK identified the self-forgiveness component as a critical part of their healing process (Purcell, Burkman, et al., 2018; Purcell, Griffin, et al., 2018).

Other Forgiveness

For those who present for treatment after witnessing or being the victim of others' immoral acts, an intervention designed to promote forgiveness of others could provide a beneficial adjunct to treatment as usual. In their definitional review, Webb et al. (2017) derived the following definition of *other forgiveness*:

> Forgiveness occurs over time and is a deliberate, volitional process involving a fundamental shift in affect, cognition, and/or behavior in response to negative feelings regarding an acknowledged offensive experience, without condoning, excusing, or denying the transgression(s)—at a minimum, an absence of ill will toward an offender. (p. 220)

In light of differences observed across various scholars' definitions of forgiveness, Worthington (2005) concluded that several different types of forgiveness exist. For example, when considering the personal experiences of victims who grant forgiveness to others, forgiveness of another person with whom a victim is not in a close relationship is widely believed to involve only the release of ill will toward the other, whereas forgiveness of others with whom a victim is in an ongoing close relationship involves replacement of negative emotions (e.g., anger, resentment, spite) with positive, other-oriented emotions (e.g., compassion, love, warmth). Furthermore, the distinct cognitive, affective, and behavioral components of forgiveness are related but do not necessarily occur simultaneously. A victim might decide to forgive another person by forming a behavioral intention to neither avoid nor seek revenge against a transgressor, though the resolution of emotional distress may occur after the initial decision to forgive is made (Worthington et al., 2007).

Whereas interventions designed to promote self-forgiveness are still in a nascent stage of development, interventions designed to promote forgiveness of others have been thoroughly investigated. Interventions designed to promote forgiveness of others have been administered in various modalities (e.g., individual, conjoint, group, community-based, self-directed therapies) and with a wide range of populations (e.g., couples following romantic affairs, survivors of interpersonal trauma, adult children of alcoholics), though not specifically with military service members or veterans. Several empirically supported approaches are available, including Enright's (2001) PROCESS model, Worthington's (2001) REACH forgiveness model, and Luskin's (2003) forgive for good model. Wade et al. (2014) meta-analyzed 54 published and unpublished reports of interventions designed to promote forgiveness ($N = 2,323$). Participants who completed a forgiveness intervention made stronger gains in forgiveness relative to those who received no treatment ($\Delta_+ = 0.56$ [0.43, 0.68]) or an alternative treatment ($\Delta_+ = 0.45$ [0.21, 0.69]). Effect sizes comparing forgiveness interventions with no-treatment groups also indicated moderate to large effects for decreasing depression ($n = 10$ studies) and increasing hope ($n = 6$ studies).

In a content analysis of group interventions designed to promote forgiveness, Wade and Worthington (2005) discussed a variety of strategies that may assist clinicians who intervene to promote forgiveness of others with their patients. Exercises that were common across therapeutic approaches included the following: first, defining what forgiveness is and is not (e.g., asking the patient to describe their definition of forgiveness and explaining how forgiveness and reconciling or forgiveness and excusing differ), and second, providing a safe and supportive environment for patients to remember an offense in a helpful way. Techniques including active listening and asking probing questions can help patients to establish an accurate appraisal of others' responsibility for an offense by exploring the offender's intent and relevant situational constraints. Therapists might also seek to assist patients in identifying important moral beliefs or expectations that were violated by a perceived transgression and conduct a self-assessment of the meaning and implications of the transgression for the patient's future (e.g., What are the benefits and drawbacks of holding a grudge against someone who wronged you?).

Third, therapists can encourage their patients to build empathy for others who have wronged them using strategies such as discussing a common humanity shared by the patient, therapist, and perceived wrongdoer; reflecting on one's wrongdoing and failures to gain perspective; and remembering what it felt like in the past when the patient received forgiveness from another person or when the patient has previously forgiven others. Finally, therapists can help patients by encouraging the commitment to forgive. Providers may invite the patient to write a letter of forgiveness that can be shared with a benevolent other or shared in session during an imaginal dialogue or simulated interaction between the patient and their transgressor. Psychoeducation about the salubrious association between forgiveness and better health may also be shared with the patient to bolster his or her commitment to the forgiveness he or she has experienced.

BARRIERS TO THE CLINICAL APPLICATION OF FORGIVENESS FOR MORAL INJURY

We have argued that intense and persistent moral pain may contribute to problematic outcomes among military personnel and veterans who sustain a moral injury, especially among those who were exposed to potentially morally injurious events they appraise as more severe and less amenable to repair. Although it is but one of many ways to cope with moral pain, forgiveness appears to be adaptive because it might facilitate meaningful interpretation of transgression-related distress coupled with the release of the psychological and emotional burdens associated with moral pain. However, there are several barriers to the implementation of forgiveness interventions for military-related moral injury.

First, victims' and perpetrators' experiences of moral pain may depend on one another to be resolved, especially for those in continued relationships, according to prior research (Worthington, 2005). For instance, outside of the military setting, a victim's unforgiveness and a transgressor's self-condemnation may be resolved through a mutual exchange of offering and accepting an apology. But those involved in immoral acts that occur in military settings frequently have varying levels of willingness or ability to address the perceived transgression. In an opinion piece published in *The Washington Post*, Marine Captain Timothy Kudo (2013) put it like this: "It's impossible [for me] to forget what happened, and the only people who can forgive me are dead." Military personnel may have insufficient information to reach those who were affected by their transgression, and those who experienced harm may be geographically isolated, unwilling to accept an apology, or even deceased. When one feels personally responsible for an immoral act and perceives that it is impossible to make amends, potentially adaptive feelings of guilt and remorse that typically promote repair may evolve into a chronic and pervasive condemnation of one's global self (Leach & Cidam, 2015). In these cases, clinicians may assist patients in identifying reparative activities that are possible and congruent with the patients' values. For example, a veteran who reported feeling responsible for the death of a child might write a letter to the deceased child or their family, volunteer in his or her community in a way that benefits children (e.g., join a community-based project to build a playground), or even commit themselves to being a supportive parent to her or his children.

Second, for service members and veterans who present for treatment after witnessing or being the victim of another person's immoral actions, individuals may be less motivated to forgive if there is little incentive to maintain a bond with the perpetrator or if contacting the perpetrator opens a possibility of future exploitation or further hurt (Burnette et al., 2012). In these situations, it is vital to differentiate forgiveness, which happens "within one's skin," when one processes and releases condemning emotions directed toward others, from reconciliation, which occurs when trust is restored between victims and perpetrators of offense to reestablish a previously ruptured relationship. Whereas reconciliation may not be possible, prudent, or safe in all cases, a victim might seek to forgive for his or her own benefit. One's motivation to forgive others can be enhanced by emphasizing the health benefits associated with forgiveness in these situations. That is, individuals who choose to release the emotional burden of victimization by practicing forgiveness typically report better physiological health, psychological well-being, higher quality relationships, and more meaningful lives (for a review, see Toussaint et al., 2015).

DISTAL OUTCOMES ASSOCIATED WITH FORGIVENESS FOR MORAL INJURY

If intense and pervasive moral pain is a potential source of psychological and functional problems, and forgiveness is one way to cope with moral pain, attempts to cope with a transgressive event by practicing forgiveness may alleviate the stress-related problems associated with a transgression and facilitate moral repair. We, therefore, discuss several potential outcomes of practicing forgiveness.

First, intervening to promote one type of forgiveness may incidentally promote other types of forgiveness as well. For example, in a longitudinal study of individuals managing alcohol dependence, Krentzman et al. (2018) found that increases in other forgiveness at an earlier unit in time promoted increases in self-forgiveness at a later point in time, and vice versa. Also, patients who blame themselves for a perceived transgression and identify as religious or spiritual may seek and receive forgiveness from whoever or whatever they consider to be sacred, such that receiving divine forgiveness can be a foundation for forgiving oneself. Those who witnessed or were the victim of others' immoral acts may even experience anger toward the sacred or feel a need to forgive the sacred for failing to prevent the harm that they or others suffered (see Chapter 3). In either case, receiving divine forgiveness and granting forgiveness to that which one believes is sacred may be a catalyst for forgiving oneself or others.

Second, the resolution of moral pain via forgiveness may facilitate intrapersonal restoration. According to Toussaint et al. (2015), individuals who forgive report reduced stress-related threats to well-being, including psychological problems (e.g., depression, anxiety) and physiological ailments (e.g., cardiovascular risk, immunodeficiency). Forgiveness has also been associated with enhanced psychological resources, such as resilience and hope. Thus, forgiveness may be a generative source of therapeutic effects that can facilitate repair and optimize treatment benefits.

Third, forgiveness might also contribute to interpersonal restoration. Core moral beliefs and values are often internalized from close others, and people tend to affiliate with others who are like-minded (see Chapters 2 and 3, this volume). Violation of internalized values may consequently result in actual or perceived rejection by important others (e.g., family of origin, romantic partners, members of one's religious or spiritual organization). Forgiveness of morally transgressive events that occurred during one's deployment, especially when coupled with forgiveness for and from close others negatively affected by difficulties experienced during a transition from military to civilian life, might, therefore, enhance belonging and increase perceived social support and interpersonal connection.

CONCLUSION

In summary, the literatures on moral injury and forgiveness have developed largely independent of each other. The purpose of this chapter was to provide an adapted stress-and-coping model to introduce forgiveness as a strategy to cope with intense and persistent moral pain. Our analysis suggests that forgiveness may be uniquely suited to alleviate the emotional burden of intense and persistent moral pain experienced by many survivors of military-related moral injury, without minimizing the person's commitment to their moral beliefs and values. We, therefore, conclude that forgiveness of oneself and others may be a critical mechanism of moral repair for service members and veterans who sustain military-related moral injuries.

REFERENCES

Bryan, A. O., Theriault, J. L., & Bryan, C. J. (2015). Self-forgiveness, posttraumatic stress, and suicide attempts among military personnel and veterans. *Traumatology*, *21*(1), 40–46. https://doi.org/10.1037/trm0000017

Bryan, C. J., Bryan, A. O., Anestis, M. D., Anestis, J. C., Green, B. A., Etienne, N., Morrow, C. E., & Ray-Sannerud, B. (2016). Measuring moral injury: Psychometric properties of the moral injury events scale in two military samples. *Assessment, 23*(5), 557–570. https://doi.org/10.1177/1073191115590855

Burnette, J. L., McCullough, M. E., Van Tongeren, D. R., & Davis, D. E. (2012). Forgiveness results from integrating information about relationship value and exploitation risk. *Personality and Social Psychology Bulletin, 38*(3), 345–356. https://doi.org/10.1177/0146167211424582

Bussing, A., Recchia, D. R., & Toussaint, L. L. (2018). German soldiers' needs to clarify open aspects in their life, to talk about fears and worries, and to forgive and be forgiven as a matter of life reflection. *Frontiers in Psychiatry.* https://doi.org/10.3389/fpsyt.2018.00582

Cornish, M., Griffin, B. J., & Morris, G. (2019). Promotion of self-forgiveness. In E. L. Worthington, Jr., & N. G. Wade (Eds.), *The handbook of forgiveness* (2nd ed., pp. 288–298). Routledge. https://doi.org/10.4324/9781351123341-27

Cornish, M. A., & Wade, N. G. (2015a). A therapeutic model of self-forgiveness with intervention strategies for counselors. *Journal of Counseling and Development, 93*(1), 96–104. https://doi.org/10.1002/j.1556-6676.2015.00185.x

Cornish, M. A., & Wade, N. G. (2015b). Working through past wrongdoing: Examination of a self-forgiveness counseling intervention. *Journal of Counseling Psychology, 62*(3), 521–528. https://doi.org/10.1037/cou0000080

Davis, D. E., Ho, M. Y., Griffin, B. J., Bell, C., Hook, J. N., Van Tongeren, D. R., DeBlaere, C., Worthington, E. L., Jr., & Westbrook, C. J. (2015). Forgiving the self and physical and mental health correlates: A meta-analytic review. *Journal of Counseling Psychology, 62*(2), 329–335. https://doi.org/10.1037/cou0000063

Enright, R. D. (2001). *Forgiveness is a choice: A step-by-step process for resolving anger and restoring hope.* American Psychological Association.

Farnsworth, J. K., Drescher, K. D., Evans, W., & Walser, R. D. (2017). A functional approach to understanding and treating military-related moral injury. *Journal of Contextual Behavioral Science, 6*(4), 391–397. https://doi.org/10.1016/j.jcbs.2017.07.003

Frankfurt, S., & Frazier, P. (2016). A review of research on moral injury in combat veterans. *Military Psychology, 28*(5), 318–330. https://doi.org/10.1037/mil0000132

Galatzer-Levy, I. R., Huang, S. H., & Bonanno, G. A. (2018). Trajectories of resilience and dysfunction following potential trauma: A review and statistical evaluation. *Clinical Psychology Review, 63*, 41–55. https://doi.org/10.1016/j.cpr.2018.05.008

Gray, M. J., Nash, W. P., & Litz, B. T. (2017). When self-blame is rational and appropriate: The limited utility of Socratic questioning in the context of moral injury: Commentary on Wachen et al. (2016). *Cognitive and Behavioral Practice, 24*(4), 383–387. https://doi.org/10.1016/j.cbpra.2017.03.001

Griffin, B. J., Moloney, J. M., Green, J. D., Worthington, E. L., Jr., Cork, B., Tangney, J. P., Van Tongeren, D. R., Davis, D. E., & Hook, J. N. (2016). Perpetrators' reactions to perceived interpersonal wrongdoing: The associations of guilt and shame with forgiving, punishing, and excusing oneself. *Self and Identity, 15*(6), 650–661. https://doi.org/10.1080/15298868.2016.1187669

Griffin, B. J., Purcell, N., Burkman, K., Litz, B. T., Bryan, C. J., Schmitz, M., Villierme, C., Walsh, J., & Maguen, S. (2019). Moral injury: An integrative review. *Journal of Traumatic Stress, 32*(3), 350–362. https://doi.org/10.1002/jts.22362

Griffin, B. J., Worthington, E. L., Jr., Davis, D. E., Hook, J. N., & Maguen, S. (2018). Development of the self-forgiveness dual-process scale. *Journal of Counseling Psychology, 65*(6), 715–726. https://doi.org/10.1037/cou0000293

Harris, J. I., Park, C. L., Currier, J. M., Usset, T. J., & Voecks, C. D. (2015). Moral injury and psycho-spiritual development: Considering the developmental context. *Spirituality in Clinical Practice, 2*(4), 256–266. https://doi.org/10.1037/scp0000045

Krentzman, A. R., Webb, J. R., Jester, J. M., & Harris, J. I. (2018). Longitudinal relationship between forgiveness of self and forgiveness of others among individuals with alcohol use disorders. *Psychology of Religion and Spirituality, 10*(2), 128–137. https://doi.org/10.1037/rel0000152

Kudo, T. (2013, January 25). I killed people in Afghanistan. Was I right or wrong? *The Washington Post.* https://www.washingtonpost.com/opinions/i-killed-people-in-afghanistan-was-i-right-or-wrong/2013/01/25/c0b0d5a6-60ff-11e2-b05a-605528f6b712_story.html

Lazarus, R. S., & Folkman, S. (1984). *Stress, appraisal, and coping*. Springer.

Leach, C. W., & Cidam, A. (2015). When is shame linked to constructive approach orientation? A meta-analysis. *Journal of Personality and Social Psychology, 109*(6), 983–1002. https://doi.org/10.1037/pspa0000037

Litz, B. T., Contractor, A. A., Rhodes, C., Dondanville, K. A., Jordan, A. H., Resick, P. A., Foa, E. B., Young-McCaughan, S., Mintz, J., Yarvis, J. S., & Peterson, A. L. (2018). Distinct trauma types in military service members seeking treatment for posttraumatic stress disorder. *Journal of Traumatic Stress, 31*(2), 286–295. https://doi.org/10.1002/jts.22276

Litz, B. T., Stein, N., Delaney, E., Lebowitz, L., Nash, W. P., Silva, C., & Maguen, S. (2009). Moral injury and moral repair in war veterans: A preliminary model and intervention strategy. *Clinical Psychology Review, 29*(8), 695–706. https://doi.org/10.1016/j.cpr.2009.07.003

Luskin, F. (2003). *Forgive for good: A proven prescription for health and happiness.* HarperCollins.

Maguen, S., Burkman, K., Madden, E., Dinh, J., Bosch, J., Keyser, J., Schmitz, M., & Neylan, T. C. (2017). Impact of killing in war: A randomized, controlled pilot trial. *Journal of Clinical Psychology, 73*(9), 997–1012. https://doi.org/10.1002/jclp.22471

Purcell, N., Burkman, K., Keyser, J., Fucella, P., & Maguen, S. (2018). Healing from moral injury: A qualitative evaluation of the impact of killing treatment for combat veterans. *Journal of Aggression, Maltreatment & Trauma, 27*(6), 645–673. https://doi.org/10.1080/10926771.2018.1463582

Purcell, N., Griffin, B. J., Burkman, K., & Maguen, S. (2018). "Opening a door to a new life": The role of forgiveness in healing from moral injury. *Frontiers in Psychiatry, 9*, 498. https://doi.org/10.3389/fpsyt.2018.00498

Ramage, A. E., Litz, B. T., Resick, P. A., Woolsey, M. D., Dondanville, K. A., Young-McCaughan, S., Borah, A. M., Borah, E. V., Peterson, A. L., & Fox, P. T. (2016). Regional cerebral glucose metabolism differentiates danger- and non-danger-based traumas in post-traumatic stress disorder. *Social Cognitive and Affective Neuroscience, 11*(2), 234–242. https://doi.org/10.1093/scan/nsv102

Schorr, Y., Stein, N. R., Maguen, S., Barnes, J. B., Bosch, J., & Litz, B. T. (2018). Sources of moral injury among war veterans: A qualitative evaluation. *Journal of Clinical Psychology, 74*(12), 2203–2218. https://doi.org/10.1002/jclp.22660

Shay, J. (2014). Moral injury. *Psychoanalytic Psychology, 31*(2), 182–191. https://doi.org/10.1037/a0036090

Smigelsky, M. A., Malott, J. D., Veazey Morris, K., Berlin, K. S., & Neimeyer, R. A. (2019). Latent profile analysis exploring potential moral injury and posttraumatic stress disorder among military veterans. *Journal of Clinical Psychology, 75*(3), 499–519. https://doi.org/10.1002/jclp.22714

Strelan, P. (2019). The stress-and-coping model of forgiveness: Theory, research, and the potential of dyadic coping. In E. L. Worthington, Jr., & N. G. Wade (Eds.), *Handbook of forgiveness* (2nd ed., pp. 63–73). Routledge. https://doi.org/10.4324/9781351123341-7

Toussaint, L., Worthington, E., & Williams, D. R. (Eds.). (2015). *Forgiveness and health: Scientific evidence and theories relating forgiveness to better health.* Springer. https://doi.org/10.1007/978-94-017-9993-5

Vitz, P. C., & Meade, J. M. (2011). Self-forgiveness in psychology and psychotherapy: A critique. *Journal of Religion and Health, 50*, 248–263. https://doi.org/10.1007/s10943-010-9343-x

Wade, N. G., Hoyt, W. T., Kidwell, J. E., & Worthington, E. L., Jr. (2014). Efficacy of psychotherapeutic interventions to promote forgiveness: A meta-analysis. *Journal of Consulting and Clinical Psychology, 82*(1), 154–170. https://doi.org/10.1037/a0035268

Wade, N. G., & Worthington, E. L., Jr. (2005). In search of a common core: A content analysis of interventions to promote forgiveness. *Psychotherapy: Theory, Research, & Practice, 42*(2), 160–177. https://doi.org/10.1037/0033-3204.42.2.160

Webb, J. R., Bumgarner, D. J., Conway-Williams, E., Dangel, T., & Hall, B. B. (2017). A consensus definition of self-forgiveness: Implications for assessment and treatment. *Spirituality in Clinical Practice, 4*(3), 216–227. https://doi.org/10.1037/scp0000138

Witvliet, C. V., Phipps, K. A., Feldman, M. E., & Beckham, J. C. (2004). Posttraumatic mental and physical health correlates of forgiveness and religious coping in military veterans. *Journal of Traumatic Stress, 17*(3), 269–273. https://doi.org/10.1023/B:JOTS.0000029270.47848.e5

Woodyatt, L., & Wenzel, M. (2014). A needs-based perspective on self-forgiveness: Addressing threat to moral identity as a means of encouraging interpersonal and intrapersonal restoration. *Journal of Experimental Social Psychology, 50*, 125–135. https://doi.org/10.1016/j.jesp.2013.09.012

Woodyatt, L., Worthington, E. L., Jr., Wenzel, M., & Griffin, B. J. (Eds.). (2017). *Handbook of the psychology of self-forgiveness*. Springer. https://doi.org/10.1007/978-3-319-60573-9

Worthington, E. L., Jr. (2001). *Five steps to forgiveness: The art and science of forgiving*. Crown.

Worthington, E. L., Jr. (2005). *Handbook of forgiveness*. Routledge.

Worthington, E. L., Jr., Witvliet, C. V., Pietrini, P., & Miller, A. J. (2007). Forgiveness, health, and well-being: A review of evidence for emotional versus decisional forgiveness, dispositional forgivingness, and reduced unforgiveness. *Journal of Behavioral Medicine, 30*, 291–302. https://doi.org/10.1007/s10865-007-9105-8

Wortmann, J. H., Eisen, E., Hundert, C., Jordan, A. H., Smith, M. W., Nash, W. P., & Litz, B. T. (2017). Spiritual features of war-related moral injury: A primer for clinicians. *Spirituality in Clinical Practice, 4*(4), 249. https://doi.org/10.1037/scp0000140

5

Case Conceptualization for Moral Injury

Jacob K. Farnsworth

A three-person Marine Corps fire team was ordered to help clear an apartment building in Iraq that insurgents had reportedly been using as a location for launching mortars. While clearing the apartment building, the marines breached a door and found a 9-year-old boy holding a rifle with what appeared to be his mother and two sisters behind him. Having taken a few steps into the room, the team leader, Corporal Ramirez, hesitated in surprise on seeing the boy. As the second marine, Lance Corporal Smith, entered through the open door behind her, the boy fired, killing him instantly. The third and last marine, Lance Corporal Howe, seeing his comrade fall, entered the room and returned fire on the boy, striking him in the chest. After securing the boy's weapon and clearing the rest of the apartment, the two marines called for medical support. As they waited, they watched the Iraqi boy slowly die despite their attempts to stop the profuse bleeding from his chest wounds. In the background, they could hear his sisters screaming and his mother cursing the marines as infidels. There was a terrified look in the boy's eyes as he passed away.[1]

Consider this event from the perspectives of Corporal Ramirez and Lance Corporal Howe. Despite both being present in the same situation, unique features of their backgrounds and roles during this event mean that this incident will likely impact them in different ways. Many clinicians are trained to assess these impacts as they manifest in the form of psychological symptoms and, if appropriate, assign corresponding mental health diagnoses. However, in addition to exploring clinical diagnoses, which attempt to describe what is

---

[1]The clinical examples included in this chapter have been derived from a combination of clients and details have been changed to preserve anonymity.

https://doi.org/10.1037/0000204-006
Addressing Moral Injury in Clinical Practice, J. M. Currier, K. D. Drescher, and J. Nieuwsma (Editors)

similar across individual patients, clinical case conceptualization seeks also to understand what is distinct and idiosyncratic between cases. More specifically, individual case conceptualization takes raw clinical information and relates it together in a way that is meaningful and coherent and that informs treatment planning for a particular patient. Although case conceptualization often is accomplished through the lens of a specific theoretical model, it may also be argued that certain clinical and conceptual issues that are pertinent to a wide array of theoretical models play a crucial role in moral injury. Accordingly, this chapter highlights special considerations that may assist a variety of therapeutic orientations in clinically conceptualizing moral injury.

ASSUMPTIONS FOR CONCEPTUALIZING MORAL INJURY

The particular approach articulated in this chapter rests on three key assumptions. First, general case conceptualization can be theoretically inclusive. Looking beyond any one particular treatment framework, especially during the early stages of treatment, allows for consideration of multiple intervention options. Doing otherwise risks attentional bias on the part of providers who might only attend to the elements that support their preferred treatment framework. Once the best fitting therapeutic approach is decided, providers can then implement that approach with appropriate levels of fidelity.

The second key assumption is that moral injury exists as a biopsychosocial process alongside ethical–moral issues. This assumption implies that moral injury is optimally addressed through a holistic and contextually sensitive framework, including biological, psychological, and social processes, as well as ethical and existential issues, including spirituality (see Chapter 3, this volume).

The third key assumption is that mental health providers operate according to evidence-based principles of care. Because the scientific study of moral injury is relatively new, empirical findings to guide case conceptualization are still accumulating. Yet, early findings can guide assessment approaches and treatment recommendations. Clinicians should continue to familiarize themselves with emerging research and be judicious in how they apply existing findings as the construct of moral injury develops. Before proceeding further, I present two important conceptual issues to help provide a foundation for the case conceptualization framework presented later.

Differentiating Moral Injury and Posttraumatic Stress Disorder

In contrast to mental health diagnoses included in the *Diagnostic and Statistical Manual of Mental Disorders* (5th ed.; *DSM-5*; American Psychiatric Association, 2013), moral injury is not currently considered a mental health disorder. Although preliminary research has suggested that moral injury may be associated with a range of psychological problems (Currier et al., 2014; Maguen et al., 2010, 2012), much of this research has explored moral injury in the context of posttraumatic stress disorder (PTSD; Bryan et al., 2018; Currier et al., 2019; Jordan et al., 2017). It is, therefore, important to clarify the relationship between moral injury and the diagnostic entity of PTSD. Existing research and commentaries on PTSD and moral injury suggest basic similarities that are informative for case conceptualization. In particular, theoretical accounts of moral injury suggest at least three components that generally parallel PTSD: (a) exposure to a precipitating stressor, (b) automatic and involuntary stress reactions, and (c) maladaptive coping responses that prolong or exacerbate the negative impact of these stress reactions on individual well-being and functioning.

These similarities also make room for a number of differences between PTSD and moral injury, a subset of which is discussed here. First, as a mental health disorder, PTSD describes a pathological condition that reflects a deficit in psychological functioning posttrauma. In contrast, some conceptualizations of moral injury maintain that some moral reactions in response to a potentially morally injurious event (PMIE) may not be signs of pathology but instead are the natural and expected outgrowth of a functioning internal moral system (Farnsworth et al., 2017, Litz et al., 2009). Second, although *DSM-5* expanded criteria to include emotions such as shame and guilt, PTSD remains largely a fear-based disorder. The predominant role of fear in PTSD can be observed in the *DSM-5* definition of a traumatic stressor, which emphasizes threat to physical safety as its central defining feature. This emphasis on threat-based trauma, though conceptually important for understanding trauma-related hyperarousal symptoms, excludes events that may generate substantial moral distress and yet not include acute physical danger. Third, cognitions in *DSM-5* PTSD are specifically described as "distorted," "exaggerated" (American Psychiatric Association, 2013, p. 272), or "erroneous" (Friedman et al., 2011, p. 758), emphasizing a focus on the descriptive accuracy of trauma-related beliefs (e.g., "I caused this trauma to happen"). In contrast, beliefs in moral injury also include prescriptive judgments about how things ought to be (i.e., "I should have acted differently"). Whereas descriptive beliefs can be falsified by appealing to objective evidence, prescriptive moral judgments are instead subjective and, therefore, impossible to categorize as "distorted," "exaggerated," or "erroneous" as required by the *DSM-5* criteria for PTSD (Farnsworth, 2019).

Despite these differences, it is likely that moral injury and the diagnosis of PTSD will frequently be intertwined. Factor analytic approaches to PTSD reveal a highly multidimensional construct (Armour et al., 2015), and even the more condensed *DSM-5* PTSD symptom clusters include symptoms that are hypothesized to reflect heterogeneous biological and psychological processes such as memory, Pavlovian conditioning, dissociation, sympathetic hyperarousal, and cognitive schemas. With such a variety of processes represented, it is perhaps not surprising that PTSD symptoms may often reflect content associated with moral injury (Bryan et al., 2018; Jinkerson, 2016), especially in cases wherein PTSD symptoms and morally injurious reactions share the same precipitating event. For example, when considering the vignette included at the start of the chapter, it can be observed that the event the marines were exposed to meets PTSD's definition of a Criterion A traumatic event. Thus, in addition to moral reactions, clinicians should also attend to potential signs of PTSD, such as nightmares, intrusive memories, and hyper-vigilance. In sum, although researchers and clinicians should take care to appreciate definitional distinctions between PTSD and moral injury, it must also be recognized that symptoms of PTSD and signs of moral injury are likely to share important content and themes for individual patients.

Attending to Both Content and Function

In the following sections, the experiences of Corporal Ramirez and Lance Corporal Howe from the opening vignette will be compared to demonstrate how clinical case conceptualization can be used to individually tailor treatment planning for moral injury. To begin, consider the chief complaints of each patient as they present for their initial psychotherapy appointments (see Table 5.1).

When clinicians encounter a patient, the first clinical data they will likely encounter is how he or she phrases the chief complaint. In the case of moral injury, the chief complaint may directly reflect moral themes such as "I need to forgive myself" or "I need to let go of the guilt and anger." Other times, the chief complaint may center on impairments in functioning connected to the moral injury, such as Corporal Ramirez's statement "I don't sleep very well." In listening to a patient's statements, including chief complaints, it is useful for clinicians to approach these issues from at least two levels of analysis.

Perhaps the simplest and most intuitive level of analysis is that of content, wherein the patient's statements are taken at face value. In this approach, the clinician listens to the semantic meaning of the patient's wording. In the example of Lance Corporal Howe, the statement, "All people disgust me; they'll abandon you the second they get the chance," may indicate that trust in others is the central clinical issue to address in treatment. At the same time, another approach to patient statements is to observe their function. Whereas content-level analysis attempts to understand what a patient's statement means, a functional approach asks instead what a patient's statement does. Said another way, what role or purpose is it serving in how the patient relates to her or his context? In the example, although trust in others may be clinically salient for the patient, by expressing cynicism about others' loyalty, the patient may also be discouraging others from exploring his emotional pain in more depth. Early on in the therapeutic relationship, it is unlikely that the functions of a particular patient's language will become immediately clear to the provider. However, it may be useful for clinicians to make hypotheses regarding the function of language and behaviors that can be tested during therapy to refine case conceptualization. As discussed later, among the most common functions of such behaviors in traumatized populations is experiential avoidance, which may

TABLE 5.1. Comparison of Moral Injury Process Components

Cpl. Ramirez	LCpl. Howe
Chief complaint	
"I don't sleep very well. The nightmares wake me up every night."	"People disgust me; they'll abandon you the second they get the chance."
Psychosocial Information	
Cpl. Ramirez is a 40-year-old married Hispanic woman. She was raised, and also currently resides with her husband and 10-year-old son, in an urban setting. She has served one 10-month combat deployment and is still serving on active duty as a commissioned officer in the Marine Corps. She was raised and still identifies as Roman Catholic and meets the full criteria for PTSD.	LCpl. Howe is a 36-year-old divorced White male veteran living alone in a rural part of the United States. He completed three deployments to Iraq as an enlisted marine, each with high levels of combat exposure. He self-identifies as an atheist and meets the criteria for PTSD and alcohol use disorder.
Process Component 1: Exposure to a Morally Injurious Event	
"When we breached the door, the last thing I expected to see was a boy holding an AK-47. He was terrified. His eyes were so big, and I just froze. I let that kid shoot LCpl. Smith right in front of me. Then LCpl. Howe fired at him, and I watched him die."	"I heard three shots as I came through the door. I saw Smith on the ground and blood coming out of his head, and this kid is standing there, pointing a rifle at me. I didn't even think twice about it. Just squeezed off two rounds, and he dropped to the floor."
Process Component 2: Reactions to a Morally Injurious Event	
"The shame . . . it's always there. I froze. I let him die. What kind of terrible leader lets that happen? I see that little boy everywhere . . . I can't stop crying about it. I just feel like there's this condemnation for me . . . like God is pointing his finger at me . . . at what I did."	"I killed that kid, but I would do it the same way if I had to go back. No question. I know I did the right thing. . . . Still, I replay that moment over and over, and it just pisses me off. We were never supposed to be over there, to begin with. It just makes me think, 'What's the point?'"
Process Component 3: Patient Responses to Moral Reactions	
"I used to go to mass every week and pray all the time, but now I can't stand to set foot inside a church or take out my rosary beads."	"I drink way too much. I know that, but it seems like it's the only way to numb me out. It helps with the anger too. Life's just easier if I've been drinking."
"I have a hard time at work being in command now. It's like I know I'm going to freeze again, so I just avoid taking on responsibilities whenever I can."	"I don't like anyone being in charge of me. I've been failed too many times by people who were supposed to look out for me. Never again."
"The worst part is that I've pulled away from my son. He's 10 now, and I love him, but every time I look at him, I see the face of that Iraqi boy. How do I hold him when he reminds me of something like that?"	"I get really protective of kids now. I don't have any of my own, but if I see a parent being rough with their kid, even strangers in public, I'll go off on them. I punched a guy out once in front of his whole family."

involve avoidance of specific states, such as guilt, shame, helplessness, or aversive memories or thoughts (Hayes et al., 1996).

The task of case conceptualization is made more complex by the manner in which it can unfold across sessions. In most clinical contexts, the patient's chief complaint is typically the first clinical information the clinician receives. It is only later through subsequent assessment and interventions that the full meaning and significance of the patient's chief complaint become evident. This meaning is informed in part by the patient's wider context and personal history. For example, consider the psychosocial information in Table 5.1 for the two marines in our scenario.

Although this information provides additional context, it is not yet clear what clinical significance it might hold for treatment. It is not uncommon that details and implications of the moral injury may initially be omitted or unappreciated by patients and their significance revealed only later as the therapeutic process progresses. Case conceptualization must accordingly be an ongoing process that occurs collaboratively with the patient. Using a general framework can help organize clinical information as it unfolds. Broad case conceptualizations for Corporal Ramirez and Lance Corporal Howe are provided as examples of how to tailor this general framework to particular patients and inform treatment planning.

A PROCESS MODEL OF MORAL INJURY COMPONENTS

One question currently under study is whether there exists a discrete set of clinical indicators that reliably define moral injury as a clinical syndrome. For example, extant research has indicated that individuals exposed to a morally injurious event are more likely to report signs of distress, such as guilt, shame, and anger, and also be diagnosed with additional mental health disorders (Wisco et al., 2017; see also Farnsworth et al., 2014, for a review). Some researchers have even attempted to define syndromes associated with experiencing a morally injurious event (Jinkerson, 2016; MacNair, 2002). This general approach emphasizes defining moral injury by identifying a constellation of behaviors and experiences observed at a given point. In contrast, process-based approaches are more concerned with how behaviors and experiences unfold across time. For example, rather than identifying particular thoughts and emotions as problematic, process-based approaches pay more attention to the behavioral antecedents and consequences surrounding thoughts and emotions and whether those behavioral patterns enhance or detract from the patient's well-being.

It should be emphasized that content-based and process-based approaches, though distinct, are not antagonistic to one another. Rather, process-based approaches require clinical content to observe across time to identify such patterns. Focusing on changes across time can allow for more flexibility in the nature of content that might be identified as part of the clinical pattern being observed. Such flexibility is helpful when approaching moral injury, in that the broad and complex nature of human morality suggests a high degree of variability in thoughts and emotions that may be expressed in individuals following a morally injurious event (Farnsworth et al., 2014). Furthermore, process-based approaches enable clinicians to attend to how a particular behavior or experience might be functioning for a given client, thereby helping to tailor individual case conceptualization. Process-based approaches to understanding moral injury can thus accommodate a range of moral emotions, thoughts, and behaviors while simultaneously informing treatment planning.

Given that research in content-based approaches to moral injury is ongoing, this chapter does not attempt to answer the question of whether there is a distinct syndrome indicative of moral injury. Instead, this chapter focuses on presenting a broad framework for case conceptualization that focuses on the necessary processes involved in the development and maintenance of a moral injury, regardless of the particular form the moral injury takes. This approach is meant to support the key assumption of theoretical inclusivity. It is, therefore, intended that the process components identified in the following sections will be compatible with a broad array of theoretical models and orientations.

Component 1: Exposure to a Potentially Morally Injurious Event

As in PTSD, conceptualizations of moral injury require a precipitating PMIE as an antecedent to subsequent morally injurious reactions. Although there is not a universally accepted definition of morally injurious events, early research indicates the use of lethal force, abusive violence, and betrayals by others are commonly identified precipitants of a moral injury (Drescher et al., 2011). And yet, exposure to such events does not automatically guarantee the development of a moral injury. Recognizing this distinction, Frankfurt and Frazier (2016) recommended morally injurious events be distinguished from any subsequent mental health impacts that these events may trigger for the individual patient.

Assessment for exposure to military-related PMIEs can be assisted by the use of combat-specific self-report scales such as subscales of the Deployment Risk and Resilience Inventory-2 (Vogt et al., 2013) or the Combat Exposure Scale (Keane et al., 1989). Furthermore, the Morally Injurious Events Scale (Nash et al., 2013) and the Moral Injury Questionnaire (MIQ; Currier et al., 2015) both measure self-reported exposure to morally injurious events. The MIQ is particularly helpful for assessing PMIE exposure in that it involves a range of discrete event types to which patients may have been exposed during their military service.

Exposure to PMIEs can also be assessed with interview questions. Given the sensitive nature of PMIEs, the framing of this discussion is critical. Because many patients may perceive stigma related to their PMIE, it can be useful to remember that a trained professional assessing for PMIE exposure in the context of a psychotherapy session provides a sense of safety that is absent when a nonprofessional insensitively asks the patient about these deeply personal experiences. Second, in assessing for PMIEs, it may be helpful for the clinician to consciously use a vocal tone and body language that is both sincere and affectively neutral to avoid implying emotional or moral reactions that the patient might not be experiencing. Third, asking the patient's permission shows respect to them and the subject matter. This can be accomplished through language such as, "War-zone experiences are often life changing and can also be deeply personal. If it's all right, I'd like to ask about some difficult experiences and hard choices that you may have been confronted with. Is that okay?"

It should be acknowledged that permission to explore morally injurious events may be implicit in some clinical contexts, such as part of a formal PTSD assessment or a trauma-focused treatment. Once permission has been granted, the provider can ask direct questions with simple, descriptive language that leaves little room for implied judgment. In my experience, the phrase "violated values" is both descriptive and neutral enough to convey the concept of morally injurious events. Unless introduced first by the patient, morally evocative terms such as "murder," "atrocity," "sin," and "transgression" should be avoided. Morally injurious events can be directly assessed through interview questions such as the following examples. Endorsements of any of these questions should prompt follow-up questions to explore specific details of these events:

- Have you ever done something in the military that seriously violated your values or morals?

- Have you ever seriously injured or taken the life of another person? (Do any of these situations bother you today?)

- Have you ever witnessed something others did that violated your values or morals?

- Have you ever felt that someone else betrayed you in a way that violated your values or morals?

In response to assessment for PMIEs, Corporal Ramirez and Lance Corporal Howe might provide responses such as those included in Table 5.1.

Component 2: Reactions to the Morally Injurious Event

The second component of this case conceptualization framework involves exploring the patient's psychological reactions to the PMIE itself. These reactions include the patient's involuntary appraisals, emotions, behavioral urges, and physical sensations associated with the PMIE. These reactions are the automatic and unconscious product of internal biological and psychological systems that have evolved to respond to morally salient situations. At the level of physiology, neuroscience has documented how regions of the brain can imbue morally salient events, such as the use of lethal force, with negative emotional experiences (Greene, 2013). Building on this evidence, Farnsworth et al. (2014) reviewed the extant research on how different classes of moral emotion may manifest following military trauma. In addition to the presence of painful self-conscious emotions (guilt, shame), other-condemning emotions (anger, contempt, disgust) might also emerge following PMIEs. These emotional reactions are calibrated by the individual's social and historical experiences and operate to a large degree outside a person's direct conscious control.

Reflexive cognitive reactions linked to the initial appraisal of moral wrongness are likely to be present along with moral emotions (Lancaster & Erbes, 2017). These cognitive reactions can include evaluations, judgments, labeling, or the consequences perceived to be attached to these reactions. For example, common examples of morally salient cognitions might include "I'm a monster," "Nothing matters," "I'm unforgivable," or "Others will judge me for this." Such evaluations exist within and reciprocally influence the individual's larger systems of meaning. When a PMIE jeopardizes or violates an individual's core meanings, the resulting loss of coherence and orientation with respect to one's worldview can interfere with the individual's sense of identity, purpose, and bearing in life (Park, 2010).

Although emotional and cognitive moral reactions often create discomfort for the individual, it is important not to pathologize these automatic reactions for at least two reasons. As highlighted in Chapter 2, the first reason is that social–functionalist perspectives of morality have emphasized that moral reactions have evolved to promote community living (Keltner et al., 2006). In these perspectives, moral reactions exist to enhance sociality by preventing selfishness and promoting selflessness (see Chapter 2, this volume). For example, a meta-analytic review by Leach and Cidam (2015) showed that shame, an emotion historically considered by psychology to be damaging, can, under certain situations, be associated with a constructive approach orientation. Likewise, other research indicates that contacting the experience of shame can be an important step in reducing future moral violations (Woodyatt & Wenzel, 2014). Therefore, even painful emotions can serve useful social functions in appropriate contexts.

A second reason against pathologizing moral reactions is that as purely descriptive tools, quantitative scientific methods provide no empirical way to determine the moral correctness of a given thought, emotion, or behavior. Accordingly, there is no scientifically justifiable basis for categorizing moral reactions as "appropriate" or "inappropriate." Rather, these labels themselves constitute moral judgments that reflect culturally and historically rooted social and professional conventions about issues such as responsibility, blame, punishment, and restitution. Although the actual practice of scientific research within psychology is by no means value neutral, the American Psychological Association's (APA's; 2017) *Ethical Principles of Psychologists and Code of Conduct* simultaneously protects against the imposition of clinician values onto the patient. As discussed later, rather than superimposing value judgments that assume a patient's moral reactions are inherently maladaptive, providers can engage in a collaborative dialogue with patients about how involuntary moral reactions relate to therapeutic goals.

Few self-report instruments currently exist to measure moral reactions in the context of military-related moral injury. Some instruments, such as the self-blame subscale of the Posttraumatic Cognitions Inventory (Foa et al., 1999) and the Trauma-Related Guilt Inventory Warzone Version (Kubany et al., 1997), tap moral cognitions about potentially traumatic events. More recent instruments specifically assessing moral reactions to PMIEs include the Expressions of Moral Injury Scale—Military version (EMIS–M; Currier et al., 2018). Clinical interviewing can also be used in assessing these reactions. Such interview questions assume exposure to a PMIE has previously been addressed between the patient and provider. Examples of questions that address moral reactions may include the following:

- When did you first realize that you had changed? How could you tell?
- How did the event change how you see yourself, others, or the world?
- What emotions do you connect to this event?
- When you think back to this event, what do you feel?

Clinical examples of responses from Corporal Ramirez and Lance Corporal Howe to such questions are also included in Table 5.1. Even though both marines were exposed to the same PMIE, the differences in their roles have important implications for their moral reactions to the event. On the one hand, Corporal Ramirez is consumed with shame and the belief that she is responsible for the death of the Iraqi boy. On the other hand, Lance Corporal Howe also takes responsibility for the event but can cognitively justify his choice to shoot the boy. Furthermore, rather than shame, his prominent reactions are anger and moral cynicism.

Component 3: Patient Responses to Moral Reactions

To help distinguish between these automatic moral reactions and the intentional behaviors that patients enact in response to them, Farnsworth et al. (2017) differentiated between moral pain and moral injury (see Introduction). *Moral pain* is defined as the experience of dysphoric moral emotions and cognitions (e.g., self-condemnation) in response to a PMIE. By contrast, Farnsworth et al. reserved the term *moral injury* to refer to expanded social, psychological, and spiritual suffering stemming from costly or unworkable attempts to manage, control, or cope with the experience of moral pain. This distinction helps to prevent unwarranted pathologization of involuntary moral reactions while allowing maladaptive and dysfunctional behaviors to be targeted clinically. Regarding the latter, diversity of human experience makes it impossible to comprehensively describe in one chapter the variety of ways that patients may dysfunctionally respond to their moral pain. However, some prominent patterns of behavior that are likely to emerge in morally injured patients are briefly reviewed next.

Human beings instinctively desire to minimize painful experiences. When faced with moral pain, it is, therefore, common for individuals to engage in strategies to avoid or control their discomfort. Common examples of avoidant behaviors include substance use, social isolation, and various forms of distraction. Although such behaviors can be temporarily effective at reducing discomfort, they often fail to help the individual form adaptive meanings about the morally injurious event and their associated moral responses. Such behaviors can also be costly in terms of the patient's quality of life when applied in a rigid or excessive manner. For example, avoiding moral pain through social isolation increases the likelihood that a morally injured individual will further transgress their values as they move away from important roles and responsibilities to loved ones or neglect personal interests and passions. Avoiding moral pain thus has the potential to become malignant, creating additional value violations beyond that of the original PMIE.

At other times, patients may ruminate on a PMIE and associated moral reactions in an attempt to resolve the discrepancy they experience between their existing schemas and the PMIE. In some cases, patients may rigidly apply their preexisting or revised moral frameworks to themselves or others after a PMIE has occurred. For example, patients with preexisting values of justice or fairness may seek revenge or self-punishment as a way to compensate or atone for the original violation. On experiencing a PMIE and subsequent moral reactions, other patients may consciously enact radical shifts in their moral worldviews. This may manifest as a profound attitude of moral disillusionment or cynicism toward moral ideas and authorities. In this disillusionment, patients may abandon previously held moral practices, such as displays of respect toward others, religious or spiritual practices, or active community participation.

It is, therefore, critical that clinicians assess not only the content of a patient's behavior but also the function or purpose of that behavior. As can be seen in the earlier examples, two individuals may engage in the same behavior (e.g., ceasing religious participation) but for very different reasons. Whereas one patient may stop attendance to religious and community events to avoid experiencing feeling shame or social judgment, another patient may do so as a form of self-punishment or as an expression of moral disillusionment. It is, therefore, important that providers attend to the function of a patient's particular behaviors to inform treatment.

As with moral reactions, there are currently few self-report instruments that specifically assess responses to moral reactions. Some items on the EMIS–M specifically include references to avoidance or maladaptive responses (e.g., "I sometimes feel so bad about things that I did/saw in the military that I hide or withdraw from others"). However, assessing responses to moral reactions can be further clarified through clinical interview. Examples of questions that may help identify responses to moral reactions include the following:

- What do you think it means that you have these [thoughts/emotions]?
- How much do you believe that [moral thought]?
- How have you been dealing with the pain of this event?

- When you feel [moral emotion], what do you typically do?
- What do you think is the purpose of [this behavior]? What does [the behavior] help you to do?

In observing the responses of Corporal Ramirez and Lance Corporal Howe, as described in Table 5.1, it can be observed that although both service members are attempting to manage painful aspects of their moral reactions, they are doing so in notably different ways.

INTERVENTION SELECTION

The primary purpose of clinical case conceptualization is the selection of interventions appropriate to the cultural background and specific features of the patient. Accordingly, the process of assessing PMIE exposure, moral reactions, and behavioral responses should ideally provide clarity to the clinician on the interventions and methods of service delivery that would best fit the data presented by the patient. This outcome assumes that providers are aware of a variety of interventions and their relative strengths and limitations for addressing an array of clinical problems related to moral injury. Hence, the competent selection of interventions requires that providers engage in comparing and matching the characteristics of the patient and the aims and strategies of the intervention.

First and foremost, the selection of treatments for moral injury should follow the principles of shared decision making (Elwyn et al., 2012). In this process, patients are informed of the options for treatment and then invited to take an active role in selecting the intervention that they feel best reflects their beliefs and values, needs, and goals. Taking a primarily supportive role, the clinician provides information and a forthright description of the evidence for different treatment approaches to maximize the patient's ability to exercise informed consent for their treatment. The selection of interventions for moral injury must also be determined in collaboration with the patient's treatment goals. Assessing these goals may be done through such questions as "How would you hope things to be different as a result of doing this work? What do you want to get out of this experience? What are the most important things you want to focus on?" Such questions provide necessary guidance for clinicians to tailor interventions in a way that is meaningful for patients. See Table 5.2 for how Corporal Ramirez and Lance Corporal Howe might have responded to such inquiries.

Mechanisms for therapeutic change in moral injury have only begun to be systematically explored. Accordingly, there is currently little empirical evidence to support one approach over others. However, some conceptual guidance in selecting interventions might be helpful. As noted earlier, moral cognitions can be separated from other types of cognitions in part by their prescriptive focus. That is, prescriptive cognitions generally pertain to moral rules or values salient to the PMIE. At the same time, it must be acknowledged

TABLE 5.2. Examples of Moral Injury Treatment Goals

Cpl. Ramirez	LCpl. Howe
"The guilt and the shame are crushing me. I want to get a handle on it somehow, so I can go to work and be with my family without getting sucked into that day, to be able to enjoy my son and hold him without totally losing it. I don't want to have that day playing over and over in my mind 24/7. I'd like to have more confidence, too—be able to lead people again and not be consumed with worry that someone is going to die while I'm on watch."	"To feel something besides anger. I'm just pissed off all the time, and it seems like I take it out on whoever is around me. I want to stop drinking so much too, just be able to put my deployments behind me and move forward with life, so I can feel like I'm doing something meaningful, for a change."

that prescriptive beliefs are influenced by an individual's descriptive understanding of the PMIE—that is, an understanding of the objective facts and details of the event itself. This interplay between the patient's descriptive and prescriptive beliefs presents an important dynamic that can assist clinicians in selecting and sequencing appropriate interventions for moral injury.

In articulating the descriptive–prescriptive distinction with respect to moral injury, I also distinguished between descriptively oriented and prescriptively oriented interventions (Farnsworth, 2019). *Descriptively oriented interventions* explore the descriptive nature of the event in an effort to provide patients with a more complete and accurate set of facts on which to base moral judgments. Common examples of descriptive techniques can include Socratic dialogue or designing behavioral experiments to help patients test whether negative expectations will be confirmed. These descriptive techniques are well-represented in existing evidence-based psychotherapies for PTSD. Clinicians can introduce these interventions to patients using wording such as the following:

> Often, these events are so painful that we spend a lot of energy trying not to experience the thoughts or feelings connected to them. Unfortunately, when that happens, we sometimes spend so much effort avoiding what the event might mean, that we never look at all the pieces long enough to see other possibilities that may actually fit the event better.

By engaging in descriptively oriented interventions, such as Socratic dialogue or behavioral experiments, new facts may be identified that alter the patient's understanding of the PMIE and shift moral judgments accordingly. For example, after Socratic dialogue, a patient who initially blamed themselves for not foreseeing a PMIE may realize that no one could have reasonably anticipated the event. Thus, descriptively oriented interventions can be powerful tools in helping patients experience significant shifts or reductions in painful moral cognitions and emotions.

In contrast, *prescriptively oriented interventions* explore the moral implications of a PMIE in an effort to support the patient moving toward their valued domains of life. Common examples of prescriptive interventions include values identification, acceptance and forgiveness techniques, and reengaging in value-consistent activities. These interventions can be introduced using wording such as the following:

> Sometimes, even after looking at the event from a new perspective, you may still feel like there was something that violated your values and continues to cause you pain. In that case, we can focus on what value was violated for you and what you want that to mean for you going forward.

Notably, prescriptive interventions are not designed to alter a patient's understanding of the event itself but rather assume a present-centered stance in their attempts to help patients move forward in the face of the PMIE's reality.

In reviewing the clinical data for Corporal Ramirez and Lance Corporal Howe, it can be observed that their presentations may call for different degrees of descriptively and prescriptively oriented interventions. Corporal Ramirez's beliefs that she let the boy die and that she is an awful leader and a terrible mother all present opportunities for a descriptive intervention. In particular, given the degree of avoidance she appears to be exhibiting, a clinician might rightly question whether she has fully explored all facts of the event and so might be over- or underemphasizing important details. Such an approach may help her contextualize the event itself as well as her subsequent struggles. Moreover, Corporal Ramirez's explicit description of her religious faith as an important part of her identity and recovery suggests that incorporating some form of spiritually integrated intervention (i.e., Vieten et al., 2016; chaplaincy) may also be beneficial (see Chapters 3 and 13, this volume). Such spiritual interventions may implement prescriptively oriented interventions to supplement the descriptive interventions previously discussed for Corporal Ramirez.

In contrast, Lance Corporal Howe's clinical presentation suggests a relative absence of targets for descriptive intervention. Although Lance Corporal Howe reported moral distress related to his PMIE, assessment of his clinical picture revealed no obvious indications of distorted thinking or exaggerated blame regarding the event itself. Rather, the patient reported a sense of social isolation, emotional avoidance, and costly behaviors related to his value of protecting children. Given the absence of clear targets for descriptive interventions, it may be more clinically indicated for Lance Corporal Howe to focus instead on prescriptively oriented tasks of constructing adaptive meanings for his moral pain, identifying his values, and exploring the most effective ways to enact them going forward. His statements suggest that in addition to treating moral injury, Lance Corporal Howe may benefit from the treatment of his problematic alcohol use.

Although it is helpful in distinguishing categories of therapeutic tasks for moral injury, clinicians should take care not to apply the descriptive–prescriptive distinction too rigidly. Because psychotherapy is often a non-linear process, there will likely be an ongoing interplay between descriptive and prescriptive elements throughout treatment. Neither the patient nor the provider can assess during their first meeting what additional insights or information will be uncovered during treatment and how these will, in turn, impact the patient's moral reactions to the PMIE. For example, it is not unusual for a patient to revise goals over the course of treatment, and providers must likewise be ready to assess and revise their case conceptualization to accommodate new clinical data.

Finally, although it is beyond the scope of this chapter to discuss in detail, it can be noted this discussion of moral injury only acknowledged the negative ways in which moral injury can impact patients. However, separation of moral reactions from the individual's responses to those reactions allows for the possibility that some individuals may respond constructively toward their moral pain. For example, experiencing the pain of moral violations may lead some individuals to reassert their commitment to their moral values and standards. Hence, in parallel to the concept of posttraumatic growth, this process-component model also allows for strengths-based assessments of patient resilience and values in the face of PMIEs. Exploration of such constructive responses is an area that awaits further empirical investigation because it may reveal important dimensions of moral resilience and coping for military service members.

CONCLUSION

Case conceptualization involves going from the general to the specific. The clinician enters the professional relationship with a general set of skills and knowledge that are then applied to patients' particular worldviews and chief complaints to help patients move toward their goals. In the case of moral injury, this chapter attempted to provide a process-based framework that clinicians can use to inform and structure treatment planning, including the selection of specific evidence-informed interventions. Although moral injury has been argued to be as old as humanity itself (see Introduction, this volume), the scientific and clinical study of the construct remains in its infancy. Therefore, the framework presented here presents a general approach to case conceptualization for moral injury to which future evidence is likely to add important insights.

REFERENCES

American Psychiatric Association. (2013). *Diagnostic and statistical manual of mental disorders* (5th ed.). https://doi.org/10.1176/appi.books.9780890425596

American Psychological Association. (2017). *Ethical principles of psychologists and code of conduct* (2002, amended effective June 1, 2010, and January 1, 2017). https://www.apa.org/ethics/code/index.aspx

Armour, C., Tsai, J., Durham, T. A., Charak, R., Biehn, T. L., Elhai, J. D., & Pietrzak, R. H. (2015). Dimensional structure of *DSM–5* posttraumatic stress symptoms: Support for a hybrid Anhedonia and Externalizing Behaviors model. *Journal of Psychiatric Research, 61*, 106–113. https://doi.org/10.1016/j.jpsychires.2014.10.012

Bryan, C. J., Bryan, A. O., Roberge, E., Leifker, F. R., & Rozek, D. C. (2018). Moral injury, posttraumatic stress disorder, and suicidal behavior among National Guard personnel. *Psychological Trauma: Theory, Research, Practice, and Policy, 10*(1), 36–45. https://doi.org/10.1037/tra0000290

Currier, J. M., Farnsworth, J. K., Drescher, K. D., McDermott, R. C., Sims, B. M., & Albright, D. L. (2018). Development and evaluation of the Expressions of Moral Injury Scale—Military version. *Clinical Psychology & Psychotherapy, 25*(3), 474–488. https://doi.org/10.1002/cpp.2170

Currier, J. M., Holland, J. M., Drescher, K., & Foy, D. (2015). Initial psychometric evaluation of the Moral Injury Questionnaire—Military version. *Clinical Psychology & Psychotherapy, 22*(1), 54–63. https://doi.org/10.1002/cpp.1866

Currier, J. M., Holland, J. M., Jones, H. W., & Sheu, S. (2014). Involvement in abusive violence among Vietnam veterans: Direct and indirect associations with substance abuse problems and suicidality. *Psychological Trauma: Theory, Research, Practice, and Policy, 6*(1), 73–82. https://doi.org/10.1037/a0032973

Currier, J. M., McDermott, R. C., Farnsworth, J. K., & Borges, L. M. (2019). Temporal associations between moral injury and PTSD symptom clusters in military veterans. *Journal of Traumatic Stress, 32*(3), 382–392. https://doi.org/10.1002/jts.22367

Drescher, K. D., Foy, D. W., Kelly, C., Leshner, A., Schutz, K., & Litz, B. (2011). An exploration of the viability and usefulness of the construct of moral injury in war veterans. *Traumatology, 17*(1), 8–13. https://doi.org/10.1177/1534765610395615

Elwyn, G., Frosch, D., Thomson, R., Joseph-Williams, N., Lloyd, A., Kinnersley, P., Cording, E., Tomson, D., Dodd, C., Rollnick, S., Edwards, A., & Barry, M. (2012). Shared decision making: A model for clinical practice. *Journal of General Internal Medicine, 27*(10), 1361–1367. https://doi.org/10.1007/s11606-012-2077-6

Farnsworth, J. K. (2019). Is and ought: Descriptive and prescriptive cognitions in military-related moral injury. *Journal of Traumatic Stress, 32*, 373–381. https://doi.org/10.1002/jts.22356

Farnsworth, J. K., Drescher, K. D., Evans, W., & Walser, R. D. (2017). A functional approach to understanding and treating military-related moral injury. *Journal of Contextual Behavioral Science, 6*(4), 391–397. https://doi.org/10.1016/j.jcbs.2017.07.003

Farnsworth, J. K., Drescher, K. D., Nieuwsma, J. A., Walser, R. B., & Currier, J. M. (2014). The role of moral emotions in military trauma: Implications for the study and treatment of moral injury. *Review of General Psychology, 18*(4), 249–262. https://doi.org/10.1037/gpr0000018

Foa, E. B., Ehlers, A., Clark, D. M., Tolin, D. F., & Orsillo, S. M. (1999). The posttraumatic cognitions inventory (PTCI): Development and validation. *Psychological Assessment, 11*(3), 303–314. https://doi.org/10.1037/1040-3590.11.3.303

Frankfurt, S., & Frazier, P. (2016). A review of research on moral injury in combat veterans. *Military Psychology, 28*(5), 318–330. https://doi.org/10.1037/mil0000132

Friedman, M. J., Resick, P. A., Bryant, R. A., & Brewin, C. R. (2011). Considering PTSD for *DSM–5*. *Depression and Anxiety, 28*(9), 750–769. https://doi.org/10.1002/da.20767

Greene, J. D. (2013). *Moral tribes: Emotion, reason, and the gap between us and them.* Penguin.

Hayes, S. C., Wilson, K. G., Gifford, E. V., Follette, V. M., & Strosahl, K. (1996). Experimental avoidance and behavioral disorders: A functional dimensional approach to diagnosis and treatment. *Journal of Consulting and Clinical Psychology, 64*(6), 1152–1168. https://doi.org/10.1037/0022-006X.64.6.1152

Jinkerson, J. D. (2016). Defining and assessing moral injury: A syndrome perspective. *Traumatology, 22*(2), 122–130. https://doi.org/10.1037/trm0000069

Jordan, A. H., Eisen, E., Bolton, E., Nash, W. P., & Litz, B. T. (2017). Distinguishing war-related PTSD resulting from perpetration- and betrayal-based morally injurious events. *Psychological Trauma: Theory, Research, Practice, and Policy, 9*(6), 627–634. https://doi.org/10.1037/tra0000249

Keane, T. M., Fairbank, J. A., Caddell, J. M., Zimering, R. T., Taylor, K. L., & Mora, C. A. (1989). Clinical evaluation of a measure to assess combat exposure. *Psychological Assessment, 1*(1), 53–55. https://doi.org/10.1037/1040-3590.1.1.53

Keltner, D., Haidt, J., & Shiota, M. N. (2006). Social functionalism and the evolution of emotions. In M. Schaller, J. A. Simpson, & D. T. Kenrick (Eds.), *Evolution and social psychology* (pp. 115–142). Psychology Press.

Kubany, E. S., Abueg, F. R., Kilauano, W. L., Manke, F. P., & Kaplan, A. S. (1997). Development and validation of the Sources of Trauma-Related Guilt Survey—War-Zone Version. *Journal of Traumatic Stress, 10*(2), 235–258. https://doi.org/10.1002/jts.2490100206

Lancaster, S. L., & Erbes, C. R. (2017). Importance of moral appraisals in military veterans. *Traumatology, 23*(4), 317–322. https://doi.org/10.1037/trm0000123

Leach, C. W., & Cidam, A. (2015). When is shame linked to constructive approach orientation? A meta-analysis. *Journal of Personality and Social Psychology, 109*(6), 983–1002. https://doi.org/10.1037/pspa0000037

Litz, B. T., Stein, N., Delaney, E., Lebowitz, L., Nash, W. P., Silva, C., & Maguen, S. (2009). Moral injury and moral repair in war veterans: A preliminary model and intervention strategy. *Clinical Psychology Review, 29*(8), 695–706. https://doi.org/10.1016/j.cpr.2009.07.003

Maguen, S., Lucenko, B. A., Reger, M. A., Gahm, G. A., Litz, B. T., Seal, K. H., Knight, S. J., & Marmar, C. R. (2010). The impact of reported direct and indirect killing on mental health symptoms in Iraq war veterans. *Journal of Traumatic Stress, 23*(1), 86–90. https://doi.org/10.1002/jts.20434

Maguen, S., Metzler, T. J., Bosch, J., Marmar, C. R., Knight, S. J., & Neylan, T. C. (2012). Killing in combat may be independently associated with suicidal ideation. *Depression and Anxiety, 29*(11), 918–923. https://doi.org/10.1002/da.21954

MacNair, R. M. (2002). Perpetration-induced traumatic stress in combat veterans. *Journal of Peace Psychology, 8*(1), 63–72. https://doi.org/10.1207/S15327949PAC0801_6

Nash, W. P., Marino Carper, T. L., Mills, M. A., Au, T., Goldsmith, A., & Litz, B. T. (2013). Psychometric evaluation of the Moral Injury Events Scale. *Military Medicine, 178*(6), 646–652. https://doi.org/10.7205/MILMED-D-13-00017

Park, C. L. (2010). Making sense of the meaning literature: An integrative review of meaning making and its effects on adjustment to stressful life events. *Psychological Bulletin, 136*(2), 257–301. https://doi.org/10.1037/a0018301

Vieten, C., Scammell, S., Pierce, A., Pilato, R., Ammondson, I., Pargament, K. I., & Lukoff, D. (2016). Competencies for psychologists in the domains of religion and spirituality. *Spirituality in Clinical Practice, 3*(2), 92–114. https://doi.org/10.1037/scp0000078

Vogt, D., Smith, B. N., King, L. A., King, D. W., Knight, J., & Vasterling, J. J. (2013). Deployment Risk and Resilience Inventory–2 (DRRI-2): An updated tool for assessing psychosocial risk and resilience factors among service members and veterans. *Journal of Traumatic Stress, 26*(6), 710–717. https://doi.org/10.1002/jts.21868

Wisco, B. E., Marx, B. P., May, C. L., Martini, B., Krystal, J. H., Southwick, S. M., & Pietrzak, R. H. (2017). Moral injury in U.S. combat veterans: Results from the National Health and Resilience in Veterans Study. *Depression and Anxiety, 34*(4), 340–347. https://doi.org/10.1002/da.22614

Woodyatt, L., & Wenzel, M. (2014). A needs-based perspective on self-forgiveness: Addressing threat to moral identity as a means of encouraging interpersonal and intrapersonal restoration. *Journal of Experimental Social Psychology, 50*, 125–135. https://doi.org/10.1016/j.jesp.2013.09.012

6

Clinician Issues in Treating Moral Injury

Brian J. Klassen, Michael B. Brennan, and Philip Held

In comparison with the application of existing and novel treatments for moral injury–based distress, the therapeutic relationship has received far less attention. This is an unfortunate oversight because, as many readers will be aware, there is a sizable body of literature that shows that the therapeutic relationship has at least an equal, if not greater, contribution to clinical outcomes as specific therapeutic techniques (Flückiger et al., 2018; Norcross, 2002). Given the important role of the therapeutic relationship across patient populations, presenting problems, and therapeutic modalities, the relationship between therapist and patient may well be an essential consideration in work with moral injury–based distress among military service members and veterans (SM/Vs).

A comprehensive review of the decades of empirical work on therapist factors and therapeutic relationship variables that influence psychotherapy outcome is outside the scope of this chapter. Instead, we highlight, from our experience, the specific aspects of the therapeutic relationship that may be most pertinent to clinical work with morally injured SM/Vs. We hope that this chapter will not only function as a conceptual foundation to guide clinician reflection on the various contours of the therapeutic relationship with morally injured service SM/Vs but also encourage theoretical and empirical work on moral injury and the therapeutic relationship. To that end, we review the therapeutic alliance, military culture, and therapist stuck points as they relate to the effective treatment of moral injury–based distress in military populations. Because this literature is sparse or nonexistent, we attempt to

https://doi.org/10.1037/0000204-007
Addressing Moral Injury in Clinical Practice, J. M. Currier, K. D. Drescher, and J. Nieuwsma (Editors)

blend knowledge from relevant empirical studies with our clinical observations from active practice with SM/Vs.

THERAPEUTIC ALLIANCE IN TREATING MORAL INJURY–BASED DISTRESS

Bordin (1979) defined the *therapeutic alliance* as a dynamic interpersonal process between a therapist and patient that consists of three components: (a) agreement on the goals of therapy (i.e., what therapy is supposed to accomplish), (b) agreement on the tasks of therapy (i.e., the actual content of what is discussed in session and how it is addressed), and (c) the quality of the emotional bond between the therapist and patient (i.e., whether the therapist and patient like and respect each other and whether the patient perceives the therapist's empathy and nonjudgmental acceptance). In the following subsections, we delineate each component of Bordin's conceptualization of the therapeutic alliance and provide examples of how these concepts might apply to clinical practice with SM/Vs with moral injury–based distress.

Agreement on Goals

In our experience, SM/Vs typically do not come to therapy with an explicit request to process morally injurious events; rather, presenting complaints often focus on typical concerns for military-connected populations, such as posttraumatic stress disorder (PTSD) or depression or broader symptoms such as poor sleep, anger, and social alienation, among others. Only through careful assessment and case formulation (see Chapter 5, this volume) can a therapist and SM/V collaboratively understand the potential impact of morally injurious events on their presenting issues. Treatment goals in psychotherapy frequently shift, however, so therapists may have to occasionally reorient the patient to the focus of therapy (or at least what the therapist thinks it is) and solicit feedback from the patient. In our experience, these brief moments in sessions may provide opportunities to shift the conversational focus toward morally injurious events, if so indicated by the therapist's case conceptualization.

On this point, a 29-year-old U.S. Marine Corps veteran with a combat deployment to Iraq came to therapy because his explosive anger was frightening his spouse. On intake, he was quite guarded about his deployment experiences, saying, "I killed someone with my bare hands. Is that what you want to know? I've never talked with anybody about this stuff before, and I don't see how it is relevant." He was more interested in the here-and-now concerns in his marriage, so the veteran and his therapist collaboratively decided on two treatment goals: (a) establishing safety in the veteran's marital relationship through the use of time-outs and distress tolerance skills and (b) focusing on better understanding his problem through regular functional analysis of conflict with his spouse that had occurred throughout the week. After three sessions, the veteran reported that the frequency and intensity of the arguments had decreased, so the therapist initiated the following discussion:

THERAPIST: So, it seems like we've done some good work on reducing the arguments you have with your spouse. I'm curious about something, though.

VETERAN: What?

THERAPIST: Well, I don't know that much about your combat experiences, but I've seen how those things can really stay with somebody and affect their current relationships. Since things seem to be doing better, I wonder if now is the time to talk more about what you went through on your deployment.

VETERAN: Yeah. . . . (sighs). . . . You're making sense.

THERAPIST: Okay. Seems like we could keep talking about different things to try in your relationship, or we could switch gears for a few sessions and see if processing thoughts and emotions associated with your combat experiences can further reduce your anger. What would you think of making that a treatment goal?

In sum, goal consensus can provide a means of initial engagement for an SM/V with a history of morally injurious events. As shown in nonveteran studies, successful goal consensus is inversely related to premature dropout and therapeutic deterioration (Saxon et al., 2017). Although the early stages of therapy may not ostensibly focus on moral injury, it is important that therapists be prepared to reorient their patients to the purpose of therapy and provide opportunities to make moral injury a more explicit focus, if clinically indicated. For instance, although the veteran in the example was certainly experiencing a moral injury, the therapist collaboratively joined with him to first target conflict in his marital relationship before raising the possible benefit of processing morally injurious events.

Agreement on Tasks

Reaching agreement on the tasks of therapy is a complex process that assumes agreement on the goals of therapy. Even if the processing of thoughts and emotions related to morally injurious events is a treatment goal, we have observed that the actual way that therapy proceeds may vary, depending on the SM/V's stage of change (cf. Prochaska & Norcross, 2002). As readers may be aware, *stages of change* refers to a nonlinear, stage-based process that individuals undertake when attempting to affect a lasting behavior change. Each stage varies according to an individual's awareness of a problem and commitment to work on the problem. For example, a patient in the precontemplation stage may have sought treatment at the insistence of others with little motivation to engage in therapy, whereas someone in the action stage could be quite insightful about the problem and its negative impacts on his or her life and feel eager for advice and guidance on how to change.

Although stages of change have not been specifically examined among SM/Vs presenting for treatment of moral injury–related distress, Prochaska and Norcross (2002) estimated that across a broad array of mental health conditions, individuals in the action stage (i.e., ready and willing to begin focused work on changing their problems) make up only 10% to 20% of cases. In contrast, individuals in the contemplation stage (i.e., aware they have problems but not committed to a specific plan of change) make up 30% to 40% of individuals, and those in the precontemplation stage (i.e., not aware they have problems) are estimated to be 50% to 60% of individuals. So, although therapists who work with moral injury–based distress in SM/Vs have to be well-versed in action-oriented, change-focused therapies, it is also likely that many patients with moral injury–based distress may need an approach that focuses on building motivation for change, as well as clarity about why behavior change may be needed.

Disagreement regarding the goals and tasks of treatment between patients and clinicians is commonplace (between 37.5% and 46.8% of the time in one study), especially among trauma survivors; however, productively resolving these disagreements might promote improved outcomes (Haugen et al., 2017). This dynamic may well prove to be the case with morally distressed SM/Vs as well. Another major clinical application when considering agreement on tasks is that the choice of treatment methods cannot be the sole decision of the therapist; rather, the therapist has a responsibility to fairly explain the treatment options available to the patient and any available research to support the use of certain treatments (e.g., effectiveness research). The therapist should then help the patient decide which approach is best for them, given their stage of change and life circumstances.

Therapist–Patient Bond

Although the bond between the therapist and patient is a critical component of the therapeutic alliance, it may be particularly challenging during therapy for moral injury–based distress. As discussed elsewhere, the constellation of moral injury sequelae includes barriers to the kind of vulnerable relationship that is often needed in psychotherapy, such as loss of trust, guilt, anger, and shame (Farnsworth et al., 2014; Litz et al., 2009). In our view, approaching the therapeutic relationship through an emphasis on shared goals and tasks probably helps build the necessary rapport between the SM/V and therapist. As Bordin (1979) conceptualized the alliance, however, the quality of the affective bond between the patient and therapist is also critical.

In facilitating a therapeutic bond, therapists have to be aware of the pressure on SM/Vs to stay silent about morally injurious events. In some cases, this pressure may be because some patients believe that they have been involved in war crimes, and they may not disclose these events out of concern for legal consequences. In other cases, patients may worry that the events are so traumatic or morally complicated that disclosing them will negatively affect the therapist. For example, one veteran who struggled with guilt because he used black humor to cope with processing human remains after a mortar explosion explained how he rejected what seemed like genuine expressions of concern from his peers. He described the desire—which is generally present among those in military leadership positions—to protect others and not appear weak:

> Nobody wanted to show signs of weakness, so we didn't talk about things and just moved on. Once people found out what I was doing [processing human remains], a couple of them came over to me and were like "hey man, you ok? What happened?" I was not ready, so I told them "naw, man, it's not as bad as you would have thought," so I kind of protected myself through protecting them. (Held, Klassen, Hall, et al., 2018, p. 5)

Although this veteran initially protected his peers by stating the situation was not as gruesome as people feared, later on in treatment, this individual also attempted to protect the therapist from some of the gruesome details. This dynamic only became apparent after he disclosed to his therapist that he had "held back" on the description of the event.

Empathy may be essential in working with SM/Vs with moral injury–based distress for several reasons. First, therapist empathy is important, regardless of the type of psychotherapy (Bohart et al., 2002). Second, empathy facilitates a number of basic conditions in the therapeutic relationship. For example, patients who feel understood are much less likely to prematurely drop out of treatment (Saxon et al., 2017). Although this has not been empirically confirmed to our knowledge, early termination of therapy or frequent missed appointments and no-shows may be a primary concern for those with moral injury, given the common role of avoidance-based coping and the frequency of isolation and social alienation (Litz et al., 2009). A crucial function of empathy is to check the understanding of the therapist so that the patient's concerns are understood appropriately. In other words, empathy facilitates the accurate perception of a patient's therapeutic goals and the tasks they are willing to undergo in therapy. As highlighted in the following exchange with an army medic with a number of combat deployments to Iraq, collaboration on goals and tasks of therapy may build the necessary trust to move therapy forward with a morally injured SM/V:

VETERAN: I just sit and wonder sometimes what my friends who were never in the military think about. What are their biggest regrets? What do they worry about?

THERAPIST: You feel so distant from them at times.

VETERAN: Yeah, exactly. That's why I feel like I have no one to talk to.

THERAPIST: Sounds like you wish you were more connected to the people around you.

VETERAN: Yes.

THERAPIST: What if we made that a treatment goal? We could try and figure out what the barriers are, and we could work on strategies
on how to feel closer with your family and friends.

Third, it has been argued that empathy felt from the therapist may assist
some patients in developing a sense of understanding and compassion for
themselves (Greenberg & Paivio, 2003), which is often needed in morally
injured patients who struggle with self-blame and negative beliefs about
themselves (Held et al., 2017). Empathy from the therapist may also deepen
the patient's experience of adaptive primary emotions (e.g., sadness, fear) by
gently guiding them toward these experiences and giving them language to
articulate their emotional experiences, making it feel safer to experience these
avoided emotions. In the following example, the therapist uses empathy to
make a conjecture about the veteran's understanding of a morally injurious
event, thereby broadening the veteran's experience of the event:

VETERAN: What bothers me most is that the patrol should have never
happened! The only reason we went outside the wire that day
and the only reason my buddy died was so that our captain
could put in for his combat action badge.

THERAPIST: You haven't said this yet, but I wonder . . . it almost sounds like
you feel betrayed by your captain for sending you out.

VETERAN: That's what it is! They were supposed to take care of us.

THERAPIST: But you feel that they didn't and that they only cared about
their careers.

VETERAN: Damn right! [*Expression of primary anger*]

THERAPIST: It sounds like you have a lot of built-up anger over this.

In the following example, an officer is guided, through the use of therapist
empathy, to acknowledge the primary emotion of sadness at the loss of a dear
friend to an improvised explosive device while in a convoy under his command. Before this exchange, this individual described his emotional experience only in terms of anger or numbness about the event:

VETERAN: I don't know what you want from me! The patrol had to go out.
I needed somebody in that seat. That means somebody had to
die that day. War sucks! It isn't fun. If it wasn't him, it would
have been someone else.

THERAPIST: I hear you. You're saying you did everything by the book.
Everything was done to a very high standard. That's absolutely
the kind of leader you are. If I may . . . it seems to me that
you're not feeling guilty so much as sad that you lost someone you cared a lot about. And, to have lost him like that, so
suddenly and violently . . . well, it makes the loss all the more
painful.

VETERAN: (Softening) Yes, it does. (Silence) You know what kills me? I've been to so many funerals . . . more than I could count. But, I didn't go to his . . . I just couldn't bear it.

Last, empathic understanding from the therapist may help SM/Vs access different ways of thinking about themselves and their experiences, which is particularly important when dealing with shame (Greenberg & Paivio, 2003). Empathic reflections from the therapist may give the patient a slightly different view into a situation or give them a new label for their experience in a way that invites further exploration and reflection. In other words, accurate empathy may help a patient bypass avoidance, which has been understood as a maintaining factor in moral injury (Litz et al., 2009). In the following example, the therapist uses empathic reflections to broaden the veteran's understanding of his feelings of disgust and to foster some curiosity about their origin. Fostering curiosity about the origin of the veteran's feelings of disgust may be one way to bypass a tendency to avoid and not reflect on those reactions.

VETERAN: Sometimes, when my wife looks at me lovingly, I feel disgusting inside, you know?

THERAPIST: Like you don't deserve her?

VETERAN: Yeah! That's exactly where my brain goes.

THERAPIST: That's interesting because you both seem to really care about each other. I wonder: Where do you think those beliefs came from?

In summary, a sense that one is listened to and understood may foster safety and warmth in connection to the therapist that may lead to additional depth of disclosure. Maintaining a relationship that facilitates disclosure of painful memories and emotions is critical, given the lengths SM/Vs can go to avoid sharing some morally injurious events with others for fear of judgment (Held, Klassen, Hall, et al., 2018). Others have found the sense of safety and warmth may also serve as a precondition for patients agreeing to more challenging (and, thus, growth-producing) forms of therapeutic work, such as exposure therapy (Hundt et al., 2015). Drawing on the discussion of stages of change earlier in this chapter, empathic understanding of the SM/V may also ensure that interventions selected by the therapist are the most appropriate fit, given the motivations and presenting concerns of the patient. For example, this therapist accurately reflects the desperation for relief the veteran feels and pairs this reflection with a more intensive treatment recommendation:

VETERAN: I'm so fucking sick of feeling like this! I feel stuck. Why can't I move past this?

THERAPIST: You're willing to do whatever it takes to feel better.

VETERAN: Yeah. I've got shit to do. I can't waste any more time cooped up at home.

THERAPIST: Maybe it's time to revisit our plan for more intensive work on the guilt you feel about the lives you took in combat.

KNOWLEDGE OF MILITARY CULTURE AND ITS ROLE IN MORAL INJURY TREATMENT

Just as cultural competence is an important pillar of ethical mental health practice, we have found that detailed knowledge of military customs, ethics, and norms on the part of the provider can help SM/Vs engage in the demanding work of resolving moral injury (Held, Klassen, Hall, et al., 2018). Specifically, in the United States, there is a widening gap between civilian and military populations. For example, an estimated 7.7% of the general public has served in the military (U.S. Census Bureau, 2017), with less than 1% currently serving on active duty (U.S. Census Bureau, 2000). The gap between civilian and military populations may contribute to stigma, misperceptions, and lack of trust, which can also negatively affect the therapeutic relationship.

Knowledge of various operational procedures, such as concept of operations brief, rules of engagement (ROE), and after-action reviews, can provide rich contextual information for further processing morally injurious events. When morally injurious events take place, they never occur in a vacuum. In military operations, there is always a chain of command, peers, and a mission to consider in addition to the thoughts and actions of any one individual. While on an operation, military personnel are governed by the ROEs, which provide guidance on how military personnel are to conduct themselves with enemy forces. ROEs are context dependent, and they try to distill many competing interests (e.g., the safety of military personnel, diplomatic goals). For example, ROEs during the beginning of the Iraq war differed vastly from the ROEs that are in place for combat operations in Iraq today; some veterans have described to us operating in situations with poorly defined ROEs (e.g., Iraq, 2003, during the initial invasion) versus situations with strict ROEs (e.g., Iraq in 2011). It is important for providers to have a general idea of what the ROEs were for the specific morally injurious situations that are being worked on in therapy. If specific ROEs appear to have played a role in the morally injurious events discussed during therapy, and the provider is unsure of the specific ROEs at that time, it may be helpful to directly ask the SM/V to understand better what rules they were operating under and how these rules might have influenced their behavior, as well as the behavior of their team.

THERAPIST USE OF EFFECTIVE TREATMENT AND ATTITUDES TOWARD MORAL INJURY

Therapists' knowledge of and willingness to use existing evidence-based trauma-focused treatments with morally injured SM/Vs when indicated is also worth attention. Although there are no specific guidelines for the treatment of distress resulting from morally injurious situations, several existing evidence-based trauma-focused psychological treatments have been shown to be effective for veterans affected by a potential moral injury (e.g., Held, Klassen, Brennan, & Zalta, 2018, Smith et al., 2013; Wachen et al., 2017). Many of these treatments are described in the following chapters of this book.

Some providers may hold beliefs that interfere with the effective treatment of moral injury–based distress. These beliefs are similar to maladaptive beliefs our patients hold that may drive their symptoms and interfere with functioning. Following Resick et al. (2017), we refer to the treatment-interfering beliefs providers hold as *therapist stuck points*. In the following subsections, we discuss several therapist stuck points that have arisen during self-reflection on our sessions, as well as discussions with our trainees. In addition to highlighting how therapist stuck points can interfere with the therapeutic relationship, we provide suggestions for therapists and supervisors on how to begin to challenge these beliefs.

Therapist Stuck Point 1: "All Veterans and Service Members Have Moral Injury"

A myth among some mental health service providers may be that all SM/Vs must have experienced some degree of moral injury that contributes in some way to their current problems. This belief is at odds with the currently available empirical literature, however. Wisco and colleagues (2017) found that a significant minority of a nationally representative sample of combat veterans endorsed a history of morally injurious events (10.8%–25.0%, depending on the nature of the perceived transgression). These rates may be much higher among treatment-seeking veterans (Held et al., 2019), but even in a highly distressed clinical sample, a significant number of veterans do not endorse morally injurious events.

Furthermore, it is implicit in the current theoretical model of moral injury (Litz et al., 2009) that exposure to morally injurious events does not always equate to distress or impairment; this conceptualization of moral injury has also been supported by empirical research showing a mediating role for meaning making (Currier et al., 2015), negative posttraumatic cognitions (Held et al., 2017), and religious and spiritual struggles (Evans et al., 2018). Some important questions therapists might ask themselves to address this stuck point are "What are my reasons for believing this patient has experienced a moral injury?" and "Have I properly drawn a connection between a morally injurious event and this individual's current symptoms?"

Therapist Stuck Point 2: "My Patient Has Done Something Morally Wrong; They Should Feel Guilty"

Guilt is a core experience of moral injury (Litz et al., 2009). In most cases, the guilt is associated with actions or inactions that led to negative consequences (e.g., feeling guilty for shooting a noncombatant). Trying to reevaluate or "right size" an individual's guilt is not the same as treating all guilt or shame as pathological (Finlay, 2015). On the contrary, feelings of guilt are a natural response to these circumstances, and guilt can ensure that individuals will not repeat the same negative actions. In some circumstances, however, many clinicians may believe the patient "should feel guilty." Although it is generally true that guilt is an appropriate response to morally injurious events, it is still important for the therapist to attempt to evaluate the magnitude of the guilt objectively and how and to whom the veteran or service member assigns blame. Guilt and blame are appropriate and functional as long as the patient can consider what they truly are responsible for. Often, patients assign excessive blame to themselves without fully considering the context in which the morally injurious event occurred.

As therapists, it is important to go into these clinical encounters as unbiased as possible and help the patient explore what they believe they or others have done wrong. In turn, patients may need support to determine whether the assignment of blame is truly warranted or may have resulted from ignoring important parts of the situation (e.g., it may not have been immediately clear that the individual was a noncombatant). A question therapists can ask themselves when noticing beliefs similar to the previous one is, "What important aspects of the situation is my patient taking the blame for that may not have been apparent at the time or that he or she may not be to blame for after all?"

Therapist Stuck Point 3: "My Patient Should Have Known What They Were Signing up for"

Unfortunately, we hear that patients "should have known what they were signing up for" more often than we would like, especially from providers who do not frequently work with individuals who have served in the U.S. Armed Forces. Although individuals may know the potential risks and received substantial training, morally complex situations are often vastly different than training scenarios (Grossman, 2009). Describing the moment of his moral injury, an Iraq combat veteran remarked to us

> No matter how much training you do leading up to that, it just never prepares you for when, like, it actually happens. You are kind of in a daze about it. Almost like you are seeing it, but you cannot believe it is happening. (Held, Klassen, Hall, et al., 2018; p. 5)

Like the therapist stuck point discussed previously, it is critical to understand why a particular situation involving a transgression is bothersome to the individual and be mindful to avoid making assumptions and conceptual leaps about why they are distressed. For example, we have worked with individuals who took several lives and seemed to have successfully integrated these experiences into their belief systems (e.g., "I had to take life to protect my friends"). Yet, despite taking many lives, there may be some incidents that continue to haunt an individual for various reasons (e.g., a situation did not go according to plan). Thus, it is important for therapists to recognize that just because someone signed up for the U.S. Armed Forces and received training, they may not have been prepared for situations they encountered. A helpful question for therapists to ask themselves to begin challenging their own stuck point could be, "What experiences may be associated with moral distress, despite years of training?" We have found reading veterans' accounts of their experiences helpful in this regard (e.g., Klay, 2014).

Therapist Stuck Point 4: "Existing Evidence-Based Treatments Are not Effective for Moral Injury"

The belief that existing evidence-based treatments are not effective for moral injury may lead to some confusion about how to choose the best treatment. No published study to date has conclusively shown that moral injury–based distress cannot be effectively addressed using existing treatments. Further, there is evidence suggesting that symptoms commonly associated with moral injury (e.g., guilt, shame) and overlapping disorders (e.g., PTSD and depressive disorders) can be addressed effectively by the treatments outlined in earlier chapters of this book. Although it can be challenging to apply existing treatments to moral injury, it is not impossible, and research has shown they can be effective (Held, Klassen, Brennan, & Zalta, 2018). Therapists can challenge this stuck point by asking themselves, "What studies or literature conclusively support the belief that existing treatments are not effective for moral injury?" In so doing, it is also important for therapists to continue to consult existing treatment guidelines and seek the support of colleagues and experts in the field.

When considering the formation of a therapeutic alliance, it is also possible that the current use of an evidence-based treatment may not correspond to the patient's identified goals at the time. This mismatch is not evidence for the therapy's lack of effectiveness; rather, it is a sign to "regroup" and seek agreement on goals and tasks of therapy with the patient or reassess their stage of change. A question therapists in this situation might ask themselves could be, "In what ways have I gotten ahead of my patient?" Overall, although other authors in this book may disagree, we believe that unless treatment guidelines suggest certain treatments do not work for moral injury–based distress, clinicians should continue to use the evidence-based treatments with demonstrated efficacy for the clinical disorders resulting from the morally injurious events.

Therapist Stuck Point 5: "If I Help My Patient Feel Better About What They Did, I Become an Accomplice"

This stuck point assumes that effective therapy, which reduces symptoms associated with moral injury–based distress, will make a therapist an accomplice or imply that the therapist is sanctioning or approving of the moral transgression. Frequently, this belief is driven by the clash between the patient's experiences and the therapists' moral beliefs and values. Depending on the flexibility of these deeply held beliefs and values, therapists may ask themselves, "In what ways can I still be opposed to the transgressions that happened and help to reduce my patient's emotional suffering appropriately?" If the therapist finds they cannot reconcile the discrepancy, they should refer to another provider who is open to working with such morally charged situations.

One important piece of information to keep in mind when working with a patient who is seeking help for moral injury–based distress is that this individual would have likely not sought therapy if he or she did not feel some sort of guilt or remorse. Indeed, in our experience, guilt is often the most painful emotion that leads morally injured SM/Vs to seek therapy. In other words, patients who either enjoyed or are not bothered by moral transgressions would not seek therapy for any negative emotions associated with these experiences. We have treated individuals who found they enjoyed violence and combat, only to feel ashamed of their reaction afterward (see Grossman, 2009); it is important to remember that these individuals still had clear emotional reactions, which can serve as possible treatment targets.

Therapist Stuck Point 6: "My Patient Cannot Tolerate Talking About the Morally Injurious Event"

This is, perhaps, the most common stuck point we have heard as trainers and supervisors. We frequently draw parallels between the belief that patients cannot tolerate talking about the morally injurious event and the notion that discussing traumas may harm or retraumatize patients, even though this has been shown not to be the case (Jayawickreme et al., 2014). Sometimes, in the thick of moral injury treatment, therapists have said that the discussions of morally injurious events have provoked personal feelings of sadism. We have felt this way too, so it is important to acknowledge that, although some directions in therapy are not easy, they are ultimately what is best for the patient. It may be the case that sometimes therapists, like their patients, lose the distinction between the memory of the event and the event itself that exposure therapy is meant to restore (Foa et al., 2007). A helpful question at this juncture is, "What are the differences between talking about morally injurious events and actually experiencing them again?" We have found Olatunji et al.'s (2009) views on the ethics of exposure therapy instructive because it raises a helpful question for us: "What is more compassionate? Helping a patient resolve their feelings of guilt and self-blame, even though it is personally difficult, or avoiding these difficult discussions in favor of providing a more pleasant, but superficial, course of therapy?"

In sum, the therapist stuck points discussed in this section are what we have observed as the most representative sample of unhelpful beliefs that may hinder therapists' efficacy in addressing moral injury. It is critical for therapists to continuously evaluate potential biases or hesitations about working with individuals who have experienced morally injurious events, as well as examine their potential biases about the military, war, and the individuals who serve.

When therapists recognize biases that will prevent them from providing the most effective care to a patient, they are encouraged to refer this individual to a colleague who is willing to work with such presenting concerns. It is important to keep in mind that most therapists have their own stuck points running through their minds from time to time. Having such beliefs is not the issue, but it is critical for a therapist to be self-aware and challenge these beliefs to promote the best outcomes for their patients.

PREMATURE REASSURANCE AS A BARRIER TO EFFECTIVE MORAL INJURY TREATMENT

We use the term *premature reassurance* to describe a natural, yet unhelpful, therapist response when engaging SM/Vs in detailed discussions of morally injurious situations. Discussions of morally charged situations often provoke powerful feelings of guilt, shame, and self-loathing from the patient. It is frequently the case that detailed exploration of morally injurious events provokes discomfort in the therapist as well, either because of the therapist's moral response evoked by the patient's discussions or as a result of seeing the patient experience significant emotional pain associated with the morally injurious event. As a result, therapists might seek to relieve a patient's distress rather quickly by saying things such as "You did all you could" or "You didn't have another choice" or offering some other form of reassurance. The desire to offer this reassurance is often driven by an unresolved therapist stuck point, such as "My patient can't tolerate discussing the moral injury." Although these reassuring statements might seem helpful and be factually true, they may ultimately be unhelpful or even harmful because they may only temporarily alleviate discomfort and ultimately prevent more in-depth processing of the morally injurious events. As such, premature reassurance can be viewed as a form of therapist-induced avoidance. As discussed extensively elsewhere in this book, avoidance has been strongly linked with the maintenance of symptoms. Premature reassurance may also be thought of as similar to the "righting reflex" in the motivational interviewing literature (cf. Miller & Rollnick, 2013), in that both the righting reflex and premature reassurance may prevent attempts at deeper emotional processing.

As an example, we (Held, Klassen, Brennan, & Zalta, 2018) detailed the case of a 43-year-old Latino U.S. Army veteran named Carlos who shot a young Iraqi girl who was coerced by insurgents to approach an American checkpoint while wearing an explosive vest. To preserve the veteran's identity, certain identifying details of his case were changed in a way that does not alter the nature of the following therapeutic interaction. After some preliminary work to build rapport and decide on treatment goals, the veteran and therapist decided on a course of prolonged exposure (see Chapter 7) to decrease the veteran's intrusive memories regarding the event. The following exchange occurred in the fourth session of prolonged exposure. After about

45 minutes of imaginal exposure to the traumatic memory, the therapist transitioned to helping the veteran process the memory.

THERAPIST: How was that for you today?

VETERAN: I'm really fucking angry right now!

THERAPIST: Oh? Tell me more.

VETERAN: (Silence for about 2 minutes) I was in that country to help people like her. I wasn't there to shoot little kids! She was helpless! . . . I didn't go into that situation wanting her to die! (Begins to tear up)

THERAPIST: What did you want to happen that day?

VETERAN: I don't know, but not that.

The therapist in this situation typified the nondirective style of processing that is recommended following imaginal exposures (Foa et al., 2007; Smith et al., 2013). In so doing, the therapist created space in the session for the veteran to contextualize the moral injury appropriately, add new information about his intention during that situation (e.g., save the little girl), as well as to express natural affect regarding the situation (e.g., sadness). It was apparent later in the session that the veteran, up until this point, had not considered that his intention in the situation was not to harm the young girl and that he actually cared a great deal for her. The veteran had been unable to access this appraisal because of self-blame.

Compare the previous exchange with a hypothetical exchange in which the therapist, having either been made uncomfortable by listening to the imaginal exposure or assuming that he or she knows exactly what drove the veteran's actions and does not follow the nondirective style of processing. The therapist then attempts prematurely to convince the veteran that he had no other option. Rather than inviting further exploration of possible ways to reappraise the situation, the exchange mostly becomes an unhelpful back and forth about who understands the situation more clearly.

THERAPIST: How was that for you today?

VETERAN: I'm really fucking angry right now!

THERAPIST: I know you didn't want to shoot this little girl, but you had to keep your unit safe. You did the right thing. [*Premature reassurance*]

VETERAN: How can you say that?

THERAPIST: I don't see that you had any other options. If you didn't shoot her, she would have gotten too close and maybe killed some of your friends. [*Premature reassurance*]

VETERAN: Maybe you're right. I still feel like shit.

Treatment for moral injury–based distress is difficult work and likely to provoke discomfort in the therapist from time to time. We have described premature reassurance as a natural, yet unhelpful, therapist response to this discomfort because it may ultimately stifle the patient's deeper emotional and cognitive processing of the morally injurious event.

VICARIOUS TRAUMA AND MORAL INJURY TREATMENT

It seems reasonable to assume that clinicians who regularly work with m distressed SM/Vs may also be susceptible to vicarious trauma, although there is no published literature linking the two (to our knowledge). Although "vicarious trauma" is often used interchangeably with other terms such as "secondary posttraumatic stress" and "compassion fatigue," *vicarious trauma* has more broadly referred to the gradual development of distress and negative cognitive, emotional, and relational consequences for the therapist as a result of routine exposure to traumatic material (Lipsky & Burk, 2009). Common signs of vicarious trauma may include preoccupation with patients outside of session, reexperiencing images from patients' traumatic material through intrusive thoughts or dreams, hyperarousal, somatic complaints, and coping through substance use (Cohen & Collens, 2013; Lipsky & Burk, 2009). Others have further articulated a broader array of signs that seem relevant for therapists who are steeped in moral injury treatment, including lack of trust in others, heightened sense of vulnerability, hopelessness, and loss of personal meaning and coherence in one's life and work (Lipsky & Burk, 2009).

Left unmanaged, vicarious trauma may negatively affect the therapy relationship as well. Trippany et al. (2004) observed that vicariously traumatized clinicians might easily become angry with their patients, leading to additional, unproductive therapeutic ruptures. Further, therapists who treat moral injury–based distress may lose the ability to contextualize the morally injurious event adequately and may behave in ways that implicitly and inappropriately hold the SM/V responsible for their role in the moral transgression. Likewise, their attunement with the patient's goals for therapy may become lost, and the therapist may either inappropriately challenge the patient or underestimate the individual's strengths and innate resilience by not challenging the SM/V at all. Whatever the precipitating factors, this miscalibration of the therapist and patient may lead to the selection of inappropriate interventions that ultimately do not benefit the patient (Greenberg & Paivio, 2003).

Although estimating prevalence rates for therapists who may be affected by vicarious trauma is difficult, the sense that vicarious trauma presents an ever-present professional hazard for clinicians working with SM/Vs seems uncontroversial (Branson, 2018; Lipsky & Burk, 2009). A range of prevention strategies have been proposed, including ongoing supervision–peer consultation, leaving adequate time in one's schedule for reflection, and adhering to a structured work–rest schedule (see Branson, 2018, for a review). Moreover, several authors have explored the notion that if vicarious trauma exists, then vicarious posttraumatic growth may exist as well (Hyatt-Burkhart, 2014); indeed, some clinicians remarked that, although trauma work was demanding, they had noticed an immense sense of professional satisfaction in watching patients improve. Likewise, many clinicians noted that they had become more grateful for positive relationships and experiences in their lives (Cohen & Collens, 2013; Hyatt-Burkhart, 2014). The relationship between therapists and their work with moral injury may be a future area for fruitful empirical exploration.

In our setting, we have been fortunate to have multiple venues for both informal peer support and formal supervision to discuss the rigors and challenges of our work but also the "success stories." This may contribute to a workplace culture where it is expected that the work with traumatized and morally injured veterans will deeply affect each clinician at points but that these reactions are openly discussed in a normalized, nonjudgmental way. As pointed out by Hyatt-Burkhart (2014) and others (e.g., Cohen & Collens, 2013), it is important to leave room for the personal growth that is possible when working with SM/Vs who are morally distressed. Seeing these individuals find some degree of peace with the past and reconnect with their families and communities is enormously satisfying to bear witness to.

CONCLUSION

In this chapter, we have attempted to provide the beginnings of a conceptual framework for therapists and supervisors to examine and reflect on how therapist factors may affect the treatment of moral injury–based distress for SM/Vs. Bordin's (1979) conceptualization of the working alliance, knowledge of military culture, and various therapist stuck points were all proposed and reviewed as essential components of this conceptual framework. In the short run, we hope that this chapter inspires therapists to think more intentionally about their contributions to their patients' recovery from moral injury. In the long run, we hope this chapter provides some incentive for further theoretical and empirical work on the contributions of therapist factors to moral injury treatment. The remarkable growth of interest in the treatment of moral injury–based distress has surely been a positive development, but more theoretical and empirical attention to therapist factors is certainly needed in the coming years.

REFERENCES

Bohart, A. C., Elliott, R., Greenberg, L. S., & Watson, J. C. (2002). Empathy. In J. C. Norcross (Ed.), *Psychotherapy relationships that work: Therapist contributions and responsiveness to patients* (pp. 89–108). Oxford University Press.

Bordin, E. S. (1979). The generalizability of the psychoanalytic concept of the working alliance. *Psychotherapy: Theory, Research, & Practice, 16*(3), 252–260. https://doi.org/10.1037/h0085885

Branson, D. C. (2018). Vicarious trauma, themes in research, and terminology: A review of literature. *Traumatology, 25*(1), 2–10. https://doi.org/10.1037/trm0000161

Cohen, K., & Collens, P. (2013). The impact of trauma work on trauma workers: A metasynthesis on vicarious trauma and vicarious posttraumatic growth. *Psychological Trauma: Theory, Research, Practice, and Policy, 5*(6), 570–580. https://doi.org/10.1037/a0030388

Currier, J. M., Holland, J. M., & Malott, J. (2015). Moral injury, meaning making, and mental health in returning veterans. *Journal of Clinical Psychology, 71*(3), 229–240. https://doi.org/10.1002/jclp.22134

Evans, W. R., Stanley, M. A., Barrera, T. L., Exline, J. J., Pargament, K. I., & Teng, E. J. (2018). Morally injurious events and psychological distress among veterans: Examining the mediating role of religious and spiritual struggles. *Psychological Trauma: Theory, Research, Practice, and Policy, 10*(3), 360–367. https://doi.org/10.1037/tra0000347

Farnsworth, J. K., Drescher, K. D., Nieuwsma, J., Carolina, N., Walser, R. B., & Currier, J. M. (2014). The role of moral emotions in military trauma: Implications for the study and treatment of moral injury. *Review of General Psychology, 18*(4), 249–262. https://doi.org/10.1037/gpr0000018

Finlay, L. D. (2015). Evidence-based trauma treatment: Problems with a cognitive reappraisal of guilt. *Journal of Theoretical and Philosophical Psychology, 35*(4), 220–229. https://doi.org/10.1037/teo0000021

Flückiger, C., Del Re, A. C., Wampold, B. E., & Horvath, A. O. (2018). The alliance in adult psychotherapy: A meta-analytic synthesis. *Psychotherapy, 55*(4), 316–340. https://doi.org/10.1037/pst0000172

Foa, E. B., Hembree, E. A., & Rothbaum, B. O. (2007). *Prolonged exposure therapy for PTSD: Emotional processing of traumatic experiences. Therapist guide.* Oxford University Press. https://doi.org/10.1093/med:psych/9780195308501.001.0001

Greenberg, L. S., & Paivio, S. C. (2003). *Working with emotions in psychotherapy.* Guilford Press.

Grossman, D. (2009). *On killing: The psychological cost of learning to kill in war and society.* Little, Brown.

Haugen, P. T., Werth, A. S., Foster, A. L., & Owen, J. (2017). Are rupture–repair episodes related to outcome in the treatment of trauma-exposed world trade center responders? *Counselling & Psychotherapy Research, 17*(4), 276–282. https://doi.org/10.1002/capr.12138

Held, P., Klassen, B. J., Bagley, J., & Pollack, M. (2019). *Prevalence rates of morally injurious event exposure among veterans presenting for outpatient mental health treatment* [Unpublished manuscript]. Department of Psychiatry and Behavioral Sciences, Rush University Medical Center.

Held, P., Klassen, B. J., Brennan, M. B., & Zalta, A. K. (2018). Using prolonged exposure and cognitive processing therapy to treat veterans with moral injury-based PTSD: Two case examples. *Cognitive and Behavioral Practice, 25*(3), 377–390. https://doi.org/10.1016/j.cbpra.2017.09.003

Held, P., Klassen, B. J., Hall, J. M., Friese, T. R., Bertsch-Gout, M. M., Zalta, A. K., & Pollack, M. H. (2018). "I knew it was wrong the moment I got the order": A narrative thematic analysis of moral injury in combat veterans. *Psychological Trauma: Theory, Research, Practice, and Policy, 11*(4), 396–405. https://doi.org/10.1037/tra0000364

Held, P., Klassen, B. J., Zou, D. S., Schroedter, B. S., Karnik, N. S., Pollack, M. H., & Zalta, A. K. (2017). Negative posttrauma cognitions mediate the association between morally injurious events and trauma-related psychopathology in treatment-seeking veterans. *Journal of Traumatic Stress, 30*(6), 698–703. https://doi.org/10.1002/jts.22234

Hundt, N. E., Mott, J. M., Miles, S. R., Arney, J., Cully, J. A., & Stanley, M. A. (2015). Veterans' perspectives on initiating evidence-based psychotherapy for posttraumatic stress disorder. *Psychological Trauma: Theory, Research, Practice, and Policy, 7*(6), 539–546. https://doi.org/10.1037/tra0000035

Hyatt-Burkhart, D. (2014). The experience of vicarious posttraumatic growth in mental health workers. *Journal of Loss and Trauma, 19*(5), 452–461. https://doi.org/10.1080/15325024.2013.797268

Jayawickreme, N., Cahill, S. P., Riggs, D. S., Rauch, S. A. M., Resick, P. A., Rothbaum, B. O., & Foa, E. B. (2014). Primum non nocere (first do no harm): Symptom worsening and improvement in female assault victims after prolonged exposure for PTSD. *Depression and Anxiety, 31*(5), 412–419. https://doi.org/10.1002/da.22225

Klay, P. (2014). *Redeployment*. Penguin.

Lipsky, L., & Burk, C. (2009). *Trauma stewardship: An everyday guide to caring for self while caring for others*. Berett-Koehler.

Litz, B. T., Stein, N., Delaney, E., Lebowitz, L., Nash, W. P., Silva, C., & Maguen, S. (2009). Moral injury and moral repair in war veterans: A preliminary model and intervention strategy. *Clinical Psychology Review, 29*(8), 695–706. https://doi.org/10.1016/j.cpr.2009.07.003

Miller, W. R., & Rollnick, S. (2013). *Motivational interviewing: Helping people change* (3rd ed.). Guilford Press.

Norcross, J. C. (2002). Empirically supported therapy relationships. In J. C. Norcross (Ed.), *Psychotherapy relationships that work: Therapist contributions and responsiveness to patients* (pp. 3–16). Oxford University Press.

Olatunji, B. O., Deacon, B. J., & Abramowitz, J. S. (2009). The cruelest cure? Ethical issues in the implementation of exposure-based treatments. *Cognitive and Behavioral Practice, 16*(2), 172–180. https://doi.org/10.1016/j.cbpra.2008.07.003

Prochaska, J. O., & Norcross, J. C. (2002). Stages of change. In J. C. Norcross (Ed.), *Psychotherapy relationships that work: Therapist contributions and responsiveness to patients* (pp. 303–313). Oxford University Press.

Resick, P. A., Monson, C. M., & Chard, K. M. (2017). *Cognitive processing therapy for PTSD: A comprehensive manual*. Guilford Press.

Saxon, D., Barkham, M., Foster, A., & Parry, G. (2017). The contribution of therapist effects to patient dropout and deterioration in the psychological therapies. *Clinical Psychology & Psychotherapy, 24*(3), 575–588. https://doi.org/10.1002/cpp.2028

Smith, E. R., Duax, J. M., & Rauch, S. A. M. (2013). Perceived perpetration during traumatic events: Clinical suggestions from experts in prolonged exposure therapy. *Cognitive and Behavioral Practice, 20*(4), 461–470. https://doi.org/10.1016/j.cbpra.2012.12.002

Trippany, R. L., Kress, V. E. W., & Wilcoxon, S. A. (2004). Preventing vicarious trauma: What counselors should know when working with trauma survivors. *Journal of Counseling and Development, 82*(1), 31–37. https://doi.org/10.1002/j.1556-6678.2004.tb00283.x

U.S. Census Bureau. (2000). *Military service*. https://www.census.gov/population/www/cen2000/censusatlas/pdf/12_Military-Service.pdf

U.S. Census Bureau. (2017). *Selected social characteristics in the United States: 2013–2017 American Community Survey 5-year Estimates*. https://factfinder.census.gov/faces/tableservices/jsf/pages/productview.xhtml?src=bkmk

Wachen, J. S., Dondanville, K. A., & Resick, P. A. (2017). Correcting misperceptions about cognitive processing therapy to treat moral injury: A response to Gray and colleagues (this issue). *Cognitive and Behavioral Practice, 24*(4), 388–392. https://doi.org/10.1016/j.cbpra.2017.06.001

Wisco, B. E., Marx, B. P., May, C. L., Martini, B., Krystal, J. H., Southwick, S. M., & Pietrzak, R. H. (2017). Moral injury in U.S. combat veterans: Results from the National Health and Resilience in Veterans Study. *Depression and Anxiety, 34*(4), 340–347. https://doi.org/10.1002/da.22614

7

Moral Injury, Posttraumatic Stress Disorder, and Prolonged Exposure

Kelsey R. Sprang Jones, Sheila A. M. Rauch, Erin R. Smith, Andrew M. Sherrill, and Afsoon Eftekhari

Although recently the use of the term "moral injury" has significantly surged, the concept has been a part of trauma research and theory since its beginnings. Janoff-Bulman's (1989) foundational work on social cognition and its influence on the impact of trauma through shattered assumptions about the self and world speaks to this very concept—people who survive trauma often feel that their whole sense of a just world is undermined. Both cognitive processing therapy (CPT; Resick et al., 2016) and prolonged exposure (PE; Foa et al., 2007) were strongly influenced by this theory and other work in this area. In addition, moral injury partially overlaps with other concepts, such as perceived perpetration and bystander guilt (Smith et al., 2013). Smith et al. (2013), defined *perceived perpetration* as

> occurring when a trauma survivor, in the context of his/her trauma, (a) acted with potentially violent and/or lethal force or failed to act when violence was occurring to others, and (b) interprets his/her behavior as perpetration or as violating his/her moral code, and (c) acted as a consequence of the trauma context and not as a premeditated act or with instrumental intent to victimize. (p. 462)

This chapter focuses on the implementation of PE for posttraumatic stress disorder (PTSD) with traumatic events that include a moral injury. We first discuss PE and the evidence base for the intervention. We then discuss the importance of assessment and differential diagnosis in determining whether PTSD is driving the patient's distress. Finally, we provide a case example to highlight cases of how PE can be effective in the treatment of moral injury–related PTSD. Consistent with other chapters in this book, *moral injury* refers to a

https://doi.org/10.1037/0000204-008
Addressing Moral Injury in Clinical Practice, J. M. Currier, K. D. Drescher, and J. Nieuwsma (Editors)

characteristic of an event experienced by an individual that entails a violation of their moral values or beliefs for which the individual feels a sense of either personal agency or responsibility (either through their action or inaction at the time) or a sense of need to rectify the wrong committed by the self or others.

As would be expected, the experience of moral injury during or following an event leads to strong emotional reactions and thoughts about the self, others, and the world. On the basis of our observations, this concept has resonated with military service members and veterans. However, other trauma survivors also may experience moral injury, including child sexual abuse survivors (who report that their sense of caregiver trust was violated) and natural disaster survivors (who indicate their neighbors became hostile competitors in the aftermath of loss). Differential diagnosis should determine the course of treatment. If morally injurious events result in PTSD (a traumatic memory that is "stuck" with avoidance and hyperarousal), PE is an appropriate and effective treatment. If depression or generalized anxiety disorder (GAD) or another diagnosis better describes the mental health issues, another treatment is warranted.

Some PTSD researchers have asserted that moral injury requires its own treatment and focus outside of current well-established PTSD interventions, such as PE and CPT. Specifically, in regard to PE, some of the concern comes from the early misconceptualization of emotional processing theory (EPT) as addressing only fear-based emotions (Foa & Kozak, 1986). In fact, the EPT model in PTSD, as early as 2006, expanded and clearly included all emotions, including guilt, shame, sadness, and anger, that may have been present at the time of the trauma (Rauch & Foa, 2006). Effective PTSD treatment requires activation of the trauma memory that is driving the PTSD intrusive symptoms. This occurs through revisiting the memory in imaginal exposure, allowing for emotional processing of all thoughts, behaviors, and emotions associated with the trauma. It also occurs through the new learning that happens during in vivo exposure. Once the memory is activated, all emotions can be experienced without avoidance. This allows for a reduction in the intensity of negative affect as well as other alterations in the meaning of the trauma. The veteran can contextualize and make meaning of their actions at the time of the trauma and after. Therapeutic change occurs through the reduction in negative affective intensity and increased ability to tolerate negative affect, as well as through alterations in the meaning of the trauma in reference to the self and the world (for additional detailed discussion about mechanisms of change in PE, see Rauch & Foa, 2006; Sripada et al., 2016). Despite the expansion of EPT to describe the process of PE better, many continue to misconceptualize the intervention as being solely for fear-based emotions.

SCIENTIFIC BASIS OF PROLONGED EXPOSURE THERAPY FOR PTSD WITH MORAL INJURY TRAUMA

Providing effective treatment to military service members and veterans is a priority area for research and intervention for the U.S. Department of Veteran Affairs (VA) and Department of Defense (DoD). With generations of individuals struggling with PTSD in the VA and DoD systems, the most recent VA/DoD guidelines identify first-line effective treatments for PTSD (VA/DoD Clinical Practice Guideline Working Group, 2017), with exposure-based therapies among those with the highest level of support. PE is one of the most studied and demonstrated effective treatments for PTSD and related psychopathology. Numerous studies support the use of PE with men and women with various types of trauma exposure and comorbidity (Lee et al., 2016; Watts et al., 2013). Most interesting, studies related to moral injury have examined the impact of PE on secondary outcomes, such as anger, guilt, and health outcomes (Foa & Rauch, 2004; Resick et al., 2002).

Although the term "moral injury" entered the PTSD literature more recently, studies looking at the impact of evidence-based practices such as PE on secondary treatment outcomes, including guilt and shame, are well established. Guilt and shame are strongly related to moral injury because they reflect perceptions and feelings about the self in relation to certain events. Specifically, we previously mentioned that moral injury is a characteristic of an event experienced by an individual that entails a violation of their moral values and beliefs for which the individual feels a sense of either personal agency or responsibility (either through their action or inaction at the time) or the need to rectify the wrong committed. *Guilt* similarly refers to a sense of remorse or regret for having violated one's moral values ("I did a bad thing"), and *shame* refers to a sense of humiliation or distress experienced due to behavior that is considered morally wrong ("I am a bad person"). These concepts are closely tied to the consequences of a morally injurious event.

In fact, qualitative data do not support that morally injurious events impede treatment response for those with a primary diagnosis of PTSD (Held et al., 2018). Clinical experience and case studies support the use of first-line interventions such as PE in cases of PTSD that include moral injury (Held et al., 2018; Smith et al., 2013). To date, there have been no randomized controlled trials directly comparing treatments specific to moral injury and PE or other evidence-based treatments for PTSD. However, in the literature, two prominent arguments challenge the appropriateness of PE and CPT to address PTSD that involved a moral injury. There are concerns around definitional issues related to the current understanding of PTSD, specifically that (a) moral injury does not fit within the concept of PTSD as a fear-based disorder, and (b) the thought processes that underlie moral injury–based PTSD do not align with fear-based cognitions that are assumed to maintain trauma symptoms. Therefore, some propose that adaptive treatments are needed to account for these issues.

Held et al. (2018) identified these arguments, provided alternative explanations, and demonstrated how moral injury–based PTSD can be theoretically conceptualized and treated within PE and CPT. With moral injury, the stimulus and response elements of cognitive and emotional processing become fused with meaning elements that drive guilt and global shame. These emotions create space for both cognitive and behavioral avoidance and maintaining maladaptive cognitive structures about self ("I am a bad person,"

"I am a murderer"). This avoidance prevents opportunities for these beliefs to be challenged and restructured.

Therefore, in PE for PTSD related to moral injury, exposure serves to activate this memory structure and creates discrepancies with these unhelpful cognitions ("I was following orders from someone I trusted," "According to information I had at the time, that kid was a potential threat"). This contradiction ultimately allows for a shift in the relationship between the stimulus, response, and meaning elements of these experiences. Similarly, psycho-education creates a new context that destigmatizes trauma reactions, in vivo exposure challenges avoidance driven by negative self-evaluation and initiates habituation, and imaginal exposure and processing continues reduction in negative affect and further integration of the trauma context. These PE elements create the pathways for effectively addressing moral injury and PTSD.

Guilt is understood to comprise thoughts and feelings regarding moral transgressions perceived by the patient and the consequent behavioral components of situational self-blame (Smith et al., 2013; Tilghman-Osborne et al., 2010). Blame can be helpful when it moves individuals toward reparations and emotional resolution. Blame can be unhelpful when it becomes generalized to global negative self-evaluations and shame. In the context of treatment, challenging the situational guilt and separating this guilt from shame and negative self-evaluation are central goals for PE. Smith et al. (2013) demonstrated how these processes manifest in PE through four clinical vignettes of service members with moral injuries. Service members explore contextual details related to their trauma to facilitate shifts in how they make sense of these experiences, habituate to guilt, and challenge those evaluations of self that maintain shame.

COMPONENTS AND SESSIONS OF PROLONGED EXPOSURE

PE for PTSD typically includes eight to fifteen 90-minute individual sessions that are delivered weekly or twice weekly. Recent adaptations of the treatment in an intensive 2- to 3-week model and four to six brief sessions in primary care have shown promise in clinical practice and some clinical trials (Cigrang et al., 2017; Yasinski et al., 2017). Foa et al. (2007) synthesized the empirical support for the intervention and provided a comprehensive guide for effective implementation of PE in *Prolonged Exposure Therapy for PTSD: Emotional Processing of Traumatic Experience, Therapist Guide*. Here, we provide a session-by-session breakdown of how PE treatment components are clinically implicated and special considerations for individuals with co-occurring PTSD and moral injury (Foa et al., 2007). Treatment components include (a) education about trauma, PTSD, and how PE addresses PTSD symptoms; (b) in vivo exposure; and (c) imaginal exposure with emotional processing. The treatment is broken down into Session 1 (treatment overview, trauma interview, breathing retraining, homework), Session 2 (homework review, common reactions to trauma, rationale for exposure, Subjective Units of Distress Scale [SUDS], in vivo hierarchy),

Session 3 (homework review, rationale for imaginal exposure, complete imaginal exposure, processing), intermediate sessions (homework review, imaginal exposure, "hot spots," processing, in vivo planning), and final session (homework review, imaginal, review progress, planning, termination). However, the first step in any treatment plan is assessment followed by differential diagnosis. Although PE is effective for moral injury related to PTSD, another treatment may be indicated if the moral injury results in a different diagnosis or concern, such as depression or panic disorder. In those cases, appropriate intervention for the identified primary diagnosis is warranted. This section addresses how PE can be used when the primary diagnosis is PTSD.

Assessment

Because diagnostic criteria overlap, it is important to distinguish the etiology of the symptoms and whether they are driven by the traumatic event. There are several key components for effective trauma assessment. Assessment should include confirmation of trauma history, symptom frequency, and symptom severity through a structured interview for PTSD or self-report and then a review with the clinician to ensure the accuracy of the responses. Structured interviews for PTSD are a good investment of time because the information gathered on examination will inform the clear differential diagnosis and specifics of the treatment course. Assessment also provides time to establish rapport. Specifically, the therapist can use the symptoms reported during assessment as a basis for exposure targets, motivational targets, and rapport building if they progress to PE. The Clinician-Administered PTSD Scale for *DSM-5* (CAPS-5; Weathers et al., 2015) and the Posttraumatic Stress Symptom Interview (Foa et al., 2016) are the most used primary PTSD structured interviews. In addition, assessment should include other common comorbid disorders, such as depression, GAD, and panic disorder. Structured diagnostic interviews, such as the DIAMOND (Diagnostic Interview for Anxiety, Mood, and OCD and Related Neuropsychiatric Disorders), can be helpful in assessing past and present comorbidities or primary complaints (Tolin et al., 2018).

During assessment and treatment planning, it is important to establish what presenting complaints are primary to provide the best chance that treatment will be effective. If the patient has another issue, such as imminent suicidal risk or significant substance misuse, those issues may have to be addressed to prevent them from interfering with PTSD treatment progress. Suicidality and homicidal urges should be carefully explored and addressed before engagement with trauma exposure. If a service member is at high risk of acting on suicidal or homicidal ideation or engaging in self-injurious behavior that places them at risk, stabilization should be prioritized before beginning trauma-focused treatment or consideration of a combined dialectical behavior therapy–PE protocol can be implemented (Harned et al., 2014). Similarly, stabilization of psychotic or bipolar symptoms increases the likelihood of safety in exposure therapy.

Rumination is common in both GAD and depression, and although driven by different mechanisms, it can often be confused with reexperiencing. *Reexperiencing* or *intrusive symptoms* are cued or uncued unwanted thoughts, emotions, and sensory memories related to a specific trauma, whereas *rumination* is characterized by intentionally going over the trauma and/or what preceded this event to solve or fix what happened. Reexperiencing is effectively treated with imaginal exposure, whereas rumination related to depression or GAD is best addressed through other targeted treatments, such as worry exposures. Importantly, PE is appropriate for individuals with PTSD, even with other co-occurring issues such as depression, anxiety, guilt, and shame. However, good case conceptualization can prepare the patient and therapist for the obstacles that are likely to arise and help to overcome those obstacles by adding elements from other treatments (worry exposures during PE) or an additional treatment course following PE (an episode of care focused on depression if those symptoms continue following PE).

When assessing a veteran or service member who endorses a morally injurious index trauma (Criterion A, according to the *Diagnostic and Statistical Manual of Mental Disorders, Fifth Edition; DSM-5*; American Psychiatric Association, 2013), certain elevations on particular criteria have been noted. These specific criteria may include persistent and/or exaggerated beliefs or expectations about oneself, others, or the world (Criterion D2: "I'm a murderer"); persistent distorted cognitions about the cause or consequences of the traumatic event that lead the individual to blame self or others (Criterion D3: "I am completely to blame"); and persistent negative emotional states (Criterion D4: guilt and shame). When assessing for traumatic events, clinicians should not discount events related to acts of violence. Often, such acts can occur due to the combat context or other situational factors that are common in moral injury. For instance, some service members had the experience of killing or harming others to protect themselves or others. Some trauma survivors may have committed violent acts out of grief or anger that may have exceeded the level necessary, such as service members who exceeded the rules of engagement in times of grief. For example, some trauma survivors were forced to victimize others out of fear their attacker would hurt or kill them. Such incidents often have a significant negative impact on the survivor. Clinicians may assess for how the service member made sense of these actions during and after the event and whether they felt their life was in danger if they had not acted. This allows the provider to effectively determine core emotions and cognitions driving current symptoms. Because of the stigma, it is common for service members to hesitate in disclosing these experiences and sometimes even to not disclose the full details until later in treatment. During the disclosure of trauma experiences, it is essential to remain nonjudgmental.

Although PE is a flexible and individualized treatment that can address complex patient presentations, there are some groups for whom the evidence base is less established, such that providers should proceed with caution, consultation, and support. For instance, PE requires sufficient memory of the traumatic event to generate an effective narrative for imaginal exposure. This does not have to be extensive. Indeed, memories of just a few minutes in duration can fuel PTSD and respond well to PE, but there has to be some type of memory that is stuck for PTSD to be present and PE to be appropriate. If patients present with imminent risk of harm to self or others, current unmanaged psychosis or bipolar disorder, and current ongoing risk of assault or abuse, clinicians should proceed with caution and consultation. PE may still offer the best treatment course, but additional assessment and intervention to reduce risk may be warranted. Although not specifically exclusionary, other potential barriers that may require special consideration include substance use, an unsafe or unstable living environment, dissociation, and personality pathology.

Following a comprehensive assessment, if appropriate, one can begin with the three components of PE. First, psychoeducation lays the groundwork for engagement and a global understanding of the treatment. Information regarding PTSD symptoms and treatment is provided, emphasizing the role of avoidance in maintaining symptoms and keeping the trauma memory "stuck," exploring how exposure allows for emotional processing and consequent trauma recovery, and explaining the role of exposure and emotional processing in the recovery process. For service members with a morally injurious index trauma, discussing guilt, blame, and negative self-perception allows for further assessment of the impact of moral injury on their posttrauma experiences, as well as normalizing and providing validation. Discussion of how exposure to avoided and/or distressing stimuli blocks negative reinforcement of cognitive and behavioral avoidance allows for a reduction in negative affect, provides the opportunity to differentiate the traumatic event from nonthreatening situations, and makes sense of the traumatic experience considering the full context of their life circumstance.

Second, in vivo exposure involves approaching distressing trauma-related stimuli (people, places, situations, emotions) and working to increase functional engagement in life. Targets for in vivo exposure are individualized to the activating stimuli and can address guilt, shame, and negative self-perceptions that result from moral injury. Finally, imaginal exposure with emotional processing involves intentionally approaching the trauma memory while engaging with the emotional (i.e., guilt, shame, anger), cognitive (i.e., negative beliefs about others), and sensory information that was present at the time of the trauma and then exploring the experiences with in vivo and imaginal exposures as a way to make sense of the traumatic experience and its current lived impact. This allows for an often-ignored context to be incorporated into the lens through which the service member interprets these events.

All PE sessions begin with a discussion of homework. Moreover, it is recommended that PTSD and depression symptoms be regularly monitored throughout treatment to provide measurement-based care and create real-time responses to emerging issues or concerns. The PTSD Checklist for *DSM-5* for PTSD (Weathers et al., 2013) and Patient Health Questionnaire (Kroenke et al., 2001) for depression are brief screeners that can easily be administered before each session to track response to treatment and allow for potential shifts to be made.

Session 1

Session 1 lays the groundwork for therapeutic change by orienting the patient to the intervention through psychoeducation about traumatic stress and exposure and normalizing the process of ongoing assessment. The session begins with an overview of the treatment program and rationale for PE imaginal and in vivo exposure. The role of cognitive and behavioral avoidance in keeping trauma "stuck" and maintaining unhelpful beliefs are collaboratively explored. A trauma interview is completed to identify the target trauma for exposure by soliciting a trauma history and the service member's reactions to these events. The target trauma is conceptualized as the one that causes the most distress, reexperiencing, and avoidance symptoms over the most recent past (either 2 weeks or month). To evaluate the presence of moral injury, the clinician should assess the judgments that service members make about their actions both during the event and over time, as well as subsequent emotions that are attached to these cognitions such as fear, guilt, shame, and anger. This session concludes with teaching and practicing the breathing retraining technique, which will be practiced three times per day as homework. Moreover, service members are encouraged to listen to an audio recording of the session one time and read the "Rationale for Treatment" handout.

Session 2

During Session 2, service members receive continued psychoeducation and plan for their first in vivo exposures. The session begins with a review of homework and the presentation of the agenda. The handout "Common Reactions to Trauma" provides service members with the opportunity to explore the impact of their trauma experience on their daily life and views about self, world, and others. This discussion is tailored to the service member's experience. With morally injurious experiences, service members may be impacted by negative self-perception, self-blame, and strained relationships. Exploration of these common reactions with a nonjudgmental attitude works to normalize and validate them. Next, the rationale for exposure is expanded, specifically related to in vivo exposure, and an in vivo hierarchy is created. Incorporating exposure to guilt and shame can be especially powerful opportunities for service members with moral injury to integrate new learning and consequently work to shift cognitive structure surrounding the index trauma. In vivo may also include activities related to making amends for what the service member considers their responsibility. Such activities may include writing a letter that is never sent, visiting a grave, or other activities that may be congruent with the service member's culture and values (e.g., volunteering or giving to charity). For homework, per standard protocol, service members are asked to continue daily breathing practice, read *Common Reactions to Trauma*, add to their in vivo hierarchy, begin in vivo assignments, record SUDS, and listen to the audio recording of the session one time.

Session 3

Session 3 introduces imaginal exposure into the therapeutic process. In reviewing homework, considerable time should be spent discussing the in vivo exposure homework and eliciting the service member's experience and perspective regarding exposure. Offering praise for efforts helps to positively reinforce engagement with the intervention. If it appears the service member inappropriately completed their exposure or engaged in avoidance, it is important to identify something they did well before engaging in problem solving for the next in vivo session. This can be especially important with moral injury so as not to feed or reinforce guilt, shame, and low self-efficacy. In vivo targets are selected for the following week, and depending on the service member's engagement, additional planning on how to increase the success of the exposure should occur. As per standard protocol, the rationale for imaginal exposure and then 45 to 60 minutes of imaginal exposure to the target trauma are completed. Throughout exposure, providers can provide prompts to help the service member connect to the context of the trauma by eliciting relevant details, thoughts, and feelings present at the time of the event. Postimaginal processing then provides space to emotionally and cognitively process or discuss the exposure and how it impacts how they see the trauma, see themselves at the time of the trauma, and see themselves now. With moral injury, these processing portions tend to focus on the discussion of the context of the trauma and the situational details that led to the morally injurious act. For instance, if a veteran reports his trauma as having killed an adolescent who he thought had a gun, processing may include talking about who gave the order, what the veteran saw at that moment, and what the veteran saw afterward. For homework, service members are asked to engage daily in breathing, listening to recordings of imaginal exposure, recording their pre–peak–post SUDS, completing in vivo exposures, and listening to the tape of the session one time.

Intermediate Sessions

Intermediate sessions (four to nine or more) provide a continuation of in vivo exposure, imaginal exposure, and postimaginal processing. During this phase of treatment, the provider helps the service member increase and maintain engagement while working their way up the in vivo hierarchy. In vivo targets are selected for the following week. Imaginal exposure continues to focus on the trauma, with the therapist working toward optimal emotional engagement and inclusion of key contextual variables that will allow for therapeutic progress. At Session 5 or 6, it is expected that all details of the trauma have been included, and the imaginal exposure has narrowed down to the "hot spots"—the most distressing moments of the memory. In cases of moral injury, these are typically the moments when the most shame, guilt, or moral distress is evident. As service members progress through treatment, cognitive shifts will likely begin to occur as new perspectives regarding the target event emerge.

Final Session

The final session provides space to complete in-session imaginal exposure while reflecting on progress achieved throughout the treatment program. Homework is reviewed, and a final imaginal takes place. Through postimaginal processing, the service member is able to reflect on behavioral and cognitive shifts that have taken place through approaching avoidance. The service member and provider collaboratively engage in relapse prevention planning to increase the likelihood of the continued application of skills.

SPECIAL ISSUES IN THERAPIST TRAINING

Best practices in PE clinical training support a combination of didactics and case consultation or supervision (Karlin et al., 2010). However, given that evidence-based practice requires evidence-based assessment (Hunsley & Mash, 2005), successful PE training assumes the clinician has basic skills in administering and interpreting empirically supported PTSD-specific assessment tools to formulate an appropriate case conceptualization and treatment plan. Therefore, before learning and implementing PE skills, trainees are recommended to first demonstrate basic skills in PTSD assessment and differential diagnosis.

For any psychotherapeutic modality, trainees are encouraged to be culturally responsive and self-reflective to ensure their morals and values are not infringing on their patients' autonomy. As a trainee explores a patient's problematic responses to apparent violations of morals, the trainee must also monitor their boundaries of what is right and wrong. In PE, one of the most critical dialogues with patients is the patient's first disclosure of the traumatic event. During the first disclosure, the patient closely monitors the clinician's reaction, which can signal how the patient reacts. Three common problematic reactions by trainees are horror, sadness, and indifference. Therapists should do their best to maintain a nonjudgmental stance even in the face of difficult disclosures. Keep in mind that discussion with colleagues after a session can be helpful if a clinician is concerned about whether the incident has room for therapeutic change. Strong emotional reactions from the therapist can make it difficult to elicit the "R-rated version" of the event that is required for imaginal exposure. The patient should detect that the clinician is present and attentive. Rather than providing evaluations or interpretations of the trauma, the clinician should acknowledge the difficulty of disclosing the event with a stranger and how that speaks to their desire to move forward. Reinforcing engagement is critical in the beginning stages of PE.

Trainees new to PE should be reminded that the process of extinction occurs within the trainee, not just the patient. Similarly, the ability to manage emotional responses in the context of treatment generalizes to other patients. Part of learning PE is developing skill in responding to trauma narratives without judgment or distracting displays of emotion. PE clinicians must be a steady and safe presence for patients as they discuss the worst days of their lives, especially events involving perceived perpetration that tend to evoke shame. Until that skill is developed, trainees should anticipate that hearing intimate details of traumatic events can be aversive. To be clear, trainees should aim to be perceived as steady and safe, not stoic and unemotional. The clinician's emotions can be an excellent tool within PE; the challenge is for clinicians to use their coping skills and consultation resources to address any distressing feelings related to the patient's traumas.

Trainee avoidance of therapeutic elements of treatment (e.g., imaginal exposure, in vivo exposure) can negatively impact patient care in profound ways. Just as PE clinicians are trained to not "fragilize" their patients, trainees are encouraged not to fragilize themselves. The patient is disclosing the trauma to the clinician because the patient perceives the clinician as a person who can handle it. Trainees may fully believe in the robust empirical literature supporting PE but may lack confidence until they have experienced using PE. Supervisors and consultants can normalize this reaction and share experiences of how they built confidence. One strategy is to ask trainees to start by "acting as if" they had confidence, and then, after a handful of successful cases, notice that confidence is occurring naturally. PE supervisors and consultants who are confident in the treatment model will often ask their trainees to "borrow confidence" from them until it is no longer needed.

SPECIAL ISSUES IN TREATMENT DELIVERY

PE trainees are encouraged to have a firm understanding of EPT and to actively use this framework not just to conceptualize their cases but to make moment-to-moment decisions in session. For PE and moral injury, service members often do not appreciate the full context in which the event occurred. Effective processing begins with imaginal exposures that are guided by the inclusion of context. The aim of imaginal exposure is not to activate post-event evaluations but internal and external information during the event. It is important to give patients room to express the truth as they understand it, not what you or they want to hear. A patient might have greatly enjoyed getting revenge or eliminating a threat and being a "good soldier" and later feel ashamed for their internal reactions. Engaging with that part of the memory during imaginal exposure will make room for a new perspective that diminishes shame.

Following imaginal exposures, processing can continue to be emotionally activating. Patients may continue to experience strong emotion and articulate negative judgments about self, the world, and others. The clinician's job is to avoid reassurance while keeping a window of vulnerability open to make perspectives flexible and open to change. New learning grows from shifts in unhelpful beliefs. Trainees are often tempted to discover the "magical cognition" that will set their patients free. However, only the patient can arrive at new perspectives—an achievement that may take time. Most often, this occurs through a chipping away at problematic thoughts over time and a continued approach to the memory, rather than pushing it away. Trainees have to focus on setting up a context for patients to view what happened without unhelpful judgments.

In cases of moral injury, processing guilt can be particularly challenging for trainees. First, trainees might experience distress when observing a patient experiencing inappropriate guilt. There may be a motivation to move the patient along quickly. This is more about addressing the trainee's distress than the patient's needs. Second, trainees may experience an urgency to "fix" guilt when it does not appear to change well into the protocol. Guilt signals what is important and motivates the individual to change (e.g., making amends). If the guilt seems somewhat justified and fits with the patient's cultural preferences, trainees should explore with patients how to make guilt more adaptive. However, trainees should be encouraged to be less permissive of shame. With shame, the goal is to "chip away" at the cognitive bridge between judging the event and judging the person (e.g., doing something "bad" does not make you "bad"). With a reduction of shame, the patient can determine their responsibility and refine a perspective that can positively influence their future behavior.

Last, although trainees should be encouraged to use contextual information to make new meaning, trainees can often get overly focused on making meaning of the event while neglecting the patient's current self-concept. Trying to change the perspective on past events can sometimes feel remote, such as trying to rewrite a previously incorrect history. PE is ultimately about the person's current functioning through exposure and new learning. It is helpful to have a present-moment focus during processing—for example, after the patient experiences an insight or displays a novel emotional response, asking how it feels to be vulnerable or tolerate distress. For those experiencing a reduction in guilt within a session, there is a great therapeutic opportunity to make new meaning about the self (e.g., removing shame). Such changes can lead to huge differences in functioning as the patient begins to see that he or she can handle negative emotion and directly address difficult situations.

CASE SUMMARY

The following applies the overall recommendations made earlier to a specific case. This case example is based on our collective clinical experiences in treating, supervising, and consulting on PE cases. Elements of the case example have been modified to protect the patient's privacy.

John was a 38-year-old married White man working in security management. He enlisted in the military following graduation from high school and served two tours in Afghanistan. At the start of treatment, he was struggling with symptoms of PTSD related to an incident that occurred during his second tour. He reached out for treatment because of increased PTSD-related social, marital, and occupational difficulties.

As an infantryman, John regularly patrolled villages near his forward operating base. His job was to watch for possible threats and report anything he saw. On one summer afternoon, John's unit was patrolling, and he was struck by the emptiness of the normally crowded street. There was no one on the street except a child walking toward them from the other side of the village. The unit began to take fire from a house at the end of the street near where the child was walking. John attempted to yell and wave the child away out of the danger, but the child continued to advance in the unit's direction. John stood up to wave to get the child's attention, but she did not stop. John was forced to take cover because of the fire. As the child got closer, John was ordered to shoot her because she appeared to have something concealed under her clothing, and he had to stop her before she got to his unit. John fired, and the child fell. The unit was able to take over the house, and two armed men were killed. Members of the unit went into the house next door and carried out two young men. They began to yell at the two men and beat them. John watched them hitting the young men, and he yelled "enough" but was told to "shut up." After things died down, John went to look at the child's body, and he was crushed to see that the child was dead, and there was no sign of a bomb. John immediately felt a tremendous amount of guilt for killing her and a sense of loss of humanity because of how his fellow soldiers treated the other villagers.

Case Conceptualization

This incident meets the criteria for Criterion A, according to *DSM-5*. In addition, the event is morally injurious for John in both perpetrating violence (killing a child) and failing to prevent the perpetration of violence (not intervening to stop the beating of the two men). Soon after this incident, John began to experience nightmares of being ordered to shoot the child and watching the child fall. He reported seeing the image of the girl's face and blood in the street many times each day. After returning from the combat zone, he avoided children and places where children might be present. This was particularly painful for his young children, who he began to feel that he could not be around because "I am not a safe person. I have hurt a child." He also avoided fellow soldiers from his unit. On intake, he reported that he felt completely to blame for killing the child. He stated, "I am a monster. I killed an innocent child."

After his discharge, he avoided anyone with prior service, individuals in uniforms, and any media that depicted combat or soldiers. John expressed a belief that he was a "coward" to not stand up to the soldiers who were beating the men, believing he should have stopped that attack. He felt deep guilt and perceived himself as "weak" and "as bad as the guys who were hitting them." He also stated that he felt that "American soldiers are supposed to be the good guys. But we weren't." He felt betrayed by the members of his unit who participated in the beating. Despite this event shaking his whole world, John did not tell anyone about the event, not even his spouse or family members. He indicated that he believed "they wouldn't love me if they knew I murdered a child," and "people will think I'm a monster." John felt emotionally disconnected from his family and friends and struggled to find any meaning in his job. He stopped attending church with his family because he felt "unforgivable."

At the time of intake, John met the criteria for PTSD related to this event. The trauma had violated his deeply held moral values and beliefs about the use of violence. His experience of this event and development of PTSD severely impacted social and interpersonal relationships, as well as his psychological and spiritual well-being.

Application of PE

During assessment, John was ambivalent regarding disclosing the details of his index trauma. The therapist asked direct questions regarding the content of this event (who, what, when, where, emotions) because it normalized John's experience and maintained unconditional positive regard. As John told his story, the therapist maintained warm affect and did not react negatively to details of the trauma. Throughout the administration of the CAPS-5, John's experience of shame was palpable, observed by his posture and avoidance of eye contact. Moreover, he made comments regarding his deservedness to access treatment. The therapist made note of this as a potential barrier during treatment and something to continue to reassess.

The therapist entered Session 1 following a comprehensive assessment and determined that PTSD was primary with comorbid depression. During the overall rationale, the therapist discussed how the memory got stuck, exploring the role of both avoidance and beliefs in maintaining his symptoms. John resonated with the memory being stuck and reflected that he could see the girl's face like it was happening again. He thought he was crazy. When discussing the role of unhelpful thoughts and beliefs, John reported, "I am a monster. I killed an innocent child," and "I have done something that is unforgivable." They explored how these beliefs developed from a violation of morals and resulted in negative emotions, such as guilt and shame. John gave voice to the difficulties he had experienced since this event, noting his disconnection from others. The therapist intentionally maintained a nonjudgmental, empathic stance toward the service member throughout this discussion to serve as an opportunity for corrective information and new learning. This is especially important in cases in which moral injury is present and allows for initial shifts in unhelpful beliefs. After eliciting examples regarding how his

PTSD was developed and maintained, John and the therapist collaboratively explored how PE effectively addressed these complaints.

In the second session, the therapist collaboratively led John through the common reactions to trauma discussion and introduced in vivo exposure. Because of the presence of moral injury, special attention was given to his experience of guilt, shame, and low self-esteem. This normalized his feelings and beliefs that maintained his PTSD. At one point, he stated, "I have done something that is unforgivable." The therapist understood the weight this could hold. As such, the therapist guided John to better understand the emotions that this belief produced and how it impacted his life. The therapist also assessed for the presence of shame, such as global evaluations of the self as a "monster, murder, unsafe person to be around children," and so forth. While noting it was challenging to initiate treatment and to "show up," John expressed some relief in an increased understanding of his symptoms.

During the second half of Session 2, the in vivo rationale was revisited, and specific targets were explored. John had previously noted avoiding engaging with his children, faith, and military reminders. For in vivo, John targeted taking his children to the park to address his guilt and associated anxiety about being "unsafe" around children. This allowed him to have a corrective experience and to challenge the belief "I am not a safe person. I have hurt a child." As indicated during assessment, John struggled with believing he deserved forgiveness and, during a session, stated, "I have done something unforgivable." For in vivo, he discussed forgiveness and morality with a leader from his faith community. They discussed his experiences, beliefs about himself, and what forgiveness could entail. He was able to consider forgiveness from a different perspective and acknowledge that he was, in fact, deserving and explored ways to make amends. Other in vivo targets that were named during his PE included attendance at church services, meditation or prayer, and visiting gravesites or memorials for individuals killed in overseas conflicts. John decided to write a letter to the girl he had shot, expressing his emotions and asking for forgiveness. He also donated money to an organization that helps war refugees, as a way to make amends.

John believed "American soldiers are supposed to be the good guys. But we weren't." His avoidance of reminders and individuals he served with was addressed directly through connecting with military personnel, images of service members, and his fellow service members. As John engaged in these in vivo exposures, he quickly began to enjoy "getting out there" again, and his discomfort around military reminders disappeared. He was able to be around these military reminders again. His decisions about what he wanted to do came out of interest instead of fear or memories of the day he had to shoot a child. He was able to let go of the guilt of not being able to help the two young men as well.

At the top of his hierarchy was disclosing his trauma to his wife and others in his life. He believed "they wouldn't love me if they knew what I did." Before these conversations, the therapist planned with John how he might respond if the individual had an adverse reaction to the discussion. Despite the outcome of in vivo exposures, new learning can occur, and the therapist wanted to ensure this learning was healing. John learned several things from this disclosure. First was that his wife did not react with judgment, but rather compassion. His behavior was never viewed as good or bad by many people, but as a product of a combat environment in which hard choices are made minute to minute. John reported that through the continued practice of in vivo exposure, he felt more engaged in his life and noted decreases in distress symptomatology.

In Session 3, John engaged in his first imaginal exposure. For John, imaginal exposure allowed for the inclusion of the context of his actions (shooting the child) and nonactions (not interrupting the attack) during the traumatic event, as well as his emotional state at the time of the trauma. This allowed John to attend to previously ignored or discounted elements of the event that contributed to the how and why of his actions. As he explored these new elements, his distress was further reduced. Initially, John focused only on inflicting harm, confirming his belief that "I am a monster." This discounted his exposure to enemy fire in attempts to warn the child, his delays in response to orders to kill the child, and the very real possibility that the girl could have been a threat or instructed or coerced to be a distraction. The therapist elicited additional context by asking, "What are you thinking? What are you seeing? What are you feeling?" This challenged John to engage with a full description of what was happening at the time of the event and chaotic combat situations in which he was making quick decisions. Moreover, John behaviorally exhibited shame during imaginal exposure through crossing his arms, directing his head away from the therapist, and holding his head in his hands. After John came into contact with this shame for several sessions, he was asked to "act the opposite to shame" and sit up straight and uncross his arms. This allowed new information to be included with the memory, such as his ability to manage negative emotion associated with the memory.

In postimaginal processing, the therapist explored previously unattended elements, including his attempts to warn the child, the delay in shooting, and his attempt to stop the beating. After these elements were presented in exposure, the therapist discussed what this meant to John by asking, "What does it mean about you that you stood up to warn the child?" or "What does it mean that you told them to stop?" The therapist highlighted aspects of the event that John had ignored. In addition, when John left out certain elements, the therapist would discuss in the processing portion of the session by saying, "I noticed that you did not include today that . . . ." Once, John did not include that those engaged in the beating all outranked him, and his team leader had told him to shut up. Without the inclusion of the contextual details, self-judgment and attributions of guilt, shame, and distress continued, but once these details were presented and discussed, the guilt began to dissipate. Through imaginal exposure and processing new interpretations of the event, PTSD symptoms subsided. John was able to see how his actions occurred within the context of combat trauma and reflected that situation and the chaos of combat much more than his character did.

CONCLUSION

Moral injury changes the lives of veterans and service members who experience it. By definition, moral injury disrupts their moral foundation and sense of who they are in the world and the safety of the world in general. For many survivors of trauma who experience moral injury, PTSD is also a consequence. In this chapter, we have shown how PE is a robust, flexible, and highly efficacious treatment for PTSD, including when moral injury is present. Since the first studies in PTSD, trauma survivors have reported shame and guilt related to events, now identified as moral injury. This term is new, but the concept has long been a part of trauma and PTSD. Working with trauma survivors in PE enables them to reexamine the context of the trauma and their actions at the time of the trauma and since then. This allows the survivor to see the event more fully and see their actions within the combat or other trauma context instead of judging from a position of everyday life. Through PE, patients are able to take back their lives from PTSD and reengage with their community, family, and life.

REFERENCES

American Psychiatric Association. (2013). *Diagnostic and statistical manual of mental disorders* (5th ed.). https://doi.org/10.1176/appi.books.9780890425596

Cigrang, J. A., Rauch, S. A., Mintz, J., Brundige, A. R., Mitchell, J. A., Najera, E., Litz, B. T., Young-McCaughan, S., Roache, J. D., Hembree, E. A., Goodie, J. L., Sonnek, S. M., & Peterson, A. L. (2017). Moving effective treatment for posttraumatic stress disorder to primary care: A randomized controlled trial with active duty military. *Families, Systems & Health, 35*(4), 450–462. https://doi.org/10.1037/fsh0000315

Foa, E. B., Hembree, E. A., & Rothbaum, B. O. (2007). *Prolonged exposure therapy for PTSD: Emotional processing of traumatic experiences, therapist guide.* Oxford University Press. https://doi.org/10.1093/med:psych/9780195308501.001.0001

Foa, E. B., & Kozak, M. J. (1986). Emotional processing of fear: Exposure to corrective information. *Psychological Bulletin, 99*(1), 20–35. https://doi.org/10.1037/0033-2909.99.1.20

Foa, E. B., McLean, C. P., Zang, Y., Zhong, J., Rauch, S., Porter, K., Knowles, K., Powers, M. B., & Kauffman, B. Y. (2016). Psychometric properties of the Posttraumatic Stress Disorder Symptom Scale Interview for *DSM–5* (PSSI-5). *Psychological Assessment, 28*(10), 1159–1165. https://doi.org/10.1037/pas0000259

Foa, E. B., & Rauch, S. A. M. (2004). Cognitive changes during prolonged exposure versus prolonged exposure plus cognitive restructuring in female assault survivors with posttraumatic stress disorder. *Journal of Consulting and Clinical Psychology, 72*(5), 879–884. https://doi.org/10.1037/0022-006X.72.5.879

Harned, M. S., Korslund, K. E., & Linehan, M. M. (2014). A pilot randomized controlled trial of Dialectical Behavior Therapy with and without the Dialectical Behavior Therapy Prolonged Exposure protocol for suicidal and self-injuring women with borderline personality disorder and PTSD. *Behaviour Research and Therapy, 55,* 7–17. https://doi.org/10.1016/j.brat.2014.01.008

Held, P., Klassen, B. J., Brennan, M. B., & Zalta, A. K. (2018). Using prolonged exposure and cognitive processing therapy to treat veterans with moral injury-based PTSD: Two case examples. *Cognitive and Behavioral Practice, 25*(3), 377–390. https://doi.org/10.1016/j.cbpra.2017.09.003

Hunsley, J., & Mash, E. J. (2005). Introduction to the special section on developing guidelines for the evidence-based assessment (EBA) of adult disorders. *Psychological Assessment, 17*(3), 251–255. https://doi.org/10.1037/1040-3590.17.3.251

Janoff-Bulman, R. (1989). Assumptive worlds and the stress of traumatic events. *Social Cognition, 7*(2), 113–136. https://doi.org/10.1521/soco.1989.7.2.113

Karlin, B. E., Ruzek, J. I., Chard, K. M., Eftekhari, A., Monson, C. M., Hembree, E. A., Resick, P. A., & Foa, E. B. (2010). Dissemination of evidence-based psychological treatments for posttraumatic stress disorder in the Veterans Health Administration. *Journal of Traumatic Stress, 23*(6), 663–673. https://doi.org/10.1002/jts.20588

Kroenke, K., Spitzer, R. L., & Williams, J. B. W. (2001). The PHQ-9: Validity of a brief depression severity measure. *Journal of General Internal Medicine, 16*(9), 606–613. https://doi.org/10.1046/j.1525-1497.2001.016009606.x

Lee, D. J., Schnitzlein, C. W., Wolf, J. P., Vythilingam, M., Rasmusson, A. M., & Hoge, C. W. (2016). Psychotherapy versus pharmacotherapy for posttraumatic stress disorder: Systemic review and meta-analyses to determine first-line treatments. *Depression and Anxiety, 33*(9), 792–806. https://doi.org/10.1002/da.22511

Rauch, S., & Foa, E. (2006). Emotional processing theory (EPT) and exposure therapy for PTSD. *Journal of Contemporary Psychotherapy, 36*(2), 61–65. https://doi.org/10.1007/s10879-006-9008-y

Resick, P., Monson, C., & Chard, K. (2016). *Cognitive processing therapy: A comprehensive manual.* Guilford Press.

Resick, P. A., Nishith, P., Weaver, T. L., Astin, M. C., & Feuer, C. A. (2002). A comparison of cognitive-processing therapy with prolonged exposure and a waiting condition for the treatment of chronic posttraumatic stress disorder in female rape victims. *Journal of Consulting and Clinical Psychology, 70*(4), 867–879. https://doi.org/10.1037/0022-006X.70.4.867

Smith, E. R., Duax, J. M., & Rauch, S. A. M. (2013). Perceived perpetration during traumatic events: Clinical suggestions from experts in prolonged exposure therapy. *Cognitive and Behavioral Practice, 20*(4), 461–470. https://doi.org/10.1016/j.cbpra.2012.12.002

Sripada, R. K., Rauch, S. A., & Liberzon, I. (2016). Psychological mechanisms of PTSD and its treatment. *Current Psychiatry Reports, 18*(11), 99. https://doi.org/10.1007/s11920-016-0735-9

Tilghman-Osborne, C., Cole, D. A., & Felton, J. W. (2010). Definition and measurement of guilt: Implications for clinical research and practice. *Clinical Psychology Review, 30*(5), 536–546. https://doi.org/10.1016/j.cpr.2010.03.007

Tolin, D. F., Gilliam, C., Wootton, B. M., Bowe, W., Bragdon, L. B., Davis, E., Hannan, S. E., Steinman, S. A., Worden, B., & Hallion, L. S. (2018). Psychometric properties of a structured diagnostic interview for *DSM–5* anxiety, mood, and obsessive-compulsive and related disorders. *Assessment, 25*(1), 3–13. https://doi.org/10.1177/1073191116638410

VA/DoD Clinical Practice Guideline Working Group. (2017). *VA/DoD clinical practice guideline for the management of posttraumatic stress disorder and acute stress disorder.* VA Office of Quality and Performance.

Watts, B. V., Schnurr, P. P., Mayo, L., Young-Xu, Y., Weeks, W. B., & Friedman, M. J. (2013). Meta-analysis of the efficacy of treatments for posttraumatic stress disorder. *The Journal of Clinical Psychiatry, 74*, e541–e550. https://doi.org/10.4088/JCP.12r08225

Weathers, F. W., Blake, D. D., Schnurr, P. P., Kaloupek, D. G., Marx, B. P., & Keane, T. M. (2015). *The Clinician-Administered PTSD Scale for* DSM–5 *(CAPS-5)—Past Month*. National Center for PTSD.

Weathers, F. W., Litz, B. T., Keane, T. M., Palmieri, P. A., Marx, B. P., & Schnurr, P. P. (2013). *The PTSD Checklist for* DSM–5 (PCL-5). National Center for PTSD.

Yasinski, C., Sherrill, A. M., Maples-Keller, J. L., Rauch, S. A. M., & Rothbaum, B. O. (2017). Intensive outpatient prolonged exposure for PTSD in post-9/11 veterans and service members: Program structure and preliminary outcomes of the Emory Healthcare Veterans Program. *Trauma Psychology News, 12*(3), 14–17.

8

Cognitive Processing Therapy for Moral Injury

Jennifer Schuster Wachen, Wyatt R. Evans, Vanessa M. Jacoby, and Abby E. Blankenship

Exposure to morally injurious events is related to increased risk of negative mental health outcomes, including depression, suicidal ideation, and post-traumatic stress disorder (PTSD; Bryan et al., 2016; Evans et al., 2018; Wisco et al., 2017). Cognitive processing therapy (CPT) is a manualized, trauma-focused cognitive behavioral treatment for PTSD and comorbid symptoms (Resick, Monson, & Chard, 2017). CPT was first developed to treat survivors of sexual assault (Resick & Schnicke, 1992, 1993) but has been supported for use in other populations at risk of encountering morally injurious events, such as combat veterans (e.g., Monson et al., 2006) and active duty military (e.g., Resick, Wachen, Dondanville, et al., 2017; Resick, Wachen, Mintz, et al., 2015). CPT is one of the primary evidence-based treatments for PTSD and has been recommended as a first-line treatment in clinical guidelines from the Department of Veterans Affairs, Department of Defense, and American Psychological Association. Although CPT was not developed as a treatment for moral injury specifically, its theoretical model and evidence base support its use for treating PTSD and other comorbidities resulting from exposure to morally injurious events.

THEORETICAL BACKGROUND OF CPT

CPT is based on the constructivist, cognitive model of PTSD that focuses on the cognitions developed as a result of the trauma and the role that inaccurate or distorted cognitions have on emotional responses and behavior. The primary

https://doi.org/10.1037/0000204-009
Addressing Moral Injury in Clinical Practice, J. M. Currier, K. D. Drescher, and J. Nieuwsma (Editors)

goals of CPT are to encourage the expression of natural emotions and reduce manufactured emotions (emotions resulting from distorted cognitions) related to the trauma; to identify and challenge dysfunctional cognitions ("stuck points") about the traumatic event(s), as well as current thoughts about self, others, and the world; and to promote a more balanced set of beliefs about oneself, others, and the world.

The CPT conceptual model frames PTSD as a disorder of nonrecovery (Resick, Monson, & Chard, 2017). That is, following a traumatic event, symptoms of posttraumatic stress are expected and natural. Over the days and weeks following the event, most trauma survivors will experience a natural remission of these symptoms. However, remission does not occur for all survivors. To explain this process, CPT is rooted in social cognitive theory (Benight & Bandura, 2004), which highlights how individuals' efforts to incorporate the experience of trauma into existing beliefs may go awry and lead to ongoing distress and impairment. In instances of successful natural recovery, trauma survivors alter preexisting beliefs to incorporate (i.e., accommodate) new information learned as a result of the traumatic events in a reality-based and balanced manner.

When natural recovery does not occur, it is likely that this process of attempting to incorporate the new information (i.e., the trauma memory) into preexisting beliefs has led to erroneous or problematic understandings of the causes and consequences of the events (i.e., assimilated stuck points), as well as distorted or unhelpful beliefs about oneself, others, and the world (i.e., overaccommodated stuck points). Accordingly, facilitating cognitive flexibility and restructuring toward more reality-based, balanced beliefs is the primary mechanism leading to recovery from PTSD. By shifting unhelpful beliefs to be more balanced and evidence based, distressing emotions that result from these maladaptive beliefs (i.e., "manufactured" emotions) are relieved. Moreover, the CPT therapist guides the patient toward awareness and approach of "natural" emotions that are the direct result of the event (e.g., sadness) rather than the interpretation, which diminish naturally over time.

The establishment of reality-based, balanced beliefs remains the primary mechanism when targeting moral injury in CPT. Following a morally injurious event, the same cognitive processes may occur wherein new information must be squared with existing beliefs. In cases when beliefs resulting from the trauma represent a failure to accurately and/or comprehensively incorporate contextual information, the goal of CPT is to explore these incomplete or distorted thoughts (via Socratic questioning or dialogue) and incorporate missing information or resolve discrepancies between available evidence and the beliefs. The target result of this exploration is a fuller, more reality-based set of beliefs about the event, oneself, others, and the world. When trauma-related cognitions represent not an erroneous belief but a troubling, accurate thought about a past moral violation, the goal of CPT is not to challenge that realistic thought. Instead, it is to encourage the service member or veteran (SM/V) to accept the reality of the situation and feel the natural emotions associated with the event that may have been avoided in the context of PTSD.

Often, after experiencing a morally injurious traumatic event, individuals (SM/Vs) will assign blame to themselves or others as a way of trying to make sense of the trauma. These distorted perceptions and associated exaggerated emotions can often be resolved via cognitive restructuring. In many cases, using Socratic questioning, the perceived transgression may be nullified by the additional contextual information, once the patient is able to resolve erroneous self- or other-blame about the event. In a smaller subset of cases, the violation (by self or others) was intentional and solely or primarily the responsibility of the perpetrator(s). In these cases, the objective of CPT is categorically not to minimize true culpability, rationalize wrongdoing, or deflect blame. When self-blame is appropriate and accurate, guilt is not a manufactured emotion. When other-blame is appropriate and accurate, contempt and even anger may be natural rather than manufactured emotions. The focus of CPT is then to experience the related natural emotions openly and to establish a balanced belief that acknowledges the reality of the situation (i.e., the moral violation) and facilitates optimal functioning and quality of life going forward.

Perhaps most common, SM/Vs present with beliefs that include both erroneous or distorted interpretations, as well as reality-based perceptions. Once again, the goal of CPT is to establish a balanced belief, accepting the reality of the event (even the painful parts) while also amending any distorted beliefs. Beliefs that arise about the event following moral violations by oneself typically involve thoughts about what one "should" or "should not" have done. Similarly, following moral violations by others, thoughts commonly center on what others "should" or "should not" have done. Simple though the word may be, what one "should" do is complex and informed by rules, laws, customs, personal values, group values, cultural values, and morality. However, Socratic questioning, when used effectively, is a particularly well-matched tool for unpacking these statements. This strategy can help the therapist understand the values of the SM/V that are contributing to his or her interpretation of the situation while guiding the SM/V to a more objective perspective of the event. The purpose of Socratic questioning is to explore complex situations in search of a holistic perception and response. Achieving this balanced perspective often involves reappraisal of certain aspects of the traumatic experience and acceptance of certain (perhaps painful) realities.

For cases of moral injury in which actions or inactions of self or others represent a violation of one's deeply held moral values, overaccommodated stuck points represent significant sources of distress. Significant changes in beliefs about self, others, and the world may stem from the "just world" belief: Good things happen to good people, and bad things happen to bad people. Often, these overaccommodated beliefs fall into one of the five categories addressed in CPT—safety, trust, power and control, esteem, and intimacy. SM/Vs who have violated their moral values may describe themselves as "morally contaminated," "unworthy of love," or "a monster." SM/Vs whose moral values have been violated by others may describe people or the world as "evil" or "disgusting."

When addressing these types of overaccommodated stuck points, Socratic questioning and the CPT worksheets are used to help SM/Vs establish a balanced and holistic perception of self, others, and the world. These tools may help patients gain flexibility in previously rigid patterns of thinking and may help disconfirm overgeneralized beliefs by broadening the scope of appraisal beyond the morally injurious event. Importantly, this dialogue may also function to facilitate processes often important for moral healing, including acceptance, forgiveness, and compassion for self and others. For example, after exploring the stuck point "I am a monster" that developed after a moral violation by the self, a new balanced belief that facilitates acceptance of past moral transgressions and forgiveness may read, "I have done monstrous things, and I plan to atone by doing good things in the future." In this way, Socratic dialogue in the context of CPT is a flexible tool that may facilitate moral healing via both cognitive change and acceptance. Indeed, helping the SM/V to identify ways in which he or she might atone for past wrongdoings may also help the patient move past the moral transgression toward moral healing.

THE SCIENTIFIC BASIS OF CPT FOR MORAL INJURY

There is an extensive literature supporting the efficacy of CPT in a number of diverse populations in which moral injury is likely to be prevalent, including victims of physical and sexual assault (e.g., Resick et al., 2002), survivors of childhood sexual abuse (Chard, 2005), military veterans (e.g., Forbes et al., 2012; Monson et al., 2006; Morland et al., 2014), and active duty service members (Resick, Wachen, Dondanville, et al., 2017; Resick, Wachen, Mintz, et al., 2015). It should be noted that CPT was designed to be a treatment for PTSD, not a treatment for moral injury specifically. Accordingly, the extant literature examining the efficacy of CPT has focused on the primary outcome of PTSD symptomatology. We acknowledge that although moral injury and PTSD often go hand in hand, not all individuals experiencing moral injury go on to develop PTSD and vice versa. However, given the strength of the research supporting the use of CPT for PTSD, we highlight some of the major research findings that may also support the use of CPT to address moral injury in the course of PTSD treatment.

The first randomized controlled clinical trial (RCT) of CPT compared CPT, prolonged exposure (PE), and a wait-list (WL) control group in a sample of 171 female rape survivors (Resick et al., 2002). Results showed that both CPT and PE groups demonstrated significant reductions in PTSD and depressive symptoms between pre- and posttreatment compared with the WL condition. There were few differences between the two active treatments, although CPT resulted in greater improvement in symptoms of guilt, suggesting that CPT may be particularly well-suited to addressing the guilt cognitions that may be associated with moral injury. These improvements were sustained at the 3-month and 9-month follow-ups. A subsequent long-term follow-up assessment of these participants (Resick et al., 2012) revealed no significant change in PTSD symptoms 5 to 10 years following original study participation, indicating that treatment gains were maintained over an extended period. This suggests that the benefits of CPT have lasting effects and that the treatment does not merely offer short-term reassurance.

A growing body of evidence supports the use of CPT in addressing PTSD in veteran and active duty military samples. In the first RCT conducted with a veteran sample, Monson and colleagues (2006) found veterans receiving CPT demonstrated improvements in PTSD symptoms compared with treatment as usual through a 1-month follow-up. Improvements in co-occurring symptoms of depression and anxiety, affect functioning, guilt distress, and social adjustment also were found, indicating CPT benefitted more than just PTSD symptoms. Forbes and colleagues (2012) examined the effectiveness of CPT compared with treatment as usual in three veterans' clinics across Australia. Results showed greater improvements in PTSD, anxiety, and depression for the CPT group. Recently, Morland et al. (2014) found CPT delivered by telehealth intervention to rural veterans to be noninferior to CPT delivered in person, providing additional support to the efficacy of CPT in a veteran population.

Active duty service members may be particularly prone to exposure to morally injurious events, given the nature of the environment in which they are embedded and the evolution of warfare tactics. Recent research supports the efficacy of CPT in treating PTSD in this population, as well. In the first study of CPT in military personnel, Resick and colleagues (2015) compared group CPT with group present-centered therapy (PCT) in a sample of 108 active duty soldiers. Group CPT resulted in significantly higher reductions in PTSD symptoms than PCT. A later study (Resick, Wachen, et al., 2017) examined group and individual CPT in an active duty sample of 268 soldiers. Participants in both conditions showed significant reductions in PTSD symptomatology with large effect sizes ($d = 0.7$ group, $d = 1.3$ individual), although individual treatment produced significantly greater treatment gains. These studies lend support to the efficacy of CPT in active duty military populations.

Although moral injury has not been the primary focus of existing RCTs examining CPT, several commentaries and case studies have also supported the use of CPT for moral injury. For example, Wachen et al. (2016) described special considerations in using CPT with active duty military based on clinical experience from conducting an RCT with this population. It was noted that many types of traumas experienced during military service, such as betrayal by leadership or peers, mistreatment of enemies, and friendly fire may be conceptualized by an SM/V as a transgression of his or her moral code. Moreover, military ethos and its potential impact on an individual's sense of responsibility may inadvertently promote the development of stuck points related to self- or other-blame. Wachen et al. discussed how strategies used in CPT may successfully address these unhelpful beliefs. Further, Held and colleagues (2018) published a case example of a military veteran who was successfully treated with CPT for PTSD resulting from a morally injurious traumatic event. Data collected during the case example indicated the patient demonstrated a clinically significant, 52-point reduction in PTSD Checklist (Weathers et al., 1993) scores, from 65 at pretreatment to 13 at posttreatment. Although this large improvement cannot be guaranteed for all who undergo CPT following a morally injurious event, this case example provides strong preliminary evidence that CPT can be used effectively to treat PTSD resulting from this type of trauma.

COMPONENTS AND SESSIONS OF CPT

CPT can be delivered in an individual or group therapy format or a combination of the two. CPT is typically conducted once or twice per week in 50- to 60-minute individual sessions or 90- to 120-minute group sessions. Practice assignments are completed in the interval between sessions. Although the original CPT protocol (Resick & Schnicke, 1993) included a written account of the trauma memory, a dismantling study of CPT determined that CPT without the account (formerly called CPT-C) was equally effective (Resick et al., 2008). Therefore, the most recent CPT manual (Resick, Monson, & Chard, 2017) includes the written account as an optional addition to the treatment (CPT+A). Although CPT is traditionally delivered in 12 sessions, the use of a variable-length version of CPT (Galovski et al., 2012) was also shown to improve outcomes. Therefore, CPT may be extended to include extra sessions if needed, or patients may complete treatment before finishing all 12 sessions if they are demonstrating good functioning.

CPT is divided into three phases: education, processing, and challenging. In the first phase, patients are provided with psychoeducation about the symptoms of PTSD and the development and maintenance of PTSD from a social cognitive perspective. Patients learn the connection between thoughts and emotions and how to recognize their beliefs resulting from the traumatic event. The second phase of treatment focuses on processing the traumatic event through engagement with the trauma memory, through the use of Socratic questioning and the written account, if used. The goal of this phase is for patients to identify and generate more balanced alternatives to their assimilated beliefs, particularly in the areas of blame, shame, and hindsight bias about the event. In the third and final phase of treatment, patients are taught to examine further their stuck points about the trauma, as well as beliefs that have become overgeneralized from the traumatic events (overaccommodated beliefs). The goal of this phase is to generate healthier, more accurate beliefs in relation to the event, self, others, and the world. The following are brief descriptions of the content of CPT for each session.

Session 1

The first session of CPT is dedicated to psychoeducation about PTSD, cognitive theory, natural and manufactured emotions, and the role of avoidance in inhibiting the natural psychological recovery process following a trauma. The therapist introduces the concept of a *stuck point*, which is a thought or belief that causes ongoing distress or impairs one's ability to engage in valued or important life activities. The therapist explains how, as a response to trauma, individuals may develop an unrealistic belief about the cause of the event (an assimilated stuck point) or overaccommodate their beliefs about themselves, others, or the world to the extreme on the basis of their traumatic experiences. The therapist then describes how these maladaptive beliefs can lead to longstanding manufactured emotions, such as guilt or shame, which do not lessen over time because they are manufactured by a person's maladaptive beliefs, rather than an external event. Manufactured emotions are contrasted with natural emotions, which do reduce in intensity over time and are critical in the natural recovery process following a trauma. Last, the therapist assigns the SM/V to write a one-page impact statement that describes (a) why he or she believes the trauma happened and (b) how beliefs about self, others, and the world have changed in the broad areas of safety, trust, power and control, esteem, and intimacy.

Session 2

The first half of Session 2 focuses on helping the SM/V identify stuck points and build a stuck point log to track stuck points throughout treatment. The SM/V reads the impact statement aloud, and the therapist and SM/V identify assimilated and overaccommodated stuck points resulting from the trauma. SM/Vs with morally injurious experiences may identify assimilated stuck points about the unfairness of the event (e.g., "I shouldn't have been in that situation," "Children should never be killed"), stuck points about themselves (e.g., "I am a monster because of what I have done"), or stuck points about others (e.g., "All human beings are cruel"). In the second half of Session 2, the therapist introduces the SM/V to the cognitive behavioral theoretical connection between events, thoughts and beliefs, and emotional responses. Last, the ABC worksheet is introduced, which asks the SM/V to write about an activating event (A), the beliefs related to that event (B), and the emotional reaction (C) to those beliefs to help the SM/V build skills of identifying thoughts and emotions and increasing awareness of how thoughts contribute to emotional responses.

Session 3

Session 3 is dedicated to using ABC worksheets to (a) continue to build skills in identifying emotions and the connection between thoughts and emotions, (b) continue to identify stuck points to be added to the stuck point log, and (c) introduce the concept of challenging one's beliefs by engaging the SM/V in gentle Socratic dialogue. The key goal of this session is to ensure that the SM/V can accurately identify underlying thoughts and related emotions. Additional stuck points are generated on the basis of the identified thoughts and added to the stuck point log. The therapist then guides the SM/V in a Socratic dialogue to gently challenge identified stuck points. For practice throughout the week, the SM/V is again assigned an ABC worksheet to complete each day, focused specifically on the index trauma.

Session 4

Session 4 is composed of a combination of psychoeducation about common trauma-related stuck points and skill building in the self-challenging of unhelpful trauma-related beliefs. The ABC practice worksheets are reviewed, with a focus on Socratic questioning of trauma-related stuck points. Several concepts likely to be salient in moral injury are introduced in this session, including hindsight bias and the difference between responsibility and intent. Socratic dialogue is used to help the SM/V reduce unwarranted self-blame and instead place blame on the appropriate party, if there is one. The therapist then introduces the Challenging Questions Worksheet, which guides the SM/V through a series of questions to evaluate the veracity of a single identified stuck point.

Session 5

Much of Session 5 is dedicated to helping build the skill of challenging stuck points using the Challenging Questions Worksheets. The therapist begins to shift from being the leader of the Socratic questioning to helping the SM/V lead him- or herself through the Socratic method. In the latter part of this session, the SM/V is introduced to a final new skill, identifying problematic patterns of thinking. The therapist presents the SM/V with the Problematic Patterns of Thinking Worksheet and explains each type of problematic thinking pattern, which represent common cognitive distortions (e.g., jumping to conclusions, exaggerating, or minimizing). The SM/V is assigned Problematic Patterns of Thinking Worksheets to categorize his or her stuck points.

Session 6

This session marks the halfway point in CPT. Here, the SM/V shifts from learning new skills to practicing the skills together to generate balanced, realistic, and more helpful thoughts. After reviewing the SM/V's Problematic Patterns of Thinking Worksheet, the SM/V is introduced to the Challenging Beliefs Worksheet (CBW) that will be used by the SM/V daily until the end of treatment. The CBW contains all the content of the previous worksheets, with the addition of ratings of how much the SM/V believes the identified stuck point (0% to 100%) and how intense the emotional response to the thought is, also from 0% to 100%. Last, the SM/V is asked to generate a new, alternative thought to their stuck point as a result of challenging the belief. Once an alternative thought has been generated, the SM/V rates (0% to 100%) the belief in the new thought, the belief in the original stuck point after challenging the thought, and new emotional responses to the new thought. SM/Vs often notice a reduction in their manufactured negative emotions at the end of the worksheet and sometimes identify new positive emotions related to their new alternative thought. Particularly among SM/Vs experiencing moral injury, alternative beliefs may bring about new negative but natural (as opposed to manufactured) emotions, such as sadness, disappointment, or grief, as they come to an acceptance of the reality of their trauma. For practice, the SM/V is assigned to complete one CBW each day, prioritizing any unresolved stuck points specifically about their index trauma.

Session 7

Much of Session 7 is devoted to the continuation of practice using the CBWs. By the end of the session, the goal is to resolve all assimilated stuck points focused specifically on the traumatic event because the following sessions are designed to focus on overaccommodated stuck points. However, if SM/Vs continue to have unresolved assimilated stuck points at this point in treatment, they are encouraged to continue focusing on these stuck points, as well as the stuck points related to the new session content. The first theme, safety, is introduced. The SM/V is given a handout related to this theme and is asked to use it to identify stuck points that have developed related to a sense of safety for self and others.

Session 8

The content of Session 8 includes challenging safety-related stuck points using the CBWs. For SM/Vs with moral injury from trauma, stuck points in this area tend to be less about their safety and are more often related to viewing themselves as dangerous or as a failure in protecting others. Examples include "I should not be around children because I will harm them," or "I am an unsafe leader." In this session, the CBWs can help the SM/V challenge these thoughts by highlighting the instances where they have, for example, been around children and not harmed them. This Socratic process can help the SM/V see that the stuck point overgeneralizes from a context-specific (i.e., combat) and highly emotional event. Thus, the SM/V may identify a more realistic thought, such as "I have never harmed a child outside the context of a life-or-death combat situation." Here, it is important to support the SM/V in processing any natural emotions that emerge from this thought, such as sadness or grief for the loss. The end of the session is devoted to introducing the SM/V to the next theme, trust.

Session 9

Session 9 builds on Session 8, which focuses on physical safety, to include trusting others to provide "emotional safety," as well as trust in one's judgment and decision making. Trust is commonly disrupted by trauma. This is especially true for SM/Vs with a moral injury because the nature of a morally injurious event often involves a betrayal in the trust of oneself or others to adhere to a moral value. For example, for an SM/V who experienced an event involving a self-directed moral injury, a stuck point might be "I cannot trust myself to make ethically sound decisions." After reviewing the psychoeducation handout and the CBWs, the therapist engages the SM/V in a Socratic dialogue facilitated by the Trust Star Worksheet. This sheet teaches the SM/V to examine their trust in others in a multifaceted, multidimensional, and dynamic way, rather than in "all-or-none" terms. Lingering trust-related stuck points are then challenged using CBWs. Last, the therapist introduces the theme of power and control.

Session 10

Session 10 focuses on the SM/Vs' beliefs about how much power they have over events in their lives, ability to exhibit self-control, and their perceived control of others. Trauma can lead individuals to "swing the pendulum" to the extreme in their beliefs about power and control in several ways. Some may begin to believe that because they could not control or prevent their index trauma, they have no control over any events in their lives, leading to helplessness or despair. Alternatively, some conclude they must be in complete control of all things at all times (including other people) or else something bad will happen. This can be true for some SM/Vs with a moral injury related to others if they perceived the trauma to be caused by another's lack of moral control or strength. Last, some begin to question whether they can control their behaviors, which often leads to fear, shame, and isolation from others. This is common for those with a self-directed moral injury. The esteem theme is introduced at the end of the session.

Session 11

Session 11 focuses on self-esteem and esteem for others. Traumatic events can disrupt one's concept of themselves and lead to destructive self-focused beliefs, such as "I am a bad or damaged person," or "I deserve bad things to happen to me." If spiritual or religious, an SM/V with a moral injury may believe that God has given them symptoms of PTSD to punish them. Equally, trauma has the potential to disrupt one's beliefs about the goodness of others and can lead to extreme beliefs such as "humanity is evil" or "people are only out for themselves." Self- and other-esteem stuck points are especially salient for those with a moral injury. Because moral injury, by nature, involves oneself or another engaging in an act that goes against what is perceived as morally good or right, beliefs about this experience can overgeneralize to "self as a whole" or "humanity as a whole." Through guidance from the CBWs and Socratic dialogue, the goal for an SM/V with moral injury is to disengage from overgeneralized or "all-or-none" thinking in regard to their own or others' behavior. Following this discussion, the final theme, intimacy, is introduced.

Moreover, the SM/V is asked to write a final impact statement reflecting the changes in his or her beliefs about the traumatic event.

Session 12

The first half of Session 12 is dedicated to working through stuck points related to intimacy, as well as any lingering stuck points not fully resolved through previous CPT work. Disrupted beliefs about intimacy are common for those with moral injury. Stuck points related to self-intimacy can include thoughts such as "I don't deserve to care for myself." Unhelpful beliefs about intimacy with others might include, "If I become close with someone, they will betray me." The rest of this session focuses on summarizing progress, learning consolidation, and preventing relapse. The SM/V is asked to read the final impact statement, and this is compared with the original impact statement. The SM/V processes the experience of CPT, discusses positive changes made, and identifies any remaining stuck points and future goals.

CPT TRAINING AND TREATMENT DELIVERY FOR MORAL INJURY

There are a number of important considerations when targeting trauma-focused interventions to address moral injury. Many of those have been elucidated in this book, and some have been addressed already in this chapter. However, there are a few salient considerations in the delivery of CPT, as well as in the training of new CPT therapists, that we highlight here. Specifically, we want to emphasize the importance of titrating pacing and directivity in guided inquiry, preventing the imposition of personal values by the therapist and acknowledging SM/Vs' important cultural values.

First, it is requisite for all CPT providers and those training new providers to develop strong Socratic questioning skills to target in-session inquiry and the cognitive restructuring process effectively. An effective CPT therapist uses this procedure as part of the broader process of collaborative empiricism to guide discovery and foster awareness and curiosity in their SM/Vs. Although open-ended questions should steer SM/Vs toward reality-based thinking, it is frequently ineffective to move too quickly from a focus on developing awareness of thoughts, feelings, and reactions to challenging problematic beliefs. This may be especially detrimental to treatment for SM/Vs with moral injury. Painful moral judgments are, by their nature, tied to deeply held moral values and may be more resistant to rapid change.

Moving too quickly from exploration to challenging beliefs (or, worse, confronting SM/Vs about their beliefs) may also result in the therapist missing important nuances in the beliefs. As we discussed earlier, stuck points that develop after morally injurious events frequently comprise both evidence-based and distorted components. A therapist who moves too quickly from exploration to challenging may inadvertently miss or even reject the reality of the values violation that occurred in an effort to amend distorted interpretations or right-size perceived culpability. Similarly, therapists who overshoot this process of guided discovery altogether, becoming directive or telling the SM/V what they "should" think or feel, are likely to damage the therapeutic relationship and impede the overarching goal of fostering cognitive flexibility. When serving SM/Vs with moral injury, it is essential to tactfully titrate pace and directivity to facilitate the skill-learning process for the SM/V and provide the therapist with time and space to develop an awareness of his or her experience, perspective, and values.

Relatedly, another pitfall in working with moral injury is poor navigation of differences in values between SM/V and therapist. Given the role of CPT therapists as guides, shepherding the SM/V to more balanced beliefs, therapists must be aware of their values, as well as their SM/Vs', including similarities and differences between them. For example, a veteran may be distressed by having killed a child in combat, given his or her values of respect for human life and caring for those in need. If a CPT provider holds superordinate values of duty and protection and defense, they may feel pulled to "convince" the SM/V that their actions were just, right, or appropriate. These interpretations, however, are based on the therapist's moral values, not the SM/V's. Exploration and awareness of personal values, as well as flexibility in responding to SM/Vs with discrepant values, are important for any therapist and perhaps especially important for those providing CPT to SM/Vs with moral injury.

Therapists should also be aware of the values of cultures with which SM/Vs identify, the moral rules prescribed by these cultures, and the way these rules may be applied (or misapplied) in different contexts. For example, civilian providers should seek education or training in military cultural values that might influence the development and maintenance of stuck points in military personnel and veterans. It is important for a CPT therapist not to seek to undermine those values but, instead, to help SM/Vs identify how rigid beliefs about moral rules are keeping them stuck in their efforts to make meaning of the events and/or negatively impacting their functioning across contexts. Moreover, awareness of cultural values will help therapists better target their interventions. For example, in working with a Christian whose actions led to a fatal car accident, awareness of the value of preserving human life (i.e., "Thou shalt not kill") may help the therapist guide the SM/V toward beliefs that facilitate forgiveness rather than exclusively focusing on potential mitigating factors that, even if present, do not nullify that reality of the SM/V's role in the death. In this way, awareness of values is necessary for optimal application of CPT, which entails both reappraising inaccurate beliefs and accepting the (often painful) reality of the event.

With regard to acceptance, another important consideration when delivering CPT with an SM/V with a moral injury is not to assume that all cognitions related to the event are erroneous. The nature of moral injury means that, at times, guilt and remorse are natural emotions resulting from responsibility and intention to harm. The SM/V should be encouraged to label and experience these natural emotions. Here, it is important not to attempt to challenge the veracity of these cognitions, but rather to allow the SM/V to acknowledge the reality of the event, but within the larger context of the SM/V's existence. Although it may be a fact and not a stuck point that the SM/V intentionally acted against his or her moral values, the therapist can use Socratic questioning to help the SM/V recognize the context of the morally injurious action and understand that it does not define the entirety of his or her existence. Moreover, the concept of self-forgiveness becomes important in these situations. The therapist may explore stuck points regarding what it would mean for the SM/V to forgive him- or herself for the transgression. The therapist also may explore with the SM/V how he or she could make amends or perform acts of restitution as a means of moving toward self-forgiveness.

CASE SUMMARY

The following example represents a case in which CPT was used to address PTSD resulting from a morally injurious traumatic event. "Joe" was a 40-year-old White Sergeant First Class infantryman in the U.S. Army. Joe deployed in support of five post-9/11 combat operations, totaling 63 months in theater. When Joe presented for treatment, he was undergoing medical evaluation for discharge. Joe reported that he was finally seeking treatment for PTSD to prepare him for transitioning from military to civilian life.

Joe joined the Army and participated in the initial invasion of Iraq. He was a fast-tracking soldier and quickly became a squad leader. After his first deployment to Iraq, he left the Army and spent 6 months working as a security guard. Joe was drinking heavily, and his first wife filed for divorce, eventually gaining sole custody of their two children. At this time, Joe had difficulty adjusting to civilian life, felt misunderstood, and decided to reenlist. He had four more deployments, a second marriage and divorce, a third marriage, and two children with his third wife. Importantly, Joe identified as a "born-again Christian" and reported that his religious belief system conflicted with his warrior belief system. Although Joe had multiple childhood and combat traumas, he endorsed an event that occurred during his first combat tour as the most upsetting and distressing. This event was the focus of treatment.

The index trauma occurred during the initial invasion of Iraq. Joe was a new squad leader in charge of soldiers guarding a checkpoint. His orders were to stop all vehicles, and vehicles that did not comply with the checkpoint would be warned and then fired on if they attempted to leave the area. One evening while on guard duty, Joe and his soldiers observed a truck rapidly approaching the checkpoint. Joe and his soldiers fired warning shots and tracers, but the truck did not stop. As a result, the squad fired on the vehicle. There was a small explosion, and the truck caught on fire. The squad celebrated this outcome. However, on investigation, the squad discovered two men with a weapon, two women, and three children (including two infants).

In Session 1, Joe recognized his experience of many symptoms of PTSD. He endorsed feelings of guilt and self-blame about the event and expressed thoughts about how he could have prevented the outcome. At Session 2, Joe came to session with a two-page written impact statement. In so doing, Joe highly emphasized the fact that he was a new squad leader and the role his inexperience might have played. He also was distressed because he could not remember whether he had actually given the order to fire on the truck. Joe believed that if he had not given the order to fire, and his squad fired anyway, he had lost control of his squad, and he was fully to blame for the deaths of the women and children in the car. However, he also believed that if he did give the order, he was also fully to blame for their deaths.

From the impact statement, Joe and his therapist identified a number of assimilated stuck points related to the event, including "If I wasn't a new squad leader, then innocent civilians would have not have been killed"; "If I hadn't lost control of my squad, then innocent civilians would not have been killed"; "If I gave the order to fire, then it's my fault that innocent civilians are dead"; and "If we celebrated then, it means we didn't respect the lives of the innocent civilians." Joe also endorsed a number of overaccommodated stuck points, particularly around the themes of self-trust and esteem. His beliefs included "I cannot be trusted to make decisions," and "I am evil because I killed." Joe also believed that he had to carry his feeling of guilt to honor the memory of those who were killed: "If I don't feel guilty, then it is disrespectful to the women and children who died."

Sessions 3 and 4 used Socratic questioning to identify and challenge assimilated stuck points, as well as to encourage Joe to feel the natural emotions (e.g., sadness, remorse) related to the event he had been avoiding. On one ABC worksheet, Joe identified these thoughts: "Innocent women and children were killed," and "It's my fault they are dead." A discussion about the differences between his thoughts (fact vs. stuck point) and resulting emotions then followed. Joe identified that feeling sad and remorseful for the deaths of the women and children who died was likely a natural response, one that should not be avoided. At the same time, he began to reevaluate his beliefs that it was entirely his fault, opening up the possibility for a reduction in guilt. The goal of these sessions was to help Joe to feel the natural emotions, while also challenging the stuck point that he was solely to blame for their deaths.

For Session 4, Joe brought in ABC worksheets he had completed between sessions. During the review of these worksheets, Joe began to consider parts of the event he had not appreciated at the start of therapy, including that the driver did not heed warnings to stop. The following is a dialogue between Joe and the therapist about his second set of ABC worksheets:

THERAPIST: What was it like doing all of your ABC worksheets on the trauma?

JOE: Well, I noticed I had some thoughts I haven't had before, based on our discussion from last time. For this one, I started thinking about things a little differently. Under "A," I wrote, "Burned bodies of women and children." Under "B," I wrote, "Men driving should have stopped," "There was a weapon," "Was the weapon for their protection?" "Children should not witness war." Lastly, I wrote the emotions "sad," "angry," and "doubtful."

THERAPIST: Which thoughts are tied to "sad" and "angry"?

JOE: Thinking about the bodies made me sad. But I get angry when I think that the men should have stopped, and there was a weapon.

THERAPIST: What about "doubtful"?

JOE: I am feeling doubtful that the weapon was just for their protection.

THERAPIST: What emotion was related to "children should not witness war?"

JOE: Guilt. I just can't stop feeling guilty.

THERAPIST: It sounds like you are beginning to think about the role the driver might have had in the death of the women and children.

JOE: Yeah, when I think about that, I guess it makes it seem like it might not be all my fault that they died. The driver knew he should have stopped. And since he had a gun, he might have had plans to hurt someone.

THERAPIST: However, you also notice that you still feel very guilty.

JOE: It wouldn't be respectful to the women and children to not feel guilty.

THERAPIST: Might that be another stuck point to work on?

During this session, Joe began to contextualize his role in the death of the women and children better and then demonstrated an increase in flexibility when the therapist introduced the CBWs. In challenging the stuck point "It's my fault the innocent civilians are dead," he recognized that it was largely the actions of the driver that directly contributed to the death of the civilians. He also acknowledged that he did not know there were women and children in the car and that he did not have the intention to harm innocent civilians. This change in his thinking allowed him to shift his blame to the driver of the car, who did not heed the warning shots. He was also able to acknowledge the sadness from the fact that the civilians died and remorse for the role he and his unit did play, and he could begin to let those natural emotions run their course.

In Session 5, Joe continued to challenge his assimilated stuck points related to self-blame. He also recognized that many of these stuck points were related to old automatic, habitual patterns of problematic thinking. He identified "If I wasn't a new squad leader, then innocent civilians would have not have been killed" as jumping to conclusions; "If I gave the order to fire, then it's my fault that innocent civilians are dead" as disregarding important aspects of the situation (in particular, the role of the driver of the truck); and "I am evil" as oversimplifying.

During Session 6, the CBW was introduced, and Joe revisited the idea that if he had not been a new squad leader, the women and children would not have been killed. At the beginning of the worksheet, he believed this thought at 50% and felt numb at 40% and anger at 70%. As Joe worked through the CBW with the therapist, he was able to identify that rules of engagement required him to shoot and/or order others to shoot if someone were to run a checkpoint. He also recognized that others played a role in the deaths of the women and children, that he did not know that women and children were in the car, and that being new and giving the order or not giving the order were factors unlikely to change the outcome of what happened that day.

Once Joe's assimilated stuck points had been resolved, Sessions 7 to 11 focused on addressing his overaccommodated stuck points. Because he no longer believed that it was all his fault that innocent civilians had died, his stuck points related to self-trust and esteem were not as firmly entrenched. Because he was able to recognize that he made an appropriate decision by following orders, he began to regain confidence in his ability to make good decisions. However, he continued to have significant difficulty letting go of his feelings of guilt. In particular, Joe continued to believe that he should always feel guilty and that if he didn't feel guilty, he wasn't showing respect to the women and children who died. This was closely tied to his religious beliefs. Joe was asked to complete a CBW on "If I do not feel guilty, then I am being a bad Christian." The following is the dialogue that ensued:

THERAPIST: Joe, I am so glad that you worked on this stuck point. As we discussed last time, believing that you must feel guilty may be making it more difficult for you to actually begin to make this new way of thinking a habit. I see you wrote in "B" that "If I do not feel guilty, then I am a bad Christian" and that you believe that 95% and that this makes you feel angry 100%, guilty 100%, and sad 95%. Tell me, what is the evidence for this thought?

JOE: God says, "Thou shalt not kill." In war, it's okay to kill an enemy combatant, but not innocent people. So, if you kill an innocent person, then you should feel guilty. You should feel guilty forever; otherwise, you're disrespecting the dead.

THERAPIST: Going back to the work you did earlier, did you know that there were women and children in the car?

JOE: No, but there were, and now I must pay for that.

THERAPIST: Walk me through that. What does that look like?

JOE:	Feeling guilty, I guess. Asking for forgiveness every day. Being a better person.
THERAPIST:	You have a son who has since joined the Army. If he were to find himself in a similar situation where he was forced to follow the rules of engagement and discovered later that women and children were killed the process, would you tell him that he needed to feel guilty for the rest of his life?
JOE:	I would tell him he couldn't have known and to pray for the dead and their families. I would tell him to still try to live a good life and maybe to do something in their honor. I know where you are going with this. I wouldn't tell him that he deserves to feel guilty for the rest of his life, especially if he didn't know.
THERAPIST:	I think that is great advice. What have you learned from your own advice?

By the end of treatment, Joe was still working on replacing his guilt with natural sadness and anger. He was also learning not to "beat himself up" but rather to pray for the deaths of the women and children and their families according to his religious beliefs. Last, in an effort to live a good life in the memory of innocent people lost or injured in war, Joe worked as a youth minister for disadvantaged children at his church.

At Session 12, Joe's final impact statement reflected his shift in beliefs regarding who was to blame for the deaths of the civilians. He placed responsibility on the driver, who chose not to stop after warning shots were fired. Joe recognized his actions were in accordance with his orders. He recognized the natural emotion of sadness from acknowledging the painful fact that innocent civilians died and noted he is working on continuing to feel sadness and remorse instead of guilt. He expressed an intention to move forward and honor the victims by living a good life. He also noted improvements in his trust, self-esteem, and intimacy with his wife.

CONCLUSION

CPT is a gold-standard treatment for PTSD, currently included in clinical practice guidelines as one of the first-line recommended treatments. Although CPT was not developed as a primary treatment for moral injury, it has been shown to be effective in a number of populations in which moral injury is prevalent. The proposed mechanism underlying CPT is well-suited to addressing issues that arise from moral injury. Specifically, Socratic questioning is a flexible tool that can be used to facilitate a more realistic context for resulting beliefs and to guide an SM/V toward acceptance and forgiveness related to moral violation. Cognitions that are deemed inaccurate are challenged and replaced with more balanced beliefs, whereas thoughts that are grounded in realistic but painful truths are acknowledged, and the SM/V is encouraged to work toward acceptance. Future research including more specific measures of moral injury will provide a greater understanding of how CPT may address PTSD and comorbid symptoms related to moral injury in diverse SM/V populations.

REFERENCES

Benight, C. C., & Bandura, A. (2004). Social cognitive theory of posttraumatic recovery: The role of perceived self-efficacy. *Behaviour Research and Therapy, 42*(10), 1129–1148. https://doi.org/10.1016/j.brat.2003.08.008

Bryan, C. J., Bryan, A. O., Anestis, M. D., Anestis, J. C., Green, B. A., Etienne, N., Morrow, C. E., & Ray-Sannerud, B. (2016). Measuring moral injury: Psychometric properties of the Moral Injury Events Scale in two military samples. *Assessment, 23*(5), 557–570. https://doi.org/10.1177/1073191115590855

Chard, K. M. (2005). An evaluation of cognitive processing therapy for the treatment of posttraumatic stress disorder related to childhood sexual abuse. *Journal of Consulting and Clinical Psychology, 73*(5), 965–971. https://doi.org/10.1037/0022-006X.73.5.965

Evans, W. R., Stanley, M. A., Barrera, T. L., Exline, J. J., Pargament, K. I., & Teng, E. J. (2018). Morally injurious events and psychological distress among veterans: Examining the mediating role of religious and spiritual struggles. *Psychological Trauma: Theory, Research, Practice, and Policy, 10*(3), 360–367. https://doi.org/10.1037/tra0000347

Forbes, D., Lloyd, D., Nixon, R. D., Elliott, P., Varker, T., Perry, D., Bryant, R. A., & Creamer, M. (2012). A multisite randomized controlled effectiveness trial of cognitive processing therapy for military-related posttraumatic stress disorder. *Journal of Anxiety Disorders, 26*(3), 442–452. https://doi.org/10.1016/j.janxdis.2012.01.006

Galovski, T. E., Blain, L. M., Mott, J. M., Elwood, L., & Houle, T. (2012). Manualized therapy for PTSD: Flexing the structure of cognitive processing therapy. *Journal of Consulting and Clinical Psychology, 80*(6), 968–981. https://doi.org/10.1037/a0030600

Held, P., Klassen, B. J., Brennan, M. B., & Zalta, A. K. (2018). Using prolonged exposure and cognitive processing therapy to treat veterans with moral injury-based PTSD: Two case examples. *Cognitive and Behavioral Practice, 25*(3), 377–390. https://doi.org/10.1016/j.cbpra.2017.09.003

Monson, C. M., Schnurr, P. P., Resick, P. A., Friedman, M. J., Young-Xu, Y., & Stevens, S. P. (2006). Cognitive processing therapy for veterans with military-related posttraumatic stress disorder. *Journal of Consulting and Clinical Psychology, 74*(5), 898–907. https://doi.org/10.1037/0022-006X.74.5.898

Morland, L. A., Mackintosh, M. A., Greene, C. J., Rosen, C. S., Chard, K. M., Resick, P., & Frueh, B. C. (2014). Cognitive processing therapy for posttraumatic stress disorder delivered to rural veterans via telemental health: A randomized noninferiority clinical trial. *The Journal of Clinical Psychiatry, 75*(5), 470–476. https://doi.org/10.4088/JCP.13m08842

Resick, P. A., Galovski, T. E., Uhlmansiek, M. O., Scher, C. D., Clum, G. A., & Young-Xu, Y. (2008). A randomized clinical trial to dismantle components of cognitive processing therapy for posttraumatic stress disorder in female victims of interpersonal violence. *Journal of Consulting and Clinical Psychology, 76*, 243–258. https://doi.org/10.1037/0022-006X.76.2.243

Resick, P. A., Monson, C. M., & Chard, K. M. (2017). *Cognitive processing therapy for PTSD: A comprehensive manual.* Guilford Press.

Resick, P. A., Nishith, P., Weaver, T. L., Astin, M. C., & Feuer, C. A. (2002). A comparison of cognitive-processing therapy with prolonged exposure and a waiting condition for the treatment of chronic posttraumatic stress disorder in female rape victims. *Journal of Consulting and Clinical Psychology, 70,* 867–879. https://doi.org/10.1037/0022-006X.70.4.867

Resick, P. A., & Schnicke, M. K. (1992). Cognitive processing therapy for sexual assault victims. *Journal of Consulting and Clinical Psychology, 60*(5), 748–756. https://doi.org/10.1037/0022-006X.60.5.748

Resick, P. A., & Schnicke, M. (1993). *Cognitive processing therapy for rape victims: A treatment manual.* Sage.

Resick, P. A., Wachen, J. S., Dondanville, K. A., Pruiksma, K. E., Yarvis, J. S., Peterson, A. L., Mintz, J., & STRONG STAR Consortium. (2017). Effect of group vs individual cognitive processing therapy in active-duty military seeking treatment for post-traumatic stress disorder: A randomized clinical trial. *JAMA Psychiatry, 74*(1), 28–36. https://doi.org/10.1001/jamapsychiatry.2016.2729

Resick, P. A., Wachen, J. S., Mintz, J., Young-McCaughan, S., Roache, J. D., Borah, A. M., Borah, E. V., Dondanville, K. A., Hembree, E. A., Litz, B. T., & Peterson, A. L. (2015). A randomized clinical trial of group cognitive processing therapy compared with group present-centered therapy for PTSD among active duty military personnel. *Journal of Consulting and Clinical Psychology, 83*(6), 1058–1068. https://doi.org/10.1037/ccp0000016

Resick, P. A., Williams, L. F., Suvak, M. K., Monson, C. M., & Gradus, J. L. (2012). Long-term outcomes of cognitive-behavioral treatments for posttraumatic stress disorder among female rape survivors. *Journal of Consulting and Clinical Psychology, 80*(2), 201–210. https://doi.org/10.1037/a0026602

Wachen, J. S., Dondanville, K. A., Pruiksma, K. E., Molino, A., Carson, C. S., Blankenship, A. E., Wilkinson, C., Yarvis, J. S., & Resick, P. A. (2016). Implementing cognitive processing therapy for posttraumatic stress disorder with active duty U.S. military personnel: Special considerations and case examples. *Cognitive and Behavioral Practice, 23*(2), 133–147. https://doi.org/10.1016/j.cbpra.2015.08.007

Weathers, F. W., Litz, B. T., Herman, D. S., Huska, J. A., & Keane, T. M. (1993, October). *The PTSD Checklist (PCL): Reliability, validity, and diagnostic utility* [Conference session]. Annual Convention of the International Society for Traumatic Stress Studies, San Antonio, TX, United States.

Wisco, B. E., Marx, B. P., May, C. L., Martini, B., Krystal, J. H., Southwick, S. M., & Pietrzak, R. H. (2017). Moral injury in U.S. combat veterans: Results from the National Health and Resilience in Veterans Study. *Depression and Anxiety, 34*(4), 340–347. https://doi.org/10.1002/da.22614

9

Acceptance and Commitment Therapy

Using Mindfulness and Values in the Treatment of Moral Injury

Robyn D. Walser and Emily Wharton

Pain is a part of life. Most people recognize that at some point during their lifetime, they will experience psychological and emotional difficulties. Losses, change in circumstance, death, and other factors of living can lead to personal struggle. Encountering emotional pain seems to be the one irrefutable truth in living. That said, however, certain forms of pain cut to the core of whom we imagine ourselves to be. Some pain not only interferes with how we function daily but also seems to tear at the fabric of our understanding of others, our social experience, and the world. Moral injury, an experience following the violation of deeply held values often occurring during a traumatic event, is one of these types of pain. Often, individuals who experience moral injury view themselves as fundamentally flawed and unable to recover following the morally injurious event. They may view healing as unattainable because they believe they deserve their suffering—a fitting punishment for the behavior that led to the violation. It is in the experience of pain, however, that healing can emerge.

Acceptance and commitment therapy (ACT; Hayes et al., 2012) is a behavioral intervention that focuses on changing the relationship to and function of pain in a person's life. Rather than changing moral pain's form through efforts to rid, reduce, or avoid the experience, ACT seeks to change its function.

https://doi.org/10.1037/0000204-010
Addressing Moral Injury in Clinical Practice, J. M. Currier, K. D. Drescher, and J. Nieuwsma (Editors)
In the public domain.

Indeed, even the intense pain of moral injury can serve as an essential reminder of deeply held personal values and lead to recovery, moving those experiencing moral injury back into a purposeful life filled with what is most meaningful.

In this chapter, we explore ACT as an intervention for moral injury. We describe how the therapy changes one's relationship with internal experiences, such as thoughts, emotions, sensations, and memories, in such a way that they are no longer the material of a fundamental personal flaw resulting from a morally injurious event. Instead, they are the material of what it means to be human, even if the actions during the morally injurious event seem to counter that idea. Through mindfulness and acceptance processes, as well as commitment and behavior change processes, ACT supports the individual in creating a relationship to themselves and others that is open, aware, and engaged—allowing healing to begin.

THEORETICAL BACKGROUND OF ACT AND MECHANISMS OF CHANGE

ACT is a "third-wave" behavioral intervention (Hayes, 2004) that focuses on reducing the harmful functions of verbal behavior (for the theory of verbal behavior, see relational frame theory; Hayes et al., 2001), viewing this behavior as one of the leading causes of suffering. As well, ACT procedures and processes are designed to target the function of behaviors, not necessarily their forms (e.g., how the words "I am worthless" function in a person's life vs. the words themselves). Although there is no consensus on the definition of moral injury (Griffin et al., 2019), Farnsworth et al. (2017) applied the functional approach of ACT to moral injury, proposing a definition that specifically points to the focus of treatment. *Moral injury* from this perspective is defined as "expanded social, psychological, and spiritual suffering stemming from costly or unworkable attempts to manage, control, or cope with the experience of moral pain" (p. 392). Through language and social conditioning, we are taught to avoid negative internal experience. However, avoidance of this nature is often paradoxical; if someone with a moral injury is wishing to stop thinking about the event, they must first think about the event. Thus, instead of focusing on the event itself (although this, too, is a part of treatment), ACT focuses on the problem of excessive and unworkable control (avoidance of internal experience). Indeed, the emotions occurring during the event and after are viewed as normal and, therefore, not in need of reduction, fixing, or elimination.

Moral pain, as defined by Farnsworth and colleagues (2017), is the "experience of dysphoric moral emotions and cognitions (e.g., self-condemnation) in response to a morally injurious event" (p. 392). As highlighted in the Introduction, moral pain itself is viewed as a healthy response to a distressing and often horrific situation; it is a reflection of emotional health for an individual to feel sadness or guilt, even horror, after killing an innocent civilian, for example. However, the process of moral injury occurs when an individual's attempts to control moral pain (e.g., reduce, eliminate, forget about) through rigid rules and unhelpful behaviors, such as self-condemnation, substance use, isolation, and so on, leads to ongoing suffering. Indeed, the Latin etymology of the word "injury" comes from *iniurius*, meaning wrongful, unjust, or harmful (see https://www.etymonline.com/word/injury#etymonline_v_9282). Moral injury, in this sense, is about the long-term struggle with a wrongful action, its fallout, and a desire for that struggle to ease. From an ACT perspective, it is about the relationship one has with the internal experience of moral pain—whether it is one of acceptance and realignment with values or one of ongoing insult and harm carried forward by the person who experienced the morally injurious event.

Finally, the functional definition supports the normality of an individual's thoughts, emotions, and behaviors, rather than emphasizing any syndromal aspect of moral injury, as in other definitions (Jinkerson, 2016). As such, the goal of treatment is to increase one's willingness to experience moral injury–related emotions, thoughts, and sensations in the service of reclaiming violated values. The goal of ACT is not to "feel better" per se but to help individuals make choices that are consistent with their values while flexibly responding, depending on the context (Nieuwsma et al., 2015).

ACT treatment, then, includes transforming one's relationship to moral pain using behavioral principles tucked inside six core processes (see Figure 9.1; Luoma et al., 2017). These processes make up the three pillars of ACT: openness, awareness, and engagement. ACT guides individuals in counteracting their ineffective behaviors by reengaging in meaningful areas of their life. Healing is promoted through accepting the reality of past events, opening to difficult emotions embedded in moral pain. Therapists acknowledge the appeal of wanting to avoid painful thoughts and emotions but remain steadfast in examining rigid patterns of behavior, exploring the costs and loss of vitality. ACT works by creating psychological flexibility and the freedom to pursue values-based activities while remaining open to human internal experience. Indeed, increases in psychological flexibility improve well-being overall (Kashdan & Rottenberg, 2010).

SCIENCE AND ACT AS AN INTERVENTION

The evidence base for ACT in the arenas of mental and behavioral health, as well as social functioning (e.g., performance at work, reductions in prejudice), has proliferated over the past decade. To date, there have been nearly 300 randomized controlled trials on ACT (for a partial list, see http://contextualscience.org/ACT_Randomized_Controlled_Trials), and many more are underway. ACT is considered an evidence-based intervention for several disorders (see American Psychological Association, Division 56, https://www.div12.org/psychological-treatments/) and has been rolled out nationally in the Veterans Health Administration (VA) for the treatment of depression (Walser et al., 2013). Despite its growth and the proliferation of trials evaluating its effectiveness, to date, only

FIGURE 9.1. The Hexagon Model of Psychological Flexibility

Commitment and
behavior change
processes

Flexible attention to the
now

Acceptance

Values

Psychological
Flexibility

Defusion

Committed
action

Flexible perspective taking
(self-as-context)

Mindfulness and
acceptance processes

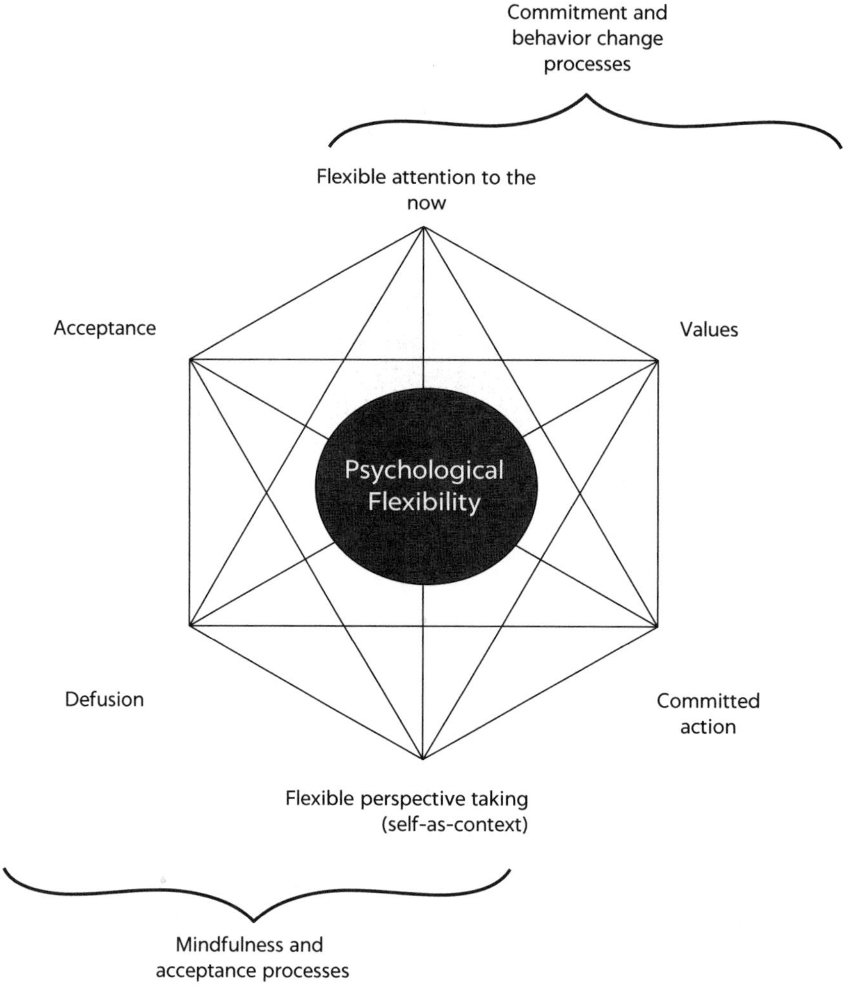

From *Learning ACT: An Acceptance and Commitment Therapy Skills-Training Manual for Therapists*, (2nd ed., p. 25), by J. B. Luoma, S. C. Hayes, & R. D. Walser, 2017, New Harbinger. Copyright 2017 by Steven C. Hayes. Reprinted with permission.

one pilot study evaluating the application of ACT in treating moral injury has been published (Farnsworth et al., 2017). Given the relatively new interest in addressing moral injury as a legitimate endeavor, the lack of trials, broadly speaking, is not surprising. Nonetheless, the data from the pilot study are promising, and the authors of the study, along with other colleagues in VA, are now conducting a funded trial.

Farnsworth and colleagues (2017) evaluated the feasibility and acceptability of ACT for moral injury in group treatment format. The group model was selected specifically to help address the social nature of moral emotions (see Nieuwsma et al., 2015). The study included 11 veterans in a posttraumatic stress disorder (PTSD) treatment program. Treatment consisted of six 75-minute sessions and was conducted by therapists with expertise in ACT and moral injury. All participating veterans were assessed for moral injury using the Moral Injury Questionnaire (Currier et al., 2015). Qualitative interviews and quantitative assessment provided support for the acceptability and feasibility of ACT in treating moral injury.

Group members generally reported experiencing benefits from ACT. Several participants expressed appreciation for specific clinical elements of ACT, such as creating a new relationship with their thoughts (defusion) and reconnecting to their values. Comments on the effects of the intervention included, "It's still there. However, I will be in the now, be in the present. I can't live by my thoughts. I'm learning now not to let the thoughts run my life"; and "I'm going to forgive myself and understand that I'm not the same person that was there when it happened. That's just a part of me" (Farnsworth et al., 2017, p. 395). Quantitative data from the trial (Walser et al., 2020) indicated (a) a significant increase in the ability to remain nondefensively open to the present moment while flexibly engaging in values-based behavior ($p = .014$), (b) a significant increase in the ability to observe thoughts and feelings as temporary ($p = .029$), and (c) clinically significant change (defined as improvement in the expected direction greater than one standard deviation) in nine of the 11 completers.

Meta-analyses have also found ACT to be effective in treating many disorders (see A-Tjak et al., 2015, for the most recent review), several associated or comorbid with moral injury. For instance, pilot studies show promising results for ACT with PTSD (Williams, 2006; Woidneck et al., 2014). ACT has also been found to reduce suicidal ideation in veterans (Walser et al., 2015) and has been shown to be effective in reducing shame (Luoma et al., 2012), a commonly reported experience in moral injury (Litz et al., 2009). Mindfulness, one of the core components of ACT, has been evaluated for its potential protective nature against the negative effects of moral injury and was found to have significant attenuating effects on the relationship between moral injury and substance use (Davies et al., 2019). Thus, the use of mindfulness within ACT may help reduce the negative effects of moral injury. Combined, the pilot data and the effectiveness of ACT in targeting the psychological fallout of moral injury suggest that ACT is, at this point, a promising treatment for moral injury.

DESCRIPTION OF THE ACT INTERVENTION

The three foundational pillars of ACT—working with clients to become open, aware, and engaged—are used to support and create psychological flexibility. *Psychological flexibility* is defined as the ability to contact the moment as a fully conscious human being and on the basis of the demands of the current situation and change behavior such that it is in the service of personal values (Hayes et al., 2012). The treatment encourages a compassionate approach toward self and others, while also connecting to a broader sense of self that is whole and remains undamaged by the moral injury or other associated thoughts and feelings.

The six core components of ACT that make up the processes and procedures for the three pillars are typically depicted in a term developed by the ACT founders called the "hexaflex" (see Figure 9.1). These processes are fluidly integrated into therapeutic sessions. In this work, no effort is made by the therapist to insist or convince the client that they must feel differently than they do. However, behaving differently is essential.

Therapy begins with assessment (see Chapter 5) and typically continues to unfold by exploring the client's current struggles in terms of moral emotions and thoughts, as well as the efforts they have made to try to control, manage, suppress, or otherwise no longer have those experiences. Many clients with moral injury have been struggling for an extended period, and often, they have tried different strategies to overcome their history. Strategies can range in nature from quite positive, such as implementing coping skills, to the more problematic, such as long-term substance use. Assessing these control strategies in terms of their effectiveness is important: Have they made the moral dilemma resolve? Often the answer is "no." Indeed, if the client is seeking mental health services for moral injury, clearly the past strategies have not paid off in any significant way. Therefore, therapists collaborate with clients to relinquish excessive and misapplied control of internal private events, and acceptance or willingness to experience is offered as an alternative—but only in the service of values-based living.

The broader clinical goals of ACT are based on the human capacity to know the world in two separate ways: verbal knowledge and experiential knowledge. Verbal knowledge is all that the mind does (i.e., problem solving, talking). Experiential knowledge is the knowledge we gain through direct experience and practice. For example, we learn how to walk by experience. It is not verbally instructed. Experiential knowledge continues to grow throughout our lifetimes. We experientially learn that emotions and thoughts do not destroy or harm us (it is behavior that is problematic), that they are experiences that move through us. However, we tend to lose contact with the experiencing self once the mind begins to form and verbal knowledge takes over. We begin to live our lives "in our heads." We become so involved with the verbal world (mind) that we begin to suffer at its hands.

Among other things, minds are evaluative and judgmental. This can be a positive aspect, keeping us out of danger and functioning socially. However, this same process can lead to intense suffering. Those who have experienced moral injury are a good example. After moral violation, the injured person can sink deeply into a personal evaluative "rabbit hole"—consumed with judgment and the associated emotions linked to the violation, losing contact with what matters and moving further away from engagement in life. Suffering begins as the morally injured person works to control or eliminate the violation by trying to forget or avoid it, hiding and isolating psychologically, emotionally, and physically to deal with the shame, guilt, disgust, anger, and other experiences that arise through moral injury. Through an ACT lens, these problematic behaviors can look like trying to avoid or restrict feelings of grief or guilt, ruminating about the injurious event, worrying that others will find out, buying into thoughts of worthlessness, over-identifying with seeing oneself as "ruined" or deserving of punishment, lacking values clarity, and stopping living one's values (Nieuwsma et al., 2015). ACT identifies these problematic and inflexible behaviors that clients engage in as a response to their moral pain and assists them in understanding how these behaviors can exacerbate moral injury fallout. Reconnecting to values and the actions that instantiate them and flexibly responding to the context instead of merely responding to emotion and mind may help the client in moving forward.

ACT works by helping clients to get back in touch with their experiential way of knowing the world. Here, they can observe and notice the ongoing flow of changing experience, both felt in the body and observed in the mind. ACT clients are supported in viewing themselves as a context, place, or perspective, where the ongoing flow of internal experiences occurs. Clients are supported in observing the morally injurious internal experiences without efforts to make them come, go, or stay. Simultaneously, clients are invited to get back in touch with their values, including those that were violated during the morally injurious event, clarifying and defining them, recognizing their social nature and working both personally and interpersonally to live consistently with these values once again. Specific behavioral actions are taken to bring these values to life. Acceptance and values-based action are brought together flexibly and interactively to help the client in their recovery from the moral injury.

Per the available protocols, ACT is typically 12 sessions in length. However, there are brief interventions (i.e., focused ACT; Strosahl et al., 2012) that last five to six sessions. It is also possible to conduct therapy for more extended periods, depending on the client's situation. ACT is also well-suited for group intervention (see Westrup & Wright, 2017, for tips on group work), and we argue, given that morality is mostly a social issue (Farnsworth et al., 2017), that group ACT is particularly compelling when addressing moral injury. The social nature of the group can assist in the healing process as members recognize acceptance among and between each other.

SPECIAL ISSUES IN TRAINING AND TREATMENT DELIVERY OF ACT FOR MORAL INJURY

Informed by contextual behavioral science (Zettle et al., 2016), ACT's foundation is based on the philosophical assumptions of contextualism (Biglan & Hayes, 2016) and is recasting itself in evolution science principles (Hayes et al., 2017). Relational frame theory (Hayes et al., 2001) augments and informs this contextual behavioral method. These components work together to support a broad understanding of human psychological functioning and the role of learning and language in human suffering.

Given this broad scope, training in ACT is essential in understanding its model and intricacies. For some clinicians, learning ACT means a notable change in their theoretical understanding of humans' relationship with internal experience. It may mean grappling with language-based processes that lead to harmful fusion with the mind. This will involve learning that cognition changes through addition, not subtraction. A memory cannot be unlearned. It can be encountered and related to differently. Anxiety and sadness (as well as joy and love) are not struggled with in attempts to make them come, stay, or go away; instead, they are there to be experienced, while also moving forward in life with values-based actions. This work, for some, is a significant shift in understanding how to treat emotional and psychological pain. Indeed, the intervention is less focused on "symptom" elimination and instead holds building a meaningful life as the key goal.

Given that ACT is tied to a broader set of philosophical assumptions, principles of behavior, and clinical procedures, it is recommended that the interested clinician engages in diverse types of training, including reading, workshops, and supervision. ACT has been extensively written about in training-oriented books designed for clinicians (see, e.g., Luoma et al., 2017). Books have been written about using language as intervention (Villatte et al., 2015), using the processes in a flexible and process-based way (Walser, 2019), and perspective taking (see McHugh et al., 2019). Finally, personal psychological flexibility can aid in the development and maintenance of strong therapeutic relationships. Indeed, recent studies (Gifford et al., 2011; Walser et al., 2013) show flexibility accounts for therapeutic outcomes over and above a measure of the alliance, suggesting the importance of building personal flexibility and instantiating it in the relationship with the client.

Last, ACT is also an incredibly flexible model; it is not simply designed to be about techniques and exercises. The interpersonal and intrapersonal process, as well as the six core processes of ACT, are woven together in whole cloth. An ACT case conceptualization guides the overarching process and arc of the therapy. Starting with the techniques and basics gets the interested clinician moving, but it is hoped that a longer-term plan for understanding the model will be pursued.

CASE SUMMARY: ACT WITH DAVID

ACT is similar for both group and individual work for moral injury; therefore, we have chosen to show an individual session for ease and the purposes of this chapter. The client's identity and details have been altered to protect confidentiality. David is a White 64-year-old Vietnam veteran. He is married and has three adult children and two grandchildren. He presented to therapy with a long history of substance abuse and diagnoses of PTSD and depression. He also noted that most of his family relationships were strained. He had been through years of treatment, including two inpatient stays for PTSD. He was also taking multiple psychotropic medications to help him sleep and feel less depressed. He noted strong feelings of guilt with thoughts of self-hatred.

In his intake assessment, David revealed that he was "haunted" by an incident that occurred while he was in Vietnam. He had not shared this memory with others and described himself as a coward for not acting differently years ago. He had come to see himself as deserving of his circumstances and said that it was better for him to push others away or isolate himself so that his "evil would not rub off on them." Although he struggled with many thoughts and emotional difficulties, he noted that this memory "plagued" him the most. He had used substances throughout his post-Vietnam experience to help numb "the shame."

During assessment, David was asked only to give a brief overview of his morally injurious event (witnessing other soldiers defile dead bodies); more details emerged as the therapy went ahead. In the first phase, the therapist focused on the efforts David had tried to control, eliminate, or avoid his internal experiences associated with the moral injury and the workability of those efforts. This work in ACT is called *creative hopelessness*, named not to create a feeling of hopelessness, but to point to the unworkable agenda of misapplied and excessive internal control of emotions, thoughts, and sensations. The hopelessness is about the agenda of internal control, not the client. Indeed, there is hope for recovery for the client.

Given that rigidity and inflexibility are the "enemies" of psychological health and well-being, ACT targets each using processes that promote psychological and behavioral flexibility. In the case of moral injury, there are two specific behavioral goals:

- Promote acceptance of emotion, thought, and sensation such that they no longer keep David stuck in unworkable patterns of behavior. The processes of willingness, defusion, present moment, and self-as-context or perspective taking support this goal.

- Promote values-based living with a focus on actions that instantiate those values. The goal is to help David in building patterns of behavior linked to his values, assisting him in leading a fuller and more meaningful life.

Functional Analysis of Behavior

It is essential to keep in mind that the work done in session with David was based on a functional analysis (FA) of his behavior. That analysis involved exploring larger patterns of behavior, as well as smaller in-session behaviors. An FA establishes the relationship between an antecedent, behavior, and its consequences. For instance, David's larger patterns of behavior involved avoidance that reinforced escape behaviors. Nearly every time he began to dwell on the memory of his morally injurious event (antecedent), he would distract himself by watching TV for hours on end (behavior), getting some relief (consequence); or when David felt anxiety, often triggered by the thought of being evil (antecedent), he would pour himself a drink (behavior), calming his "nerves" (consequence). These three-term contingency analyses reveal the function of David's behavior: David distracts himself and drinks alcohol to avoid painful memories, thoughts, and anxiety related to the moral injury.

Behavior can also be assessed for its function during session. When a painful emotional topic was approached (antecedent), David changed the subject and spoke more quickly (behavior), and if not observed and interrupted by the therapist, he felt relief (consequence) from the uncomfortable feeling, reinforcing the escape behavior. The therapist worked to detect internal avoidance behaviors (e.g., distraction), overt emotional control avoidance behaviors (e.g., drinking), and in-session avoidance behaviors (e.g., changing the topic). Further conceptualization involved detection of fusion with thoughts, disconnection from the present moment, an inability to engage different perspectives, lack of values clarity, and lack of committed action (see Luoma et al., 2017, for case conceptualization).

Acceptance

ACT views acceptance as the ability to be open to one's internal experience (Hayes et al., 2010). In working with moral injury, ACT brings clients into contact with their moral pain. The therapist helps clients see the utility of painful emotions, such as guilt reminding them of their values, potentially informing them about future behavior. Clients learn to observe their internal experience, seeing that their emotions are not intrinsically dangerous.

THERAPIST: You have shared with me a number of ways that you have tried to control what you think and feel, especially as it relates to what happened. Alcohol, isolation, therapy, TV, the whole list. Is there anything else I should add?

DAVID: I have tried it all. Sometimes I even just yell at myself.

THERAPIST: Okay, so we can add yelling at yourself as another strategy to fix this pain. What else?

DAVID: Well . . . I don't talk about it at all. Even if people ask—they say I have that far-off look and ask me why . . . and I just say, "Oh, nothin'" and try to get out of the conversation.

THERAPIST: So, pretending that nothing is going on inside is also a strategy?

After obtaining a full list of positive and negative strategies, a single question was asked: "Which of these strategies took away the pain?" The point here is to undermine internal control, helping David recognize that each of these efforts, even if they worked for a brief time, did not rid him of the pain. The quicksand metaphor (Walser & Westrup, 2007) can often be used here.

THERAPIST: What does your mind tell you to do when you have fallen into quicksand?

DAVID: To get out.

THERAPIST: And so, what do you do?

DAVID: Start to thrash around, but that only causes you to sink further.

THERAPIST: Right. What if trying to escape your internal experience, your emotions and thoughts, is like being in quicksand—the harder you try to get out, the more you sink. To float in quicksand, you have to hold still, to lay out in it.

After fully developing internal control as the problem, the therapist and client can begin to explore the alternative to control of internal events: acceptance. Using exercises and metaphors (see Hayes et al., 2012; Stoddard & Afari, 2014), they can start the journey of openness to experience, letting go of unworkable and painful strategies.

DAVID: It's just too hard to live with this. Too painful.

THERAPIST: (Respectfully) You are right. I can't fully understand what happened and how it has made you feel. But I can see that you are living with it . . . just in a very painful way.

DAVID: (Somewhat defiant) Yeah . . . but I deserve this pain; I created this.

THERAPIST: Something happened that you regret. You took an action that didn't line up with your own expectations of yourself, which led to pain, guilt, and shame. But there is another layer I would like us to look at. A layer of suffering—a relationship with you and others has unfolded that seems to be about that original event but is perhaps a layer beyond that event.

DAVID: I am not sure what you mean.

THERAPIST: You have the event and then years of judging yourself. You are in a long-lasting tug-of-war with this memory, and it seems you can never win. You have the pain, plus the fight with the pain.

DAVID: I can never forgive myself.

THERAPIST: Yeah, I don't think we are quite ready to consider forgiveness yet. But I do wonder what it would be like if you dropped the rope.

Here, the therapist is inviting the possibility of something different. She might note that dropping the rope does not mean the "monster" on the other side of the pit goes away. Indeed, the guilt can stay as it is. The therapist collaborates with clients to contact the bodily experience of the pain fully, to notice the judgments and thoughts that arise with it. The goal is to promote openness to experience. Emotions, even challenging ones such as shame and guilt, are not enemies. The therapist discusses the function of guilt and shame, noting how they can prove quite useful by telling someone who experiences moral injury that they are still human. Indeed, it might be a bigger problem if they never felt guilt over such an event. Last, the therapist waits to approach forgiveness; it is early in therapy, and other work has to be done before considering what forgiveness might look like for David.

Cognitive Defusion

Defusion is the process by which clients learn to see their thoughts as "separate" from themselves, although they are still embodied. They are a person with thoughts; they are not the thoughts themselves. Observing the ongoing flow of thinking is the work of defusion. This process is done through a range of different exercises.

In David's case, some of the critical thoughts he struggled with had to do with judgments about himself and others. The work is not to eliminate his thoughts or make them more positive. It is to help him see the evaluations for what they are—evaluations.

THERAPIST: Tell me more about the thoughts that show up for you when you think of the event.

DAVID: (Pauses, unable to speak for a moment) I think God is punishing me. He knows that what I did is wrong. I wonder if I am going to hell. I stood there doing nothing.

THERAPIST: (Patiently) I want to look at something here. I want to notice the pain that is present as we talk about what your mind is handing you, but I also want to check on something. How many times have you had these kinds of thoughts over the years?

DAVID: Without number.

THERAPIST: (Sighs) Then I have to consider this question . . . how likely do you think it is that we are going to make them go away?

DAVID: Truthfully . . . I don't think they will ever go away.

THERAPIST: I wonder if it is possible then . . . to change your relationship with them.

The goal with David here is merely to help him get enough "distance" between himself and his thoughts—to be mindful of his thoughts—so that they no longer dictate his behavior. An exercise might include helping David to watch his thoughts "float" by as leaves might on a stream, serving to help him observe thoughts rather than get entangled in them.

Contact With the Present Moment

In this process, clients are guided to connect to their experiences in the "here-and-now." Conscious awareness of the moment is offered in contrast to the usual pattern of ruminating about the past or worrying about the future. Clients are encouraged to experience their emotions fully, noticing how their body feels in the moment. This helps clients counteract their tendency to avoid, push away, or numb their feelings of moral pain and other negative emotions.

THERAPIST: It seems like one of the places where you get most stuck is when you start to reflect on the event. It is like it grabs you and drags you into the past.

DAVID: It's like I keep playing the scene over and over again in my head.

THERAPIST: It's pulling you back to all those years ago, as if your past becomes your "now." However, it doesn't need to own this place, here and now, where you have family, friends, and something you are trying to create. I wonder if you would be willing to come back to the now.

DAVID: Let's try. . . .

THERAPIST: Okay, let's do a short exercise and see how it goes. (Therapist conducts a brief body scan)

Bringing attention back to the present assists clients in living in the moment. It supports them in responding to direct contingencies (what is happening here and now) instead of being trapped in rules about how the past should have been or about what the future may hold.

Self-As-Context or Perspective Taking

In self-as-context or perspective-taking work, the client is guided in seeing their "self" as separate from their internal experience at any given time. They are the place where experience occurs; they are not the experiences themselves. This process can help clients see a morally injurious event as something that occurred, while not being defined by the event. In the same way that a person can become fused to a thought, a person can become fused to an identity (e.g., evil, cowardly).

David continued to identify his current experience with that which happened during the morally injurious event. He often equated himself to "that guy who was a coward." This led to a cascade of other judgments about himself as "evil." Self-as-context helped David see that he had this experience, but he is not the experience itself. He was a student and a soldier before the event, and after the event, he became a husband, father, and worker. Helping David see the many roles that he plays in his life can help him to get distance from the one role that is seemingly defining him in this moral injury struggle.

THERAPIST: Let's consider chess. Imagine that the pieces stand for your thoughts, feelings, and memories. Wouldn't it be nice if you could remove the pieces from the board that represented the bad feelings and thoughts . . . so that you did not have to deal with them anymore? But no matter how you strategize, you can't get rid of the pieces. Now, imagine that you are the board. You are the place where each of these pieces, all experiences, thoughts, and feelings, both negative and positive, play out. As the board, you are in contact with the pieces, aware of your experience, but the board is not the pieces, and you are not your thoughts and feelings.

DAVID: Interesting . . . but who am I if I am not my thoughts and feelings?

THERAPIST: You are the being that holds these experiences. So, you have contacted the thought that you are evil. That piece is on your board. You have the memory of the event. That piece is on your board. But the pieces are not the board. You have millions of pieces, a lifetime of thoughts and feelings. The ones before the moral injury and the ones after the moral injury. So, although you have a moral injury, you are not your moral injury.

David can come to view himself as more than his moral injury, seeing it is as an experience he had. Through other exercises and metaphors, he can begin to experience a sense of self that is larger than the injury. He can choose to spend more time connecting to his values—a topic we turn to shortly. First, however, it is helpful to explore issues of compassion and forgiveness through perspective taking and self-as-context work.

David viewed his behavior of doing nothing during the morally injurious event as an affront to his values. He could not forgive himself for not acting against the atrocity he saw. David was asked to revisit the scene of the moral injury, but instead of looking at the men who were committing the war crime, he was asked to see himself looking at the crime unfold. It should be noted that this work is done, as with each of the processes, with respect and compassion for the client.

THERAPIST: (After introducing the exercise and asking David to close his eyes and picture the scene) See if you can see yourself as that soldier standing there watching this event unfold. What do you notice about you? What do you see when you look at him?

DAVID: (Speaking with his eyes closed) I see him and just want to kick his ass! I want to yell at him for not taking action. I can't believe he isn't doing anything!

THERAPIST: (After a pause) Now imagine that you are zooming in closer, and you could come right up to the face of this younger "you" watching this event unfold . . . see if you can see his face.

DAVID: (After a long pause) He's . . . he's 19. He's . . . really young. I have forgotten how young he was . . . he looks like a boy. And he is scared.

THERAPIST: What do you notice about your reaction to him now?

DAVID: (After a long pause, fighting back tears) I want to hold him.

Following this work, the therapist and David explored the meaning of holding him and recognizing what was happening at the time. He wanted to forgive his younger self. The therapist and David worked on forgiveness as an activity, not forgiveness as a feeling. He worked on being more compassionate to himself when feeling guilt, disgust, or anger. It should be emphasized that any work done with clients in this area is a process and not an outcome. There are more ways to implement the ACT core processes to address issues of forgiveness and compassion (see Evans et al., in press; Walser & Westrup, 2007). Conceptualizing issues of right and wrong, exploring forgiveness, and working on self-compassion are all parts of ACT.

Values

In values clarification, the therapist helps clients in defining what is important to them in life. Values are not concrete goals; instead, they serve as compass points for action. The therapist helps clients see that even in the face of painful emotions, they can still take actions that are in line with their values. The goal is not to take away negative feelings but to make life meaningful, which can also lead to experiences of joy. David noted that his values of protecting and honoring life and freedom were violated when he did not stop the men who were engaging in the behavior that led to the moral injury. He held himself just as responsible as those who had desecrated the bodies. During values exploration, David and the therapist explored how the values were not being lived during the incident and also how they might not be being lived now.

DAVID: I really let myself down—why couldn't I have just done something different?

THERAPIST: I understand the sentiment, but history only goes in one direction—we can't undo the past. But there is something that can be done differently now.

DAVID: I don't believe I deserve a better life.

THERAPIST: (With humility) Fortunately, belief is not required for you to deserve a better life or to live a better life [defusion]. Values go both ways. When we are living them fully, we are engaging in behaviors toward others and ourselves that bring those values to life. Today, you can choose to live these values, protect and honor, not just for others, but for you as well. It is the case that the values were violated all those years ago, but they continue to be left behind now too. There are other lives—including yours—where protecting and honoring can still be served. If you were to bring these values to life now, what might look different?

DAVID: If I were to honor myself?

THERAPIST: Yes.

DAVID: I wouldn't isolate.

Values are explored throughout ACT in terms of what values were violated during the injury and what values can be brought back to life or reengaged. Values are never attained—they are broad, abstract directions to move toward in one's life (e.g., honoring, loving, belonging); they are processes of living, not outcomes. Finally, it is essential to take action concerning values.

Committed Action

With values as the guideposts, committed action is the process of taking steps in the direction of valued living. The therapist and client clarify and define behavioral goals and actions that can be taken in the service of values. Clients learn that they can take actions consistent with their values, even in the face of negative thoughts and feelings. Acceptance and committed action intersect at this moment.

Supporting clients in behavioral change is an essential step in ACT. Collaborating with clients to delineate how they have stopped living their values—by isolating himself and drinking, in the case of David—is part of the committed action work. Committing to even small behaviors that turn the client back to values that were violated because of the moral injury is part of the process. Building ever-larger patterns of values-based behavior is the goal.

THERAPIST: Makes sense . . . one of the ways you could honor yourself involves reducing isolation. I know this can be challenging, especially given the judgments that are likely to appear when you are with your wife and children. So, part of the work here is to feel and think what you feel and think, offer compassion to yourself, and take action. If you were to lean back into the value of honoring yourself and reducing isolation, what action might you take?

DAVID: I might go over to my daughter's house . . . she has invited me a number of times.

THERAPIST: That seems like a values-based action—to honor your relationship with your daughter.

DAVID: Yes, but I get on edge. I start feeling like I don't deserve to be there.

THERAPIST: Yes, I am guessing that will show up. Are you willing to have that thought and whatever emotions that come along with it in the service of honoring this relationship?

DAVID: Whew . . . I can try.

THERAPIST: This is about living life from the feet up . . . not the head down. Getting entangled in those thoughts, fused with them, will send you into isolation.

From here, the therapist and David can work on committed actions that continue to line up with the value of honoring others (as well as working on other values). In the end, the goal is to live life fully, having compassion and working on self-forgiveness as a process while taking steps that are values aligned.

CONCLUSION

Of those who have experienced a moral injury, ACT asks, Are you willing to experience (thoughts, emotions, sensations, memories) what you experience when you experience it, fully and without defense, and do (take action) what takes you in the direction of your chosen values? Through processes of mindfulness and acceptance, behavior change and commitment, clients are invited to open to their experiential self while still being engaged in a life guided by meaning.

Ultimately, the hope is that those who experience moral injury will no longer hold tightly to the notion that they are damaged by their past actions, being held hostage by memories of the event in ways that interfere with living their values now. Instead, they choose to be present and connect to a broader perspective, a sense of self that is more than any single memory or event, recognizing that the feelings associated with moral injury indicate their humanness and point to what is essential in life. It is here that a standing invitation is given to those experiencing moral injury, to be open, aware, and engaged, living life from the feet up—taking action—as they move forward in the process of healing.

REFERENCES

A-Tjak, J. G., Davis, M. L., Morina, N., Powers, M. B., Smits, J. A., & Emmelkamp, P. M. (2015). A meta-analysis of the efficacy of acceptance and commitment therapy for clinically relevant mental and physical health problems. *Psychotherapy and Psychosomatics, 84*(1), 30–36. https://doi.org/10.1159/000365764

Biglan, A., & Hayes, S. C. (2016). Functional contextualism and contextual behavioral science. In R. D. Zettle, S. C. Hayes, D. Barnes-Holmes, & A. Biglan (Eds.), *The Wiley handbook of contextual behavioral science* (pp. 37–61). Wiley-Blackwell.

Currier, J. M., Holland, J. M., Drescher, K., & Foy, D. (2015). Initial psychometric evaluation of the Moral Injury Questionnaire—Military version. *Clinical Psychology & Psychotherapy, 22*(1), 54–63. https://doi.org/10.1002/cpp.1866

Davies, R. L., Prince, M. A., Bravo, A. J., Kelley, M. L., & Crain, T. L. (2019). Moral injury, substance use, and posttraumatic stress disorder symptoms among military personnel: An examination of trait mindfulness as a moderator. *Journal of Traumatic Stress, 32*, 414–423. https://doi.org/10.1002/jts.22403

Evans, W. R., Walser, R. D., Farnsworth, J. K. & Drescher, K. D. (in press). *The moral injury workbook: Acceptance and commitment therapy skills for moving beyond shame, anger and trauma to reclaim your values.* New Harbinger.

Farnsworth, J. K., Drescher, K. D., Evans, W., & Walser, R. D. (2017). A functional approach to understanding and treating military-related moral injury. *Journal of Contextual Behavioral Science, 6*(4), 391–397. https://doi.org/10.1016/j.jcbs.2017.07.003

Gifford, E. V., Kohlenberg, B. S., Hayes, S. C., Pierson, H. M., Piasecki, M. P., Antonuccio, D. O., & Palm, K. M. (2011). Does acceptance and relationship focused behavior therapy contribute to bupropion outcomes? A randomized controlled trial of functional analytic psychotherapy and acceptance and commitment therapy for smoking cessation. *Behavior Therapy, 42*(4), 700–715. https://doi.org/10.1016/j.beth.2011.03.002

Griffin, B. J., Purcell, N., Burkman, K., Litz, B. T., Bryan, C. J., Schmitz, M., Villierme, C., Walsh, J., & Maguen, S. (2019). Moral injury: An integrative review. *Journal of Traumatic Stress.* Advance online publication. https://doi.org/10.1002/jts.22362

Hayes, S. C. (2004). Acceptance and commitment therapy, relational frame theory, and the third wave of behavioral and cognitive therapies. *Behavior Therapy, 35*(4), 639–665. https://doi.org/10.1016/S0005-7894(04)80013-3

Hayes, S. C., Barnes-Holmes, D., & Roche, B. (Eds.). (2001). *Relational frame theory: A post-Skinnerian account of human language and cognition.* Plenum Press. https://doi.org/10.1007/b108413

Hayes, S. C., Monestès, J. L., & Wilson, D. S. (2017). Evolutionary principles for applied psychology. In S. C. Hayes & S. Hofmann (Eds.), *Process-based CBT: The science and core clinical competencies of cognitive behavioral therapy* (pp. 155–171). New Harbinger.

Hayes, S. C., Strosahl, K. D., Bunting, K., Twohig, M. P., & Wilson, K. G. (2010). What is acceptance and commitment therapy? In S. C. Hayes & K. D. Strosahl (Eds.), *A practical guide to acceptance and commitment therapy* (pp. 3–29). Springer.

Hayes, S. C., Strosahl, K. D., & Wilson, K. G. (2012). *Acceptance and commitment therapy: The process and practice of mindful change* (2nd ed.). Guilford Press.

Jinkerson, J. D. (2016). Defining and assessing moral injury: A syndrome perspective. *Traumatology, 22*(2), 122–130. https://doi.org/10.1037/trm0000069

Kashdan, T. B., & Rottenberg, J. (2010). Psychological flexibility as a fundamental aspect of health. *Clinical Psychology Review, 30*(7), 865–878. https://doi.org/10.1016/j.cpr.2010.03.001

Litz, B. T., Stein, N., Delaney, E., Lebowitz, L., Nash, W. P., Silva, C., & Maguen, S. (2009). Moral injury and moral repair in war veterans: A preliminary model and intervention strategy. *Clinical Psychology Review, 29*(8), 695–706. https://doi.org/10.1016/j.cpr.2009.07.003

Luoma, J. B., Hayes, S. C., & Walser, R. D. (2017). *Learning ACT: An acceptance and commitment therapy skills training manual for therapists* (2nd ed.). New Harbinger.

Luoma, J. B., Kohlenberg, B. S., Hayes, S. C., & Fletcher, L. (2012). Slow and steady wins the race: A randomized clinical trial of acceptance and commitment therapy targeting shame in substance use disorders. *Journal of Consulting and Clinical Psychology, 80*(1), 43–53. https://doi.org/10.1037/a0026070

McHugh, L., Stewart, I., & Almada, P. (2019). *A contextual behavioral guide to the self: Theory and practice.* New Harbinger.

Nieuwsma, J. A., Walser, R. D., Farnsworth, J. K., Drescher, K. D., Meador, K. G., & Nash, W. P. (2015). Possibilities within acceptance and commitment therapy for approaching moral injury. *Current Psychiatry Reviews, 11*(3), 193–206. https://doi.org/10.2174/1573400511666150629105234

Stoddard, J. A., & Afari, N. (2014). *The big book of ACT metaphors: A practitioner's guide to experiential exercises and metaphors in acceptance and commitment therapy.* New Harbinger.

Strosahl, K. D., Robinson, P. J., & Gustavsson, T. (2012). *Brief interventions for radical change: Principles and practice of focused acceptance and commitment therapy.* New Harbinger.

Villatte, M., Villatte, J. L., & Hayes, S. C. (2015). *Mastering the clinical conversation: Language as intervention.* Guilford Press.

Walser, R. D. (2019). *The heart of ACT: Developing a flexible and process-based practice using acceptance and commitment therapy.* New Harbinger.

Walser, R. D., Evans, W., Farnsworth, J. K. (2020). *Pilot investigation of acceptance and commitment therapy for the treatment of moral injury* [Manuscript in preparation]. National Center for PTSD, Menlo Park, CA.

Walser, R. D., Garvert, D. W., Karlin, B. E., Trockel, M., Ryu, D. M., & Taylor, C. B. (2015). Effectiveness of acceptance and commitment therapy in treating depression and suicidal ideation in Veterans. *Behaviour Research and Therapy, 74,* 25–31. https://doi.org/10.1016/j.brat.2015.08.012

Walser, R. D., Karlin, B. E., Trockel, M., Mazina, B., & Taylor, C. B. (2013). Training in and implementation of acceptance and commitment therapy for depression in the Veterans Health Administration: Therapist and patient outcomes. *Behaviour Research and Therapy, 51*(9), 555–563. https://doi.org/10.1016/j.brat.2013.05.009

Walser, R., & Westrup, D. (2007). *Acceptance and commitment therapy for the treatment of post-traumatic stress disorder and trauma-related problems: A practitioner's guide to using mindfulness and acceptance strategies.* New Harbinger.

Westrup, D., & Wright, M. J. (2017). *Learning ACT for group treatment: An acceptance and commitment therapy skills training manual for therapists.* Context Press.

Williams, L. M. (2006). *Acceptance and commitment therapy: An example of third-wave therapy as a treatment for Australian Vietnam War veterans with posttraumatic stress disorder* [Unpublished doctoral dissertation]. Charles Sturt University.

Woidneck, M. R., Morrison, K. L., & Twohig, M. P. (2014). Acceptance and commitment therapy for the treatment of posttraumatic stress among adolescents. *Behavior Modification, 38*(4), 451–476. https://doi.org/10.1177/0145445513510527

Zettle, R. D., Hayes, S. C., Barnes-Holmes, D., & Biglan, A. (Eds.). (2016). *The Wiley handbook of contextual behavioral science.* John Wiley & Sons.

10

Adaptive Disclosure

A Novel Evidence-Based Treatment for Moral Injury

Matt J. Gray, Kendal Binion, Stephanie Amaya, and Brett T. Litz

Adaptive disclosure (AD; Litz et al., 2016) was designed explicitly to address the unique outcomes and etiological factors associated with the aftermath of exposure to war-zone events, which have historically been neglected or suboptimally treated in active duty and veteran patient populations. Unlike extant evidence-based therapies for posttraumatic stress disorder (PTSD), AD was specifically developed with the warrior ethos and military culture in mind, to better meet the needs of military personnel exposed to war trauma. AD integrates emotion-focused experiential strategies with elements of cognitive behavior therapy. It is designed to flexibly treat varied principal harms, including conventional life-threat traumas, traumatic loss and grief, and—most central to this text—moral injury, which entails experiences that violate closely held moral beliefs and ethical codes. Although it includes exposure-based components, these serve to activate salient distressing appraisals and emotion-laden cognitions rather than serving an extinction function.

The AD model underscores that many traumatic events in the war zone and resulting distress and suffering entail painfully accurate and valid appraisals of culpability and responsibility, especially in the case of moral injury. As such, conventional cognitive restructuring and challenge exercises (which typically assume that appraisals are inaccurate or out of proportion) are largely supplanted by experiential exercises designed to process the meaning of the event, situate it in the past, allow for consideration of a recommitment

https://doi.org/10.1037/0000204-011
Addressing Moral Injury in Clinical Practice, J. M. Currier, K. D. Drescher, and J. Nieuwsma (Editors)

to preevent values, and allow for healing and repairing prosocial behaviors. These latter behaviors include, but are not limited to, real or symbolic amends making and behaviors designed to promote forgiveness of self and others. Although the morally injurious event cannot be undone or readily explained away, it need not be one's destiny. Service members (SMs) and veterans begin to learn and contemplate adaptive and healthy life choices that challenge conceptualizations of the self or others as globally bad.

THEORETICAL BACKGROUND

The prolonged presence of U.S. troops in Afghanistan (Operation Enduring Freedom; OEF) and Iraq (Operation Iraqi Freedom; OIF) has placed considerable demands on health care systems tasked with addressing the mental health needs of active SMs and returning veterans. Even fairly early in the trajectory of recent wars, the Mental Health Advisory Team IV (Office of the Surgeon, Multinational Force–Iraq, & Office of the Surgeon General, United States Army Medical Command, 2006) reported that 60.8% of OEF/OIF troops experienced a life-threatening situation, 33.9% witnessed human cruelty and suffering, and 53.0% experienced a traumatic loss of a close peer in theater. These experiences were associated with a greater risk of developing debilitating mental health disorders (Wilk et al., 2010). Notably, epidemiological studies have estimated that 10% to 20% of OEF/OIF veterans experience significant mental health difficulties related to their deployment (e.g., Hoge et al., 2004). Such difficulties include PTSD, depression, and anxiety, which are often compounded by associated problems, such as substance use (Jacobson et al., 2008), physical health problems (Hoge et al., 2007), and functional disability (e.g., attrition from military service; Hoge et al., 2006). Given the high likelihood of experiencing potentially morally injurious events and their pervasive effects, identifying opportunities for effective and early intervention strategies has become a major public health challenge.

Conventional cognitive behavior therapy (CBT) approaches, such as prolonged exposure (PE; Foa et al., 2007) and cognitive processing therapy (CPT; Resick et al., 2017), are widely accepted as the leading evidence-based treatments for PTSD. However, although these strategies have been successfully tested and implemented in civilian populations, trials targeting veterans with chronic PTSD have found consistently smaller effect sizes relative to civilian trials (Monson et al., 2006; Ready et al., 2008; Schnurr et al., 2007). Current treatment models may be insufficiently tailored to address the unique occupational and cultural context of the military and the unique emotional, behavioral, and psychological consequences of combat-related traumatic experiences.

Several aspects of existing CBT models may limit treatment effectiveness with veterans and active duty personnel. First, CBT for PTSD and anxiety disorders is predicated on a conditioning and learning model, which conceptualizes trauma as a fear-inducing victimization-based threat to life (Friedman, 2006). However, training and preparation in the military typically incorporate exposure to combat-related, high-fear contexts to protect against conditioned fear responses and the development of problematic schemas about safety and control. Moreover, traumatic experiences during deployment are not limited to life-threatening and victimization experiences; SMs are also exposed to horrific losses and morally injurious events associated with emotional sequelae that differ from prototypical responses to traumatic stress (Nash, 2007). These responses may range from the classical fear- and anxiety-based reactions to more combat-specific guilt, shame, grief, and moral injury (Litz et al., 2009). Although CBT-based strategies acknowledge the importance of addressing these diverse psychic injuries of war, the traditional Socratic questioning approach may not be well-suited to address distressing but accurate appraisals of perpetration events. The CPT manual suggests contextualizing perpetration events in terms of the SM's intent and making restitution (Resick et al., 2017), but there is insufficient detailed guidance provided for implementing the proposed techniques (Gray et al., 2017).

ADAPTIVE DISCLOSURE OVERVIEW

AD was designed specifically for active duty personnel, to leverage well-established, evidence-based strategies to address complications related to moral injury and traumatic loss (Steenkamp et al., 2011). The original therapy was manualized and brief (six sessions) to accommodate the high operational tempo and time constraints of active duty military personnel. AD is based on the core assumptions that, to accommodate to the military context, treatments have to (a) honor the military ethos (and clinicians have to have a reasonable degree of knowledge about the military and the realities of war-zone exposure to various stressors); (b) serve as a foundation for healing over the long haul, rather than a one-and-done "cure" conceptualization; (c) leverage military values and customs in the therapeutic setting; and (d) encourage meaning making within the context of military roles and values. The first randomized controlled trial of AD, using an eight-session variant, compared AD with CPT-C (cognitive therapy only). This noninferiority trial was positive in that AD was found to be no more or less efficacious than CPT-C (the primary aim of the trial; Litz et al., 2020).

AD integrates therapeutic techniques derived from CBT and gestalt and emotion-focused therapy approaches, modified to facilitate meaning making of combat and operational experiences. The primary conduit for disclosure in AD comprises a combination of imaginal exposure and subsequent experiential processing and meaning making. Exposure elements are designed to activate beliefs and appraisals associated with intense negative affect to allow for meaningful engagement and contemplation. This "hot-cognitive processing" (i.e., processing that is emotional, experiential, and provocative; Edwards, 1990; Greenberg & Safran, 1989) of morally injurious events moves away from a critical analysis in favor of more emotion-driven evaluations. In so doing, this strategy has the potential to bypass defensiveness that may arise when a clinician who does not share their military experience or background attempts to provide corrective appraisals to the SM. In this way, AD sets a strategic therapeutic frame for corrective and forgiveness-promoting experiences that distinguishes it from conventional strategies primarily aimed at achieving in-session extinction of distress through multiple retellings of the traumatic event.

In the gestalt therapy tradition, inducing hot cognition leads to revealing and experiencing previously ignored feelings, desires, and needs (Greenberg & Safran, 1989). As such, AD also uses two versions of a modified empty chair exercise adapted from gestalt therapy to target combat-related events associated with guilt and traumatic loss (Gray et al., 2012; Litz et al., 2016; Steenkamp et al., 2011). The modified empty chair exercises used to address moral conflicts require the imaginal confession of the morally injurious event to a safe, caring moral authority to promote hope and forgiveness-related themes, and alternative perspectives surrounding the experience are elicited. In the case of traumatic loss, patients are asked to have an imaginal dialogue with the deceased to address traumatic grief by targeting maladaptive cognitions surrounding the loss to foster acceptance and self-forgiveness. In instances where life threat, personal responsibility, and traumatic loss commingle, it is necessary to consider the external perspective that might be most healing. For example, if an SM's actions or inactions resulted in the death of a fellow combatant, consideration of what the deceased might hope for the SM and how best to honor the fallen may be more fruitful than the perspective invoked by consideration of a moral authority figure.

AD also deviates from standard attempts to correct or challenge erroneous appraisals because it explicitly recognizes that intensely distressing appraisals may be well-placed and completely valid. Instead, it is meant to promote a willingness to engage in difficult memories by demonstrating that it is possible to tolerate the emotions that these painful memories evoke. Further, it tends to be more "future-oriented" than standard treatments for combat-related PTSD. Instead of primarily focusing on challenging thoughts about a past event and reducing anxiety and arousal as a primary focus, AD is designed to promote a recommitment to predeployment values and to consider and implement a plan to live adaptively and meaningfully. The legitimacy of the harrowing nature of combat experiences is acknowledged, honored, and—perhaps most importantly—not merely explained away. In the case of perpetration-based moral injury, future orientation may involve consideration of real or symbolic amends making and prosocial engagement, among other strategies. The overarching aim of AD is to help an SM or veteran rebalance their self-schemas from the self as all bad and unworthy of connection (or buying into harsh, judgmental social exclusion), in the case of personal transgressions, and/or others as all bad (and people, in general, will always let you down), in the case of being the victim of others' transgressions. The goal is to rebalance the moral scales, reduce the prominence of severe moral emotions, and create space for hope and corrective experience in the social world.

In essence, AD's defining feature is the application of exposure-based, emotion-focused experiential therapeutic experiences that can be tailored to the SM and their primary harms (i.e., life threat, traumatic loss, or moral injury). Emotional disclosure and experiential techniques are followed by a dialogue about the meaning and implications of the patient's traumas. The therapist takes an active role in guiding emerging meanings to modify toxic thought patterns. In instances when self-blame or troubling interpretations are rational or deeply rooted in military values, the emphasis is shifted from challenging the accuracy of the belief in favor of promoting more adaptive responses and reparative action. The therapy is designed to foster acceptance of morally injurious experiences while helping the SM reclaim goodness and establish a foundation for healing and repair.

EFFICACY OF ADAPTIVE DISCLOSURE

Although evidence generally supports CBT strategies as effective PTSD treatments, these interventions tend to be less efficacious for combat trauma. A meta-analysis of existing psychotherapeutic treatments for PTSD found that although pre- versus posttreatment comparisons were significant across treatments ($d = 1.43$), the average effect size for treatment with veterans ($d = .81$) was significantly lower relative to civilian samples experiencing mixed trauma ($d = 1.24$) or assault ($d = 1.82$; Bradley et al., 2005). Notably, although pre- to posttreatment gains were significant, only five of the 26 studies included in the review evaluated treatment effectiveness for combat-related trauma. Moreover, those studies that did include combat-exposed samples did not evaluate treatment feasibility or efficacy with active duty SMs, and it is unclear whether they systematically addressed moral injury and traumatic loss.

AD was developed in response to the unique and evolving needs of veterans and active duty SMs experiencing combat-related PTSD. A condensed, six-session protocol was evaluated through an open trial with 44 active duty marines at Camp Pendleton, CA (Gray et al., 2012). Effect sizes for PTSD ($d = .79$) and depression ($d = .71$) symptom improvement were large; patients expressed high satisfaction with the treatment, indicating that they found the intervention helpful and would recommend it to other marines. Despite its notable brevity relative to the current iteration of AD, as well as best practice approaches, effect sizes for reductions in PTSD and depression ($d = .79$) were comparable to clinical trials evaluating conventional approaches with military populations ($d = .81$; Bradley et al., 2005). It is important to point out here that although effect sizes are comparable to those achieved by traditional PTSD treatments (i.e., PE and CPT), AD promoted such gains in roughly half the number of sessions that typify other treatments.

This initial version of AD was designed to be exceptionally brief so that it could be delivered in garrison between deployments. A lengthier version of AD has been developed and is currently being tested in VA settings; it is hypothesized that effect sizes will be larger than the six-session version of AD. Though additional empirical work is ongoing to evaluate the efficacy of the current AD protocol, preliminary findings have suggested that diverse presentations of military trauma are responsive to AD even in the absence of self-blame reductions (Gray et al., 2012). Specifically, consistent with central tenets of AD, self-blame was not appreciably reduced from pre- to posttreatment, but global appraisals of self did improve on the Posttraumatic Cognitions Inventory (Foa et al., 1999). Because AD typically encourages taking ownership over moral transgressions while simultaneously promoting awareness that the totality of one's identity is not dictated by a single event no matter how egregious, this is the precise pattern of results that would be expected.

ADAPTIVE DISCLOSURE TREATMENT COMPONENTS

AD possesses three main components to treatment that are customized based on each patient's unique needs: (a) an imaginal exposure component, (b) a "breakout" component intended to address loss and traumatic grief, and (c) a breakout component intended to address moral injury. Though all patients receive the imaginal exposure component of the intervention, the breakout components targeting loss or moral injury are integrated on an as-needed basis, depending on the SM's or veteran's most pressing traumatic memory. The decision to incorporate a breakout component is left to the therapist's discretion based on the traumatic event being targeted. An overview of the three treatment components is described next, followed by a session-by-session outline of the recommended eight-session approach to treatment.

Exposure

Imaginal exposure is a core component of AD in that all patients engage in disclosing a traumatic deployment experience, ideally the most distressing or reexperienced deployment event. The target traumatic event should be characterized by the clinician as one that is highly fear inducing and life threatening, related to loss or traumatic grief, or morally injurious. The execution of the imaginal exposures is similar to PE, such that the patient recounts the distressing event in detail to stimulate previously avoided thoughts and emotions related to the memory. Should the primary trauma be a highly fearful and life-threatening memory, the therapy will largely emulate PE, with the goal of promoting extinction of the conditioned fear and processing the trauma through multiple immersive retellings. Should the focus of treatment be related to war-zone loss or moral injury, however, the exposure component is necessary but is also complemented with breakout components to address the areas of psychic distress for which exposure alone is insufficient. Traumatic grief and moral injury often generate feelings of guilt, shame, self-loathing, and/or anger that cannot be fully extinguished by exposure alone, nor can they invariably be rationally disputed or challenged (for a recent review, see Griffin et al., 2019). As such, exposure to target loss and moral injury is revised to allow sustained engagement with the memories of the trauma so that the appraisals (e.g., self-loathing, guilt, shame) may be acknowledged, explored, and reconsidered. Further, immersion within an imaginal exposure exercise assists in the generation of a charged and focal emotional state. The information gained from these modified exposures is used to start the experiential breakout components for loss and moral injury.

Breakout Component: Loss and Traumatic Grief

Drawing on validated interventions for grief treatments, AD incorporates a modified empty-chair technique adapted from gestalt therapy traditions. This intervention involves a hypothetical conversation with the deceased person. This technique is used to explore and address harmful beliefs surrounding the loss by encouraging alternative perspectives from the SM or veteran through the viewpoint of the deceased. The breakout component is used following the exposure module described earlier and is completed over multiple sessions. Given the primary focus of this text on moral injury, the description of the traumatic loss breakout and processing is necessarily brief. Refer to the treatment manual for a detailed depiction of AD's treatment of combat-related grief (Litz et al., 2016).

Breakout Component: Moral Injury

When the primary traumatic event is characterized by a morally injurious act, treatment incorporates breakout component sessions to address two broad categories of war-related moral injury, namely, perpetration and betrayal-based grievances. Moral injury involving *perpetration* comprises a range of events, including the accidental or intentional killing of civilians, torture or sadistic killing, mutilation of corpses, sexual assault, and real or perceived failure to prevent the death of comrades or civilians (Litz et al., 2016). Comparatively, *betrayal-based* moral injury is related to leaders' behaviors and judgments that violated expectations of moral or ethical conduct, thereby damaging the SM's trust in authorities and often eliciting anger. SMs or veterans who have participated in or witnessed morally injurious behavior often adopt maladaptive coping strategies that lead to debilitating levels of guilt, shame, social disengagement, self-handicapping, and self-harm (Steenkamp et al., 2011).

The breakout component for morally injurious behavior uses experiential strategies, including the empty-chair technique described previously, that serve to promote an appreciation of the context of war and the acceptance of an imperfect self. Given that the existence of a moral code sometimes requires that an act be judged as bad when it does not adhere to ethical standards, the breakout component for moral injury is not meant to form or amend a moral code, nor is it meant to condone the SM's or veteran's acts. Rather, the moral injury breakout components serve to challenge extreme and rigid thinking by encouraging the recognition that although an act may be undeniably "bad," it is still possible to move forward and establish a good, moral life. For clients with intractable religious beliefs that seem to disallow consideration of forgiveness, client consultation with relevant religious authorities may be recommended as one possible homework assignment, and chaplaincy consultation may be warranted.

This intervention involves a hypothetical conversation with a compassionate and understanding moral figure who is held in the highest regard by the patient. This ethical authority should be someone who has always supported the patient and will continue to support the patient despite any potential transgression the patient has committed or witnessed. Should the SM or veteran demonstrate difficulty in identifying such a figure, it may be beneficial for the patient to identify an individual to whom they feel protective. Ideally, this figure (i.e., a moral authority or an individual by whom they feel protected and supported) would be identified during Session 1 or at the beginning of Session 2. The breakout component is implemented following the imaginal exposure module and is completed over multiple sessions. Detailed guidance in the selection of the moral authority figure is provided in the treatment manual (Litz et al., 2016), but in short, the therapist assists the client in identifying a figure that embodies benevolence, forgiveness, and kindness to invoke a third-party perspective.

It is critical to orient the SM or veteran to the purpose of the intervention and explain what will be asked of the patient during this technique. Next, the clinician guides the patient in a conversation with the moral authority figure in the present tense; this task is completed in two phases. Phase one of this dialogue involves the SM or veteran disclosing the morally injurious experience to the moral figure. It is recommended that patients fully immerse themselves in the dialogue by closing their eyes and using the present tense to promote optimal engagement with this phase. The patient is instructed to share the behavioral and emotional changes he or she has experienced since the event. The second phase of this dialogue involves allowing the patient to speak with the voice of the moral authority and to respond, in the present tense, to the disclosure. The therapist should attempt to ensure that the moral figure responds realistically to the disclosure, such as allowing for genuine surprise or disappointment. Next, the moral authority would speak with understanding, compassion, and forgiveness, directed by the clinician. For readers uncertain about or uncomfortable with the prospect of conducting a modified empty-chair technique, it is worth noting that it is merely a perspective-taking exercise that has a long, empirically bolstered tradition in both clinical and social psychological literatures. Because the morally injured are prone to "self-flagellation" and are often focused on being "unworthy" of forgiveness, invoking a third-party perspective can soften this stance. Accordingly, if present-tense dialogue is a "bridge too far" for some clients, even having them reflect on what the moral authority figure might say—without a present-tense dialogue per se—may help promote consideration of less self-vilifying and condemn-ing appraisals.

The outline of the breakout component for betrayal-based moral injury is similar in structure to morally injurious perpetration. The difference lies in the subject matter of the disclosure. Here, the content of the dialogue centers on the actions by a leader that have violated expectations of moral conduct and the impact this experience has on the SM or veteran.

OUTLINE OF SESSIONS

A session-by-session flow of AD is discussed next, with a pictorial representa-tion of active sessions (2–7) outlined in Figure 10.1. Importantly, the follow-ing description is of the eight-session version of AD that is described in greater detail in the published treatment manual (Litz et al., 2016). Recently, an extended 12-session version of AD was developed that incorporates letter writing homework to make the experiential breakouts easier to accomplish for patients and therapists, more extensive behavioral task assignments in service of an evolving healing and repair plan, and compassion training in the form of loving-kindness meditation (Litz & Carney, 2018). This new therapy is being tested in a VA clinical trial (Yeterian et al., 2017).

FIGURE 10.1. Flow Chart of Adaptive Disclosure Sessions 2 to 7

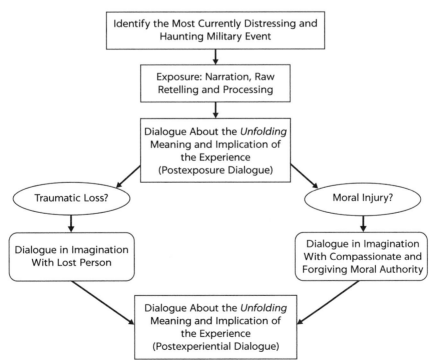

Assessment and Case Conceptualization (≈ 90 minutes)

At least one formal session should be devoted to information gathering to assist in case conceptualization and treatment planning. It is recommended that a formal clinical interview, such as the Clinician-Administered PTSD Scale (Weathers et al., 2018), be administered to aid the clinician in determining the most appropriate treatment intervention for the SM. Administration of an inventory of exposure to potentially morally injurious events—such as the Modified Moral Injury Questionnaire (Robbins et al., 2017)—is recommended, as well. Additional areas of assessment include the patient's current level of functioning, predeployment functioning, principal harm (the most distressing or reexperienced trauma), and distress tolerance techniques. AD should be considered as a primary therapeutic intervention if the central harm includes traumatic loss or morally injurious experiences, and the patient would benefit from targeting a specific trauma and processing the meanings and interpretations assigned to the event(s).

Session 1 (≈ 60 minutes)

Should the SM or veteran be considered an appropriate candidate for AD, the first session should begin with providing feedback to the patient concerning diagnosis and initial case conceptualization. As part of the case conceptualization, it is important for the clinician to identify whether the principal harm is characterized as a highly fearful and life-threatening event, a war-zone loss, or a moral injury. If this information is not yet evident, the clinician uses future exposure sessions to identify what aspect of the trauma has to be processed. The rest of the session should be devoted to introducing and describing the therapy, answering questions and concerns of the patient, and preparing the patient for the first exposure session.

Sessions 2 to 7 (≈ 90 minutes)

The start of each active treatment session begins with an imaginal exposure of the primary trauma, regardless of the event type (i.e., life-threat, loss, or moral injury). The exposure component aims to engage the patient with the details of the trauma and to access their emotions. This segment of the session should last 15 to 30 minutes; multiple iterations of the trauma narrative are not necessary as long as the patient is fully engaged with their emotions. Following the exposure exercise, the SM is provided the opportunity to return psychologically to the present and identify the experience of disclosing the trauma narrative (postexposure dialogue). Should loss or moral injury be present in the patient's narrative, the postexposure narrative is followed by the experiential breakout component. At the conclusion of the breakout component, a similar conversation to the postexposure dialogue is implemented in which the SM or veteran is provided the opportunity to share their experience of the intervention.

In cases of loss or moral injury, each active session is roughly divided into fourths: exposure, postexposure dialogue, experiential strategies (breakout component), and postexperiential dialogue. In the case of highly fearful, life-threatening traumas, sessions can allocate equal time to the exposure and post-exposure dialogue.

Session 8 (≈ 90 minutes)

The final session of AD centers on reviewing the progress that the SM or veteran has made and summarizing the process of the intervention. Given the short time frame of AD, it is crucial that the clinician and patient review how AD is intended to be used as a model learning experience and to emphasize how this intervention is used to create a foundation of adaptive coping and to promote the processing of the patient's trauma. The brief nature of this intervention may require that further processing work be continued by the SM.

SPECIAL CONSIDERATIONS

To ensure competent treatment for those seeking relief from moral injury, it is crucial for therapists to become well-versed in military cultures. Traditional treatments for traumatic stress do not explicitly consider military culture or the unique clinical issues that may arise from combat or operational exposure, losses, and traumas (Gray et al., 2012). Further, given the evidence suggesting that the therapeutic alliance is a significant predictor of outcome improvement (Lambert & Barley, 2001), military cultural competence may bolster the patient–therapist relationship with nonmilitary clinicians. Without an adequate understanding of military culture, roles, and identities, therapists may unintentionally criticize or place judgment on these experiences, understandably creating distrust in the therapeutic alliance.

Though four distinct military branches exist with their own traditions, the warrior ethos is the one transcendental ideal that connects all military SMs and veterans. The prevailing feature of the warrior ethos is the oath to live by and uphold a strict moral code. The concept of living by a moral code is not unique to SMs, but taking an oath to live by this code is not experienced by most civilians. These primary components of the warrior's ethos (e.g., dedicating oneself to live by a moral code and protecting the welfare of others) require a significant degree of selflessness in which an SM considers the well-being of others as potentially more important than one's own life.

Another aspect of the warrior's ethos is the personal relationship with suffering. SMs are taught at the outset of training how to suffer physically, mentally, and emotionally. This relationship with suffering is not necessarily enjoyed but rather is viewed as a vessel for meaning. It is important for clinicians to recognize that SMs and veterans may not wish to seek mental health care unless they can acknowledge some potential good beyond relieving their suffering.

A personal relationship with death is another aspect of the warrior ethos. The act of taking a life in battle and the witnessing of others' deaths are considered necessary rites of passage—as is facing the possibility of one's own death. By closely embracing the concept of death, SMs can be viewed as facing one of the most debilitating fears. This concept may impact the implementation of AD through the expectation of SMs that their therapist should have a similar relationship and appreciation for death. SMs and veterans, however, often acknowledge that most therapists will never have "crossed the river" to the same extent as they have. This concept of warrior ethos may also impact a patient's expectations for themselves when they experience traumatic grief because this may be misinterpreted by the SM as a weakness, ultimately threatening their warrior identity.

Finally, a shared pride, or esprit de corps, among SMs is the last component of the warrior ethos. This pride stems from the real accomplishments and abilities of a military unit and becomes essential to the successful completion of military missions. This pride originates in the admiration and then internalization of military culture so that the SM aims to become deserving of respect and pride from the organization. The degree to which an SM's positive self-regard is established in their military identity can pose a challenge when the individual leaves the military, a possible dilemma that may manifest within therapy. Military values and culture vary somewhat depending on the branch, conflict, setting, and duties of the SM, and these variations should be explored and honored. In any case, it will be necessary for the therapist to explore and understand military values and culture germane to the SM. The AD manual includes an entire appendix devoted to the diversity of military missions, branches, organizations, and relationships that may be fruitful for therapists to review (Litz et al., 2016).

CASE EXAMPLE

Sergeant Cunningham[1] is a 33-year-old White divorced marine with 13 years of active duty service. He served two tours—one in Iraq in 2004, and one in Afghanistan in 2009. He presented with severe symptoms of combat-related PTSD and also endorsed significant depressive symptoms and some suicidal ideation but no immediate intent or plans. Sergeant Cunningham stated that he was seeking help because his symptoms were not getting better, he had begun to drink more regularly and more heavily, and he was beginning to have increased bouts of rumination about the "evil that (he) caused." He had avoided treatment before presenting at the clinic.

Session 1

The first session began with a discussion of Sergeant Cunningham's current functioning, the improvements he was hoping for, and what he was like

---

[1]All identifying information was altered to ensure patient anonymity.

before his first deployment. The therapist probed for changes in Sergeant Cunningham's perceptions of self and identity, interpersonal relationships, and overall functioning. Sergeant Cunningham reported that he had noticed significant changes, particularly feeling irritable and "on edge" and having trouble sleeping due to frequent nightmares. He also expressed concern about whether he could "ever feel good about (him)self again."

The therapist made the point that although combat changes everyone, and therapy cannot "undo" all those changes, many SMs can learn to cope more effectively with difficulties they are experiencing, more successfully situate events in the past, and reclaim some of who they were before deployment so that they can move forward adaptively and pursue a life of worth and meaning. It was explicitly noted that although the therapeutic work required is difficult, the goal of AD is to help SMs recognize that a past event—no matter how horrific—does not represent the totality of self and need not forever define one's identity. Sergeant Cunningham expressed some relief but also noted that he had significant reservations about beginning this work, stating that he had never spoken to anyone about the incident that was most distressing to him.

Next, Sergeant Cunningham and the therapist together identified which traumatic deployment experience would be the focus of treatment. He was asked to think about the most difficult or impactful event and to give a brief description of what happened. It was explained that the event would be discussed during the next session in detail to get a clearer sense of the event and its meaning and how it was keeping him from moving forward. Sergeant Cunningham briefly described a number of distressing events from his first deployment before acknowledging that the most troubling event occurred during his most recent deployment when he called in an airstrike knowing that civilians and children were in the area and likely died as a result. He noted that he has been overwhelmed with guilt since coming home and feels evil and unable to move forward.

Toward the end of the first session, Sergeant Cunningham was asked to write an impact statement about the traumatic event for homework. This assignment is similar to that in CPT (Resick & Schnicke, 1993), in which the SM is asked to write at least one handwritten page on why they think the traumatic event occurred. They are not asked to provide a detailed account of the event but instead to write about the meaning of the event, why it happened, how it has impacted the SM, and what its perceived impact will be for the SM in the future. The goal is to activate appraisals and interpretations that are resulting in incapacitating guilt, shame, or distress.

Sessions 2 to 7

The second session began with Sergeant Cunningham reading his impact statement aloud. The therapist listened for beliefs about the causes and reasons for the event that required processing later in the session. Primary appraisals associated with the most significant distress and grief centered on intentionally causing death to noncombatants and the belief that some evils can never be justified or forgiven—and further that he could never be good or respectable again. He began crying as he described being unable to undo what he now considered to be an immoral act. He stated that he was weak and did not deserve relief from his suffering. The therapist acknowledged, validated, and normalized these perceptions and fear and reflected empathically how overwhelming they must be. A primary tenet of AD is that acts that violate one's core values—whether unavoidable and common in combat or not—should not be minimized or summarily attributed to the "fog of war." SMs are allowed to take ownership of their involvement and the legitimacy of their appraisals. Painful moral emotions must be honored and recognized for what they are— informational cues that one has perhaps indeed erred in extreme ways but also evidence that one has the capacity for virtue, goodness, and forgiveness. Truly evil people would not experience intense conflict or distress stemming from their actions. Although an in-session experiential exercise often happens in this session, the time necessary to validate, discuss, and process Sergeant Cunningham's emotions and appraisals was fairly lengthy. This was the first time he had discussed this event with anyone, and per his report, it was the first time he had thought about the meaning of the event in any level of detail. For a homework assignment, he was given the "totality of self" writing assignment (Litz et al., 2016) where he was asked to reflect on positive, virtuous, and moral actions before, during, and after his deployment and to comment on whether such actions would be possible in the future and what they might mean.

Beginning in Session 3 and continuing for the next several sessions, the therapist reviewed homework assignments with an eye toward the contemplation of moral repair and consideration of future behaviors and commitments reflecting core values, and that would "chisel away" at the rigid conceptualization of self as categorically evil. Following a brief review of homework exercises (described briefly later and in more detail in the AD treatment manual), most sessions involved an exposure (i.e., a retelling of the principal harm to activate relevant cognitions), followed by an experiential exercise in session. Prominently, this session used the modified empty-chair technique in which the SM engages in imagined dialogue with a compassionate moral authority figure of their choice about the transgression, its impact, and how it defines one. In Sergeant Cunningham's case, he identified his gunnery sergeant (a superior), a man whom he deeply respected and admired. In this exercise, Sergeant Cunningham was asked to describe how stuck he was, focusing on his confusion over what kind of a man he was and whether he could ever be good or moral again. Through the perspective of the gunnery sergeant, Sergeant Cunningham was able to identify how the context of battle and of that situation, in particular, could have contributed to his actions. During the conversation, the imagined perspective of the gunnery sergeant cultivated insights that not only did this horrific transgression fail to encapsulate everything about him but also that there was a mandate to make amends for his actions by helping others. This primary focus is central to an AD conceptualization. The transgression may well have been horrific and need not be altogether justified, excused, or minimized for healing to occur. The exposure component not only provides an opportunity to give voice to a "taboo" and deeply shameful experience in the presence of a caring other, but it also activates appraisals of self-condemnation and often a conceptualization of self as evil. The exposure component and the experiential exercises are designed to acknowledge and give voice to transgression and impact, and dialogue and homework assignments are designed to promote more adaptive, alternate possibilities for self in the future. The imagined dialogues with a compassionate moral authority figure are necessarily organic and idiosyncratic to the SM and the event in question but often begin—in earlier sessions—as a means of identifying rigidity and extreme condemnation to consideration of the possibility of self-forgiveness and ultimately—ideally—culminating in recognition that immobilization and self-flagellation fails to "undo" the transgression in question but does prevent opportunities for virtue and contributions to a greater good.

With respect to homework assignments, a number of strategies were used with Sergeant Cunningham. These included writing a letter to those killed in the airstrike conveying deep sorrow and regret, apology, and a deep and sincere desire for forgiveness. A subsequent letter focused on specific, concrete actions that would be taken to begin the process of symbolic amends making and contribution to others. Sergeant Cunningham identified a local charity that helped children who had recently lost a parent and set up a recurring monthly donation. It was recognized that no action could undo his transgression but that he had an opportunity and—in his view—a moral obligation to help those who had been impacted by sudden death and traumatic grief. These types of behavioral commitments to virtuous action may be thought of as "prosocial behavioral activation." By way of analogy, severely depressed individuals can begin to experience an elevation in mood by beginning to reengage with previously enjoyed but neglected activities. Having them reengage with purposeful activity can be more productive than therapeutic dialogue about depressive cognitions. In the same way, having those experiencing moral injury begin to engage in even small or minor actions that are incompatible with a conceptualization of self-as-evil may be more effective in challenging such beliefs than Socratic questioning or conventional cognitive restructuring. Beginning to behave in virtuous ways can promote recognition of new possibilities as a moral and benevolent person while not minimizing or justifying a significant transgression. Other writing assignments included consideration of self-forgiveness, with a focus on whether the refusal to do so has any larger benefit other than self-punishment and whether beginning to forgive oneself might allow a path that contributes to the well-being of others.

Session 8

During the final session, the therapist solicited feedback on what Sergeant Cunningham had learned and discussed the work that remained to be done, emphasizing the ongoing challenges ahead. The therapist reiterated that the intervention represented the beginning of a continuing process in which the therapy provided a road map of how to deal with the remaining difficulties. Potential triggers for deployment-related difficulties were discussed, and coping strategies were planned that could be used during such times. The therapist also initiated a discussion about the importance of self-care and social reengagement, delineating specific adaptive behaviors in which Sergeant Cunningham might engage. A final point that resonated especially strongly with Sergeant Cunningham was that although his transgression could never be undone and would always be a part of his history, ruminating about it and being forever incapacitated by it would not only "not undo" the event but it also would prevent positive contributions to the world and others. Ultimately, Sergeant Cunningham recognized that, because of his deployment experiences, he had a moral obligation to help and contribute to others. Although he still had nontrivial residual symptoms by the last session—to be expected, given the complexity of trauma and brevity of treatment—he had experienced significant reductions in conventional symptoms (i.e., his PTSD Checklist for *DSM-5* [Weathers et al., 2013] score dropped from 62 to 36). More important, he had identified concrete ways to recommit to predeployment values and virtues.

CONCLUSION

AD was designed to give military culture a place in the therapy room, validate the voice of the SM, accept a range of culture-consistent culpabilities, and target damage to moral identity by focusing on moral repair. AD attempts to help the SM integrate the discomfort of the moral injury through experiencing forgiveness, self-compassion, and engaging in reparative behaviors. The AD treatment manual provides numerous therapeutic prompts for processing and considering self-blame that may be tenable and well-placed, in a manner that—rather than disputing the veracity of such appraisals—encourages a recommitment to pre-event personal ethical and moral standards. It also offers several behavioral, written, and contemplative homework assignments designed to encourage self-forgiveness, taking ownership over real or perceived immoral and egregious acts, and seeking reparative action where feasible and to the extent possible. Although it is beyond the scope of this commentary to describe AD homework assignments in detail (or, for that matter, to enumerate all of them), examples include writing about self-forgiveness and compassion, real (when possible) or symbolic apologies to individuals impacted by a moral transgression, symbolic repayment for the offense (e.g., contributing to a charity representing those afflicted by this or similar transgressions), and general prosocial behavioral activation (i.e., engaging in charitable actions or philanthropic activities) to promote alternative possibilities of self (if the patient deems him- or herself to be wholly evil).

Though the morally injurious act cannot be undone, it need not be destiny, and it need not preclude virtuous acts in the future. In this manner, the patient's reality and the accuracy of his or her appraisal are honored. Rather than disputing that which may well be objectively true, the patient is encouraged to take ownership of the act, pursue real or symbolic reparative action, consider self-forgiveness, and recognize that self-flagellation and self-condemnation (e.g., "I am evil")—taken to an extreme—cannot undo the horrific act but can prevent moral and virtuous behavior in the future. The approach is designed to facilitate perspective taking and to shift beliefs from blameworthiness (which may be objectively true) to forgiveness and compassion (which are nonetheless possible) and, in doing so, to facilitate the potential for living a moral and virtuous life.

REFERENCES

Bradley, R., Greene, J., Russ, E., Dutra, L., & Westen, D. (2005). A multidimensional meta-analysis of psychotherapy for PTSD. *The American Journal of Psychiatry*, *162*(2), 214–227. https://doi.org/10.1176/appi.ajp.162.2.214

Edwards, K. (1990). The interplay of affect and cognition in attitude formation and change. *Journal of Personality and Social Psychology*, *59*(2), 202–216. https://doi.org/10.1037/0022-3514.59.2.202

Foa, E. B., Ehlers, A., Clark, D. M., Tolin, D. F., & Orsillo, S. M. (1999). The Posttraumatic Cognitions Inventory (PTCI): Development and validation. *Psychological Assessment*, *11*(3), 303–314. https://doi.org/10.1037/1040-3590.11.3.303

Foa, E. B., Hembree, E. A., & Rothbaum, B. O. (2007). *Prolonged exposure therapy for PTSD: Emotional processing of traumatic experiences, Therapist guide*. Oxford University Press. https://doi.org/10.1093/med:psych/9780195308501.001.0001

Friedman, M. J. (2006). Posttraumatic stress disorder among military returnees from Afghanistan and Iraq. *The American Journal of Psychiatry*, *163*(4), 586–593. https://doi.org/10.1176/ajp.2006.163.4.586

Gray, M. J., Nash, W. P., & Litz, B. T. (2017). When self-blame is rational and appropriate: The limited utility of Socratic questioning in the context of moral injury: Commentary on Wachen et al. (2016). *Cognitive and Behavioral Practice*, *24*(4), 383–387. https://doi.org/10.1016/j.cbpra.2017.03.001

Gray, M. J., Schorr, Y., Nash, W., Lebowitz, L., Amidon, A., Lansing, A., Maglione, M., Lang, A. J., & Litz, B. T. (2012). Adaptive disclosure: An open trial of a novel exposure-based intervention for service members with combat-related psychological stress injuries. *Behavior Therapy*, *43*(2), 407–415. https://doi.org/10.1016/j.beth.2011.09.001

Greenberg, L. S., & Safran, J. D. (1989). Emotion in psychotherapy. *American Psychologist*, *44*(1), 19–29. https://doi.org/10.1037/0003-066X.44.1.19

Griffin, B. J., Purcell, N., Burkman, K., Litz, B. T., Bryan, C. J., Schmitz, M., Villierme, C., Walsh, J., & Maguen, S. (2019). Moral injury: An integrative review. *Journal of Traumatic Stress*, *32*(3), 350–362. https://doi.org/10.1002/jts.22362

Hoge, C. W., Auchterlonie, J. L., & Milliken, C. S. (2006, March 1). Mental health problems, use of mental health services, and attrition from military service after returning from deployment to Iraq or Afghanistan. *JAMA*, *295*(9), 1023–1032. https://doi.org/10.1001/jama.295.9.1023

Hoge, C. W., Castro, C. A., Messer, S. C., McGurk, D., Cotting, D. I., & Koffman, R. L. (2004, July 1). Combat duty in Iraq and Afghanistan, mental health problems, and barriers to care. *The New England Journal of Medicine*, *351*, 13–22. https://doi.org/10.1056/NEJMoa040603

Hoge, C. W., Terhakopian, A., Castro, C. A., Messer, S. C., & Engel, C. C. (2007). Association of posttraumatic stress disorder with somatic symptoms, health care visits, and absenteeism among Iraq war veterans. *The American Journal of Psychiatry, 164*(1), 150–153. https://doi.org/10.1176/ajp.2007.164.1.150

Jacobson, I. G., Ryan, M. A. K., Hooper, T. I., Smith, T. C., Amoroso, P. J., Boyko, E. J., Gackstetter, G. D., Wells, T. S., & Bell, N. S. (2008, August 13). Alcohol use and alcohol-related problems before and after military combat deployment. *JAMA, 300*(6), 663–675. https://doi.org/10.1001/jama.300.6.663

Lambert, M. J., & Barley, D. E. (2001). Research summary on the therapeutic relationship and psychotherapy outcome. *Psychotherapy: Theory, Research, & Practice, 38*(4), 357–361. https://doi.org/10.1037/0033-3204.38.4.357

Litz, B., & Carney, J. R. (2018). Employing loving-kindness meditation to promote self- and other-compassion among war veterans with posttraumatic stress disorder. *Spirituality in Clinical Practice, 5*(3), 201–211. https://doi.org/10.1037/scp0000174

Litz, B. T., Lebowitz, L., Gray, M. J., & Nash, W. P. (2016). *Adaptive disclosure: A new treatment for military trauma and moral injury.* Guilford Press.

Litz, B. T., Rusowicz-Orazem, L., Grunthal, B., Gray, M., Nash, W., & Lang, A. (2020). *A randomized controlled non-inferiority trial comparing adaptive disclosure, a combat-specific PTSD treatment, and cognitive-processing therapy in deployed Marines* [Manuscript in preparation]. Department of Psychiatry, Boston University School of Medicine.

Litz, B. T., Stein, N., Delaney, E., Lebowitz, L., Nash, W. P., Silva, C., & Maguen, S. (2009). Moral injury and moral repair in war veterans: A preliminary model and intervention strategy. *Clinical Psychology Review, 29*(8), 695–706. https://doi.org/10.1016/j.cpr.2009.07.003

Monson, C. M., Schnurr, P. P., Resick, P. A., Friedman, M. J., Young-Xu, Y., & Stevens, S. P. (2006). Cognitive processing therapy for veterans with military-related posttraumatic stress disorder. *Journal of Consulting and Clinical Psychology, 74*(5), 898–907. https://doi.org/10.1037/0022-006X.74.5.898

Nash, W. P. (2007). Combat/operational stress adaptations and injuries. In C. R. Figley & W. P. Nash (Eds.), *Combat stress injury: Theory, research, and management* (pp. 33–63). Routledge.

Office of the Surgeon, Multinational Force–Iraq, & Office of the Surgeon General, United States Army Medical Command. (2006, November 17). *Mental Health Advisory Team (MHAT) IV Operation Iraqi Freedom 05–07: Final Report.* https://ntrl.ntis.gov/NTRL/dashboard/searchResults/titleDetail/PB2010103335.xhtml

Ready, D. J., Thomas, K. R., Worley, V., Backscheider, A. G., Harvey, L. A. C., Baltzell, D., & Rothbaum, B. O. (2008). A field test of group based exposure therapy with 102 veterans with war-related posttraumatic stress disorder. *Journal of Traumatic Stress, 21*(2), 150–157. https://doi.org/10.1002/jts.20326

Resick, P. A., Monson, C. M., & Chard, K. M. (2017). *Cognitive processing therapy for PTSD: A comprehensive manual.* Guilford Press.

Resick, P. A., & Schnicke, M. K. (1993). *Cognitive processing therapy for rape victims: A treatment manual.* Sage.

Robbins, A. T., Kelley, M. L., Hamrick, H. C., Bravo, A. J., & White, T. D. (2017, May 25–28). *Modifying the Moral Injury Questionnaire: Including core symptomatology* [Poster presentation]. Association for Psychological Science, Boston, MA.

Schnurr, P. P., Friedman, M. J., Engel, C. C., Foa, E. B., Shea, M. T., Chow, B. K., Resick, P. A., Thurston, V., Orsillo, S. M., Haug, R., Turner, C., & Bernardy, N. (2007, February 28). Cognitive behavioral therapy for posttraumatic stress disorder in women: A randomized controlled trial. *JAMA, 297*(8), 820–830. https://doi.org/10.1001/jama.297.8.820

Steenkamp, M. M., Litz, B. T., Gray, M. J., Lebowitz, L., Nash, W., Conoscenti, L., Amidon, A., & Lang, A. (2011). A brief exposure-based intervention for SMs with PTSD. *Cognitive and Behavioral Practice, 18*(1), 98–107. https://doi.org/10.1016/j.cbpra.2009.08.006

Weathers, F. W., Bovin, M. J., Lee, D. J., Sloan, D. M., Schnurr, P. P., Kaloupek, D. G., Keane, T. M., & Marx, B. P. (2018). The Clinician-Administered PTSD Scale for *DSM–5* (CAPS-5): Development and initial psychometric evaluation in military veterans. *Psychological Assessment, 30*(3), 383–395. https://doi.org/10.1037/pas0000486

Weathers, F. W., Litz, B. T., Keane, T. M., Palmieri, P. A., Marx, B. P., & Schnurr, P. P. (2013). *The PTSD checklist for* DSM-5 *(PCL-5)*. https://www.ptsd.va.gov

Wilk, J. E., Bliese, P. D., Kim, P. Y., Thomas, J. L., McGurk, D., & Hoge, C. W. (2010). Relationship of combat experiences to alcohol misuse among U.S. soldiers returning from the Iraq war. *Drug and Alcohol Dependence, 108*(1–2), 115–121. https://doi.org/10.1016/j.drugalcdep.2009.12.003

Yeterian, J. D., Berke, D. S., & Litz, B. T. (2017). Psychosocial rehabilitation after war trauma with adaptive disclosure: Design and rationale of a comparative efficacy trial. *Contemporary Clinical Trials, 61*, 10–15. https://doi.org/10.1016/j.cct.2017.07.012

11

Impact of Killing

A Treatment Program for Military Veterans With Moral Injury

Kristine Burkman, Shira Maguen, and Natalie Purcell

Among military veterans of multiple service eras, killing in war is associated with increased risk of moral injury, as well as posttraumatic stress disorder (PTSD), alcohol abuse, suicide, and postwar functional difficulties (MacNair, 2002; Maguen et al., 2009; Van Winkle & Safer, 2011). Veterans with higher numbers of killing experiences have twice the odds of suicidal ideation compared with those with few or no killing experiences, even after adjusting for demographic variables, PTSD, depression, substance use disorders, and general combat exposure (Maguen et al., 2012). Despite high rates of killing in war (Hoge et al., 2004) and associated outcomes (Fontana & Rosenheck, 1999; Fontana et al., 1992; Maguen et al., 2010, 2011), veterans are not routinely assessed for killing experiences, even though such assessment could assist with prevention and treatment efforts.

When veterans are invited to share their thoughts and feelings after combat, many describe killing another person or people as a transformative experience that profoundly altered their perception of themselves and their world (Purcell et al., 2016). Reactions to killing in war include a wider range of psychological and spiritual sequelae than is captured by the diagnostic criteria of PTSD (Bryan et al., 2018; Kopacz et al., 2015); these include shame, guilt, and spiritual distress. Nonetheless, veterans may not talk about killing and moral injury, even in therapy, due to uncertainty about whether killing is an

This chapter was coauthored by employees of the United States government as part of official duty and is considered to be in the public domain. Any views expressed herein do not necessarily represent the views of the United States government, and the authors' participation in the work is not meant to serve as an official endorsement.

https://doi.org/10.1037/0000204-012
Addressing Moral Injury in Clinical Practice, J. M. Currier, K. D. Drescher, and J. Nieuwsma (Editors)
In the public domain.

appropriate discussion topic and concern about judgment from providers who are primarily civilians and may be perceived as being unable to understand (Purcell et al., 2016). Veterans Health Administration (VHA) trauma clinicians may also avoid the topic due to concerns about stigma, fears of their reactions, and concerns that they are inadequately trained to address the topic of killing and associated moral and spiritual issues (Burkman et al., 2018).

We (KB & SM) developed the Impact of Killing (IOK) treatment program in response to research finding that veterans who kill in war are at a uniquely high risk of negative mental health outcomes (Maguen et al., 2009, 2010, 2011). IOK development was informed by focus-group input from combat veterans of all eras (Purcell et al., 2016), and the protocol was refined through initial pilot testing (Maguen et al., 2017) and qualitative analysis of both veteran (Purcell, Burkman, et al., 2018) and provider feedback (Burkman et al., 2018). We believe that IOK fills a specific yet critically important gap in our field by directly addressing the guilt, shame, self-sabotaging behaviors, functional difficulties, and moral and spiritual distress directly associated with killing. IOK is also easily integrated into existing systems of trauma care, creating a stepped model of treatment for moral injury. This chapter describes the theoretical background, development, and content of the IOK treatment to inform its further implementation.

THEORETICAL BACKGROUND FOR IOK

Moral injury has been defined as "perpetrating, failing to prevent, bearing witness to, or learning about acts that transgress deeply held moral beliefs and expectations" (Litz et al., 2009, p. 697). For many veterans, killing in war transgresses moral, spiritual, or religious beliefs, creating a sense of dissonance and internal conflict known as moral injury (Purcell et al., 2016). In the moral injury model proposed by Litz and colleagues (2009), killing-related cognitions associated with guilt, shame, and self-condemnation act as mediators within a larger framework of psychological distress and functional impairment. We posit that healing from killing-related moral injury involves the identification of a wide range of cognitions related to killing and other morally injurious events (MIEs) and a focus on understanding the functional impact of those cognitions in treatment. Many of these cognitions, we argue, must be addressed with the understanding that a transgression has occurred—that is, that the individual's reaction to crossing a moral line is not necessarily a distortion that must be challenged but rather a reality to be accepted and integrated. This shifts the lens from mainly focusing on distortions to jointly acknowledging the harm done and working toward acceptance.

In evidence-based psychotherapies (EBPs) for PTSD, exposure (in vivo and imaginal) and Socratic questioning of trauma reactions are powerful interventions that can challenge erroneous relationships made in the aftermath of traumatic events. These approaches offer much-needed clarity related to context and responsibility but are insufficient when the source of moral distress is not cognitive distortions but rather valid perceptions of potential wrongdoing or real harm (Maguen & Burkman, 2013). IOK goes beyond current EBPs by acknowledging the need for acceptance and grief work related to veterans' acts of commission and/or omission. IOK is explicit in the process of differentiating beliefs that can be challenged (to reveal a more balanced truth) from beliefs that must be acknowledged as painful realities (and thus earmarked for self-forgiveness and amends work).

Self-forgiveness is a critical link in the moral injury framework (Litz et al., 2009), and we conceptualize it as a key healing ingredient that is not formally captured in other treatments (Purcell, Griffin et al., 2018). IOK explicitly fosters self-forgiveness, which is strongly associated with positive physical and mental health outcomes (Davis et al., 2015; Purcell, Griffin, et al., 2018). We draw from Hall and Fincham's (2005) model of self-forgiveness, which requires acknowledging the wrong or harm done, processing negative feelings triggered by the offense (e.g., guilt, remorse), and achieving an internal acceptance of oneself. Self-forgiveness entails taking responsibility for that wrongdoing, yet also recognizing that prior actions alone do not define who a person will be moving forward. Self-forgiveness is often raised in the context of profound functional impairment and a long history of self-punishing or self-sabotaging behaviors. It is not the role of the therapist to adjudicate whether veterans should or should not be forgiven but, rather, to help identify the reasons veterans are unable to self-forgive and to reflect the impact that their decision or stance may have on their lives. IOK also engages veterans in conciliatory behaviors—an important part of the authentic self-forgiveness process (Carpenter et al., 2014).

Definitions of forgiveness and self-forgiveness and approaches to conciliatory behaviors are often inextricably linked with moral, spiritual, and religious beliefs. Spiritual issues are not directly addressed in current EBPs for PTSD, which is a concerning gap, given that spiritual functioning is associated with PTSD severity and suicidal behavior in veterans (Kopacz et al., 2016). There is a growing awareness in the field that religious and spiritual distress contributes to negative mental health outcomes (Aist, 2012), and yet clinicians continue to report they avoid discussions of spirituality or religion for fear of stepping outside their scope of practice or feeling inadequately prepared to address spiritual matters (Burkman et al., 2018). IOK entails inquiring and learning about a veteran's moral, spiritual, or religious beliefs (Vieten et al., 2013; see also Chapter 3, this volume). The IOK therapist's role is to help veterans collaboratively explore their moral and spiritual conflicts as well as options for additional spiritual support and healing (see Chapter 13).

Recognizing that moral injury often results in profound self-condemnation and social withdrawal, IOK begins with a cognitive behavioral framework and incorporates elements of gestalt, existential, and relational psychotherapies. We use experiential exercises and written assignments to foster empathy toward enemy soldiers and/or civilians, as well as reconciliation with aspects of oneself. Leveraging a veteran's sense of compassion and esteem for a fellow soldier or a younger version of themselves can shift or overcome barriers to self-compassion and self-forgiveness. Given the level of stigma associated with the topic of killing and veterans' concerns about being judged or condemned, the therapeutic relationship can serve as a powerful tool to allow veterans to test their beliefs about what would happen if others learned about what they did. When processing events they describe as unforgivable, veterans ideally experience acceptance and compassion reflected by their therapist.

In IOK, conciliatory behaviors and community integration are encouraged through an "amends plan" to counteract social withdrawal. These behaviors can facilitate authentic healing that is consistent with a veteran's core moral values (Carpenter et al., 2014). Engaging in prosocial activities, giving back to others, and connecting with other human beings can offer experiences and generate emotions and thoughts that bolster the reclaimed moral self and can thus assist with healing. Veterans with moral injury often isolate themselves from spiritual communities or loved ones. When possible, reconnecting with those communities and loved ones offers a profound emotional experience of belonging that can facilitate forgiveness. It also begins an important process of building or reinforcing external supports outside the therapeutic relationship that can support improved long-term functioning and quality of life.

SCIENTIFIC BASIS OF IOK

The IOK treatment protocol reflects the culmination of nearly 10 years of research on the topic of killing in war and moral injury. We began by examining the impact of killing through a mixed-method approach, using quantitative and qualitative work to inform next steps. Our quantitative research examined mental health outcomes associated with killing in war, showing that those who killed in war were at increased risk of PTSD, alcohol abuse, suicide, and functional difficulties after returning home, even after adjusting for the impact of general combat (Maguen et al., 2009, 2010, 2011, 2012). We found that killing is a unique risk factor that is associated with poor mental health outcomes.

We then conducted focus groups with veterans of multiple war eras (post-9/11, Persian Gulf, Vietnam, Korea, and World War II), discussing their experiences with killing, how killing continued to impact their lives postdeployment, and whether killing experiences were addressed in existing PTSD treatments. Veteran feedback was analyzed to determine common experiences, beliefs, and barriers to addressing moral injury in existing models of treatment (Purcell et al., 2016). Focus group findings also allowed us to develop the Killing Cognition Scale (KCS), a self-report measure assessing beliefs about killing in war that highlights prominent themes revealed in focus groups (e.g., guilt or shame, self-betrayal of morality, loss of spirituality, condemned self). Focus group findings also allowed us to develop an initial treatment protocol (six to eight sessions) addressing key clinical issues not captured in existing EBPs for PTSD. This treatment protocol was designed to follow EBPs for PTSD with the understanding that killing in war often happens in the context of life-threatening situations and is complicated by life threat–based traumatic experiences.

We tested our initial treatment protocol in a randomized controlled pilot study (Maguen et al., 2017) with combat veterans from multiple eras (Korea, Vietnam, Gulf, post-9/11) who were diagnosed with PTSD, endorsed being distressed by killing or feeling responsible for the death of others, and completed an EBP for PTSD. In an intent-to-treat analysis ($n = 33$), we found that, compared with controls, the IOK treatment group experienced a significant improvement in PTSD symptoms, general psychiatric symptoms, and quality-of-life functional measures. Veterans who received the treatment were more likely to endorse taking part in community events or celebrations and were more likely to confide or share personal thoughts and feelings with loved ones. For example, veterans described reconciling with adult children they had not spoken to in years, reaching out and apologizing to ex-partners for their behavior postcombat, volunteering, visiting meaningful sites (e.g., the gravesite of a fallen soldier, Vietnam), and even returning to places of worship after decades away. Veterans who received IOK also demonstrated significant decreases in their level of distress regarding various killing-related beliefs such as "I deserve to suffer for killing" and endorsed greater understanding of the factors that led to killing. All veterans who received IOK reported that the treatment was acceptable and feasible.

We also solicited qualitative feedback from all participants who completed the IOK pilot study (Purcell, Burkman, et al., 2018) and surveyed 10 trauma providers who reviewed the IOK treatment protocol to refine the treatment further (Burkman et al., 2018). Overwhelmingly, both veterans and providers indicated that IOK served a need not addressed by existing EBPs for PTSD, and they felt many veterans could benefit from the protocol. Veterans felt that the treatment should be longer, spending more time on the area of self-forgiveness, and we revised the protocol accordingly (expanding it to 10 sessions). Another consistent and powerful finding from our qualitative analysis of veterans' and providers' responses to the protocol was the importance of tailoring treatment to fit individual veterans' specific needs. Morality, spirituality, and killing in war are profoundly personal; although IOK offers a containing and structured frame, it allows providers to be flexible, creative, and collaborative in their approach. Future research will include a 4-year, multisite randomized controlled trial of the expanded protocol among regionally diverse veterans.

DESCRIPTION OF IOK COMPONENTS AND SESSIONS

IOK is a cognitive behaviorally based intervention that consists of 10 sessions of weekly individual psychotherapy lasting 60 to 90 minutes each, facilitated by a therapist who has specialized training in trauma and traumatic stress. Ideally, veterans will have either completed an EBP for PTSD or engaged in some form of trauma-focused psychotherapy before engaging in IOK. This is due partly to the brevity in which we review the cognitive behavioral model and the intensity of emotion associated with moral injury. We are aware that some veterans may struggle to connect with or complete existing EBPs for

PTSD and that moral injury may coexist with depression, general anxiety, or a substance use disorder. Clinical judgment is key, and we have found that veterans tend to engage more fully and get more out of the treatment if they have experience approaching difficult emotional material to reach a new understanding or experience.

The treatment starts with completing the KCS. We feel this is a critical step based on feedback from both veterans (Purcell, Burkman, et al., 2016, 2018) and providers (Burkman et al., 2018) regarding the challenge they experience in initiating discussions of killing. We explain to intervention recipients that the items on the KCS reflect common thoughts and beliefs that combat veterans of all eras have shared; some may resonate, others may not. We tailor the treatment to focus on the areas of greatest conflict, distress, and/or functional impairment on the basis of their responses. Table 11.1 provides examples of the various categories and items captured in the KCS.

A major goal for the first session is to set the tone for what veterans should expect from IOK (see Table 11.2), which includes informing them of the range of emotions that may arise and the importance of self-care and safety planning to protect against self-harming or self-sabotaging behaviors. We also highlight the importance of collaboration with the therapist and explain that assignments in future sessions will be determined on the basis of how the veteran responds to various measures, session content, and initial between-session assignments. Finally, we stress that IOK is designed to be a springboard for ongoing work toward moral repair outside of therapy. We assess attempts the veteran has made on their own to heal from moral injury, both to identify potentially self-destructive tendencies and to reinforce and validate any gains made through previous therapy, spirituality, or personal pursuits. As best we can, we validate steps already taken and encourage veterans to view IOK as an opportunity to take stock and map out steps toward acceptance, self-forgiveness, and moral repair.

TABLE 11.1. Killing Cognition Scale Categories and Example Cognitions

Category	Example cognition
Guilt	"I had feelings that I should not have had at the time when I killed."
Shame	"I worry about what my family and friends would think of me if they knew I killed someone."
Self-Blame	"I deserve to suffer for killing."
Responsibility	"I was responsible for an unjustified killing."
Loss of meaning	"Nothing seems important anymore after killing."
Contamination and self-loathing	"I am forever tainted because of killing."
Remorse or regret	"I wish I could have changed the outcome after seeing the humanity of the person I killed."
Moral violation	"No good person would have done what I did."
Spiritual disillusionment	"I wonder where God was when the killing happened."
Disgust or dismay	"It bothers me that I felt a rush when I killed."
Other	"I don't trust my own anger after killing."

TABLE 11.2. Impact of Killing Treatment Session-by-Session Outline

Session	Description	Content
1	Pretreatment Evaluation	Assessment, past work, barriers to treatment, coping skills
2	Common responses to killing	Physiology, instinctual decisions, initial reactions, emotions, behaviors, beliefs
3	Killing cognitions, Part 1	Killing cognitions, meaning of killing
4	Killing cognitions, Part 2	Maladaptive killing cognitions (continued), behavioral activation, introduction to acceptance
5	Acceptance and moral injury	Acceptance (continued), role of self-betrayal in moral injury, related sequelae
6	Defining forgiveness	Defining forgiveness and self-forgiveness, barriers to self-forgiveness, and introduction to forgiveness plan
7	Forgiveness, Part 1	Areas of forgiveness, function of self-forgiveness, gaining perspective, forgiveness letters (continued)
8	Forgiveness, Part 2	Forgiveness letters (continued), introduction to amends plan
9	Taking the next step	Forgiveness letters (continued), making amends, connection to others
10	Maintaining gains	Healing as a process, plan to continue work

To further address stigma, clinicians initiate Session 2 by providing information that other veterans have shared about their war experiences. We believe that this discussion of common reactions to killing may help veterans learn that reactions to killing that they believed were unique to them (and shameful) are more common than they realized. Common responses to killing include physiological responses, instinctual decisions, and the role of training in being able to kill and group dynamics of the unit that impact how individuals make sense of killing. We also share common, potentially concerning emotions and beliefs that may emerge minutes after killing or much later. Additional MIEs (besides killing) are often revealed in the course of treatment and are addressed as part of the individual's specific experience. At the end of this session, we assign a writing task that asks veterans to reflect on how killing has changed their view of themselves and others, as well as their sense of meaning and ability to function in life. We use beliefs generated from this assignment, as well as responses on the KCS and reactions from the common responses to killing session, to identify areas to challenge with cognitive restructuring and areas to earmark for acceptance, grief, and self-forgiveness work.

The cognitive behavioral framework is reviewed in the third session. Most veterans receiving IOK are familiar with it due to prior completion of EBPs for PTSD. Here, we focus on the beliefs about killing that are most problematic. Veterans work with therapists in session and complete between-session assignments (e.g., thought records related to killing cognitions) to gain perspective, recognize the importance of context, and more fully integrate aspects of self that may be distorted or dismissed. Thought records for IOK have four columns (situation, cognition, emotion, behavior), with automatic and "revised" rows.

In Session 4, we highlight the importance of recognizing behaviors associated with reactions to killing cognitions because they often lead to seeking out or even creating confirmatory evidence to support self-condemning beliefs. We have found that veterans often interpret the self-destructive behavior that is a consequence of killing-related cognitions as further "evidence" that they are not good people. To prepare for further sessions, it is thus imperative for veterans to understand how self-destructive behaviors contribute to long-held negative beliefs about themselves, others, and humanity and to highlight how new behaviors can catalyze new beliefs that more fully reflect their true self.

Although some beliefs related to killing can be challenged, others (i.e., appropriate guilt) are accurate and have to be acknowledged and addressed. By Session 5, therapy shifts away from cognitive restructuring and focuses instead on acceptance, self-forgiveness, and making amends. The fifth session acknowledges the range of consequences that veterans who have killed in war face (e.g., survivor guilt, self-condemnation, social isolation, suicidal ideation, self-harming and self-sabotaging behaviors, spiritual disillusionments) and focuses more directly on the definition and concept of moral injury. There is also an acknowledgment that killing often happens in the context of other morally injurious events, as well as profound loss (e.g., loss of innocence, death of a fellow service member).

We begin the conversation about forgiveness with an assignment asking the veteran to define self-forgiveness, share where they learned about it, and examine whether they apply the same standards of forgiveness toward themselves as they do toward others. Exploring veterans' moral and spiritual development is essential in understanding the personal and cultural factors that influence moral injury and moral repair. Veterans may reject the concept of self-forgiveness because they believe it equates to condoning actions they feel are wrong or "letting them off the hook." Others feel forgiveness (of self or others) is not possible without justice, often resulting in self-punishment. Some believe only the individual harmed or God can offer forgiveness and that self-forgiveness is akin to violating one's faith. The goal here is not to reach agreement on a universal definition of forgiveness but rather to allow veterans to define it for themselves and take specific actions to understand better what is needed to move toward forgiveness of self and others. Through carefully understanding how veterans define forgiveness, why they apply forgiveness to others differently than they do themselves, and what specific barriers they identify as preventing self-forgiveness and forgiveness of others, veterans can develop a forgiveness plan with specific steps they can take to work through and with these challenges.

A powerful next step involves writing forgiveness letters. The first letter is generally written to an individual killed, harmed, or not saved (e.g., with medics). Veterans are instructed to state the wrong they committed and their understanding of the impact of that wrong and to ask for forgiveness. In nearly all circumstances, these letters are to individuals who are dead or completely inaccessible (e.g., an unidentifiable civilian who was assaulted or killed during combat). The goal is to use the memory of these individuals and events to fully access emotions around the transgression, including individuals' shared humanity (vs. the dehumanization that often facilitates killing). The letters also help veterans to adopt and examine another's perspective, which can alter ingrained ways of perceiving the identified morally injurious situation.

Additional letters are assigned to target different areas of forgiveness—for example, a letter from the perspective of a trusted other guiding the veteran on how to move forward in her or his life and a letter to the prewar version of oneself asking for forgiveness. We encourage therapists to work collaboratively with the veteran to ascertain whether writing additional letters (e.g., to family members of killed enemy soldiers or civilians or loved ones who were harmed over the years by veterans' self-destructive and isolative tendencies) would be helpful. Identifying the subject(s) of forgiveness letters is a collaborative process and rests heavily on providers' clinical judgment. The point is to ensure that veterans are engaging in an authentic process of seeking forgiveness versus an exercise in self-punishment or false or forced forgiveness based on the feeling it is what they should do or feel. The forgiveness letters often reveal powerful themes of remorse, loss, grief, despair, and longing for change. Letters are part of the therapeutic process rather than a product to share with others. Disclosure about letters or killing experiences is an important collaborative conversation, and disclosure is not an explicit goal of the treatment.

Letters are the cornerstone of the forgiveness plans; however, we also encourage other activities to explore the definition and function of self-forgiveness. These include generating a pros and cons list anchored on the function of self-forgiveness, various reading materials about forgiveness, consulting with the chaplaincy or other spiritual leaders, and/or practicing meditation or prayer. Veterans who completed the pilot trial shared that the forgiveness assignments were by far the most challenging part of treatment and yet also the most powerful (Purcell, Burkman, et al., 2018). We have found that vigorous exploration of forgiveness and self-forgiveness often reveals deeply held, intact moral values that we can help the veteran to honor.

The final two sessions of the protocol focus on developing a plan for veterans to make amends. Making amends is a personal process that allows for creativity. It provides veterans with a chance to incorporate cultural ideas about self-forgiveness into a concrete action plan for atonement and continued healing after formal treatment. For some, this may involve engaging in commemorative or healing rituals that can be clarified in session; for others, simply volunteering or spending more time with family or loved ones is a form of making amends. Some veterans, such as those who have participated in 12-step programs (e.g., Alcoholics Anonymous [AA]), may already have experience with making amends. Where the person or people wronged may not be available for direct amends or where a direct apology might create additional harm, the veteran can instead commit to living their life in a way that honors the spirit of what those amends might be (i.e., "living amends"). We encourage veterans in IOK to live their lives in a way that honors their articulated morals and values, and the amends plan maps out specific steps that can be taken to continue to heal. Here, many veterans wrestle with whether to tell others about their killing experience. As mentioned earlier, disclosure is not a specific goal of IOK, but it is important to help veterans examine their expectations and prepare for a range of reactions if they choose to share.

Because IOK is designed to be a springboard for ongoing healing, our last assignment is a reflection statement that asks veterans to assess what has shifted or changed since they started treatment. We also specifically ask about areas that remain conflicted and how the veteran plans to continue working toward acceptance, self-compassion, and forgiveness. By acknowledging the ongoing and persistent nature of forgiveness and self-forgiveness, we are encouraging veterans to accept that some aspects of their experiences may never be fully resolved. Cautioning that false or forced forgiveness is temporary and may only add to the wound of moral injury, we encourage greater and deeper connections with their spirituality and faith communities, social support systems, and loved ones to help support them as they continue to heal.

SPECIAL ISSUES IN TRAINING AND DELIVERY OF IOK

Because IOK is designed to follow EBPs for PTSD, we strongly encourage clinicians delivering IOK to participate in formal training in trauma conceptualization, as well as the administration of cognitive processing therapy, prolonged exposure (PE), or other trauma treatments. One of the key differences between IOK and existing EBPs for PTSD is its emphasis on distinguishing between cognitive distortions related to killing and beliefs that reflect areas for acceptance, self-forgiveness, and grief work. Discerning when Socratic questioning might be helpful versus potentially reinforcing feelings of shame and negative self-beliefs can be challenging. Moreover, veterans with moral injury may engage in behaviors (whether consciously or unconsciously) during the therapeutic process that elicit reactions of horror, judgment, or condemnation. We have found that therapists with significant trauma experience have an easier time navigating these dynamics and can skillfully catch and reflect this pattern back to veterans in a way that allows them to understand these behaviors and their potential impact better.

It is important to note that some trauma providers have reported that they were specifically trained not to ask combat veterans about killing (Burkman et al., 2018). This can be problematic. Veterans report that they prefer providers to initiate inquiry about the topic (thoughtfully and compassionately) and use direct language to address killing (Purcell et al., 2016). We recommend doing so within a broader conversation about a wide range of combat exposures (e.g., witnessing injury or killing, loss of other military personnel). As a first step, providers have to address any misgivings they may have about asking or discussing killing. Moreover, we believe clinicians have to prepare for uncomfortable therapeutic experiences, including bearing witness to discussions of violence and atrocities (Frankfurt & Frazier, 2016). Veterans from our pilot study noted the importance of a trusted, nonjudgmental therapist who could remain present and calm amid the details and intense emotions tied to discussions of morally injurious events (Purcell, Burkman, et al., 2018).

Another important consideration for providers delivering IOK is the need to address moral and spiritual concerns (see Chapters 3 and 13). Providers are encouraged to reflect on their religious and spiritual beliefs (or lack thereof) and be aware of any bias that may impact their ability to fully support veterans of diverse cultural, religious, and spiritual backgrounds. Being sensitive to how these backgrounds may contribute to moral development, injury, and repair is consistent with our professional responsibility. Reviewing a primer on various religions as it pertains to moral injury (e.g., see Wortmann et al., 2017) can be a helpful first step for providers who feel ill-equipped to approach a veteran's spiritual beliefs because of a lack of familiarity. However, ongoing curiosity and openness to veterans' experiences of morality and spirituality are essential in IOK. We also encourage providers to be proactive in helping veterans connect with various spiritual communities or resources (e.g., Veterans Affairs [VA] chaplaincy). We do not ask or encourage providers to operate outside their scope of practice but rather to see themselves as an eager collaborator with those who offer spiritual expertise and support outside the therapeutic relationship.

Finally, as discussed in Chapter 6, we urge clinicians to be mindful of potential vicarious traumatization and burnout. Providers must be able to tolerate veterans' intense feelings of guilt, remorse, disillusionment, and despair stemming not only from a distortion of reality but also from a genuine, personal understanding of humans' capacity for destruction and cruelty. This work can evoke feelings of helplessness and powerlessness in providers. We recommend consulting with colleagues for support, perspective, and empowerment.

CASE SUMMARY OF IOK

Kevin was a 71-year-old, Black combat veteran of the U.S. Army who served 22 months in Vietnam.[1] He had been in mental health treatment for over 10 years, first presenting for care following numerous episodes of angry outbursts at work that forced him into early retirement. Kevin was married for the third time, and his wife told him that if he did not address his anger and alcohol use, she would begin divorce proceedings. Before participating in IOK, Kevin had several years of participation in AA and multiple cognitive behavior and process therapy groups for substance use, anger management, and PTSD. Kevin also completed PE (3 years earlier), and his referring provider described

---

[1]Identifying information and specific details have been altered to protect the veteran's confidentiality.

significant progress over the past 10 years in maintaining his sobriety, managing his anger, and being able to speak about traumatic events without becoming overwhelmed. However, Kevin's provider was also concerned about his longstanding feelings of guilt and shame related to his military experiences, as well as his inability to set limits with family members, often overextending himself financially and emotionally.

Kevin's marriage involved significant conflict, and he frequently described emotional, verbal, and at times, physical abuse from his spouse, who he felt had every right to express her anger and disappointment in him. His relationship with his wife was causing a significant rift with his adult children from a previous marriage, whom Kevin had reconciled with over the past several years and who felt his current wife was "not good for him." Outside of his longstanding PTSD group members, Kevin had few friends, virtually none of whom were sober, and he often described feeling "safest" on the VA campus.

In his first session, Kevin's responses on the KCS highlighted significant distress associated with guilt and shame cognitions, such as "I feel ashamed that I sometimes encouraged killing," as well as self-blame and contamination and self-loathing cognitions such as "I deserve to suffer for killing," and "I feel like a monster because I killed." Kevin also endorsed distress related to moral violation with cognitions such as "No good person would have done what I did" and spiritual disillusionment cognitions, including "I wonder where God was when the killing happened." Finally, Kevin also identified disgust and dismay cognitions such as "I am afraid of what I am capable of because I killed," and "I don't believe I am a lovable person since I killed." On completing the KCS questionnaire, Kevin remarked that he was feeling tense and made a joke about how horrified his friends and family would be if they saw his answers.

After validating the significant gains he had made over the years and reviewing what was helpful in previous treatment experiences, Kevin and his therapist discussed potential barriers to completing IOK. Kevin's biggest concern was how his therapist would respond to what he told her. He was skeptical that he could change how he felt about killing because he could not "undo the killing." His therapist affirmed that, although he might not change the way he felt about the killing, she was glad he was willing to explore how he could improve his quality of life. When asked, Kevin acknowledged that he was unhappy in his marriage but unsure of what to do about it. He also wanted to spend more time with his children and grandchildren and was hoping that completing IOK would "help [him] find peace."

After reviewing common responses to killing, Kevin was more sensitive to various factors that contributed to his experiences in Vietnam. He noted how disconnected he felt from the "19-year-old kid" who went "from a chapel to a killing field" within a matter of months. In his meaning statement, themes regarding loss of spirituality, loss of innocence, self-loathing, and self-condemnation were prominent:

> Before I was drafted, I was a church kid and believed in God. I had fun with my friends, looked out for my little brother, and only really thought about baseball and girls. I can hardly remember what that feels like anymore. I became

someone else. I will never forget stepping off the plane when I got back from Vietnam. I couldn't get my uniform off quickly enough. People were giving me dirty looks, and one person called me a murderer. I guess I was. When I got home, my parents had invited all their friends over. My dad was proud of me, and my mom kept crying and hugging me. I wasn't glad to be home, and I wasn't glad to be alive. I didn't want to talk about the war. I didn't want to acknowledge I had even been there. I made up excuses to avoid seeing my friends. And when I did, I felt like an imposter. I have a hard time trusting people and feel like I don't deserve to be in a relationship. What would they think about me if they knew I killed people? I haven't even told my own wife. She already knows I am messed up. Drugs, alcohol, anger problems. Even after 8 years sober, she knows what I am. A monster. I don't go to church anymore, I don't believe God loves me, and I am not sure I love him . . . and I just don't feel right going in a church believing that. How did killing in Vietnam impact my life? It took away my belief in the good in world, it made me a monster who has caused a lot of pain to people I love. That innocent kid is dead, he never left Vietnam. And I can't stand [the person] who survived.

Kevin and his therapist addressed KCS items that mapped onto his statement (e.g., "One person called me a murderer. I guess I was"). We clarified that his most troubling thought was "I am a monster because of what I did in Vietnam." Kevin described killing an enemy combatant in close range when his unit was ambushed. He kicked the dead body out of anger and, when he and his unit were leaving the area, they passed two women who he yelled at and hit hard with the butt of his rifle to get them out of the way. He acknowledged the combatant soldier was trying to kill him, and he had to defend himself, but seeing how young the soldier was (like Kevin at the time) and then kicking the body in anger made him feel inhumane, as did mistreating civilians whom, he thought, could have been related to or knew the young soldier he killed. Kevin struggled when his therapist asked him to focus on the killing, and he explained to her that his distress was not just about the killing; it was about seeing the enemy's face, kicking the body, and yelling and hitting those women. These actions, combined with the killing, made him feel like a monster. "No good person would do what I did," he believed.

Kevin and his therapist chose to start with his beliefs that "I am a monster because of what I did in Vietnam." That is, his belief that "No good person would do what I did" seemed more multilayered, given his addiction history (i.e., how much he fed that belief over the years) and might open a larger conversation about the capacity for good and evil within human beings. To gain early traction and help Kevin reevaluate how he saw himself, his therapist chose the statement she believed that he could more readily challenge. Together, they uncovered a tremendous amount of guilt, remorse, anger, and deep sadness. By contextualizing the role of civilians in war (some deadly), Kevin's inability to grieve when he witnessed his friends die during that ambush, and his overwhelming sense of helplessness, they were able to generate compassion for all parties. By doing so, they could challenge the idea of Kevin as a monster, while acknowledging that kicking the body and hitting the women were wrongs that he deeply regretted. Here, the emotional shift from intense anger and fear to uncertainty and deep sadness was palpable.

In reviewing his thought records over the next two sessions, Kevin and his therapist discussed cultural factors impacting his experience, including his religious upbringing and the U.S. political climate when he returned from Vietnam. One theme that emerged was his profound sense of alienation from strangers, his church community, and his family. He did not feel others could relate to his experience, and he believed they would judge him harshly if he told them about what happened in Vietnam or how he was questioning God, so he withdrew. Kevin reflected on how that withdrawal led to addiction, troubled relationships, and avoiding any activities that might generate positive emotions (e.g., spending time with his children). It was critical that, in these discussions, Kevin started building some sense of compassion for what his younger self was confronting (i.e., loss of innocence, disillusionment with humanity and God).

Kevin and this therapist then moved into forgiveness work with an assignment asking him to define forgiveness and self-forgiveness. Predominant themes that emerged in his initial assignment included the importance of "making things right" and noting that only God is capable of forgiveness. Drawing from this assignment, they explored general areas of forgiveness, including Kevin's need to forgive himself for what he did in Vietnam, as well as all the years he was not emotionally or physically present for his loved ones. Kevin and his therapist also explored his complicated relationship with God following Vietnam, acknowledging ambivalence in reconnecting with a spiritual community, given his misgivings about how God could allow war to happen. They discussed barriers to self-forgiveness in detail. For example, the people Kevin wanted to apologize to were either dead or unable to be located (e.g., the two women in Vietnam). Kevin also felt that he had not "earned" the right to be forgiven, and his therapist named a lack of perceived justice as a barrier. They also acknowledged his fear that, should he forgive himself, he might "snap" and lose control again. He felt that, by continuously punishing himself, he kept himself in check, so more people would not get hurt.

Barriers to self-forgiveness often illuminate the steps needed in developing a forgiveness and amends plan. Kevin's therapist explained the process of seeking forgiveness from someone who is dead (or unable to be apologized to directly) through letter writing. This was framed as a way of being more accountable and more authentic in coming to terms with one's wrongdoings—a way of formally acknowledging the wrong committed, taking responsibility for it, and committing to change for the better.

The first letter assigned was to the soldier Kevin killed and kicked in anger after he was dead. Kevin expressed concern about being able to complete the letter, and he and his therapist reviewed coping skills and discussed the importance of naming the wrong committed to move toward forgiveness and make peace with the past. His first letter read as follows:

Dear Quân [I wanted him to have a name],

I am sorry for killing you and for disrespecting your body by kicking you over and over. I believe you were already dead when I attacked you like that, but I honestly don't know if you felt any pain during that [incident]. I hope not.

I know you understand that we had to kill to stay alive in war, and you would have killed me if you had the chance. But the way I felt about you at the time, the rage went beyond what was asked of me as a soldier. I am so sorry for disrespecting you in that way. I know this doesn't excuse what I did, but I need you to know that, to me, you were one of "them," and after seeing Jimmy and Sanchez go down, I just wanted you all dead and lost myself in rage. My rage for being in Vietnam, my rage for being shot at every day, for losing men every day, for having to walk through rotting bodies to get from point A to point B. And yet, you probably felt the same way. Please know that I am not the type of person who wants others to suffer. I will regret forever how I treated you, but I am not that man. That kid. That scared, angry, lost kid who was so pissed and sad and fed up with all the bullshit of war and took it out on you. I hope you know that I think about you and your family all the time. I know you had one. I thought about your mother when I looked at my own. I wondered if you had kids, and if not, thought about the fact that you never would. I hope you can forgive me, and I forgive you too. For Jimmy, Sanchez, for all of us. I hope you have found peace. And I hope I can too.

Reading this letter aloud brought up profound sadness for Kevin, and he and his therapist sat tearfully in silence for several minutes following his reading. Kevin softly whispered some words of prayer before making eye contact with his therapist again, and they reflected on the tremendous tragedy of war and the need to mourn and grieve for all involved. Kevin described his process of writing the letter and admitted to being surprised that he felt some compassion for himself in remembering what happened that day and how he felt. He and his therapist discussed how it might be helpful for Kevin to write another letter, this time to himself, apologizing for what he did that betrayed his morality. They reflected on how much self-punishment and suffering Kevin has endured over the past 40 years and that part of healing may be to forgive himself for the pain he caused in trying to survive and make sense of war.

In the next session, Kevin brought in his forgiveness letter to his prewar self and described a challenging week with his wife. He noted that, as he had been going through this treatment, he was becoming increasingly aware of how unhappy he has been in his relationship for the past few years. He described meeting his wife when he was still heavy in his addiction and that, since going through treatment, he felt less connection with her. He then felt tremendously guilty that as "[he] gets better, [they] get worse." Normalizing the challenge for couples when one goes through recovery, his therapist suggested they revisit this topic as they move into making an amends plan and identifying the next steps following treatment. Kevin agreed and read the letter he completed to his prewar self:

You probably can't even recognize the man I have become. I know I have a hard time seeing any of myself in you. You were a good kid, always wanting to help others, looking out for your little brother. I know how scared you were when you were sent to Vietnam, you didn't want to show it, but you were terrified. And then you saw all the killing and dying and filth and cruelty that comes with war. I abandoned you in Vietnam. I had to just to get through the days. I stopped caring after Jimmy and Sanchez. After kicking that body and knocking those women back like that—it's like I died that day too. Didn't care if I lived. Didn't really want to come home. And when I came home, I pushed away everyone you loved and made damn sure you wouldn't have a life you could be proud of. I said horrible things to Sara, I scared her with my drinking and the drugs and made sure she moved on to someone better for her. I nearly killed you with the alcohol and drugs. Landed you in jail again and again, screwed up every job you ever loved or were good at. I hurt Mom, who worried about and prayed for us for every day of her life, she died not knowing if we would be okay. She died knowing I didn't have God in my life, which broke her heart. I pushed away your children. Scared them, left them, yelled at them. I can't undo what's been done. But I can try to remember that you wanted to do good in this world. I can stop causing the people we love pain and worry. I will cherish our children and grandchildren for every single day they allow me to be in their lives. I don't want you to spend the rest of your life miserable and alone. I want more for us. I want you to feel loved again, to love others. I think you might deserve that.

Kevin read the letter aloud and clearly was conflicted; although he was sad, he also appeared nervous. He and his therapist discussed his reaction to this assignment, and he admitted to feeling guilty about even entertaining the idea that he could have more positive experiences in his life. They revisited a KCS item, "I deserve to suffer for killing," and discussed how Kevin was starting to see that decades of self-punishment did not occur in a vacuum, that he could not hurt himself without hurting people who loved him. And he did not want to hurt anyone anymore. Kevin and his therapist reflected on his core values of respect, protecting and helping others, and being dependable. When they discussed the role of amends making, Kevin expressed understanding that he needed to live a life that reflected and honored his core values and readily developed several ideas he wanted to include in his amends plan, such as volunteering with veterans groups, offering to babysit twice a week for his grandchildren, returning to AA, and possibly mentoring members new in recovery.

In their final sessions, Kevin and his therapist reflected on areas where he remained conflicted. Two main areas emerged. First, Kevin identified increased compassion for himself and others, which only complicated his ambivalence about his relationship with God. He and his therapist discussed how, as a first step, he could meet with one of the VA chaplains to discuss his mixed emotions about returning to the church and his ongoing difficulty accepting that God could allow that level of human suffering. Given Kevin's sense of shame about questioning God, he was open to starting with a VA chaplain first and then possibly approaching his younger brother (a deacon at a local congregation) about returning to church at some point. He expressed appreciation for the role faith had always played in his family and acknowledged that he missed both the feeling of faith and the sense of community.

The other area that Kevin expressed significant concern about was his relationship with his wife. He stated that he was more conflicted following IOK than before and was not sure he could stay in the relationship, which made him feel incredibly guilty because "she stood by me in my addiction." He and his therapist discussed how he and his wife could pursue couples therapy to get support for issues of communication and forgiveness for past behavior. Kevin acknowledged that a therapist might offer a more balanced perspective of what needed to be addressed in his relationship with his wife or his adult children from a previous marriage. His therapist reflected on how multiple relationships in his life could continue to heal and that couples therapy appeared to be an important next step.

CONCLUSION

Veterans with moral injury may be at the highest risk of suicide and other negative mental health outcomes, given their possible exposure to killing in war (Maguen et al., 2012). It is important that providers within the VA system and community-based setting assess for exposure to killing within a supportive environment and, in doing so, communicate an understanding that killing can be a part of the combat experience that creates significant distress and functional impairment for some. It is also crucial that VHA begins to offer treatment options, such as IOK, to help veterans struggling with moral injury begin the healing process.

IOK offers a targeted approach to treat veterans struggling with moral injury. We have found that trauma providers in a large VA health care system believe that IOK could be seamlessly woven into existing models of care and offers something of a unique approach, especially in its focus on spirituality and self-forgiveness (Burkman et al., 2018). Furthermore, veterans who completed the initial randomized controlled pilot study of IOK reported improvement in PTSD symptoms and general psychiatric symptoms, as well as increased participation in community events and disclosing their experiences to loved ones (Maguen et al., 2017).

We believe that IOK offers a unique approach to addressing moral injury resulting from killing in war. IOK also encourages increased collaboration between clinicians and other key stakeholders in the community who are invested in promoting moral repair among combat veterans. In developing IOK, we benefited from consulting with chaplains, community spiritual leaders, veterans organizations, and family members invested in helping veterans heal from the moral wounds of war. Moral injury cuts across multiple domains, and treatments that foster moral repair should reflect the inherently multifaceted nature of the wound.

REFERENCES

Aist, C. S. (2012). The recovery of religious and spiritual significance in American Psychiatry. *Journal of Religion and Health, 51*, 615–629. https://doi.org/10.1007/s10943-012-9604-y

Bryan, C. J., Bryan, A. O., Roberge, E., Leifker, F. R., & Rozek, D. C. (2018). Moral injury, posttraumatic stress disorder, and suicidal behavior among National Guard personnel. *Psychological Trauma: Theory, Research, Practice, and Policy, 10*(1), 36–45. https://doi.org/10.1037/tra0000290

Burkman, K., Purcell, N., & Maguen, S. (2018). Provider perspectives on a novel moral injury treatment for veterans: Initial assessment of acceptability and feasibility of the Impact of Killing treatment materials. *Journal of Clinical Psychology, 75*, 79–94. https://doi.org/10.1002/jclp.22702

Carpenter, T. P., Carlisle, R. D., & Tsang, J. (2014). Tipping the scales: Conciliatory behavior and the morality of self-forgiveness. *The Journal of Positive Psychology, 9*(5), 389–401. https://doi.org/10.1080/17439760.2014.910823

Davis, D. E., Ho, M. Y., Griffin, B. J., Bell, C., Hook, J. N., Van Tongeren, D. R., DeBlaere, C., Worthington, E. L., & Westbrook, C. J. (2015). Forgiving the self and physical and mental health correlates: A meta-analytic review. *Journal of Counseling Psychology, 62*(2), 329–335. https://doi.org/10.1037/cou0000063

Fontana, A., & Rosenheck, R. (1999). A model of war zone stressors and posttraumatic stress disorder. *Journal of Traumatic Stress, 12*(1), 111–126. https://doi.org/10.1023/A:1024750417154

Fontana, A., Rosenheck, R., & Brett, E. (1992). War zone traumas and posttraumatic stress disorder symptomatology. *Journal of Nervous and Mental Disease, 180*, 748–755. https://doi.org/10.1097/00005053-199212000-00002

Frankfurt, S., & Frazier, P. (2016). A review of research on moral injury in combat veterans. *Military Psychology, 28*(5), 318–330. https://doi.org/10.1037/mil0000132

Hall, J. H., & Fincham, F. D. (2005). Self-forgiveness: The stepchild of forgiveness research. *Journal of Social and Clinical Psychology, 24*(5), 621–637. https://doi.org/10.1521/jscp.2005.24.5.621

Hoge, C. W., Castro, C. A., Messer, S. C., McGurk, D., Cotting, D. I., & Koffman, R. L. (2004, July 1). Combat duty in Iraq and Afghanistan, mental health problems, and barriers to care. *The New England Journal of Medicine, 351*, 13–22. https://doi.org/10.1056/NEJMoa040603

Kopacz, M. S., Currier, J. M., Drescher, K. D., & Pigeon, W. R. (2016). Suicidal behavior and spiritual functioning in a sample of veterans diagnosed with PTSD. *Journal of Injury & Violence Research, 8*(1), 6–14.

Kopacz, M. S., Hoffmire, C. A., Morley, S. W., & Vance, C. G. (2015). Using a spiritual distress scale to assess suicide risk in veterans: An exploratory study. *Pastoral Psychology, 64*(3), 381–390. https://doi.org/10.1007/s11089-014-0633-1

Litz, B. T., Stein, N., Delaney, E., Lebowitz, L., Nash, W. P., Silva, C., & Maguen, S. (2009). Moral injury and moral repair in war veterans: A preliminary model and intervention strategy. *Clinical Psychology Review, 29*(8), 695–706. https://doi.org/10.1016/j.cpr.2009.07.003

MacNair, R. M. (2002). Perpetration-induced traumatic stress in combat veterans. *Peace and Conflict, 8*(1), 63–72. https://doi.org/10.1207/S15327949PAC0801_6

Maguen, S., & Burkman, K. (2013). Combat-related killing: Expanding evidence-based treatments for PTSD. *Cognitive and Behavioral Practice, 20*(4), 476–479. https://doi.org/10.1016/j.cbpra.2013.05.003

Maguen, S., Burkman, K., Madden, E., Dinh, J., Bosch, J., Keyser, J., Schmitz, M., & Neylan, T. C. (2017). Impact of killing in war: A randomized, controlled pilot trial. *Journal of Clinical Psychology, 73*(9), 997–1012. https://doi.org/10.1002/jclp.22471

Maguen, S., Lucenko, B. A., Reger, M. A., Gahm, G. A., Litz, B. T., Seal, K. H., Knight, S. J., & Marmar, C. R. (2010). The impact of reported direct and indirect killing on mental health symptoms in Iraq War veterans. *Journal of Traumatic Stress, 23*(1), 86–90. https://doi.org/10.1002/jts.20434

Maguen, S., Metzler, T. J., Bosch, J., Marmar, C. R., Knight, S. J., & Neylan, T. C. (2012). Killing in combat may be independently associated with suicidal ideation. *Depression and Anxiety, 29*(11), 918–923. https://doi.org/10.1002/da.21954

Maguen, S., Metzler, T. J., Litz, B. T., Seal, K. H., Knight, S. J., & Marmar, C. R. (2009). The impact of killing in war on mental health symptoms and related functioning. *Journal of Traumatic Stress, 22*(5), 435–443. https://doi.org/10.1002/jts.20451

Maguen, S., Vogt, D. S., King, L. A., King, D. W., Litz, B. T., Knight, S. J., & Marmar, C. R. (2011). The impact of killing on mental health symptoms in Gulf War veterans.

Psychological Trauma: Theory, Research, Practice, and Policy, 3(1), 21–26. https://doi.org/10.1037/a0019897

Purcell, N., Burkman, K., Keyser, J., Fucella, P., & Maguen, S. (2018). Healing from moral injury: A qualitative evaluation of the Impact of Killing treatment for combat veterans. *Journal of Aggression, Maltreatment & Trauma, 27*(6), 645–673. https://doi.org/10.1080/10926771.2018.1463582

Purcell, N., Griffin, B. J., Burkman, K., & Maguen, S. (2018). "Opening a door to a new life": The role of forgiveness in healing from moral injury. *Frontiers in Psychiatry, 9*, 498. https://doi.org/10.3389/fpsyt.2018.00498

Purcell, N., Koenig, C. J., Bosch, J., & Maguen, S. (2016). Veterans' perspectives on the psychosocial impact of killing in war. *The Counseling Psychologist, 44*(7), 1062–1099. https://doi.org/10.1177/0011000016666156

Van Winkle, E. P., & Safer, M. A. (2011). Killing versus witnessing in combat trauma and reports of PTSD symptoms and domestic violence. *Journal of Traumatic Stress, 24*(1), 107–110. https://doi.org/10.1002/jts.20614

Vieten, C., Scammell, S., Pilato, R., Ammondson, I., Pargament, K. I., & Lukoff, D. (2013). Spiritual and religious competencies for psychologists. *Psychology of Religion and Spirituality, 5*(3), 129–144. https://doi.org/10.1037/a0032699

Wortmann, J. H., Eisen, E., Hundert, C., Jordan, A. H., Smith, M. W., Nash, W. P., & Litz, B. T. (2017). Spiritual features of war-related moral injury: A primer for clinicians. *Spirituality in Clinical Practice, 4*(4), 249–261. https://doi.org/10.1037/scp0000140

12

Building Spiritual Strength

A Group Treatment for Posttraumatic Stress Disorder, Moral Injury, and Spiritual Distress

Timothy J. Usset, Mary Butler, and J. Irene Harris

Exposure to potentially morally injurious events (PMIEs) and/or trauma-related spiritual distress has been associated with more severe and longer duration of posttraumatic stress disorder (PTSD) symptoms and increased suicide risk (Bryan et al., 2018; Currier et al., 2014, 2015; Schorr et al., 2018). Current evidence-based treatment in the Department of Veterans Affairs (VA), such as prolonged exposure and cognitive processing therapy, were not specifically designed to treat moral injury or spiritual distress. Although first-line evidence-based therapies may address some symptoms of moral injury, exposure therapies focus on activating and resolving arousal, and cognitive therapies focus on altering maladaptive cognitions. Clinical recommendations for resolution of PMIEs, however, focus on value-based meaning making and reintegrating the complex, multifaceted moral contexts of combat consistent with the veteran's psychospiritual developmental capacity (Harris et al., 2015; Litz et al., 2009; Nash & Litz, 2013) Moreover, many combat veterans do not access traditional mental health services, and of those that do, as many as 39% drop out of first-line evidence-based treatments (Steenkamp et al., 2015).

Building Spiritual Strength (BSS) is an eight-session, manualized, spiritually integrated group intervention that was created to address the gaps and concerns in current treatment models. There is no published research on BSS as an individual modality. BSS seeks to use a participant's existing meaning making or faith orientation to help them heal from traumatic experiences. BSS can be facilitated by appropriately trained chaplains or mental health

https://doi.org/10.1037/0000204-013
Addressing Moral Injury in Clinical Practice, J. M. Currier, K. D. Drescher, and J. Nieuwsma (Editors)

223

professionals in VA health care systems or community settings. BSS has been tested in two randomized clinical trials, one with a wait-list control (Harris et al., 2011) and another with a present-centered group therapy (PCGT) control condition (Harris et al., 2018). In the first study, BSS participants had clinically and statistically significant reductions in PTSD symptoms compared with a wait-list control group. Further, in a study by Harris et al. (2011), individuals from ethnic minority groups (African American and Latinx) made more robust gains than Caucasian individuals. Moreover, when participants on the waiting list subsequently received BSS treatment, Harris et al. (2011) found significant reductions in their PTSD symptoms compared with their baseline during the waiting period.

In the second randomized clinical trial (Harris et al., 2018), participants in both BSS and PCGT conditions evidenced statistically and clinically significant reductions in PTSD symptoms. The primary difference in the two conditions entailed changes in spiritual distress over the study period. In the PCGT condition, participants reported increases in spiritual distress from baseline to the end of treatment, and this trend of increasing spiritual distress continued at a 2-month follow-up assessment. However, participants in the BSS group evidenced statistically significant reductions in spiritual distress over the course of treatment and further reductions at the 2-month follow-up assessment. Given the relationship between spiritual distress and suicide risk in veterans managing PTSD (Raines et al., 2017), these latter results have important implications for a potential role for BSS in preventing suicide among veterans.

THEORETICAL FOUNDATIONS OF BSS

People who have experienced trauma, particularly in a combat or military context, often encounter a collision of multiple moral contexts. Moral injury and spiritual distress can manifest when the moral context and values they bring from home are challenged by a different moral context in combat or other traumatic events. For example, in a civilian moral context, killing a child is a heinous crime; however, in a combat context, killing a child in a suicide vest may be required by the rules of engagement to save lives of comrades and other civilians. This collision of moral contexts can lead to moral injury, spiritual distress, and/or existential distress. BSS seeks to integrate service members' and veterans' (SM/Vs') psychospiritual development with different contexts to facilitate healing. Integration of multiple moral contexts allows SM/Vs to make meaning of trauma in a way that reduces the risk of dysfunctional blame, guilt, or distress.

BSS integrates exposure and developmental models to approach moral injury and spiritual distress. BSS draws primarily from James Fowler's stages of faith (Fowler, 1981; Fowler & Dell, 2006). Though Fowler uses the word "faith" to describe his stages, we expand the definition to include spiritualities and worldviews that may not be expressly religious. In Fowler's stages, spiritual reasoning develops in sequence from chaotic to concrete to ordered. Those who attain higher developmental stages are able to hold paradoxical thoughts without significant distress. Fowler's six stages of psychospiritual development are summarized in Table 12.1.

Fowler's stages provide a framework to describe how people differentiate and develop in their theological and belief process (Fowler, 1981; Fowler & Dell, 2006). As highlighted in Table 12.1, Stage 2 involves literal interpretations and practice of faith. Stage 3 moves to ordered processes and understandings of religion through specific authorities or institutions. By Stage 4, people begin to integrate faith or belief systems different from their own without experiencing debilitating distress. Because the military entrance age in the United States is as early as 17 years old, many members of the military experience trauma when they are engaging the world from the perspective of Stage 2 or 3.

When looking at a developmental model, it can be easy to idealize later stages of development as beyond the risk of harm. However, with moral injury, a person in distress could be in any of Fowler's stages. Therapists should promote interventions that are appropriate and reparative relative to the SM/V's

TABLE 12.1. Fowler's Stages of Psychospiritual Development

Stage	Definition	Approximate developmental stage
Stage 1. Intuitive-projective	Consistent with fantasy and magical thinking. Concepts are drawn from direct education and observation of parents and society.	Children under 5
Stage 2. Mythic-literal	Children learn the basic aspects of their faith and put it into practice in a literal manner.	5 until adolescence
Stage 3. Synthetic-conventional	The individual will represent the belief system through the authorities and institutions of that faith. Cognitive processes regarding issues of faith are conventional and deferent to authorities.	Adolescence, potentially through adulthood
Stage 4. Individuative-reflective	Those who move to Stage 4 begin to critically evaluate previously held religious ideas, become more willing to explore multiple spiritual perspectives, and are able to consider religious doubts without distress.	Often early adulthood
Stage 5. Conjunctive	Characterized by religious and spiritual practice that is flexible and encompasses numerous faith perspectives.	Middle to late adulthood
Stage 6. Universalizing	Rarely achieved and marked by viewing all faiths, peoples, and cultures in the context of a universal community.	Rare; typical age of onset unknown

Note. Based on data from Fowler (1981) and Fowler and Dell (2006). Adapted from "Moral Injury and Psycho-Spiritual Development: Considering the Developmental Context," by J. I. Harris, C. L. Park, J. M. Currier, T. J. Usset, and C. D. Voecks, 2015, *Spirituality in Clinical Practice*, 2(4), p. 259 (https://doi.org/10.1037/scp0000045). In the public domain.

developmental stage. A person operating at Stage 2 or 3 may not have developed the resources to make meaning of traumatic events that happened in a different moral context in a reparative way. BSS supports SM/Vs' psychospiritual development to Stages 4 and beyond. Growth from Stage 2 or 3 to 4 facilitates making meaning of traumatic events in a way that promotes healing.

To facilitate and promote the integration of multiple moral contexts, the BSS intervention makes liberal use of silence, journaling, and narrative components to facilitate a healing process for SM/Vs. These practices have been associated with posttraumatic growth and lower levels of spiritual distress (Harris et al., 2008; Ogden et al., 2011). Practicing the use of silence allows SM/Vs to process ideas, rather than responding reflexively. Often, when prevented from responding immediately, individuals are able to complete cognitive processing at a higher developmental level (Chaiklin, 2003), allowing them more opportunities to explore the multiple moral contexts relevant to spiritual distress or moral injury comorbid with PTSD. The journaling process similarly facilitates greater cognitive complexity in making meaning of traumatic experiences (Ullrich & Lutgendorf, 2002), providing new perspectives that can assist individuals in resolving moral injury and spiritual distress.

OVERVIEW OF THE BSS INTERVENTION

All groups begin and end with the agreed-on ritual or activity chosen by the group (if any). Rituals that groups have used have been activities such as observing a moment of silence, sharing high fives with the group, lighting candles, or designating a different group member each week to share a reading of scripture or other material they find important to their journey. From Session 3 onward, sessions begin with 15 to 20 minutes to process meditation or prayer logs from the previous week, and the empty-chair exercise described in Session 2 is offered as needed.

Session 1

The first session of BSS has three primary objectives: establishing ground rules for healthy group functioning, helping SM/Vs understand the learning objectives for the intervention, and building rapport and group cohesion through structured sharing and storytelling. Facilitators introduce themselves and invite brief introductions from SM/Vs, being sure to let them know that more detailed introductions will come later in the session. After introductions, facilitators guide SM/Vs to the workbook to review guidelines for healthy group functioning and ask group members whether there are any additional guidelines they would like to add to make the group more personal, such as opening and/or closing rituals. Mandated reporting requirements consistent with local state and federal laws are also reviewed.

Next, facilitators direct the group to the learning objectives outlined in the workbook. This begins by setting the standard for deliberate, inclusive language appropriate to the makeup of the group. Each group member should be queried for her or his preferred language for their meaning-making construct (e.g., higher power, G-d, life force, moral values) and pick the workbook they prefer; one version uses "G-d" language, the other uses "higher power" language. The group should be encouraged to find language that is agreeable for everyone when speaking about belief systems, religions, or spiritualities. Facilitators should be prepared to use multiple terms within the same group. SM/Vs have to be reminded that this is a group wherein different faiths and belief systems are explored to facilitate healing from trauma-related conditions. The goal in this environment is to support and learn from one another; the group is not a place for evangelism or proselytization. Different interpretations of events and belief systems are introduced to challenge a level of psychospiritual development that is not serving an individual well. The goal is always to further an SM/V's development and integration, not to change them to a different system of faith or spirituality or meaning making.

For the storytelling component of Session 1, one domain (e.g., family, spiritual, and vocational development) at a time is completed by each participant before moving to the next section. This allows for better time management and boundary setting if there is a group member who is inclined to under or oversharing. After stories are shared, the group is guided to set goals for growth and development. The homework for the week is to meditate or pray about the goal(s) they have set. The group session is then closed with the agreed-on ritual, if any. Each following session will begin and end with the group's agreed-on ritual (if any).

Session 2

This session begins with the agreed-on opening rituals(s), if any, and sharing experiences in prayer or meditation about goals. From Session 2 onward, there is no general "check-in," but there is an invitation to discuss the previous week's homework. Facilitators should remind SM/Vs of this and encourage them to complete homework if they would like time to process what happened for them in the previous week. Session 2 is where the two primary mechanisms of action in the intervention are initiated: the empty-chair exercise and the meditation or prayer logs.

Introducing alternative meaning-making processes (not alternative constructs) for the sake of psychospiritual integration is a core assumption of BSS. The empty-chair exercise starts this process. Before beginning the exercise, facilitators remind group members that this exercise can be challenging, and the point is not to change someone's belief system. It is instead an opportunity to explore meaning making from multiple perspectives. The steps of the exercise are as follows:

1. Invite a group member to bring forward a single issue causing them distress or pain in the form of a prayer or meditation.

2. Allow for a few moments of silence.

3. The facilitator(s) responds to the group member with what she or he thinks a higher power, G-d, or anthropomorphized value system might be saying.

4. Other group members are invited to respond in a manner consistent with their belief system (either from a religious or spiritual perspective or as a human being, friend, or fellow veteran).

5. The original group member who shared the issue is invited to respond to what they heard.

6. The next group member is invited to share an issue until all group members complete the exercise.

Facilitators ensure that the process is followed for each participant and must be diligent about the moments of silence. A box of tissues is needed in this session and all that follow. Tears are not an uncommon occurrence in this exercise. Facilitators should tell SM/Vs this ahead of time to normalize and give permission to experience natural emotions such as sadness and hurt.

After the empty-chair exercise is completed, SM/Vs are introduced to the second primary means of promoting psychospiritual development: meditation or prayer logs. Facilitators should remind SM/Vs to use language that is consistent with their belief system (e.g., an atheist or agnostic is far more likely to call this exercise a mediation or reflection journal than a prayer log). The process is similar to the empty-chair exercise; SM/Vs practice completing the meditation or prayer log in group with a single issue. The experience is discussed, and the group then practices with a second issue, if time allows. For homework, SM/Vs are asked to spend some time each day in meditation or prayer and be prepared to discuss the experience at the beginning of each group. Linn et al.'s (1994) book *Good Goats: Healing Our Image of God* is provided. This book takes a developmental approach from a Roman Catholic perspective to help readers explore new images of G-d that are potentially reparative.

Session 3

In this session, facilitators solve problems about and normalize any issues or concerns group members are having with the meditation or prayer logs. They especially look for any participant feeling stuck, having strong or overwhelming feelings, or experiencing other challenges with the homework. The group begins with an invitation for members to share what came up in their prayer or meditation logs. Those experiences are explored with the group for 15 to 20 minutes, and the empty-chair exercise is offered for further processing. Facilitators have to monitor their own reactions and notice how group members are engaging with one another. Differing interpretations are a key mechanism of action to promote further integration of multiple moral contexts. This has to be balanced with the group remaining a "safe enough" place and prohibiting proselytizing. Facilitators have to be watchful of group members reinforcing a negative pattern of belief or coping strategy and intervene appropriately. An example is a group member from any faith tradition pronouncing repentance as the only means of another participant recovering from their (often) inappropriate sense of guilt or an atheist telling a religious person to give up her or his faith. Facilitator responses should include profound respect for each religious perspective discussed, along with setting boundaries about denying the validity of others' perspectives.

Depending on the needs of the group and time available, the remaining time in this session is used to discuss responses to the Linn et al. (1994) reading and provide psychoeducation on symptoms of PTSD. The psychoeducation discussion is framed in a way that externalizes PTSD as a problem that causes distress and is preventing group members from further emotional and spiritual growth. Facilitators remind SM/Vs that meditation or prayer logs, as well as the empty-chair exercise, can be useful tools to work with PTSD symptoms that are causing them distress. Talking about the dynamics of moral injury and spiritual distress may also be helpful, but we advise describing them from a symptom perspective, rather than using potentially stigmatizing labels. This is done to avoid further labels or stigma toward people that have experienced trauma, but there is room for naming too if it seems it will benefit members of the group.

Session 4

In this session, more opportunities for psychospiritual development and growth happen by exploring the existence of evil in the world. This is done by inviting group members to share their thoughts and beliefs about how their belief system, faith, and/or spirituality inform how they see evil and offering different "theodicies" for discussion. That is, BSS operates from the perspective that at least certain parts of a person's theodicy or view of evil may be causing them distress. Discussion on the topic is invited not to change their theodicies completely but to invite integration with other perspectives in a way that reduces distress and offers room for psychospiritual growth in a manner consistent with the SM/V's faith identification.

Beginning in this session, addressing a possible *retributive theodicy* is one of the most challenging parts for many SM/Vs. It is defined loosely as an individual having an experience or belief that a higher power, G-d, or the world is punishing them in a manner that might fuel spiritual distress (Hale-Smith et al., 2012; Harris et al., 2018). In the case of retributive theodicy, it may be helpful for facilitators to explore other theodicies in the same faith tradition or belief system of a group member. This falls well within the bounds of ethical practice and is congruent with BSS's goals of further psychospiritual development to reduce distress and increase coping skills (American Psychological Association, 2017; VandeCreek & Burton, 2001). Homework after this session includes specific requests for SM/Vs to explore evil in their meditation or prayer logs.

Session 5

In this session, psychospiritual development is promoted by introducing and practicing three different types of active spiritual coping: seeking calm and focus, assistance, and acceptance (Bade & Cook, 2008). Facilitators should give ample time for SM/Vs to ask questions about each type and offer space to practice them in session. A fourth style of coping, a passive type, is described but not practiced. The fourth coping style should be described with care. Naming it "negative coping" may not be helpful. However, it is useful to make clear that this passive approach to spiritual coping is not associated with good outcomes (Bade & Cook, 2008).

Session 6

This session begins a two-session series on forgiveness and reconciliation. It is common to see individuals with more rigid styles of psychospiritual development adversely impacted in this area. Facilitators address this problem in three primary ways: (a) opening the door to view forgiveness as a process, rather than an event; (b) offering a number of different perspectives on forgiveness; and (c) inviting a discussion on forgiveness to bring different experiences in the room.

Conveying forgiveness as a process (and a difficult one!) is one of the most important lessons in this session. Forgiveness processes can bring up many different feelings. Facilitators talk to the group about feelings as messengers and indicators of times they had to act, pain they may be experiencing, or events for which they are still making meaning. Facilitators validate any feelings that are shared. They then educate group members on the steps of forgiveness supplied in the workbook. Facilitators describe forgiveness as a process, rather than an event, and differentiate forgiveness and reconciliation. Homework after this session includes specific requests for SM/Vs to explore forgiveness in their meditation or prayer logs and assigning the self-forgiveness workbook (Griffin et al., 2015).

Session 7

This session expands on the last and adds more exploration on reconciliation. Facilitators ask group members to describe their reactions to the nuances and difficulties of the forgiveness process outlined in the workbook. SM/Vs are invited to share forgiveness processes that went well and work through the reconciliation content of the workbook.

There is often overlap in discussion in Sessions 6 and 7. The heart of this session's work is expanding SM/Vs' viewpoints on forgiveness and reconciliation as complementary but different constructs that happen more often on a continuum, rather than a single event. Facilitators have to remind group members that this is the second to last session of the group and to think about how they would like to close their time together in the final session. Facilitators can encourage sharing thoughts and feelings about the group ending.

Session 8

More time can be allotted to explore forgiveness processes that came up in the logs and discuss responses to the self-forgiveness workbook. Facilitators remind group members that the meditation or prayer journals are a practice they can continue after completion of the group. Because this is the final session, facilitators invite group members to review the goals set during the first session and reflect on the work they have done. Facilitators should acknowledge and praise any growth and change they have observed. In some cases, if the SM/V has moved to a substantially different level of psycho-spiritual development, the original goals may no longer seem relevant; in turn, facilitators should assist the SM/V in recognizing their spiritual developmental achievement, rather than construing such a change as a failure to attain a goal. From there, facilitators invite group members to share how they will continue the work from the past 8 weeks. Each had been on a healing journey before joining the group, as well as within the group, that will continue in the months and years after the group. As such, the facilitators invite further conversation, started in Session 7, about thoughts and feelings about the group coming to an end.

Facilitators remind group members that healing is a process that will entail challenges and obstacles well after the group. Group members are encouraged to lean on the practices and insights they have developed to get them through difficult life circumstances in the future. Additional resources are offered for further therapy and spiritual and meaning making practices.

SPECIAL ISSUES IN TRAINING AND TREATMENT DELIVERY FOR BSS

This section notes several important issues to be aware of and address when facilitating a spiritually integrated trauma intervention. Additional information on mandated reporting is summarized because chaplains may or may not have received training in this area.

Working in a Pluralistic Environment

In the BBS intervention, facilitators and SM/Vs are not asked to act in a way that is contrary to their spirituality or value system. The purpose of the intervention is not to convert SM/Vs to a faith group or belief system, but to reconnect them with a spirituality or value system they find helpful. However, the process is driven entirely by the participant. Facilitators have to walk the careful line of questioning problematic areas in a participant's belief system, while not leading them to a specific faith or spirituality to answer it.

Practically, there are a number of things facilitators can do to ensure all members of the group feel welcome. In Sessions 1 and 2, facilitators have to understand the faith, spirituality, or value perspective of all SM/Vs. This allows the facilitator to address each group member appropriately with language that is consistent with her or his belief system. It is not uncommon to ask one group member how their prayer log is going and immediately ask the next member how things went in their meditation journal. Addressing the overall group in an inclusive manner is just as important as addressing individuals in that way. If the entire group comes from a similar Christian background, it is usually acceptable to speak about a higher power in language that is consistent with those traditions. In the same way, if there are SM/Vs from Jewish, Muslim, Buddhist, atheist, agnostic, Hindu, humanist, Native American, or other spiritual backgrounds, it is important to address the group with welcoming language. Inviting the group to come up with acceptable common language can be an important component in group formation and cohesion. Finally, it is not uncommon to work with a participant whose faith tradition places a high value on proselytizing or evangelism. In those cases, facilitators can strongly encourage SM/Vs to engage in that practice outside the group but not act on that commitment in the sessions themselves.

Working With Guilt From a Developmental Model

In many religious traditions, forgiveness is a significant theme to address as a minister, chaplain, or mental health professional. In this intervention, there are a few nuances when working with SM/Vs regarding forgiveness. Trauma can be an out-of-control experience for the individual who has lived through it. When working with PTSD, moral injury, and spiritual distress, guilt for perceived lack of action, which may contribute to inappropriate guilt (see Chapter 2), can be as common as guilt for conducting an action. The latest edition of the *Diagnostic and Statistical Manual of Mental Disorders* (5th ed., American Psychiatric Association, 2013) added inappropriate guilt as a symptom of PTSD. In our clinical work, we have commonly seen people try to retroactively gain control of the trauma by blaming themselves for all or part of what happened. Self-blame in such situations can help people gain control of something that was terrifying and out of control.

One example came forward in working with a Vietnam veteran. The veteran blamed himself for his platoon getting ambushed while he was away receiving medical care for a different combat injury he had sustained. In his reasoning, if he had avoided the injury, he could have prevented the ambush and saved his platoon. Listening as a third party, it was clear this veteran assumed a far greater ability to control a combat environment than is possible for any individual. Yet, his sense of guilt was real and had to be worked with deliberately through a lens of multiple moral contexts that honored his values and sense of loss.

In another example, a veteran who had repeatedly gone to his clergy to confess his failure to coach a peer to take cover fast enough felt he had caused that peer's death. Those who heard these confessions accepted his self-evaluation of blame and provided high levels of emotional support at each "confession." By using the language of confession (of sins or wrongdoings), the clergy member unintentionally reinforced a maladaptive coping strategy. In turn, this veteran's symptoms did not start to improve until a therapist called into question his true control over shells falling in his combat base and explicitly identified inappropriate guilt as a possible terror management strategy.

When considering these examples, confronting self-blame as a coping strategy and invoking an illusion of control represent key BSS interventions for resolving inappropriate guilt. In doing so, it is important for facilitators to explain the nuances of appropriate and inappropriate guilt from SM/Vs' reflective practices and pay close attention at these moments.

Assessing Suicidal Ideation

BSS can be facilitated by properly trained clergy and chaplains, as well as mental health professionals. This raises an issue about mandated reporting and suicidal ideation. Importantly, ministers, chaplains, and mental health professionals have different laws for mandated reporting, depending on their state of residence. In some contexts, ministers or chaplains may not have had any training on mandated reporting.

Mandated reporting is necessary when a law requires professionals to notify appropriate authorities or agencies when an SM/V discloses certain information. This material cannot be substituted for proper training on mandated reporting but provides a general reminder and overview. Information that requires mandated reporting can include the threat of self-harm, threat of harming another, elder or child abuse, or a pregnant woman abusing substances and refusing treatment. In all cases, it is best to check with a supervisor or local authorities immediately if there is any uncertainty because some reports have to be made within 24 hours. With self or other harm, it is most important to assess intent, plan, and means. Key questions include, Does the person intend to commit the harmful act? Do they have a plan to carry out the act? Do they have the means of carrying out the act?

Suicidal ideation is also covered by mandated reporting and is worth reviewing in more detail. Clergy and chaplains, in particular, should consult with mental health professionals to learn more about risk assessment. Several signs could indicate a person is thinking of self-harm. These include but are not limited to statements such as "Nobody will miss me when I'm gone," "I just don't think life is worth living anymore," "I wish the pain would just go away," or "I have been feeling hopeless lately."

When an SM/V's affective or verbal manner indicates potential risk, it can be a good cue to investigate the likelihood of self-harm. Questions could come from the Suicidality Tracking Scale (Coric et al., 2009). The goal of inquiry is to determine whether an individual is safe. A report or intervention should be made if thoughts of suicide are present, and the individual has a plan and the means or intent to carry it out. If a facilitator does not have a behavioral health license, it is best to refer to a supervisor or other mental health professional for a second evaluation or opinion of suicide risk.

Facilitation of BSS Groups

One question is important to ask when recruiting SM/Vs for a BSS group: Is this individual appropriate for the group? Answering that question can sometimes be difficult. At the most basic level, facilitators have to be reasonably certain the individual will not cause harm to themselves or others while in a group intervention. Active substance abuse also raises questions around a potential participant's fit for a group-based intervention focusing on trauma or moral injury. If any issues are present that raise questions about an individual's fitness for the group, a resource list should be available to refer them for appropriate treatment. If a facilitator has not worked much with groups in the past, it is important to consult with professionals who have experience in group facilitation. In addition, Yalom and Leszcz's (2005) *Theory and Practice of Group Psychotherapy* is a good resource on the basics of group facilitation.

CASE EXAMPLES OF BSS GROUP

This section summarizes three individual SM/Vs and describes their group process in BSS. Details of cases have been changed and merged together to protect client anonymity.

David

David was a European American man in his mid-70s. He grew up in a middle-income family in the northeastern United States. His family would sometimes attend services at a local Christian Protestant church on holidays, but his parents were never religiously devout, and David had never considered himself a religious person. His father served in the Second World War but rarely talked about his military service. According to David, his father seemed to cope with his war experiences by working long hours and spending time with other veterans at the local Veterans of Foreign Wars (VFW) post.

As the oldest of four children, David filled a parental role in his house because his father was frequently away. Despite his father's emotional absence, military service was held in high esteem in his immediate and extended families. When the Vietnam War started, David had just graduated from college and sought a commission in the army.

By joining the army, David thought he could continue his family's tradition of military service and gain a connection to his distant father. He completed training as an infantry platoon leader and was subsequently deployed to Vietnam. His platoon was ordered to assault a position shortly thereafter, and he organized the unit to carry out the order. The assault was called off, but the information was never relayed to David. His platoon attacked with no reinforcements, and 70% of his men were wounded or killed. This haunted David for decades, and he viewed himself as personally responsible for those who died. On his return home, he sought community with other veterans at his local VFW. Like many other Vietnam veterans, he was not welcomed home after this war-zone deployment, and he was told to return after he had fought in a "real war."

Like his father, David largely coped with his experiences of guilt and betrayal by working long hours. He did not make the connection until he retired from a career in construction management in his early-60s. He and his spouse had planned to travel in retirement; however, David began having nightmares and flashbacks and experiencing symptoms of hypervigilance and increased guilt over members of his platoon who were killed in action during the war. After a year of these symptoms and much encouragement from family members, David sought treatment at a local VA medical center. He completed prolonged exposure, which successfully reduced the frequency of nightmares, flashbacks, and hypervigilance symptoms. His experience of guilt remained, which caused him to seek out additional therapy. He was skeptical about a "spiritual" intervention because he did not identify as a religious person but decided to give it a chance after hearing that BSS did not require or expect a person to have a religious affiliation.

Courtney

Courtney was an African American woman in her early 30s. She grew up in a middle-income family in the Midwest. Her family belonged to a Baptist church where her mother sang in the choir, and her father was an elder. Religion was an important part of her day-to-day life growing up, and her faith was shaped by an image of a G-d that was closely involved in these details of her daily life. Courtney had a passion for serving others from a young age and decided to pursue a career in health care. Because education was so expensive, she decided to join the Army as a medic to get hands-on training and qualify for education benefits when she finished her contract.

Working as an Army medic was initially a fulfilling vocation for Courtney. She increased her clinical skill set working stateside in a variety of army hospitals and was excited when she got the news that she would be deploying. Her excitement was short lived. One month into the deployment, her battalion commander began making unwanted sexual advances on her. She refused, but then the commander threatened to send her friends in the unit on more dangerous missions if she did not sleep with him. Not seeing any other choice, she complied with his request to keep her friends safe. When the commander's harassment and assaults continued, she tried to file a complaint, but it was ignored by the chain of command because she was "voluntarily" sleeping with the commander.

Courtney's experience of sexual trauma caused her to feel abandoned by G-d and betrayed by the army's value structure that had initially served as a source of meaning. She went from frequently participating in public and private religious activities to avoiding them most of the time. She felt bitter, intense shame, and distant from her family, who were concerned about her lack of religious involvement. Courtney also lamented her loss of faith, which had been such an important part of her life. When she heard about a "spirituality group for trauma" at her local VA, she decided to give it a try.

Oscar

Oscar was a Latino man in his early 40s. He grew up in the southwest region of the United States as the fourth of six children. His parents did the best they could, but both worked long hours to support the needs of the family. As devout Roman Catholics, they encouraged having a strong work ethic, caring for family, and supporting the church. Oscar felt trapped in his family and wanted to see more of the world. A Marines Corps recruiter came to his high school shortly before graduation, and Oscar decided to sign up right after graduation. Many members of his extended family had served in the military, and it seemed like a good way for him to get out of the house and start a career.

His faith remained important to him, and he would attend mass and receive the Eucharist as often as possible throughout his training, missions, and deployments. He served in combat in his first deployment but felt prepared for what he experienced, and all the enemy combatants were adults. Things fell apart in his second deployment. He was sent to a region where insurgents weaponized children by throwing them in front of convoys to get vehicles to stop or strapping them with bombs and detonating them after they got close enough to a patrol. Oscar saw numerous children killed because of these tactics, including some by members of his unit who ran them over with their vehicles to avoid the more dangerous consequences of stopping.

Oscar could not overcome the extreme sense of guilt he experienced after seeing children killed in such a manner. He stopped taking the Eucharist and felt cut off from the church. He loathed himself so much that he considered suicide and felt even more guilt because he believed the Roman Catholic church viewed suicide as a "mortal" sin. Traditional approaches to trauma-focused therapy did not appeal to him because of his cultural views toward mental health care, which were reinforced in the Marines Corps. He heard about a group for people to talk about trauma that was run by the VA but that met in local churches or community centers. This appealed to him because he was not amenable to going to a hospital or mental health clinic.

BSS Group Process

Because these three members of the group came from different belief systems, it was important to establish a common language with one another. After some discussion, all three agreed that using the term "higher power" would work for any generic statements. Courtney and Oscar chose the workbook that used "G-d" language, whereas David chose the higher power workbook. For a ritual, the group decided to begin and end each group with a moment of silence to reflect on the work they were about to do and the work they had already done.

In Session 2, David shared his guilt about the deaths of his platoon members in Vietnam, Courtney shared her anger at G-d and her unit over the sexual harassment and assault from her battalion commander, and Oscar shared his intense guilt over the deaths of children he witnessed in the recent war. Facilitators provided feedback from the perspective of what a higher power might say, and the participants chose to speak to one another as fellow veterans. At the end of session, David requested his log be referred to as a "reflection log," whereas Courtney and Oscar both preferred the term "prayer log."

As the sessions continued, the process for each participant matured. Through the empty-chair exercise, David was able to sit with the terror and helplessness he experienced when his platoon was left alone, and he realized how he had coped with those feelings by blaming himself for what happened. He then used his reflection log to more overtly name values that were important to him, sit with the grief he had over his lost platoon members, contextualize the situation in which they died, and explore the experience of betrayal he had at the VFW when he returned home. He was not inclined to think of himself as a religious person, but hearing Courtney and David's beliefs helped him view himself as a person with a value and belief system (as opposed to someone who "didn't believe in a god").

In the empty-chair exercise, Courtney found it helpful to hear from David as an officer and Oscar as a fellow service member "that G-d had nothing to do with what that officer did to her, that was on that officer alone." David and Oscar naming that individual and those in her chain of command as "disgraces to the uniform" allowed her to see that there were people who wore the uniform who would not have stood for the behavior of that officer or her unit's response to her. The prayer log proved a fruitful place for her to express the anger and sense of betrayal she experienced from G-d. Paired with hearing about different theodicies in Session 4, Courtney saw how her trauma was robbing her of a valued relationship with G-d, her faith community, and family. The faith that she returned to was not the same faith she brought to the trauma, but one that had been changed and even matured by her difficult experiences and reflective work.

Oscar appreciated having a group to come to where he could talk about what happened without feeling like he was going to "therapy" or was "messed up in the head." During the empty-chair exercise, Oscar found the feedback from his peers and facilitators helpful. His peers noted that he had done his duty to the best of his ability. Facilitators pointed out from the perspective of their higher power, the concept of G-d seeing people and situations from multiple moral contexts. G-d would never celebrate the deaths of children but did not hold Oscar accountable or view him as guilty for behaving according to the rules of engagement in a terrible war situation. The facilitators knew a local Roman Catholic priest who was familiar with issues of combat veterans, and they provided Oscar with this information should he decide to return to confession. Through the feedback in the empty-chair exercise and the prayer logs, Oscar finally felt comfortable enough to approach the priest. He was able to participate in confession from a place where he was not experiencing overwhelming shame for what had happened in war but from a place of mourning the loss of innocent life. Being able to return to the church completely resolved his experience of suicidal ideation, and his military service no longer haunted him daily.

Each group member had a different journey, but there were similarities in each of their processes. For example, each member's distress came from a need to integrate different nuances in their belief systems, faith, or theodicies. By experiencing multiple perspectives in the group during empty-chair exercises and reflection or prayer logs, each veteran was able to bring together new perspectives that furthered their healing processes. All three maintained the same faith identification or belief system they brought into the group, but the nuances gained through the group helped their belief systems become sources of strength and healing, rather than pain and distress.

CONCLUSION

BSS has shown promising results in treating PTSD, moral injury, and spiritual distress in two clinical trials. It fills a needed gap in spiritually integrated, evidence-based trauma-focused treatments. Because many people prefer to consult clergy, rather than mental health providers, BSS can be a tool to engage those who may not otherwise seek mental health treatments (Ellison et al., 2006; Leavey et al., 2007). With appropriately trained chaplains as providers alongside behavioral health personnel, BSS can expand the number of professionals that can treat PTSD, moral injury, and spiritual distress (see Chapter 13). If these types of chaplain-provided services continue to prove effective, this may also be a more cost-effective way to provide mental health services, especially in rural communities that may have limited mental health resources (Roberts et al., 1999).

There are areas in which further research is needed on BSS. Although BSS services are available in many locations across the United States, especially within the VA system, formal research has only been done in the upper Midwest; it would be appropriate to determine whether results are different in other geographic regions. Another area for further research is BSS's potential role in suicide prevention for trauma survivors. Moral injury and spiritual distress are associated with suicide risk among people managing PTSD (Bryan et al., 2018; Kopacz, 2014; Kopacz, Currier, et al., 2016; Kopacz et al., 2015; Kopacz, Rasmussen, et al., 2016); tools to address such distress may be effective in reducing suicide risk.

The putative mechanism of action in BSS purportedly has to do with psychospiritual development; because measurement tools for this construct are limited, further research on relationships between psychospiritual development, PTSD, guilt for holding oneself responsible for factors beyond one's control, and suicide risk would be useful in determining appropriate applications of BSS techniques. Assessing the efficacy of BSS services across chaplains and other mental health providers would also usefully inform the use of the intervention.

In summary, there is empirical support for BSS as an effective treatment for PTSD and spiritual distress and moral injury in two randomized controlled trials (Harris et al., 2011, 2018), and the intervention is increasingly available as a treatment option. As with any intervention, it may not be the best choice for every SM/V, and it is most appropriate for those with a strong preference for spiritually integrated care. Further research will assist chaplains, clergy, and mental health providers to understand the best contexts and uses for this emerging tool.

REFERENCES

American Psychiatric Association. (2013). *Diagnostic and statistical manual of mental disorders* (5th ed.). https://doi.org/10.1176/appi.books.9780890425596

American Psychological Association. (2017). *Ethical principles of psychologists and code of conduct* (2002, amended effective June 1, 2010, and January 1, 2017). https://www.apa.org/ethics/code/index.aspx

Bade, M. K., & Cook, S. W. (2008). Functions of Christian prayer in the coping process. *Journal for the Scientific Study of Religion, 47*(1), 123–133. https://doi.org/10.1111/j.1468-5906.2008.00396.x

Bryan, C. J., Bryan, A. O., Roberge, E., Leifker, F. R., & Rozek, D. C. (2018). Moral injury, posttraumatic stress disorder, and suicidal behavior among National Guard personnel. *Psychological Trauma: Theory, Research, Practice, and Policy, 10*(1), 36–45. https://doi.org/10.1037/tra0000290

Chaiklin, S. (2003). The zone of proximal development in Vygotsky's analysis of learning and instruction. In A. Kozulin, B. Gindis, V. S. Ageyev, & S. M. Miller (Eds.), *Learning in doing: Vygotsky's educational theory in cultural context* (pp. 39–64). Cambridge University Press.

Coric, V., Stock, E. G., Pultz, J., Marcus, R., & Sheehan, D. V. (2009). Sheehan Suicidality Tracking Scale (Sheehan-STS): Preliminary results from a multicenter clinical trial in generalized anxiety disorder. *Psychiatry, 6*(1), 26–31.

Currier, J. M., Drescher, K., & Harris, J. I. (2014). Spiritual functioning among veterans seeking residential treatment for PTSD: A matched control group study. *Spirituality in Clinical Practice, 1*(1), 3–15. https://doi.org/10.1037/scp0000004

Currier, J. M., Holland, J. M., & Drescher, K. C. (2015). Spirituality factors in the prediction of outcomes of PTSD for U.S. military veterans. *Journal of Traumatic Stress, 28*(1), 57–64. https://doi.org/10.1002/jts.21978

Ellison, C. G., Vaaler, M. L., Flannelly, K. J., & Weaver, A. J. (2006). The clergy as a source of mental health assistance: What Americans believe. *Review of Religious Research, 48*(2), 190–211.

Fowler, J. W. (1981). *Stages of faith*. HarperCollins.

Fowler, J. W., & Dell, M. L. (2006). Stages of faith from infancy through adolescence: Reflections on three decades of faith development theory. In E. C. Roehlkepartain, P. E. King, L. Wagener, & P. L. Benson (Eds.), *The handbook of spiritual development in childhood and adolescence* (pp. 34–45). Sage.

Griffin, B. J., Worthington, E. L., Jr., Lavelock, C. R., Greer, C. L., Lin, Y., Davis, D. E., & Hook, J. N. (2015). Efficacy of a self-forgiveness workbook: A randomized controlled trial with interpersonal offenders. *Journal of Counseling Psychology, 62*(2), 124–136. https://doi.org/10.1037/cou0000060

Hale-Smith, A., Park, C. L., & Edmondson, D. (2012). Measuring beliefs about suffering: Development of the views of suffering scale. *Psychological Assessment, 24*(4), 855–866. https://doi.org/10.1037/a0027399

Harris, J. I., Erbes, C. R., Engdahl, B. E., Olson, R. H., Winskowski, A. M., & McMahill, J. (2008). Christian religious functioning and trauma outcomes. *Journal of Clinical Psychology, 64*(1), 17–29. https://doi.org/10.1002/jclp.20427

Harris, J. I., Erbes, C. R., Engdahl, B. E., Thuras, P., Murray-Swank, N., Grace, D., Ogden, H., Olson, R. H., Winskowski, A. M., Bacon, R., Malec, C., Campion, K., & Le, T. (2011). The effectiveness of a trauma focused spiritually integrated intervention for veterans exposed to trauma. *Journal of Clinical Psychology, 67*(4), 425–438. https://doi.org/10.1002/jclp.20777

Harris, J. I., Park, C. L., Currier, J. M., Usset, T. J., & Voecks, C. D. (2015). Moral injury and psycho-spiritual development: Considering the developmental context. *Spirituality in Clinical Practice, 2*(4), 256–266. https://doi.org/10.1037/scp0000045

Harris, J. I., Usset, T., Voecks, C., Thuras, P., Currier, J., & Erbes, C. (2018). Spiritually integrated care for PTSD: A randomized controlled trial of "Building Spiritual Strength." *Psychiatry Research, 267*, 420–428. https://doi.org/10.1016/j.psychres.2018.06.045

Kopacz, M. S. (2014). The spiritual health of veterans with a history of suicide ideation. *Health Psychology and Behavioral Medicine, 2*(1), 349–358. https://doi.org/10.1080/21642850.2014.881260

Kopacz, M. S., Currier, J. M., Drescher, K. D., & Pigeon, W. R. (2016). Suicidal behavior and spiritual functioning in a sample of Veterans diagnosed with PTSD. *Journal of Injury & Violence Research, 8*(1), 6–14.

Kopacz, M. S., Hoffmire, C. A., Morley, S. W., & Vance, C. G. (2015). Using a spiritual distress scale to assess suicide risk in veterans: An exploratory study. *Pastoral Psychology, 64*, 381–390. https://doi.org/10.1007/s11089-014-0633-1

Kopacz, M. S., Rasmussen, K. A., Searle, R. F., Wozniak, B. M., & Titus, C. E. (2016). Veterans, guilt, and suicide risk: An opportunity to collaborate with chaplains? *Cleveland Clinic Journal of Medicine, 83*(2), 101–105. https://doi.org/10.3949/ccjm.83a.15070

Leavey, G., Loewenthal, K., & King, M. (2007). Challenges to sanctuary: The clergy as a resource for mental health care in the community. *Social Science & Medicine, 65*(3), 548–559. https://doi.org/10.1016/j.socscimed.2007.03.050

Linn, D., Linn, S. F., & Linn, M. (1994). *Good goats: Healing our image of God.* Paulist Press.

Litz, B. T., Stein, N., Delaney, E., Lebowitz, L., Nash, W. P., Silva, C., & Maguen, S. (2009). Moral injury and moral repair in war veterans: A preliminary model and intervention strategy. *Clinical Psychology Review, 29*(8), 695–706. https://doi.org/10.1016/j.cpr.2009.07.003

Nash, W. P., & Litz, B. T. (2013). Moral injury: A mechanism for war-related psychological trauma in military family members. *Clinical Child and Family Psychology Review, 16*(4), 365–375. https://doi.org/10.1007/s10567-013-0146-y

Ogden, H., Harris, J. I., Erbes, C. R., Engdahl, B. E., Olson, R. H., Winskowski, A. M., & McMahill, J. (2011). Religious functioning and trauma outcomes among combat veterans. *Counselling and Spirituality/Counseling et Spiritualité, 30*, 71–89.

Raines, A. M., Currier, J., McManus, E. S., Walton, J. L., Uddo, M., & Franklin, C. L. (2017). Spiritual struggles and suicide in veterans seeking PTSD treatment. *Psychological Trauma: Theory, Research, Practice, and Policy, 9*(6), 746–749. https://doi.org/10.1037/tra0000239

Roberts, L. W., Battaglia, J., & Epstein, R. S. (1999). Frontier ethics: Mental health care needs and ethical dilemmas in rural communities. *Psychiatric Services, 50*(4), 497–503. https://doi.org/10.1176/ps.50.4.497

Schorr, Y., Stein, N. R., Maguen, S., Barnes, J. B., Bosch, J., & Litz, B. T. (2018). Sources of moral injury among war veterans: A qualitative evaluation. *Journal of Clinical Psychology*, *74*(12), 2203–2218. https://doi.org/10.1002/jclp.22660

Steenkamp, M. M., Litz, B. T., Hoge, C. W., & Marmar, C. R. (2015). Psychotherapy for military-related PTSD: A review of randomized clinical trials. *JAMA*, *314*(5), 489–500. https://doi.org/10.1001/jama.2015.8370

Ullrich, P. M., & Lutgendorf, S. K. (2002). Journaling about stressful events: Effects of cognitive processing and emotional expression. *Annals of Behavioral Medicine*, *24*(3), 244–250. https://doi.org/10.1207/S15324796ABM2403_10

VandeCreek, L., & Burton, L. (Eds.). (2001). Professional chaplaincy: Its role and importance in healthcare. *Journal of Pastoral Care*, *55*(1), 81–97. https://doi.org/10.1177/002234090105500109

Yalom, I., & Leszcz, M. (2005). *The theory and practice of group psychotherapy* (5th ed.). Basic Books.

13

Collaboration With Chaplaincy and Ministry Professionals in Addressing Moral Injury

Jason Nieuwsma, Melissa A. Smigelsky, Jennifer H. Wortmann, Kerry Haynes, and Keith G. Meador

M orality can be understood through various lenses: philosophical, anthropological, biological, psychological, developmental, theological, and cultural, to name a few. For many people, these perspectives on moral development are integrated, informed, and interpreted through the lens of religion (see Chapter 3, this volume). Religion is at least as old as recorded human history, with a large majority of the world's population belonging to a religious tradition (Pew Research Center, 2012). Even for those who may not have been raised in or actively participate as part of a religious community, they nonetheless exist in human societies whose cultural mores have been shaped in conjunction with prevailing religious beliefs and practices. The behaviors and opinions of a society frequently reflect religious formation and commitments, with their moral significance dependent on the confluence of various cultural lenses contributing to the moral and ethical commitments of individuals.

The interactions between religion and pervading cultural beliefs about morality are dynamic, which in turn matters for moral injury. Perspectives on morality are dynamically constructed over time in relation to prevailing religious and sociocultural mores, which influence the degree to which a whole range of events and actions may or may not elicit feelings of guilt, shame, and

This chapter was coauthored by employees of the United States government as part of official duty and is considered to be in the public domain. Any views expressed herein do not necessarily represent the views of the United States government, and the authors' participation in the work is not meant to serve as an official endorsement.

https://doi.org/10.1037/0000204-014
Addressing Moral Injury in Clinical Practice, J. M. Currier, K. D. Drescher, and J. Nieuwsma (Editors)
In the public domain.

other moral emotions characteristic of moral injury (Farnsworth et al., 2014). Is killing right or wrong? Is it justified in certain circumstances? Is it punishable (in this life or the next)? What are the moral responsibilities of an individual in a corrupt system or context? What is corrupt? Does God take sides in human conflicts? Does God permit or even reward certain behaviors in war? Religions offer perspectives on these and many other moral questions, both for those overtly engaged in religious and spiritual practices, as well as those more minimally aware of these dimensions of their formation. Religious views on these issues have often influenced, mitigated, or motivated wars throughout human history, including our most recent conflicts. Religious traditions and spiritual practices inevitably contribute to the psychosocial–spiritual functioning of warfighters both during and following their combat experiences.

In the United States, as elsewhere, the religious landscape continues to shift over time. Importantly, most persons in the United States are religious: 71% identify as Christian (a diverse group) and 6% as belonging to a non-Christian faith (Pew Research Center, 2015); 54% subjectively identify as either moderately or very religious (Smith et al., 2018). However, in recent decades, and particularly among younger Americans, there has been a substantial shift away from "organized religion" and an accompanying shift toward "spirituality" (see Chapter 3, this volume). According to the General Social Survey, 22% of American adults identified as having no religious affiliation in 2016, a notable increase from 6% in 1991, where it had been relatively stable since data collection began in the 1970s (Smith et al., 2018). Among Americans born after 1980 (i.e., millennials), the unaffiliated figure is most pronounced, with slightly over 1 in 3 identifying as unaffiliated (Pew Research Center, 2015). Simultaneously, more people identify as "spiritual but not religious." In just the 5 years from 2012 to 2017, the percentage of U.S. adults self-defining as such jumped from 19% to 27%. Among those who do not identify as religiously affiliated, 88% still consider themselves as at least moderately spiritual (Chaves, 2017).

These shifts have implications for engaging religious and spiritual care professionals in the care of persons with moral injury. For one, ministry professionals, such as chaplains, are now commonly understood to attend to both religious and spiritual care needs. Although there can be utility in distinguishing between religion and spirituality (e.g., for operationalizing terms to answer research questions), for most people, there is substantial entanglement between the two terms. As highlighted in Chapter 3, *religion* typically refers to tradition-oriented practices, whereas *spirituality* often refers to more subjective experiences and practices (Saucier & Skrzypińska, 2006). However, for purposes of this chapter, because religion and spirituality are intertwined with the potential for differential interpretations, we do not attempt to distinguish sharply between the two and often use "religion or spirituality" to refer to an overall domain of human experience and practice.

In what follows, we begin with an overview of ministry professionals, with a special focus on chaplains who are most likely to attend to moral injury. Next, we provide a rationale for mental health clinicians collaborating with ministry professionals in the care of moral injury, followed by an examination of some of the ways in which spiritual care providers can address moral injury in their work. To conclude, we provide some practical recommendations for enhancing collaborative care between mental health and ministry professionals.

MINISTRY PROFESSIONALS

The diversity and ongoing evolution of religious and spiritual (R/S) traditions present challenges to the categorization of ministry and spiritual care professionals. Some religious traditions place significant importance on hierarchical structures and understandings of authority, whereas others do not, and in the case of nonorganized spiritual practices, there may be no identified positions of significance whatsoever. Requirements to become a clergyperson vary across different Christian traditions and fluctuate even more substantially across the broader panoply of world religions. Thus, any attempt at classification across traditions will inevitably be riddled with multiple exceptions.

Although invariably subject to such pitfalls of oversimplification, we offer Figure 13.1 as a basic depiction of the types of ministry professionals of most relevance in this chapter. We use the terms *ministry professionals* and *spiritual care providers* to reference the broad category of persons who are professionally devoted to R/S work. Clergy make up most of this category, but also included are nonclergy who may operate in a variety of different capacities, such as with parachurch organizations (i.e., religious organizations operating largely apart from church structures). Clergy, then, are persons recognized as formal leaders within religious traditions. They are typically ordained (i.e., identified and set apart by their tradition for specific ministry and/or religious rites), especially in Christian traditions, and are broadly understood to include priests, pastors, rabbis, mullahs, imams, and the sangha. Clergy can operate in several different capacities, including many not illustrated in Figure 13.1. For purposes of this chapter, clergy who function as chaplains or community clergy are of special interest.

Chaplains are clergypersons who are often assigned to work in the context of a secular institution, such as the military, a hospital, prison, or school (Legood, 1999). With respect to addressing moral injury among service members and veterans (SM/Vs), chaplains who function in the military and Veterans Affairs (VA) are of particular relevance. In the United States, military chaplains serve all branches of the armed forces; can be active duty, reserve, or National Guard; and are assigned to the Army, Air Force, or Navy (Navy chaplains also serve the needs of the Marines and Coast Guard). Most function in operational contexts (e.g., ranging from serving in a chapel on a base to deploying with SMs to combat zones), though a small percentage (fewer than 10%) are assigned to health care settings (Nieuwsma et al., 2013). VA chaplains, by contrast, work entirely within the health care context of VA. As such, most of these chaplains have had additional clinical training through clinical pastoral

FIGURE 13.1. Types of Spiritual Care Providers

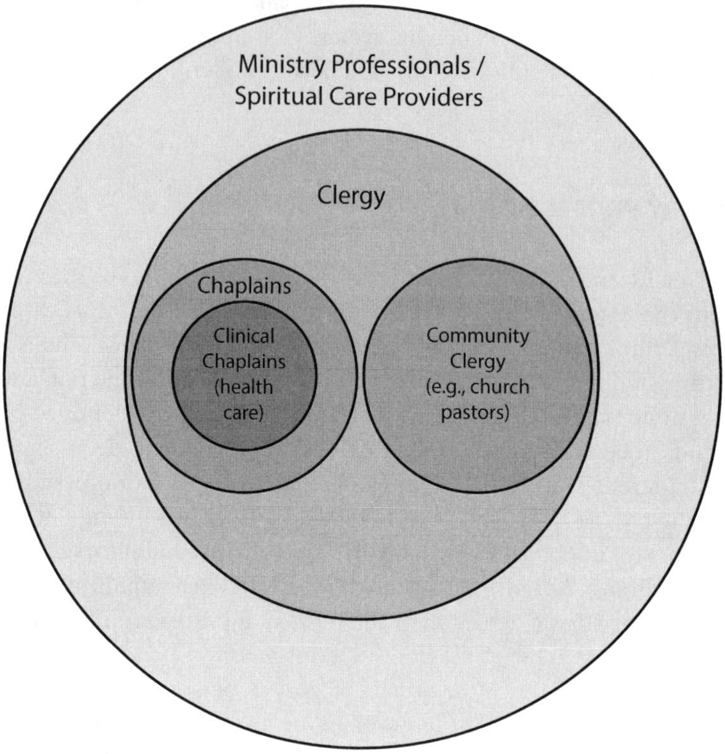

Note. Circle sizes are not intended to be proportional representations of the population.

education (CPE). One unit of CPE is equivalent to 400 hours of combined training and hands-on experience in a clinical setting, and many health care institutions, such as VA, expect their full-time clinical chaplains to have completed at least two to four units.

CPE training augments chaplains' religious or theological expertise with distinctive skills in providing care to diverse persons in clinical settings. A strong emphasis on reflection, supervision, and interpersonal dynamics in CPE differentiates this sort of chaplaincy care from that of other ministry professionals. In settings such as the military, VA, and other health care environments, chaplaincy care is not directive in aiming toward conformity to the faith of the chaplain; rather, it is centered on respecting and supporting a person's R/S practices while providing emotional and spiritual care as a chaplain.

Compared with chaplains, community clergy are not typically assigned to work as part of a secular institution. Instead, they traditionally operate within an organization of their faith tradition, often being responsible for the functioning of religious congregations (e.g., churches, synagogues, mosques). The term *community clergy* refers to what most people probably think of when they think of clergy, with the "community" modifier seeming perhaps superfluous.

In considering how to attend to the needs of persons with moral injury, though, it is helpful to distinguish between chaplains—who have specialized training to work with certain populations (e.g., veterans) and in certain contexts (e.g., health care), while not being primarily responsible for the life of a religious congregation—and community clergy, who differ from chaplains on the described attributes. Community clergy nonetheless have the potential to function in important roles in the care of those with moral injury. Although they are unlikely to receive the sort of specialized training that might equip a VA chaplain to provide veteran-centric spiritual care in the context of an integrated health care system, they are well-positioned to help a veteran reintegrate into a community of meaning and purpose. Community clergy can play pivotal roles in facilitating such belongingness while also fostering spiritual connectedness within the particularities of individual faith traditions.

Again, there are exceptions to these categorizations. For example, the Church of Jesus Christ of Latter-day Saints (Mormons) does not have dedicated clergy, though there is a process whereby individuals from this tradition can be endorsed to function as military or VA chaplains. Similarly, though Catholic nuns are not part of the clergy, they can also be endorsed to function as chaplains in some contexts, such as in some health care settings. The general organizational structure outlined here is not intended to exclude or marginalize different R/S traditions but rather to give readers unfamiliar with ministry professionals, clergy, or the intricacies of chaplaincy a basic understanding of how these persons often function.

RATIONALE FOR COLLABORATION

In the broadest sense, *morality* constitutes a system that defines what is good, right, and appropriate. For many veterans, R/S values and beliefs form a significant portion of the basis for morality that was violated by a morally injurious experience. Consequently, it is important for providers to understand and integrate a veteran's R/S into the conceptualization and treatment of moral injury (see Chapter 3). Several of the central issues in moral injury—such as perpetration, guilt, shame, betrayal, anger, despair, and forgiveness—can be spiritual and carry distinct meaning according to different faith traditions (Wortmann et al., 2017). Importantly, these meanings may or may not be consistent with psychological perspectives on these issues. Although psychologists are well equipped to intervene in cognitive, emotional, and behavioral aspects of moral injury, collaboration with community clergy and chaplains may be warranted to sufficiently understand how religion and spirituality shape internal experiences and thus how to respond appropriately and effectively.

The line between mental health and spiritual care can be blurry, particularly for the individual who is suffering. For example, grief is a universal human experience that naturally conjures questions of an existential or spiritual nature (e.g., what happens when people die?) and that may have decidedly psychological elements (e.g., anticipatory anxiety about one's death). Grief also can be a prominent experience of moral injury because morally injurious events often contain elements of death, whether being or feeling responsible for the death of another, witnessing death and destruction, or experiencing survivor guilt (Currier et al., 2015; Vargas et al., 2013). Interventions aimed at exploring existential questions, reducing anxiety, or healing from moral injury may call for dramatically different approaches depending on how R/S beliefs of the patient and provider shape the perception of the problem. In addition to personal beliefs, it can be helpful to understand different approaches to reconciling scientific and religious perspectives.

Predominant approaches to understanding the relationship between science and religion purport that the two are inherently incompatible (conflict model), concerned with separate areas of knowledge (independence model), related but in a distant way (dialogue model), or related in intimate and variable ways (integration model; Nelson, 2009). Mental health collaboration with spiritual care providers can benefit from an awareness of one's internalized model because this will affect whether and how one is likely to pursue interdisciplinary collaboration. Some psychologists receive overt training in how religious beliefs and commitments affect the psychotherapeutic dynamic—often through training programs that have religious affiliations—but most training programs offer spotty coverage of R/S, with any training in addressing R/S issues occurring primarily in the context of clinical supervision (Schafer et al., 2011).

Although there is a need for increased training on R/S issues among many mental health professionals, it is simultaneously important to be mindful of each profession's contributions and limitations. Psychologists are, first and foremost, mental health professionals—not R/S professionals. Some psychologists have strongly held personal religious or spiritual beliefs (Oxhandler et al., 2017); however, psychologists generally are less traditionally religious than those they serve (Vieten et al., 2013). Compared with other helping professionals (e.g., clinical social workers, marriage and family therapists), psychologists' R/S beliefs and practices differ more from the general public: They are less likely to believe in God, more likely to claim no religious affiliation, and less likely to report that religion is important in their lives (Oxhandler et al., 2017). Furthermore, some studies have shown psychologists to exhibit biases toward religious patients (e.g., Ruff & Elliott, 2016); however, the sparse literature on this topic is mixed, with other studies finding no evidence of bias (e.g., Harris et al., 2016).

Although psychologists as a group may tend to differ from their patients on R/S and whether it provides the primary moral framework for navigating the world, psychologists are inevitably socioculturally formed in their beliefs and assumptions about what is good or right. Further, the clinical practice of psychology necessitates making judgments about what is good and desirable in life. Is it symptom reduction? Functional improvement? Development of coping skills? Formation of new habits? The task of deciding what the most significant outcomes of treatment are—the "good" or even "right" outcomes being pursued—is inherently an intersubjective task between patient and provider in the context of a therapeutic relationship.

This intersubjective agreement matters profoundly in the treatment of moral injury, wherein fundamental assumptions about good and evil, right and wrong, even life and death, were possibly shattered (Janoff-Bulman, 1992). For example, some therapies seek to reduce or eliminate distressing emotions (e.g., guilt) because of the assumption that the experience of such emotions is harmful to the patient. This assumption is based on empirical findings linking guilt to negative outcomes such as posttraumatic stress disorder symptoms and suicidal thoughts and behaviors (e.g., Cunningham et al., 2017). Yet, although cognitive restructuring as a psychological intervention may be appropriate and helpful in many situations, it may be less so if a patient is contending with issues that, for them, constitute "sin" or failure through the lens of their R/S. Consider the following deidentified example:

> Mia, a 25-year-old White woman, came in for treatment 6 months after returning from deployment in Iraq, where she was raped by a fellow soldier. Mia's capacity for resilience was evident in the way she carried herself, looking the therapist directly in the eye and emphasizing her desire to work through the event so she could put it behind her. She described growing up in a religious family, developing a rich personal faith herself, and specifically having a strong belief that sexual intimacy should be reserved for a marriage relationship. She felt guilty because she believed she should have been a better judge of character and not agreed to be in the company of the other soldier in the first place. At first, Mia questioned whether she had "sinned" by having a sexual encounter outside of marriage and wondered whether the rape was some form of divine punishment for other sins she committed on the battlefield. Her therapist, who described herself as "spiritual but not religious" and was internally infuriated by the idea of rape as divine punishment, gently explored those beliefs with Mia. Eventually, Mia concluded that she did not act of her own volition and thus did not "sin." She further determined that she did not believe God would punish her with such a painful experience, which brought her therapist a private sense of relief.

As therapy progressed, Mia's therapist continued to work on reinforcing those cognitive shifts. She also began to incorporate discussion of Mia's values. Together, they explored her many roles (e.g., friend, sister, employee, student, runner), and Mia began keeping a diary of actions she took that were connected to those valued roles. She found that she could do things such as go to work even when she lacked motivation and interest because she remembered that she wanted to be a dependable person. Before her deployment, Mia had been an avid churchgoer, attending services every Sunday and spending daily time in her practice of prayer and scripture study. Since returning stateside, she had attended only a handful of services and reported that she rarely prayed anymore. Mia consistently expressed a desire to begin attending church regularly again and to resume her daily spiritual practice, though she said this without much apparent enthusiasm.

Mia's therapist chose to focus on areas that Mia did seem excited about, such as her local running club and monthly outing with a group of longtime friends. Several weeks went by, with weekly, then biweekly, sessions reinforcing

Mia's gains. By the therapist's assessment, and per the patient's report, Mia was doing much better. She had resumed her typical functioning, except for her spiritual practices, and Mia and her therapist agreed that the time had come for termination.

For many veterans experiencing trauma-related stress issues, including moral injury, there is a belief that suffering is punishment for sin (retribution theodicy), and thus one's suffering is interpreted as evidence of sin (Harris et al., 2018). Most faith traditions have established meanings and rituals for dealing with guilt and other emotions that result from sin or wrongdoing (e.g., confession to God or a priest, focusing on the present moment instead of guilt over actions from the past; Wortmann et al., 2017). As nonspiritual care providers, psychologists rightly should be wary of labeling an action (or inaction) as "sin." Yet, as discussed in Chapter 3 as well, to treat a problem with a spiritual dimension as purely psychological (e.g., maladaptive cognitions) risks alienating patients for whom R/S is a core part of their framework for understanding the world. Although Mia's therapist did not intentionally or explicitly disregard her R/S convictions, her limited engagement with Mia about those topics may have influenced or inadvertently challenged the legitimacy of Mia's faith (Shafranske & Cummings, 2013). Furthermore, one-dimensional (e.g., solely psychological) solutions may not be adequate to address a multidimensional problem. To illustrate this, we return to our example:

> Mia continued to practice the skills she learned in therapy, including "catching" herself engaging in maladaptive thinking patterns and using her prepared list of alternative statements. She confided in a few trusted others about what happened to her while she was deployed, and she performed well at school and in her job. She attended church sporadically, averaging less than once a month. She had not quite been able to put her spiritual discontent into words while in therapy, but she knew "all was not right" with God. She would feel uncomfortable sitting in church, singing worship songs, weighed down by a sense of unworthiness and memories of the rape. She felt as if she was pretending, going through the motions instead of connecting spiritually with God and others in her faith community. But everything else in her life seemed to be fine, so Mia tried to put her spiritual distress out of her mind.

Mia's ongoing struggle is evidence that psychotherapy did not wholly address the issues that were troubling her. She and her therapist agreed that the work was helpful and that she was considerably improved at the time of termination. By many estimations, the therapy was a success. However, Mia was someone for whom psychological distress was only a piece of the puzzle. Her therapist recognized early on that faith was a central concern for Mia, and although she did not share Mia's beliefs, she made a point of focusing on values in the latter part of therapy. The therapist felt reasonably certain that values work would help Mia connect with the deepest part of herself, the part that had been violated by the rape. She reasoned that Mia's ability to engage in values-directed action was evidence of her living her best life possible.

Despite the therapist's obvious compassion, intention, and skill, therapy addressed only a portion of Mia's suffering. The therapist stayed within her scope of practice, brushing up against the spiritual issues that concerned Mia without overstepping the boundaries of her competence. The therapist felt proud of her work with Mia yet dissatisfied by the unspoken heaviness that clung to Mia, even as she described all the things going well in her life. For many R/S individuals, there is something that transcends the individual and thus her or his inclinations regarding what is important (Pargament, 2013). This transcendent entity could be a secular construct such as "society" or "humanity"; it could be a religious body, a spiritual leader or historical figure, sacred texts, or a loosely defined higher power. For Mia, it was "God." Mia held back that part of herself in therapy. She found her therapist to be kind and helpful, but she did not see how the therapist could help her with a problem that transcended what was within Mia's control. She and her therapist had systematically tackled Mia's thoughts, feelings, and behaviors effectively, yet there was something else, something "other" that Mia could not explain. It is for patients like Mia that collaboration is key.

Collaborating with spiritual care providers in such cases, particularly in addressing moral injury, offers numerous advantages. First, they can offer a "moral authority" that psychology has generally strived to avoid. Competent psychologists may help a patient expand cognitive flexibility about notions of sin, punishment, and various theodicies to good effect. Yet in many cases of moral injury, a definitive judgment about morality sometimes is desired by the patient. Importantly, although psychologists may not regard themselves as moral authorities, patients can see them as such anyway. Ignoring this possibility risks underestimating the influence that psychologists' attitudes and treatment approaches have on their patients. Furthermore, psychologists must be mindful of moments when they might internally believe themselves to be an authority on what is right or good for a patient. Consider the following scenario:

> A veteran strongly believes that having killed an enemy combatant, despite being justifiable in the context of war and done at the command of a superior, is a sin. He engages in a variety of self-destructive behaviors, including drinking excessively and driving recklessly, stating he does not care if he dies. The psychologist, eager to help mitigate the potential harm of these behaviors, conceptualizes the thought as a stuck point and encourages the veteran to write it in his stuck point log. The veteran does so, and they return to it frequently but make no discernable progress toward changing it, much to the chagrin of the concerned psychologist. In fact, the veteran becomes increasingly irritated that they keep having the same discussion. His behaviors do not change, and eventually, he stops attending sessions.

In this scenario, the psychologist has subtly, and perhaps unknowingly, imposed a sense of moral authority by consistently suggesting the veteran consider reconceptualizing whether the action was a sin. The psychologist's difficulty or unwillingness to accept the action as sin in the eyes of the patient may have inadvertently created a barrier for reconciling his spiritual beliefs with his actions. Early collaboration with chaplaincy could potentially keep this veteran in treatment and deepen the therapeutic work by facilitating a space for R/S concerns to be addressed concurrently with an evidence-based treatment.

Another advantage of collaboration is the reality that some patients would rather work with chaplains or ministry professionals than mental health providers. Findings from the National Comorbidity Survey indicate that many persons seeking treatment for mental disorders are more likely to turn to clergy than to psychiatrists or general medical doctors (Wang et al., 2003). Mental health professionals have worked hard to combat stigma and integrate mental health into holistic views of wellness, and consequently, it can be frustrating when they are unable to provide services that would presumably be helpful. However, the persistence of such preferences presents a compelling case for collaboration. Stronger collaboration leads to easier and more natural referral processes. For example, a patient who is skeptical of mental health may be more inclined to follow through on a referral from their clergyperson if the clergyperson has a personal relationship with the mental health provider. Likewise, a patient who is reluctant to acknowledge or dive into their spiritual concerns may be willing to do so when a knowledgeable mental health professional can describe how psychological and spiritual concerns overlap and influence one another. Moreover, in cases in which a patient is struggling so much that they become a risk to themselves or others, collaboration places more eyes on the person and facilitates more opportunities for intervention.

Last, collaboration carries numerous practical advantages. Access to mental health care, particularly for at-risk patients, is a priority for health systems such as the VA. Although there are far fewer chaplains than mental health professionals in systems such as the VA, collaboration between these disciplines still offers some distinctive possibilities for reaching veterans. This may be especially useful in trauma care (including moral injury), where the push to provide treatments as effectively and efficiently as possible has limited many psychologists to disseminating time-limited, evidence-based protocols that are effective for some but certainly not all. Research demonstrating high dropout rates from cognitive processing therapy and prolonged exposure (e.g., Kehle-Forbes et al., 2016) highlights the problem. Although it is imperative that patients be offered treatments with the best evidence available, patient desires and preferences should inform the course of treatment. Engagement with spiritual care providers may help address some of the major barriers to treatment (e.g., stigma, provider availability, treatment acceptability), while also helping R/S-inclined patients to understand and address their struggles using multiple perspectives.

There is precedent within health care systems and clinical training programs for understanding the importance of integrating mental health and spiritual care. In 2010, VA and the Department of Defense (DoD) included a focus on chaplaincy as part of a large-scale, cross-departmental VA/DoD Integrated Mental Health Strategy (Nieuwsma et al., 2013), resulting in numerous and ongoing efforts to improve collaboration (Nieuwsma et al., 2014). Furthermore, training programs such as CPE, as well as the newer Mental Health Integration for Chaplain Services training offered to VA/DoD chaplains, equip chaplains to partner with mental health providers in the provision of care. Yet, for integration and collaboration to take place, mental health and spiritual care providers need a grasp of what the other offers. It is common for both professions to feel uncertain and even nervous about the language, expectations, and culture of the other.

In the following section, readers are introduced to the basics that describe what spiritual care providers can offer. However, just as mental health professionals are tremendously diverse in their work, chaplains or spiritual care providers also exhibit individual differences that shape the way they approach and deliver care. Therefore, it is essential to get to know individual spiritual care providers to build effective collaborations. As you read the following section, think about Mia and her therapist. How would you build a bridge from the work Mia and her therapist have already done to the R/S work that remains? How would you describe the possibilities to Mia? How would you consult with or refer to a spiritual care colleague? The ability to answer these kinds of questions is the beginning of R/S competence.

WHAT SPIRITUAL CARE PROVIDERS CAN OFFER

Spiritual care addresses fundamental human desires for meaning, purpose, identity, hope, and connection. Even as these broad domains overlap with concerns that may be addressed by traditional mental health providers, the spiritual care provided by chaplains and ministry professionals is enriched by a depth of theological knowledge obtained through formal training in their faith tradition. Because faith traditions inform cultural perspectives and worldviews held by veterans regardless of their current or previous religious affiliation (see Chapter 3), formal theological training equips chaplains and ministry professionals with the content expertise and authority to explore in detail the intersections of worldviews and religious doctrine with spiritual struggles and moral injury. Moreover, chaplains and ministry professionals provide pastoral and spiritual care, which is characterized by and grounded in compassion, empathy, and encouragement. Such theological exploration accompanied by compassionate care could add value to both case anecdotes presented in the previous section.

As described earlier, comprehensive spiritual care is best approached as a team effort. In a multidisciplinary health care setting, medical or mental health providers may ask screening questions to assess the relevance of faith to a person's well-being and identify unmet spiritual needs. In such a context, clinical chaplains are the spiritual care experts on the interdisciplinary team (Speck, 2012). Chaplains provide both direct spiritual care and consultation to the team on spiritual and cultural competency. Insofar as chaplains and other ministry professionals have also received specialized training to provide care in particular settings (e.g., palliative, mental health), their care may overlap with mental health providers; even so, their expertise is focused on the spiritual domain and is thus complementary to that of other providers. In the earlier scenarios, a chaplain could assist mental health professionals in understanding the relevance of notions such as sin and punishment for these persons, as well as explore those issues directly with the veteran. In these cases, spiritual care would be not only complementary but also essential.

When patient preference dictates the necessity of offering spiritual care, chaplains and ministry professionals provide options that increase access to care for more persons. For various reasons, persons may prefer to receive care from ministry professionals over traditional mental health providers. Community clergy may be more accessible logistically (e.g., having office hours, offering free services). Some individuals may perceive clergy as more approachable in terms of holding a shared worldview. Seeking counseling from clergy may also bypass the stigma of seeking mental health care, in that clergy may be perceived as being more organic to the community. For example, in communities that offer less anonymity or privacy (e.g., a person's car recognized when parked at the mental health clinic), a visit to clergy may be less noticed by others or considered more socially acceptable. Veterans, in particular, may view chaplaincy care favorably because of their familiarity with the role from their military experience.

In addition, spiritual care may appeal to persons seeking a holistic experience. In contrast, as highlighted in Chapter 3, the biomedical approach common in health care settings can result in an overemphasis on fixing problematic symptoms and an underemphasis on promoting the wholeness of the person. Even as traditional mental health providers may strive to situate their care in the context of the person's larger narrative, institutional demands can encourage providers to focus their attention on efficient assessment and promotion of change in discrete domains of functioning. Chaplains and ministry professionals, depending on their context, may have more flexibility in their schedules to provide a listening ear for an extended time, as well as longer term care on an individual or group basis. When a person experiencing moral injury engages with a ministry professional who is sensitive to issues of guilt, shame, forgiveness, and flourishing, the possibilities for healing are significant.

When addressed in the provision of spiritual care, receiving and giving forgiveness takes on a power, solemnity, and weightiness that transcends cognitive and behavioral concepts (see Chapter 4). More than an intrapsychic process of thinking differently about a morally injurious experience or a behavioral change of making amends, spiritual healing may entail reconciliation with having deeply offended God, the universe, or humanity—however the person may describe their very real experience of shame. Even though acknowledging wrongdoing and moving toward repair within a faith tradition can mirror a psychological process of genuine self-forgiveness (McConnell, 2015), the process of spiritual care can sanctify this experience. Because a spiritual care provider views the encounter in which they hear and hold a person's story of moral injury as sacred, this allows veterans to "be seen" and known, not merely fixed, when the entirety of their pain and shame has been exposed.

Following this initial response, chaplains and ministry professionals can engage religious practices in their care of persons experiencing moral injury. Drawing on symbolic rituals with light or elements such as fire or water (e.g., Antal et al., 2019) and the practice of prayer, chaplains and ministry professionals offer opportunities to sit in awareness of painful experiences and participate in symbolic cleansing. Chaplains and ministry professionals who are affiliated with particular denominations (e.g., Catholic, Orthodox) can also administer the sacrament of confession and provide the response of absolution, which for followers of these denominations further sacralizes the experience. For many R/S persons and spiritual care providers, these religious practices are engaged in for their own sake. In so doing, they participate in the mystery of faith, as opposed to mechanistically using a rite or ritual to heal a wound. At the same time, religious practices may be an important facilitator of the healing process in the context of moral injury.

In the special case of confession, it is important for traditional mental health providers to be aware that ministry professionals have varying expectations regarding confidentiality (Bulling et al., 2013). In a sacramental context, as well as under military chaplain policy, confidentiality is absolute. This expectation of complete privacy can be comforting to some service members who fear the repercussions of disclosure. Note that in other settings, however, clergy and chaplains are subject to state laws regarding mandated reporting. Moreover, in hospital settings where the chaplain is part of an interdisciplinary care team, sharing information with the team can optimize care. Chaplains and ministry professionals have to clarify initially with those in their care whether the person is making a confession and to what extent the provider is expected to document their care, as well as the potential to share information as needed within an interdisciplinary team. Traditional mental health providers who seek to refer and collaborate may be well served by communicating with ministry professional colleagues about these expectations.

R/S practice also intersects with community, where there is potential for isolation and misunderstanding to hinder recovery or alternatively for bonds to form that facilitate healing in the context of moral injury. Chaplains in hospital settings can create community experiences on a temporary basis (e.g., spirituality groups or chapel services) or in settings where communities may form over a longer period (e.g., in domiciles, community living centers, or hospice). For veterans, in particular, being together with fellow veterans can revive a lost sense of camaraderie and provide the comfort of common experience, as well as a safe place to share painful memories and provide and receive understanding. In the military setting, chaplains may participate in and foster community on a base, ship, or chapel, and their visible presence among service members can be profound in supporting morale. Some VA chaplains have created opportunities to facilitate poignant community ceremonies that transform the meaning and impact of moral injury in veterans and civilians (e.g., Antal et al., 2019).

In the more traditional setting in which community clergy practice, there is great potential to address moral injury by welcoming and fostering a sense of belonging for veterans and their families (Meador et al., 2016). In some faith communities, supporting military families is a visible mission, and the community does well to identify and involve its veterans and family members. Even with these good intentions, there is potential in faith communities to assume an all-or-nothing perspective on military experiences. One-dimensional characterizations of veterans as heroes—or villains—fails to accommodate the myriad stories of individual veterans and their family members, some of which may include experiences of moral injury. Faith communities and ministry professionals can take steps to create a place of belonging for veterans and family members. They can begin by seeking opportunities to increase knowledge of and sensitivity to some of the concerns that veterans and family members may have, including moral injury. They can reach out to individuals in their communities to make connections, taking an attitude of desiring to get to know and enjoy the whole person without prying or making assumptions. Traditional mental health providers and chaplains who routinely work with veterans can seek to partner with faith communities to collaboratively educate one another in the service of veterans and their families.

PRINCIPLES IN COLLABORATION

Health care systems have increasingly recognized the importance of interdisciplinary care, and perhaps one of the most compelling areas for collaboration between mental health professionals and spiritual care providers is moral injury (Meador & Nieuwsma, 2018; Nieuwsma, 2015). Around the same time that moral injury first began to receive attention in the psychological literature, VA established a new program office entitled Mental Health and Chaplaincy (Meador et al., 2010; Nieuwsma, 2010). This office has collaborated with numerous key partners and leaders in the field to improve the integration of mental health and chaplain services. One such effort involved bringing together teams of chaplains and mental health professionals from 14 different VA and military medical facilities across the country to systematically improve cross-disciplinary integration (Nieuwsma, King, et al., 2017). The key principles from that endeavor apply to mental health professionals and spiritual care providers seeking to collaborate in the care of moral injury and can be summarized as follows: establish awareness, communicate and coordinate care, and formalize processes (Nieuwsma, Cantrell, & Meador, 2017).

Establishing awareness is an obvious starting point and is critical for many reasons. First, mental health professionals and spiritual care professionals, be they community clergy or clinical chaplains, often do not know each other. Certainly, for interdisciplinary care to be effective within the context of a health care system, it is crucial for providers to be aware of one another and services offered by each discipline. For work with community clergy, where there is greater variability than within clinical chaplaincy, building relationships may be even more important. Ministry professionals differ in their interpretations of sacred texts and in how their theologies inform their perspectives on science and medicine. Familiarity and trust may be built via conversations among providers about these issues, and interdisciplinary training and meetings can create opportunities for important discussions.

Communicating and coordinating care is another key objective for integrating mental health and spiritual care services for those with moral injury. Communication between professionals is important for the functioning of any interdisciplinary team and can be especially important when providers are addressing common focus areas. For instance, moral injury–related anger, rage, guilt, and shame are likely targets to be addressed by both mental health and spiritual care providers. Where appropriate and possible, ongoing open communication about care processes is ideal, but when this is not feasible for some reason (e.g., confidentiality), more general types of communication are still valuable. It is useful for both care providers to understand generally how the other discipline thinks about and handles issues such as guilt and shame, for instance, so that, at a minimum, they can at least not be at cross purposes with one another. Even more generally, for the most basic coordination of care services to take place, it is crucial to understand what the other discipline does and can offer. Are moral injury groups offered? If so, what do they consist of, and who should attend? Is individual counseling available? On what kinds of things might this focus? Understanding this information allows mental health providers to inform patients about potentially beneficial care services and to conduct either formal or informal "screening" to identify patients who might be appropriate.

Finally, formalizing collaborative care processes is important if such care is to persist over time. Such formalization of processes could take many forms depending on the context. It may involve a change to the electronic medical record that allows for the placing of a certain kind of referral or a templated note that embodies an understanding of the potential for cross-disciplinary care. It may be a service agreement signed by department heads outlining ways in which mental health and chaplain services are to coordinate care. It may be the recurring offering of a training event in the community that serves to build and sustain trust between mental health and ministry professionals. It may even be as simple as developing a catalog of trusted ministry professionals to contact when collaboration is indicated. Turnover can be a significant challenge. Although trusting relationships are foundational for effective cross-disciplinary collaboration, so too is it important to have systems in place that will recurrently foster the maintenance of collaboration.

CONCLUSION

Spiritual care providers, whether chaplains or ministry professionals in the community, can provide essential and complementary care for veterans experiencing moral injury. They can provide instruction in the interpretation of sacred texts and a compassionate response that widens a veteran's perspective on their morally injurious experiences. Chaplains and ministry professionals can facilitate healing by offering rites such as corporate and individual confession followed by absolution from an authority figure, which may grant a person the mental or spiritual freedom to engage in activities they once avoided. Engagement in R/S communities can also provide opportunities to participate in activities and engage with others who seek to give and receive support. However, if veterans perceive a contradiction between their belief systems and behaviors and also struggle to engage in practices that restore the relationship with community and/or a higher power, they may encounter a barrier to healing. Exploration of these concerns with a chaplain or ministry professional may help veterans develop flexibility in their beliefs, articulate what they deeply value, and engage in behaviors that facilitate reconnection.

Mental health providers should avoid conceptualizing R/S as either a positive or negative coping resource or as mere tools to "fix" problems, manage discomfort, or even bring about healing (see Chapter 3). Willingness on behalf of mental health professionals to cultivate relationships with chaplains, clergy, and other spiritual care providers may open doors to consulting about spiritual matters and providing collaborative care to help veterans navigate discrepancies and ambiguity and assist them in discovering a potential for flourishing—even after, with, or through their moral injury.

REFERENCES

Antal, C. J., Yeomans, P. D., East, R., Hickey, D. W., Kalkstein, S., Brown, K. M., & Kaminstein, D. S. (2019). Transforming veteran identity through community engagement: A chaplain-psychologist collaboration to address moral injury. *Journal of Humanistic Psychology*. Advance online publication. https://doi.org/10.1177/0022167819844071

Bulling, D., DeKraai, M., Abdel-Monem, T., Nieuwsma, J. A., Cantrell, W. C., Ethridge, K., & Meador, K. (2013). Confidentiality and mental health/chaplaincy collaboration. *Military Psychology, 25*(6), 557–567. https://doi.org/10.1037/mil0000019

Chaves, M. (2017). *American religion: Contemporary trends* (2nd ed.). Princeton University Press.

Cunningham, K. C., Farmer, C., LoSavio, S. T., Dennis, P. A., Clancy, C. P., Hertzberg, M. A., Collie, C. F., Calhoun, P. S., & Beckham, J. C. (2017). A model comparison approach to trauma-related guilt as a mediator of the relationship between PTSD symptoms and suicidal ideation among veterans. *Journal of Affective Disorders, 221,* 227–231. https://doi.org/10.1016/j.jad.2017.06.046

Currier, J. M., Holland, J. M., Drescher, K., & Foy, D. (2015). Initial psychometric evaluation of the Moral Injury Questionnaire—Military version. *Clinical Psychology & Psychotherapy, 22*(1), 54–63. https://doi.org/10.1002/cpp.1866

Farnsworth, J. K., Drescher, K. D., Nieuwsma, J. A., Walser, R. B., & Currier, J. M. (2014). The role of moral emotions in military trauma: Implications for the study and treatment of moral injury. *Review of General Psychology, 18*(4), 249–262. https://doi.org/10.1037/gpr0000018

Harris, J. I., Usset, T., & Cheng, Z. H. (2018). Theodicy and spiritual distress among veterans managing posttraumatic stress. *Spirituality in Clinical Practice, 5*(4), 240–250. https://doi.org/10.1037/scp0000170

Harris, K. A., Spengler, P. M., & Gollery, T. J. (2016). Clinical judgment faith bias: Unexpected findings for psychology research and practice. *Professional Psychology, Research and Practice, 47*(6), 391–401. https://doi.org/10.1037/pro0000113

Janoff-Bulman, R. (1992). *Shattered assumptions: Towards a new psychology of trauma.* Free Press.

Kehle-Forbes, S. M., Meis, L. A., Spoont, M. R., & Polusny, M. A. (2016). Treatment initiation and dropout from prolonged exposure and cognitive processing therapy in a VA outpatient clinic. *Psychological Trauma: Theory, Research, Practice, and Policy, 8*(1), 107–114. https://doi.org/10.1037/tra0000065

Legood, G. (1999). *Chaplaincy: The church's sector ministries.* Cassell.

Meador, K. G., Cantrell, W. C., & Nieuwsma, J. A. (2016). Recovering from moral injury. In R. B. Kruschwitz (Ed.), *Patterns of violence* (pp. 35–42). Baylor University. https://www.baylor.edu/content/services/document.php/264312.pdf

Meador, K. G., Drescher, K. D., Swales, P., & Nieuwsma, J. A. (2010, July). *Mental health and chaplaincy: Envisioning a new paradigm for service integration* [Conference session]. Veterans Health Administration Mental Health Conference, Baltimore, MD, United States.

Meador, K. G., & Nieuwsma, J. A. (2018). Moral injury: Contextualized care. *The Journal of Medical Humanities, 39*(1), 93–99. https://doi.org/10.1007/s10912-017-9480-2

McConnell, J. M. (2015). A conceptual-theoretical-empirical framework for self-forgiveness: Implications for research and practice. *Basic and Applied Social Psychology, 37*(3), 143–164. https://doi.org/10.1080/01973533.2015.1016160

Nelson, J. M. (2009). Science, religion, and psychology. In J. M. Nelson (Ed.), *Psychology, religion, and spirituality* (pp. 43–75). Springer. https://doi.org/10.1007/978-0-387-87573-6_2

Nieuwsma, J. A. (2010). Introducing "Mental Health and Chaplaincy"—A vision for integrated health care. *Spirit of Chaplaincy, 1*(2), 9–10.

Nieuwsma, J. A. (2015). Moral injury: An intersection for psychological and spiritual care. *North Carolina Medical Journal, 76*(5), 300–301. https://doi.org/10.18043/ncm.76.5.300

Nieuwsma, J. A., Cantrell, W. C., & Meador, K. G. (2017, Fall/Winter). Designing mental health care systems for chaplain involvement. *Caring for the Human Spirit Magazine,* 16–18.

Nieuwsma, J. A., Jackson, G. L., DeKraai, M. B., Bulling, D. J., Cantrell, W. C., Rhodes, J. E., Bates, M. J., Ethridge, K., Lane, M. E., Tenhula, W. N., Batten, S. V., & Meador, K. G. (2014). Collaborating across the Departments of Veterans Affairs and Defense to integrate mental health and chaplaincy services. *Journal of General Internal Medicine, 29,* 885–894. https://doi.org/10.1007/s11606-014-3032-5

Nieuwsma, J. A., King, H. A., Jackson, G. L., Bidassie, B., Wright, L. W., Cantrell, W. C., Bates, M. J., Rhodes, J. E., White, B. S., Gatewood, S. J. L., & Meador, K. G. (2017). Implementing integrated mental health and chaplain care in a national quality improvement initiative. *Psychiatric Services, 68*(12), 1213–1215. https://doi.org/10.1176/appi.ps.201700397

Nieuwsma, J. A., Rhodes, J. E., Jackson, G. L., Cantrell, W. C., Lane, M. E., Bates, M. J., Dekraai, M. B., Bulling, D. J., Ethridge, K., Drescher, K. D., Fitchett, G., Tenhula, W. N., Milstein, G., Bray, R. M., & Meador, K. G. (2013). Chaplaincy and mental health in the department of Veterans affairs and department of defense. *Journal of Health Care Chaplaincy, 19*(1), 3–21. https://doi.org/10.1080/08854726.2013.775820

Oxhandler, H. K., Polson, E. C., Moffatt, K. M., & Achenbaum, W. A. (2017). The religious and spiritual beliefs and practices among practitioners across five helping professions. *Religions, 8*(11), 237. https://doi.org/10.3390/rel8110237

Pargament, K. I. (2013). Searching for the sacred: Toward a nonreductionistic theory of spirituality. In K. I. Pargament (Ed.), *APA handbook of psychology, religion, and spirituality: Vol. 1. Context, theory, and research* (pp. 257–273). American Psychological Association. https://doi.org/10.1037/14045-014

Pew Research Center. (2012). *The global religious landscape.* http://www.pewforum.org/2012/12/18/global-religious-landscape-exec/

Pew Research Center. (2015). *America's changing religious landscape.* https://www.pewforum.org/2015/05/12/americas-changing-religious-landscape/

Ruff, J. L., & Elliott, C. H. (2016). An exploration of psychologists' possible bias in response to evangelical Christian patients: Preliminary findings. *Spirituality in Clinical Practice, 3*(2), 115–126. https://doi.org/10.1037/scp0000102

Saucier, G., & Skrzypińska, K. (2006). Spiritual but not religious? Evidence for two independent dispositions. *Journal of Personality, 74*(5), 1257–1292. https://doi.org/10.1111/j.1467-6494.2006.00409.x

Schafer, R. M., Handal, P. J., Brawer, P. A., & Ubinger, M. (2011). Training and education in religion/spirituality within APA-accredited clinical psychology programs: 8 years later. *Journal of Religion and Health, 50,* 232–239. https://doi.org/10.1007/s10943-009-9272-8

Shafranske, E. P., & Cummings, J. P. (2013). Religious and spiritual beliefs, affiliations, and practices of psychologists. In K. I. Pargament (Ed.), *APA handbook of psychology, religion, and spirituality: Vol. 2. An applied psychology of religion and spirituality* (pp. 23–41). American Psychological Association. https://doi.org/10.1037/14046-002

Smith, T. W., Davern, M., Freese, J., & Hout, M. (2018). *General social surveys, 1972–2016* [Data set]. gssdataexplorer.norc.org

Speck, P. (2012). Interdisciplinary teamwork. In M. Cobb, C. M. Puchalski, & B. Rumbold (Eds.), *Oxford textbook of spirituality in healthcare* (pp. 459–464). Oxford University Press. https://doi.org/10.1093/med/9780199571390.003.0061

Vargas, A. F., Hanson, T., Kraus, D., Drescher, K., & Foy, D. (2013). Moral injury themes in combat veterans' narrative responses from the National Vietnam Veterans' Readjustment Study. *Traumatology, 19*(3), 243–250. https://doi.org/10.1177/1534765613476099

Vieten, C., Scammell, S., Pilato, R., Ammondson, I., Pargament, K. I., & Lukoff, D. (2013). Spiritual and religious competencies for psychologists. *Psychology of Religion and Spirituality, 5*(3), 129–144. https://doi.org/10.1037/a0032699

Wang, P. S., Berglund, P. A., & Kessler, R. C. (2003). Patterns and correlates of contacting clergy for mental disorders in the United States. *Health Services Research, 38*(2), 647–673. https://doi.org/10.1111/1475-6773.00138

Wortmann, J. H., Eisen, E., Hundert, C., Jordan, A. H., Smith, M. W., Nash, W. P., & Litz, B. T. (2017). Spiritual features of war-related moral injury: A primer for clinicians. *Spirituality in Clinical Practice, 4*(4), 249–261. https://doi.org/10.1037/scp0000140

14

Future Directions for Addressing Moral Injury in Clinical Practice

Concluding Comments

Joseph M. Currier, Kent D. Drescher, and Jason Nieuwsma

> At the start a new candidate for paradigm may have few supporters, and on occasions the supporters' motives may be suspect. Nevertheless, if they are competent, they will improve it, explore its possibilities, and show what it would be like to belong to the community guided by it. And as that goes on, if the paradigm is one destined to win its flight, the number and strength of the persuasive comments will increase. More scientists will then be converted, and the exploration of the new paradigm will go on. Gradually the number of experiments, instruments, articles and books based upon the paradigm will multiply. Still more [women and] men, convinced of the new view's fruitfulness, will adopt the new mode of practicing normal science, until at last only a few elderly hold-outs remain. (Kuhn, 1964, p. 158)

We opened this book with the observations of Thomas Kuhn, the highly esteemed philosopher of science, in describing the significance of "crises" in motivating a shift or "retooling" of paradigms that guide scientific research and inform clinical practice (Kuhn, 1964, p. 76). In turn, we discussed precipitants for the emergence of the concept of moral injury (e.g., the lower efficacy of posttraumatic stress disorder [PTSD] treatments in military service members and veterans [SM/Vs] than civilians), briefly traced the evolution of attempts to conceptualize possible health-related sequelae of military traumas, and summarized working definitions of varying components of moral injury (e.g., exposure, appraisal, outcomes). In proceeding chapters, leading researchers and clinicians then offered theoretical frameworks for conceptualizing moral injury, shared their insights about addressing prominent clinical issues, and described promising treatments for moral injury

https://doi.org/10.1037/0000204-015
Addressing Moral Injury in Clinical Practice, J. M. Currier, K. D. Drescher, and J. Nieuwsma (Editors)

with some grounding in scientific research. Although chapter authors likely disagree about whether the proliferation of interest in moral injury truly signifies a Kuhnian paradigm shift, they are each spearheading efforts to define and assess this construct, identify its mechanisms and outcomes, and develop and disseminate treatments to promote recovery and healing from the potential health-related impacts of morally injurious events. By compiling their collective knowledge in this book, we hope clinicians have received guidance about how to conceptualize moral injury and apply therapeutic strategies that may afford the greatest probability of healing with morally injured persons seeking their care.

Drawing again on Kuhn's (1964) predictions in *The Structure of Scientific Revolutions*, we now span away from a boots-on-the-ground focus on clinical issues and treatments to assume a 30,000-foot view of future directions for moral injury work. Largely inspired by our struggles and successes in caring for morally injured SM/Vs, we remember what it was like to stand among a small group of moral injury's first supporters around the time of Litz et al.'s (2009) seminal review. As we transition into the 2020s, we are astounded by the diversity of competent researchers, scholars, and clinicians who are studying moral injury and working to develop, evaluate, and disseminate interventions that may prevent and/or heal the possible emotional, social, and spiritual wounds of morally injurious events. With increasing numbers of studies, publications, and clinical strategies, acceptance and enthusiasm for the moral injury construct appears to be growing exponentially. Although these developments are exciting, this body of work is, unfortunately, progressing without empirical validation and consensus among academics and health professionals about the definition and outcomes that may signify the state of being morally injured. In turn, interdisciplinary collaboration and replicability of scientific endeavors remain challenging. If this construct will "win its fight" in psychology and other mental health fields, competent and ecologically valid research is needed to shore up fissures in the underlying foundations of this growing literature (e.g., Yeterian et al., 2019).

Even in the absence of a paradigmatic definition of moral injury, several researchers have suggested future directions for continuing scientific and clinical work. For example, Griffin et al. (2019) recently suggested helpful directions for (a) basic and epidemiological research and (b) clinical research and practice. Regarding the former domain, Griffin et al. emphasized the need to establish that purported outcomes of moral injury truly have a unique pathology and trajectory compared with life threat–based PTSD or other trauma-related mental health conditions. Given that nearly all studies on moral injury have focused on psychological outcomes, they also emphasized the utility of a biopsychosocial–spiritual model that may catalyze interdisciplinary research on potential biological, social, and spiritual mechanisms and outcomes that likely characterize this multidimensional construct. Regarding advancement of scientifically informed clinical practices, Griffin et al. also raised the need for more psychometric development of moral injury measures, development and evaluation of psychotherapies (many featured in earlier chapters), and possible training and educational resources for promoting clinical competencies and professional ethics for addressing moral injury with individuals from culturally diverse backgrounds. According to Kuhn's (1964) predictions, pursuing these directions may indeed illuminate the benefits of a moral injury paradigm for future generations of clinicians and researchers.

At present, arguably the most pressing scientific priority for advancing clinical practice is to determine whether and/or how moral injury fits with PTSD and other existing mental health diagnoses. Although the moral injury construct holds intuitive appeal and resonates with persons who work with traumatized populations (ourselves included), Litz and Kerig (2019) cautioned that we "should not assume without evidence that moral injury, as a mental or behavioral health outcome, has explanatory validity and clinical utility beyond concepts more widely recognized, such as PTSD" (p. 344). If proponents are to maintain scientific integrity, we have to be open to the possibility that research may fail to support the incremental validity of moral injury and find PTSD represents a structurally imperfect but sufficient framework for guiding clinical practice. In fact, given probable overlapping features with diagnostic criteria for PTSD (e.g., precipitated by emotionally challenging events, presence of reexperiencing of traumatic memories and avoidance trauma-related cue and reminders, negative changes in beliefs and painful moral emotions in Cluster D symptoms, potential self-handicapping behaviors in Cluster E symptoms), it will likely be challenging to disentangle morally injurious phenomenology empirically. In the absence of such findings, we urge our fellow moral injury supporters to strive for epistemic humility and avoid jumping to conclusions on the validity of the moral injury construct solely on the basis of clinical observations or theoretical speculations. It is notable that Kuhn (1964) commented on "suspect" motives at the emergence of a paradigm shift (p. 158). Importantly, as we close this book, moral injury will only "win its fight" via scientific endeavors from researchers and clinicians who possess the competence, integrity, and courage to allow their predictions to be disconfirmed.

Beyond emphasizing the importance of clinical research, there is a seemingly infinite array of other possible directions and dangers on the horizon for future work on moral injury. As we span away to a 30,000-foot view in these concluding comments, we cannot discuss all these concerns. However, we conclude this book by bringing two directions with special relevance for advancing clinical practices and other applied work with morally injured persons into clearer view: (a) expansion of moral injury to nonmilitary populations and (b) approaching moral injury from a broader public health perspective.

MORAL INJURY IN CIVILIAN POPULATIONS

In keeping with Kuhn's (1964) predictions, interest in moral injury is rapidly growing among scholarly and professional groups that might not focus exclusively on the experiences and needs of SM/Vs. When a useful scientific construct is identified within a particular population, it is inevitable that researchers and clinicians will apply it to new populations and explore the intersections with potentially related constructs. In fact, many readers of this book are likely clinicians who are seeking answers about how to address moral injury with other trauma-exposed groups. However, as psychologists who have devoted much of our careers to supporting SM/Vs, we must confess that the extension of the moral injury construct to nonmilitary populations creates some concern and apprehension. That is, given the small percentage of the U.S. population who serve in the military, we fear inquiries into moral injury in civilians will, over time, dwarf and divert attention away from the unique experiences and needs of SM/Vs. In many ways, we are still just beginning to learn about the clinical utility of this construct in SM/Vs. However, as applications to nonmilitary populations continue to progress, moral injury could come to be viewed in the future as something entirely different that no longer holds the same promise for informing clinical practice with SM/Vs who are struggling to come to terms with their traumas.

Beyond these types of practical concerns, we also perceive moral and ethical and conceptual issues that engender a sense of caution for us. Regardless of whether moral injury is ultimately conceptualized as a subtype of PTSD and/or a distinct syndrome or condition, expansion of the construct to nonmilitary traumas raises some questions about whether PTSD can or should fully accommodate all those with moral injury once research extends to civilians. The diagnosis of PTSD has traditionally been viewed as a disorder experienced by victims and survivors of trauma. However, the reality is that war has always been a special case in moral, ethical, or legal terms. Albeit in a limited manner, military personnel are vested with societal (and sometimes even religious) sanction for perpetrating violent actions and even death on others in the service of national security. Particularly in wartime, service members must follow established "rules of engagement" or experience potential consequences. However, as many clinicians come to learn from their patients in the course of therapy, the fog of war can be immensely thick in places, and much questionable moral behavior can remain hidden, unreported, and without consequence. Further, as another source of possible shame or anger, many service members might receive medals for actions that, if performed in the civilian world, would result in criminal prosecution. Legally, clinicians have the freedom to maintain confidentiality in such cases. However, an overlay of criminality in such cases could complicate engagement in treatment and quality of social connectedness.

Notwithstanding occasional calls for a subtype of PTSD for perpetrators of violence or trauma (e.g., MacNair, 2002), there has been little clamor to include perpetrators of criminal acts in the civilian sector as recipients of a PTSD diagnosis. However, although perpetration has not been included as a possible defining feature of Criterion A stressors, there is a caveat in the preceding section of the *Diagnostic and Statistical Manual of Mental Disorders* (5th ed.; *DSM-5*; American Psychiatric Association, 2013) describing peritraumatic (environmental) risk factors for the development of PTSD. That is, *DSM-5* highlights an increased risk "for military personnel, being a perpetrator, witnessing atrocities, or killing the enemy" (p. 278). This brief one-line statement seems (a) specific to military personnel, (b) vague about what types of perpetration are envisioned, (c) to possibly restrict involvement in atrocities to "witnessing" as opposed to committing them, and (d) to limit killing to "the enemy" rather than innocent civilians. This statement appears to set parameters on transgressive or self-directed acts in a manner that could exclude or marginalize certain civilian groups with the potentially highest risk of moral injury (e.g., violent offenders). As moral injury is applied to civilian traumas, we hope that researchers and clinicians will avoid exacerbating further stigmatization of these already underserved groups.

Importantly, as highlighted throughout this book, painful moral emotions can be directed at self and others. In fact, when moral systems are intact, reciprocal moral emotions tend to emerge across victims and perpetrators such that those who have witnessed a moral violation may experience anger, contempt, and/or disgust, whereas the perpetrator experiences profound guilt and shame. When the moral violation is highly intense and the outcome of the violation horrific, moral injury could then conceivably develop on both sides. For example, one of the common self-directed events in our clinical encounters with SM/Vs who served in Iraq and Afghanistan entails the deaths of children during convoy runs. That is, service members who are assigned to drive the lead vehicle in a convoy are ordered not to stop under any circumstances to avoid ambush. Along the way, imagine a child runs into the roadway, the driver follows orders, keeps his or her foot on the gas, and continues on. Mission accomplished, but a child is killed. In turn, the driver could develop PTSD (and moral injury)—not particularly related to fear or life threat but to the moral decision he or she was forced to make and its tragic consequence. However, one can also imagine both PTSD and moral injury being experienced by the parents who watched the incident and were morally horrified as the vehicle that killed their child continued on without stopping, as though nothing had happened, and their child's death did not matter to the perpetrator or U.S. military in general.

Move this scenario out of the war zone and back to civilian settings. For example, imagine the numerous cases that occur each year in which civilian parents observe their child struck and killed by a drunk driver with a history of multiple prior DUI convictions. These parents could certainly meet the criteria for PTSD and potentially for moral injury. But what about the driver? When overwhelmed by guilt, shame, and intense remorse that impairs functioning, could the driver potentially have moral injury? In such cases, society seems to generally view criminals as "other" and is somewhat reluctant to reduce the discomfort associated with their morally injurious acts and/or address mental health needs. However, drawing on backgrounds working with maximum-security inmates, Lynd and Lynd (2017) described enduring moral suffering on the part of some prisoners that appeared highly similar to depictions of moral injury from military events. When considering high incarceration rates compared with other industrialized nations, large prison populations in the United States, and general views of incarceration as punishment as opposed to rehabilitation, expansion of moral injury could compel society to acknowledge the humanity of criminal offenders who might need access to evidence-based mental health care. Looking ahead, beyond procedures and policies in mental health disciplines, the larger political and social climate will likely make a difference in how extending the construct of moral injury into these types of civilian settings will be received.

Notwithstanding these concerns, the extension of moral injury to non-military groups is already underway. To date, researchers have examined the construct in refugees (Nickerson et al., 2015), educators in high-risk settings (Currier et al., 2015), and helping professionals such as child protective services staff (Haight, Sugrue, & Calhoun, 2017; Haight, Sugrue, Calhoun, & Black, 2017). Moreover, conceptual and theoretical articles argue for the utility of the moral injury construct for educators (Levinson, 2015) and physicians struggling within the current health care system (Talbot & Dean, 2019). Further, a growing number of studies indicate civilian police officers often struggle with the moral impact of police actions that result in civilian death (e.g., Komarovskaya et al., 2011; Papazoglou & Chopko, 2017). Although no clinical research in these populations exists (to our knowledge), the construct of moral injury might also apply to other first responders (e.g., firefighters, EMTs), substance abusers coming to terms with past hurtful behaviors, women conflicted about the termination of a pregnancy, and criminal perpetrators of violence (e.g., domestic violence, sexual assault, murder) who are seeking rehabilitation. In any of these situations, individuals might experience profound moral suffering due to their decisions or actions (or lack thereof) and/or witnessing or experiencing others' acts that violate deeply held moral beliefs and values.

As highlighted in the opening chapter, Litz and Kerig (2019) proposed a heuristic continuum of experiences with varying moral intensity that might lead to moral injury, as well as other potentially less severe experiences (described as moral distress and moral frustration). The suggestion of a broad continuum of potential moral violations that might conceivably result in a similar continuum of symptom expression is extremely important for extending the moral injury construct. In the earlier examples, it is questionable whether moral injury subsequent to killing a civilian child within the context of military combat should be viewed as comparable to the experience of a recovering alcoholic who has inflicted emotional and financial harm on his family. However, both experiences may result in moral suffering and difficulty functioning in important life domains. Additional work is needed to define and operationalize varying types of morally troubling events and levels of moral pain or distress, possibly using Litz and Kerig's model. Larger discussions about content validity will be needed to advance this work, as will assessment instrumentation that might be used across civilian contexts to measure the intensity of moral violations, range of potential harm resulting from the morally injurious events, and an array of possible emotional experiences, cognitions, and moral judgments, as well as behavioral outcomes of such events (e.g., Chaplo et al., 2019; Steinmetz et al., 2019).

MORAL INJURY FROM A PUBLIC HEALTH LENS

In psychology and other mental health fields, the moral injury conversation has been framed almost entirely in diagnostic and therapeutic terms. These conversations are important for the advancement of mental health care but are less relevant to growing groups of stakeholders in moral injury. In fact, incremental diagnostic and psychotherapeutic evolutions among mental health professionals may seem relatively inconsequential to persons interested in moral injury from the vantage point of religion and spirituality, politics, or society or even from the perspective of many SM/Vs. For those viewing moral injury through a religious or spiritual lens, areas of interest are likely to revolve instead around practices for forgiveness and reconciliation, relationship to God or the divine, ways to reestablish patterns of moral living, and reintegration with faith communities. From a political perspective, individuals may wonder about the justness of war in general, justifiability of certain wars and wartime actions in particular, moral responsibility of political parties and personages for atrocities and other wartime events, and implications for political activism as related to past, present, and potential for future engagement in different wars. Societally, moral injury invites a different angle on questions about moral and social responsibility, including the degree to which societies are broadly complicit in the actions of their military forces and extent to which they bear responsibility for helping SM/Vs reintegrate into society. Finally, and most important, moral injury can take on diverse meanings for the SM/Vs experiencing it—reactions we have seen run the gamut from feeling their internal experiences were deeply validated by the term to potentially being offended by its implications. Note that all these possible reactions are constraining moral injury to a phenomenon as only experienced within a military context—the potential for broadening the conversation only grows when considering moral injury in civilian populations!

The mental health community has two basic options for responding to interest from these various sectors. The first is to isolate, which can include anything from assuming a posture of condescension (e.g., those people are misinformed or misguided and not worthy of attention) to a stance of indifference (e.g., that group is approaching this so differently that it is futile to seek out any common ground). The second is to engage, which can similarly take on different forms ranging from corrective or educational approaches (e.g., here is what moral injury is and how to think about it) to collaborative approaches that assume a posture of respect and curiosity (e.g., how can we learn from each other's views?). Different combinations of these reactions seem warranted and appropriate depending on how moral injury is being described and the degree to which it is being co-opted for different purposes—or for "suspect" motives in Kuhn's words (1964, p. 158). Not every perspective is equally valid and informed by knowledge, integrity, and wisdom. However, there could be substantial opportunities embodied within such an approach of collaborative curiosity for ongoing research and applied work across sectors for advancing our understanding of moral injury.

This opportunity might be usefully understood through a public health framework. As opposed to the more traditional psychotherapeutic frameworks that have been heavily informed by an individualistic medical model approach over recent decades, public health models attempt to take a broader societal perspective on disease, health, and wellness and focus not only on treatment but also on prevention (Porta, 2014). When applied to moral injury, prevention from this perspective could be divided into three categories: tertiary (i.e., care and intervention for persons with moral injury), secondary (i.e., early identification and intervention in response to emerging signs of moral injury), and primary (i.e., reduction of incidence of moral injury via broad-based communal efforts). Further, some public health models also add a fourth category that might also be of special relevance for moral injury: "primordial" (i.e., minimization of factors that might increase moral injury risk; Porta, 2014).

Some of the interest in moral injury from the aforementioned sectors might be conceptualized into these four prevention categories. The psychotherapeutic interventions described in this book, as well as other individual approaches to caring for morally injured persons (e.g., pastoral counseling with a clergyperson), fall into the tertiary category. Some approaches from a societal perspective, including those from individual communities (e.g., faith communities, veterans' organizations, other community organizations), concerning how to help "high-risk" individuals reintegrate could well represent examples of secondary prevention, especially if these efforts ultimately help to prevent the manifestation of more functionally impairing aspects of moral injury (e.g., social isolation, substance abuse, suicidal behavior). Primary prevention efforts, then, would aim to keep moral injury from occurring in the first place and might include carefully considering military training approaches, rules of engagement procedures, and perhaps even identification of "at-risk" individuals before exposure to situations with a higher risk of exposure to morally injurious events. Basic self-care is important at this level as well; for example, inadequate sleep places individuals at higher risk of poor decision making (Harrison & Horne, 2000), such that attempts to ensure sufficient sleep could serve as preventive interventions. Finally, insofar as moral injury is understood within a military context, primordial prevention efforts could include such macro-level strategies as political and diplomatic actions to avert the potential for war and occurrence of morally injurious events in the first place.

What is the appropriate degree of engagement for mental health professionals with these different levels of moral injury care and prevention? Of course, there is no simple or uniform answer to this question. We will undoubtedly have different perspectives on politics, religion, and wars that influence whether and how we engage in these and other domains. However, mental health professionals are generally unified around one superordinate goal—improving psychosocial outcomes for those in our care. Although precisely determining how best to define and measure psychosocial outcomes requires ample room for professional debate, the generic truth of this shared goal is so obvious as to be tautological—of course, mental health professionals seek to improve mental health and flourishing of morally injured patients!

Given that shared objective, we urge moral injury supporters to pay attention to the robust literature indicating how community engagement and social support promote psychosocial outcomes. Having a sense of social belonging is one of our most basic needs (Baumeister & Leary, 1995). When this need goes unmet, the health consequences can be numerous and severe. For example, individuals with weaker social support networks are more prone to the common cold (Cohen et al., 1997), depression (Barnett & Gotlib, 1988), substance abuse and relapse (Galea et al., 2004), and suicide (Joiner et al., 2005). At the other end of the spectrum, individuals who feel a sense of social belonging are more likely to experience a range of salubrious health outcomes (Cohen, 2004). From a public health view, we must, therefore, balance issues related to "impact" and "access" when planning and implementing interventions for moral injury. As is customary in mental health fields, this book focused on high-impact interventions for which access to such options could be limited (e.g., individual and group-based therapies). However, when considering social and communal dimensions of moral repair, there might be immense value in broadening care options for moral injury to less impactful interventions that are more economically feasible and could be applied to larger populations (e.g., peer-based programs).

Most of us who practice psychotherapy with morally injured persons hope to see them someday experience a sense of wellness, wholeness, and flourishing that is independent of their reliance on professional care providers. Looking ahead, to achieve this will in some manner require a broader engagement of community. This necessity has been recurrently recognized by generations of trauma care professionals, as well as from the beginning of work on moral injury. The words written by psychiatrist Jonathan Shay (1994) in *Achilles in Vietnam*—a book that can now be viewed as a seminal precursor to contemporary conversations about moral injury—remain as poignant now as when he wrote them a quarter-century ago:

> As much as I love what I do and consider it worthwhile, I cannot escape the suspicion that what we do as mental health professionals is not as good as the healing that in other cultures has been rooted in the native soil of the returning soldier's community. . . . We must create our own new models of healing which emphasize the communalization of the trauma. (p. 194)

Beyond concerns about scientific research and developing evidence-based practices for moral injury, however the construct will come to be someday be defined and measured, mental health professionals must begin to consider more peer- and community-based models of care that can provide opportunities for belonging and meaning outside the relationships with clinical providers.

Mental health professionals and psychotherapeutic approaches to moral injury hold substantial promise for improving the lives of many past and present military members. As we seek to refine and improve what we can offer from a psychological health care perspective, we should simultaneously challenge ourselves to consider how best to participate in and contribute to larger conversations about moral injury in religious communities and traditions, political groups, and society in general. In partnering evidence-based models and treatments to the care of moral injury with a broader public health perspective, there is substantial potential to enhance healing among those with moral injury, prevent it among those who may be at risk, and promote psychosocial–moral flourishing among all who are or might be affected in our society.

REFERENCES

American Psychiatric Association. (2013). *Diagnostic and statistical manual of mental disorders* (5th ed.). https://doi.org/10.1176/appi.books.9780890425596

Barnett, P. A., & Gotlib, I. H. (1988). Psychosocial functioning and depression: Distinguishing among antecedents, concomitants, and consequences. *Psychological Bulletin, 104*(1), 97–126. https://doi.org/10.1037/0033-2909.104.1.97

Baumeister, R. F., & Leary, M. R. (1995). The need to belong: Desire for interpersonal attachments as a fundamental human motivation. *Psychological Bulletin, 117*(3), 497–529. https://doi.org/10.1037/0033-2909.117.3.497

Chaplo, S. D., Kerig, P. K., & Wainryb, C. (2019). Development and validation of the Moral Injury Scales for Youth. *Journal of Traumatic Stress, 32*(3), 448–458. https://doi.org/10.1002/jts.22408

Cohen, S. (2004). Social relationships and health. *American Psychologist, 59*(8), 676–684. https://doi.org/10.1037/0003-066X.59.8.676

Cohen, S., Doyle, W. J., Skoner, D. P., Rabin, B. S., & Gwaltney, J. M., Jr. (1997). Social ties and susceptibility to the common cold. *JAMA, 277*(24), 1940–1944. https://doi.org/10.1001/jama.1997.03540480040036

Currier, J. M., Holland, J. M., Rojas-Flores, L., Herrera, S., & Foy, D. (2015). Morally injurious experiences and meaning in Salvadorian teachers exposed to violence. *Psychological Trauma: Theory, Research, Practice, and Policy, 7*(1), 24–33. https://doi.org/10.1037/a0034092

Galea, S., Nandi, A., & Vlahov, D. (2004). The social epidemiology of substance use. *Epidemiologic Reviews, 26*(1), 36–52. https://doi.org/10.1093/epirev/mxh007

Griffin, B. J., Purcell, N., Burkman, K., Litz, B. T., Bryan, C. J., Schmitz, M., Villierme, C., Walsh, J., & Maguen, S. (2019). Moral injury: An integrative review. *Journal of Traumatic Stress, 32*(3), 350–362. https://doi.org/10.1002/jts.22362

Haight, W., Sugrue, E. P., & Calhoun, M. (2017). Moral injury among child protection professionals: Implications for the ethical treatment and retention of workers. *Children and Youth Services Review, 82*, 27–41. https://doi.org/10.1016/j.childyouth.2017.08.030

Haight, W., Sugrue, E., Calhoun, M., & Black, J. (2017). Everyday coping with moral injury: The perspectives of professionals and parents involved with child protection services. *Children and Youth Services Review, 82*, 108–121. https://doi.org/10.1016/j.childyouth.2017.09.025

Harrison, Y., & Horne, J. A. (2000). The impact of sleep deprivation on decision making: A review. *Journal of Experimental Psychology: Applied, 6*(3), 236–249. https://doi.org/10.1037/1076-898X.6.3.236

Joiner, T. E., Jr., Brown, J. S., & Wingate, L. R. (2005). The psychology and neurobiology of suicidal behavior. *Annual Review of Psychology, 56,* 287–314. https://doi.org/10.1146/annurev.psych.56.091103.070320

Komarovskaya, I., Maguen, S., McCaslin, S. E., Metzler, T. J., Madan, A., Brown, A. D., Galatzer-Levy, I. R., Henn-Haase, C., & Marmar, C. R. (2011). The impact of killing and injuring others on mental health symptoms among police officers. *Journal of Psychiatric Research, 45*(10), 1332–1336. https://doi.org/10.1016/j.jpsychires.2011.05.004

Kuhn, T. S. (1964). *The structure of scientific revolutions.* University of Chicago Press.

Levinson, M. (2015). Moral injury and the ethics of educational injustice. *Harvard Educational Review, 85*(2), 203–228. https://doi.org/10.17763/0017-8055.85.2.203

Litz, B. T., & Kerig, P. K. (2019). Introduction to the special issue on moral injury: Conceptual challenges, methodological issues, and clinical applications. *Journal of Traumatic Stress, 32*(3), 341–349. https://doi.org/10.1002/jts.22405

Litz, B. T., Stein, N., Delaney, E., Lebowitz, L., Nash, W. P., Silva, C., & Maguen, S. (2009). Moral injury and moral repair in war veterans: A preliminary model and intervention strategy. *Clinical Psychology Review, 29*(8), 695–706. https://doi.org/10.1016/j.cpr.2009.07.003

Lynd, A., & Lynd, S. (2017). *Moral injury and nonviolent resistance: Breaking the cycle of violence in the military and behind bars.* PM Press.

MacNair, R. M. (2002). Perpetration-induced traumatic stress in combat veterans. *Journal of Peace Psychology, 8*(1), 63–72. https://doi.org/10.1207/S15327949PAC0801_6

Nickerson, A., Schnyder, U., Bryant, R. A., Schick, M., Mueller, J., & Morina, N. (2015). Moral injury in traumatized refugees. *Psychotherapy and Psychosomatics, 84*(2), 122–123. https://doi.org/10.1159/000369353

Papazoglou, K., & Chopko, B. (2017, November 15). The role of moral suffering (moral distress and moral injury) in police compassion fatigue and PTSD: An unexplored topic. *Frontiers in Psychology, 8,* 1999. https://doi.org/10.3389/fpsyg.2017.01999

Porta, M. (Ed.). (2014). *A dictionary of epidemiology* (6th ed.). Oxford University Press. https://doi.org/10.1093/acref/9780199976720.001.0001

Shay, J. (1994). *Achilles in Vietnam: Combat trauma and the undoing of character.* Scribner.

Steinmetz, S. E., Gray, M. J., & Clapp, J. D. (2019). Development and evaluation of the Perpetration-Induced Distress Scale for measuring shame and guilt in civilian populations. *Journal of Traumatic Stress, 32*(3), 437–447. https://doi.org/10.1002/jts.22377

Talbot, S. G., & Dean, W. (2019, March 15). Beyond burnout: The real problem facing doctors is moral injury. *Medical Economics, 96*(10). https://www.medicaleconomics.com/med-ec-blog/beyond-burnout-real-problem-facing-doctors-moral-injury

Yeterian, J. D., Berke, D. S., Carney, J. R., McIntyre-Smith, A., St Cyr, K., King, L., Kline, N. K., Phelps, A., Litz, B. T., & the Members of the Moral Injury Outcomes Project Consortium. (2019). Defining and measuring moral injury: Rationale, design, and preliminary findings from the Moral Injury Outcome Scale Consortium. *Journal of Traumatic Stress, 32*(3), 363–372. https://doi.org/10.1002/jts.22380

INDEX

Cognitive model of posttraumatic stress
disorder, 143–144
Cognitive processing therapy (CPT),
143–160
case example, 155–159
and cognitive behavioral model of moral
injury, 26–27
components and structure of, 148–153
dropout from, 252
goals of, 144
scientific basis of, 146–148
support for, 184
theory behind, 123, 143–146
training and treatment delivery with,
153–155, 212
Cognitive psychology, 45
Cognitive reappraisal, 23
Cognitive restructuring
and cognitive behavioral model of moral
injury, 27
in cognitive processing therapy, 153
in impact of killing program, 210
Cognitive schemas, 89
Coherence, 61
Collaborative care, 257. *See also* Chaplains
and ministers
Collaborative empiricism, 153
Combat exposure, 203
"Combat fatigue," 4. *See also* Posttraumatic
stress disorder
Combat veterans. *See* Service members and
veterans
Commitment. *See* Acceptance and
commitment therapy
Committed action, 166, 172, 178–179
Common cold, 269
Common Reactions to Trauma, 131
Community clergy. *See* Chaplains and
ministers
Comorbidity, 125
Compassion
in acceptance and commitment therapy,
167–168, 177
self-, 177
social functionalist perspective on, 37,
44
of spiritual care providers, 253
and therapist empathy, 110
Compassion fatigue, 119
Condemnation, 212
Condescension, 267
Conditioning and learning model, 184
Confession (religious practice), 255
Confidentiality, 255, 264
Conjunctive stage (psychospiritual
development), 225
Contamination, 208
Contemplation stage, 108
Contempt, 43

Contextualism, 169
Cooperation, 38–39
Coping
avoidance-based, 62, 67
behavioral, 23
and Building Spiritual Strength
intervention, 229, 230
and forgiveness, 75
passive, 230
in stress-and-coping model, 71, 74
Cornish, M. A., 78, 79
CPE (clinical pastoral education), 245, 246,
253
CPT. *See* Cognitive processing therapy
Creative hopelessness, 171
Criminality, 264
Crises, 261
Cultural factors
and military culture, 112
with religion and spirituality, 60, 64
in social functionalism, 39
Curiosity, 153
Currier, J. M., 11, 54, 68

D

Davis, D. E., 78
Death
personal relationship with, 194
and PTSD criteria, 6
Degradation, 46
Deployment Risk and Resilience
Inventory-2, 93
Depression
acceptance and commitment therapy for,
165
and adaptive disclosure, 184, 187
and bereavement, 10
and cognitive behavioral model of moral
injury, 24
and cognitive processing therapy, 147
and impact of killing program, 203, 208
monitoring of, 129–130
and prolonged exposure, 123, 128
rumination in, 128
and social functionalism, 41
and social support, 269
and therapeutic alliance, 106
Descriptively oriented interventions,
100–101
Despair, 152, 211, 213, 247
*Diagnostic and Statistical Manual of Mental
Disorders (DSM-5)*
and case conceptualization, 89
and cognitive behavioral model, 20, 28,
30
PTSD criteria in, 5, 8, 232, 264–265
and relevance of moral injury, 5–6
Diagnostic frameworks, 36–37

Silence, 226–228
Sin, 250
Sleep, 20, 106, 268
Smith, E. R., 123
SM/Vs. *See* Service members and veterans
Social adjustment, 147
Social alienation
    and characteristics of moral injury, 20
    and cognitive behavioral model of moral
        injury, 24
    and impact of killing program, 205–206
    and social functionalism, 42
    and therapeutic alliance, 106, 109
Social cognition, 123
Social cognitive theory, 144
Social conditioning, 164
Social disengagement, 189
Social functionalism, 35–49
    on emotions, 37–39
    implications of, 48–49
    on moral emotions, 39–45
    and process model of moral injury, 95
    and social-intuitional accounts of
        morality, 45–48
Social-intuitional accounts of morality,
    45–48
Social reconnection, 78
Social responsibility, 267
Social support, 78, 212, 269
Socratic dialogue
    and case conceptualization, 99
    in cognitive processing therapy, 145,
        146, 149–153, 155
    and impact of killing program, 204–205,
        212
"Soldier's heart," 4. *See also* Posttraumatic
    stress disorder
Somatic experiences, 24, 119
Spiritual care providers, 245, 253–256.
        See also Chaplains and ministers
Spiritual disillusionment, 208
Spirituality. *See* Religion and spirituality
Stages of change, 107–108
Status, 39
Stigma
    and impact of killing program, 204, 206,
        209
    and military culture, 112
    and process model of moral injury,
        93–94
    and prolonged exposure, 128
Stress, 22, 89
Stress-and-coping model, 71, 74
Stressors, 74
Stress response, 75–76
The Structure of Scientific Revolutions (Kuhn),
    262

Stuck points
    in cognitive processing therapy, 149–153,
        155
    common types of, 113–117
Subjective Units of Distress Scale (SUDS), 131
Substance use
    and adaptive disclosure, 184
    and cognitive behavioral model of moral
        injury, 24
    and impact of killing program, 208
    and prolonged exposure, 129
    and shame, 41
    and social support, 269
Subversion, 46
SUDS (Subjective Units of Distress Scale), 131
Suicidality
    and acceptance and commitment
        therapy, 167
    and Building Spiritual Strength
        intervention, 233–234
    and collaboration with chaplains/
        ministers, 249
    and impact of killing program, 203,
        206
    and religion/spirituality, 61
    and social functionalism, 41
Suicidality Tracking Scale, 233
Suicide, 4
Supervision, 119, 132
Survival, 37–38
Survivor guilt, 248
Symbolic apologies, 198
Symbolism, 39
Sympathetic nervous system, 40, 89
Sympathy, 37
Syncretism, 56
Synthetic-conventional stage (psycho-
    spiritual development), 225

T

Tasks of therapy, 107–108
Telehealth, 147
Termination, 109, 132
Terror management theory, 233
Tertiary interventions, 268
Theoretical orientations, 36
Theory and Practice of Group Psychotherapy
    (Yalom & Leszcz), 234
Therapeutic alliance, 106–112
    in adaptive disclosure, 193
    and agreement on goals, 106–107
    and agreement on tasks, 107–108
    defined, 106
    formation of, 115
    and therapist–patient bond, 108–112

Therapeutic relationship
    in acceptance and commitment therapy, 170
    impact of, 105
Thin construct, 53
Thin places, 53
Thought records, 209–210
Time management, 227
Torture, 189
Toussaint, L., 83
Training
    in acceptance and commitment therapy, 169–170
    in Building Spiritual Strength intervention, 231–234
    for clinical competence, 263
    in cognitive processing therapy, 153–155, 212
    for collaboration with chaplains/ministers, 252–253
    in impact of killing program, 212–213
    in prolonged exposure, 132–133, 212
    and social functionalism, 36
Transgressive acts, 7
Trauma, 5, 212. *See also specific headings*
Trauma-Related Guilt Inventory Warzone Version, 96
Traumatic grief, 189
Traumatic loss
    in adaptive disclosure, 183–187, 189, 192
    and forgiveness, 75
Treatment planning, 127, 132
Trippany, R. L., 119
Trust
    in cognitive processing therapy, 145, 151–152
    and collaboration with chaplains/ministers, 257
    and military culture, 112
    and social functionalism, 38
    and therapeutic alliance, 108
Trust Star Worksheet (cognitive processing therapy), 152
12-step programs, 211

U

Universalizing stage (psychospiritual development), 225
U.S. Air Force, 245
U.S. Armed Forces, 114–115
U.S. Army, 245
U.S. Department of Defense (DoD), 124–125, 143, 252–253
U.S. Department of Veteran Affairs (VA)
    and adaptive disclosure, 187–188, 191
    areas of research for, 124–125

Building Spiritual Strength intervention in, 238
    chaplains employed by, 245, 246
    and cognitive processing therapy, 143
    and collaboration with chaplains/ministers, 252–253
    establishment of Mental Health and Chaplaincy office by, 256
    and rise of PTSD rates, 3
U.S. Navy, 245

V

VA. *See* U.S. Department of Veteran Affairs
Validation, 208
Values
    in acceptance and commitment therapy, 165, 167–172, 177–178
    and case conceptualization, 99–100
    military, 185
Vastness, 45
Verbal knowledge, 168
Veterans. *See* Service members and veterans
Veterans Health Administration (VHA), 165, 204, 219. *See also* U.S. Department of Veteran Affairs
Vicarious trauma, 15, 119–120
Vietnam War
    and definitions of moral injury, 7
    formalization of PTSD diagnosis after, 5
    veteran adjustment issues after, 4
Vulnerabilities, 20, 24

W

Wachen, J. S., 147
Wade, N. G., 78–80
Warrior ethos, 193–194
Webb, J. R., 78, 79
Well-being, 78, 82, 83
Wellness, 252
Wisco, B. E., 113
Witvliet, C. V., 77
Work–rest schedule, 119
Worksheets, 146, 149–150
World War I, 4
World War II, 4, 5
Worry exposures, 128
Worthington, E. L., Jr., 80
Wortmann, J. H., 59

Y

Yalom, I., 234

Z

Zinnbauer, B. J., 56

ABOUT THE EDITORS

Joseph M. Currier, PhD, is a clinical psychologist who serves as associate professor and director of clinical training in the Combined Clinical & Counseling Psychology Doctoral Program at the University of South Alabama. Dr. Currier has been involved in research and scholarship on moral injury for roughly a decade, during which time he completed multiple research projects with Veterans Administration medical centers and other clinical or community-based settings with military veterans. Dr. Currier has led multiple grant-funded initiatives and published over 100 peer-reviewed articles on trauma, grief, moral injury, and the interplay between spirituality and mental health. He serves on the editorial boards of the American Psychological Association (APA) journals, *Psychology of Religion and Spirituality*, and *Traumatology*, and also recently coauthored a book published by the APA entitled *Trauma, Meaning, and Spirituality: Translating Research Into Clinical Practice.*

Kent D. Drescher, MDiv, PhD, was a staff member at the National Center for PTSD for 27 years (1990–2017). During that time, he was involved in trauma research, clinical education, and clinical care for veterans experiencing posttraumatic stress disorder and other related disorders. He has been involved in discussions of the emerging construct of moral injury since 2007 and, in recent years, has been active in treatment development. He has authored more than 60 peer-reviewed articles and book chapters, many related to the intersection of trauma, spirituality, and moral injury. He recently retired from federal service.

Jason Nieuwsma, PhD, is a clinical psychologist who is an associate professor in the Department of Psychiatry and Behavioral Sciences at Duke University Medical Center and serves as the associate director for mental health and chaplaincy in the Department of Veterans Affairs. His work in the area of moral injury includes epidemiological and clinical research, as well as an extensive focus on integrating spiritual care and chaplaincy services with traditional mental health care services for veterans and service members. Dr. Nieuwsma has published over 50 articles and book chapters, led multiple grant-funded initiatives, serves on the editorial board for the American Psychological Association journal *Spirituality in Clinical Practice* and as associate editor for the *Journal of Health Care Chaplaincy,* and recently served as the lead coeditor on the book *ACT for Clergy and Pastoral Counselors: Using Acceptance and Commitment Therapy to Bridge Psychological and Spiritual Care.*